The Sioux

The Peoples of America

General Editors: Alan Kolata and Dean Snow

This series is about the native peoples and civilizations of the Americas, from their origins in ancient times to the present day. Drawing on archaeological, historical, and anthropological evidence, each volume presents a fresh and absorbing account of a group's culture, society, and history.

Accessible and scholarly, and well illustrated with maps and photographs, the volumes of *The Peoples of America* will together provide a comprehensive and vivid picture of the character and variety of the societies of the American past.

Already published:

The Tiwanaku
Alan L. Kolata

The Timucua
Jerald T. Milanich

The Aztecs
Second Edition
Michael E. Smith

The Cheyenne
John H. Moore

The Iroquois
Dean Snow

The Moche
Garth Bawden

The Nasca
Helaine Silverman and Donald A. Proulx

The Incas
Terence N. D'Altroy

The Sioux
Guy Gibbon

The Sioux

The Dakota and Lakota Nations

Guy Gibbon

Blackwell
Publishing

© 2003 by Guy Gibbon

BLACKWELL PUBLISHING
350 Main Street, Malden, MA 02148-5020, USA
9600 Garsington Road, Oxford OX4 2DQ, UK
550 Swanston Street, Carlton, Victoria 3053, Australia

First published 2003 by Blackwell Publishing Ltd

2   2006

Library of Congress Cataloging-in-Publication Data

Gibbon, Guy E., 1939-
    The Sioux : the Dakota and Lakota nations / Guy Gibbon.
        p. cm. — (The Peoples of America)
Includes bibliographical references and index.
    ISBN 1-55786-566-3 (alk. paper)
    1. Dakota Indians—History.   2. Dakota Indians—Government relations.
3. Dakota Indians—Social life and customs.   I. Title.   II. Series.
    99.D1 G493 2002
    978.004'9752—dc21

                                                    2002005374

    ISBN-13: 978-1-55786-566-3 (alk. paper)

A catalogue record for this title is available from the British Library.

For further information on
Blackwell Publishing, visit our website:
www.blackwellpublishing.com

Contents

Figures

Preface and Acknowledgments

Since introductory-level histories of the Dakota, Yankton, and Lakota (Teton) Sioux are available (Bonvillain 1994, 1997; Hoover 1988), I have written *The Sioux* for advanced students and readers. By advanced, I mean students or readers who have some familiarity with the history of the Sioux, with other ethnohistories, with the rudiments of cultural anthropology, or with some combination of these different kinds of background knowledge.

Because the goal of *The Sioux* is to stimulate further study, the text is organized as a collage of ideas rather than as a history or ethnohistory, *sensu stricto*. While the chapters contain historical sketches of periods, for instance, they also contain topical issues for study. As a stimulus for further study, *The Sioux* also purposely raises many more questions than it answers and provides many more endnotes and references than is normal in a history or an ethnohistory. For the same reason, I build "models" at times about possible consequences of postulated events in the past, such as the settlement aggregation of the Sioux in the early fourteenth century. These imaginary reconstructions are not to be confused with verified histories of past events; the suggested consequences might or might not have occurred. Their purpose is to encourage readers to think creatively, to think about possibilities and consequences not considered in standard histories of the Sioux.

Stated even more plainly, *The Sioux* is not a "grand narrative" written by an "authority" to satisfy a curiosity; my intent is to prod readers into thinking deeply, critically, independently, and diligently about the history of the Sioux. Chapter 1 offers a philosophical and pragmatic rationale for this approach.

The historical sketches within the text are organized by periods, from the emergence of the Sioux as an identifiable group in late prehistory to the year 2000. There is nothing sacrosanct about these periods. The beginning and end dates of each period mark important external events that affected the Sioux people. Examples are the Louisiana Purchase of 1803 that opened a large portion of the West to American settlement, the beginning (1850) and end (1889) of the Sioux Wars with the US military, and the Reorganization Act of 1934. Others would organize these divisions according to their own understandings and interests. Likewise, they would choose other topical issues for review, for only imagination limits their number.

Historical ethnographies are normally written by cultural anthropologists who work backward through time from "the ethnographic present." As an archaeologist who has studied the material remains of Siouan-speaking groups for many years, I have worked "downstream" toward the present. I acknowledge with appreciation, then, the detailed remarks that I received from reviewers on a manuscript version of the text.

Special thanks to the College of Liberal Arts at the University of Minnesota, which provided a research leave of absence during fall 2001 to complete the manuscript. I was also awarded a Graduate Research Partnership Program grant in summer 2001 by the College of Liberal Arts to gather information on recent Sioux history. Karri Plowman, whose thesis topic is Indian identity in urban settings, was my capable research partner for this grant. Special thanks as well to Blackwell's Ken Provencher and to Juanita Bullough, the manuscript's copyeditor, for their help in preparing *The Sioux* for publication; to Debbie Schoenholz of the Science Museum of Minnesota for her help in selecting illustrations for the text; and to my wife Ann, who has endured life with an academic with graciousness and humor.

To encourage comment on the text by individual Sioux and by other American Indians, a version of the text was serialized in *Native American Press/Ojibwe News*, a bi-monthly newspaper. Many thanks to Bill Lawrence, the publisher of the newspaper, and to Clara Niiska, a reporter, for this opportunity. I also discussed the appropriateness of parts of the text with Faith Bad Bear of the Science Museum of Minnesota. Comments from all of these sources and from two reviewers have been incorporated into the text where possible.

G. G.

one
Reading the Sioux

The most common image of American Indians throughout the world is that of the bison-hunting Sioux. Warrior horsemen on the northern Plains of North America, they became the best known of all Indian nations through paintings and photographs, confrontations with the US military, Wild West shows, and hundreds of movies. Sitting Bull, Crazy Horse, Red Cloud, and other Sioux leaders are among the most famous of all Indians, and the battle at Little Bighorn ("Custer's Last Stand") in 1876 and the massacre at Wounded Knee in 1890 are among the most widely known events in US history. For most people in the world, the very symbol of Indianness is the Sioux eagle-feather headdress. Even other Indian people throughout North America wear some version of this headdress at powwows as a symbol of Indian unity. In 1973, the Sioux brought the plight of Indian people to the attention of the world again in a second confrontation at Wounded Knee. For all of these reasons, the Sioux are the prototype of Indian people in the Americas.

However, these famous horsemen of the Plains were only one division of a larger Sioux nation, and the lifeway of their popular image lasted only a little over 100 years. Earlier, before the horse appeared on the Plains, their ancestors lived for hundreds of years in the forests of central Minnesota and northwestern Wisconsin, where they hunted deer and harvested wild rice. Later, their descendants lived for decades in poverty and misery on small reservations in the northern Plains and Minnesota. Today, the Sioux are an increasingly vibrant people who are forging a new lifeway in which their cultural heritage has a central role. To understand the Sioux as a people, then, it is necessary to view the entire panorama of their history, not just a few romanticized "highlights."

As you will discover, this is a problematic and difficult undertaking. It is an illusion to believe that we can "understand" the Sioux – or any other people, for that matter – by reading a few ethnographies and histories of one period of their history in the nineteenth century. Since the goal of this book is to help the reader become aware of what an understanding of the Sioux involves, issues of cultural translation and of understanding another culture are its focus. Although the text is easy to read, its concepts are challenging. Effort, reflection, persistence, and thought are essential equipment in the journey ahead.

This chapter provides a general introduction to Sioux history and to some of the core issues involved in its study. The brief conventional overview of Sioux history sketched in the first section of the chapter serves two purposes. As an overview, it makes the historical content of other chapters in the book more meaningful by situating them within the flow of history. In addition, given its conventional nature, it is a convenient target for introducing core problems of cultural translation, of writing histories and ethnographies, and of cultural understanding in general in the following three sections of the chapter. The final section of Chapter 1 reviews the strategy of the text and the content of each chapter.

Basic Sioux History

Today the Sioux are a loose alliance of tribes in the northern plains and prairies of North America. They speak Siouan, a linguistic family that at contact was among the most commonly spoken language stocks north of Mexico. They became known as the Sioux or a word like it in the seventeenth century, when the Ojibwa told the French that that was what they were called. The word derives from the Ojibwa *na-towe-ssiwa*, which means "people of an alien tribe." The French spelled the word *Naudoweissious*, and the English and Americans shortened it to Sioux. Both spellings have been used since that time, with Sioux the more commonly used of the two versions of "people of an alien tribe."[1]

The Sioux alliance of tribes has three main divisions, the Dakota to the east, the Yankton–Yanktonai in the middle, and the Lakota to the west, with the latter now more numerous than the others combined. Individuals within these divisions commonly refer to themselves as Dakota (Dakota and Yankton-Yanktonai) or Lakota, words that roughly mean "Indian" or The People in their dialects. There are four Dakota subdivisions, the Mdewakanton, Wahpekute, Sisseton, and Wahpeton, and two Yankton-Yanktonai subdivisions, the Yankton and Yanktonai ("Little Yankton"). Each of these subdivisions and the Lakota are divided still further into smaller political units.

The seven principal subdivisions – the Mdewakanton, Wahpekute, Sisseton, Wahpeton, Yankton, Yanktonai, and Lakota – are recognized by the Sioux as ancestral political units, the Seven Council Fires (*Oceti Sakowin*), whose origins extend back to their homeland in the present state of Minnesota. In recent years, some Sioux, like many other Indian people, have made a concerted effort to replace their imposed, non-Indian name, here "the Sioux," which is derived from an Ojibwa word, by the names they call themselves. For example, the Sisseton-Wahpeton Sioux tribe recently became the Sisseton-Wahpeton Dakota tribe, and other tribes are proposing changes in their name, too. The label Sioux is used here because there is no agreed-upon alternative, it is the most appropriate label for their language, and the word (as opposed to Lakota–Dakota) is recognized throughout the world. However, readers should constantly be aware that there are more appropriate and acceptable names for these Indian people than the word "Sioux."

Europeans first encountered the Dakota, the eastern division of the Sioux, in the seventeenth century in the mixed hardwood forests or northwoods of central Minnesota and northwestern Wisconsin. Since that time this region has been regarded as the late prehistoric ancestral homeland of the Sioux people. Because the prehistory of the Sioux before this encounter is poorly documented, contending interpretations of their past based on oral narratives, reconstructed written histories, and archaeological evidence exist. An interpretation of the archaeological evidence suggests that they emerged relatively suddenly as an alliance of tribal groups in the late thirteenth or early fourteenth century ad. At that time, scattered family groups aggregated into a small number of clustered, probably palisaded, villages situated beside the larger lakes and rivers in the region. There they harvested wild rice, their principal grain, in the fall, made maple sugar in the early spring, and hunted deer. Once or twice a year they entered the prairies to the west to hunt bison.

In the mid-seventeenth century, the Sioux began drifting westward and southward. Both "push" and "pull" processes seem to have been involved. Turmoil in New England and the eastern Great Lakes pushed tribes west around Lakes Michigan and Superior. By the time the fur trade became established in the western Great Lakes and Upper Mississippi Valley in the early eighteenth century, many of these tribes were competing with one another and the Sioux for furs and the benefits of the French trade. Pressure from the Ojibwa, who gradually moved into Minnesota from the Lake Superior area, pushed some Sioux southward and perhaps westward.

The Dakota, for example, were apparently pushed and pulled into the southern one-third of the state, where they settled along the Minnesota and Mississippi rivers. By contrast, the western Sioux, the Lakota and Yankton-Yanktonai, had already crossed the Red River into the eastern Dakotas between 1700 and 1725. Greater game resources and the promise of the horse, which was present on the southern prairie-plains by 1650 and was being used by other Siouan speakers south of the Dakotas by

1700, might have drawn them. While some western Sioux bands had a few horses by 1707 if not earlier, the Lakota (the Sioux of the West) did not become Plains horsemen until 1750–75, by which time Lakota foraging parties had crossed the Missouri River. By the late 1700s, because of "pulls" and "pushes," all of the Sioux had left their ancestral homes in the mixed hardwood forests of central Minnesota and northwestern Wisconsin.

As each of the three divisions adapted to different prairie-plains environments, their lifeways changed and diverged from one another, and while they spoke the same language, each developed its own dialect. The Middle Sioux, the Yankton-Yanktonai, became middlemen in a far-flung

Figure 1.1   Sitting Bull (F. F. Barry photograph, 1885. Minnesota Historical Society Photograph Collection)

trade system between the Lakota, who had pushed westward as far as Wyoming and eastern Montana, and the Dakota (the Sioux of the East), who were closely involved in the French fur trade. While the Lakota became bison-hunting, nomadic horsemen and the principal grain of the Dakota shifted from wild rice to maize (corn), some Yankton-Yanktonai adopted many of the traits of their Mandan, Hidatsa, and Arikara neighbors, including earthlodge dwellings and their style of dress. With the horse for transportation, the Lakota prospered and their numbers grew until, by the nineteenth century, they outnumbered all other Sioux bands combined. Because of limitless bison herds, their horsemanship, and their nomadic, warrior existence, they became the last, great barrier to Euro-American domination of the Plains.

In the first half of the nineteenth century, American pressure on the resources of the Sioux became increasingly intense and demanding. Fort Snelling was established at the junction of the Mississippi and Minnesota rivers in 1819 to keep peace between the Sioux and Ojibwa, and to keep non-Indian settlers off Indian lands and British fur traders out of American territory. Soon after, Indian agents initiated a long-term process of preparing the neighboring Dakota for participation in the Euro-American way of life. Reading and writing English and farming were encouraged by the US government, and, in the 1820s, missionary teachers were allowed to come and assist in this process.

In 1837, the Dakota succumbed to mounting pressure and sold their land east of the Mississippi River to the US government. Among the pressures were debts that the government was using to force land sales and a desire by missionaries to anchor the mobile Dakota to small reservations where education in reading, writing, and farming would be easier and under closer control. Treaties signed at Traverse des Sioux and Mendota in 1851 took away their remaining land in Minnesota except for a small reservation along the Minnesota River. American settlers, who had reached Minnesota in the 1840s, poured into Minnesota Territory in the 1850s. Meanwhile, much of the money paid to the Dakota for their land was given directly to fur traders to settle debts, and promised food rations were not always supplied on time or in sufficient quantity. These and other inequities led to the Dakota Conflict of 1862. At the end of the conflict, the remaining land of the Dakota was seized and opened to homesteading. The surviving Dakota fled the state, were removed to Crow Creek on the Missouri River in South Dakota, were sent to prison, or were otherwise dispersed.

A similar pattern of initial land acquisition, subsequent movement to ever-smaller reservations, stress on learning non-Indian ways, and deprivation was experienced by the Yankton-Yanktonai and Lakota to the west. During the first half of the nineteenth century, at the very time the horse-riding nomadic way of life of the Lakota was flourishing, Euro-American traders and US troops, and many thousands of eastern Indians after 1830, moved into the grasslands of the Great Plains. One of the largest of these Indian displacements resulted from the Chicago Treaty of 1833, which removed the Potawatomi, Kickapoo, Sauk, Miami, Illini, and other eastern tribes from Michigan, Indiana, Illinois, and Wisconsin to Kansas and Oklahoma. By mid-century, the Euro-American colonization front reached Kansas, and, following a clamor for new land, both Kansas and Nebraska were opened to colonization in 1854. To end the "Indian problem," the US government initiated an aggressive military policy in the Plains in the Civil War years of the 1860s. This policy included building additional military posts and hunting "renegade" groups that refused to settle on reservations. Both of these activities further inflamed relationships and stressed the limited food resources of the region. After completion of the transcontinental railroad in 1869, herds of bison were slaughtered for their hides, which were shipped back east in boxcars. By the mid-1870s, bison were nearly extinct in the central Plains, and by the mid-1880s, they had disappeared in the northern Plains.

Even though many of these developments occurred first south of Dakota Territory, the Western and Middle Sioux were soon subjected to similar processes. In 1868, the Lakota were restricted to the Great Sioux Reservation, which was that part of Dakota Territory west of the Missouri River. By the 1870s, intolerable pressure led to a series of "Indian Wars," the most famous of which was the annihilation of Custer's Seventh Calvary at the Battle of the Little Bighorn in 1876 by Sitting Bull's Lakota and by Cheyenne forces and other allies. With the disappearance of the bison herds in the northern Plains by 1885, the foundation of the Lakota's nomadic lifeway was destroyed and decades of dependence on reservation annuities began for all Sioux. Their holdings were further diminished and scattered by the Dawes Allotment Act of 1887, which forced families and individuals onto 160-acre or smaller allotments and opened the remaining land to non-Indian settlement. The massacre of Big Foot's band at Wounded Knee Creek in 1890 and the killing of Sitting Bull by Indian policemen the same year symbolize the end of the freedom and preferred nomadic lifeway of the Lakota and some other western Sioux bands.

The 1890s were revolutionary years for the Sioux. Besides being confined to reservations where indifferent and self-serving Indian agents appointed for political favors often controlled them, they were expected to farm arid land. Worse, some of their children were shipped to boarding schools, such as Carlisle in Pennsylvania, where they were taught manual skills, urged to abandon their Indian ways, and made to speak English. While the Sun Dance, which had reached its peak of popularity during the war years of the mid-nineteenth century, was now forbidden, other religions, such as the Ghost Dance and Peyotism, spread in the 1890s as integrating mechanisms for crowded and deprived Indian societies. Besides reaffirming the value of the Indian experience, they taught accommodation to Euro-American patterns of life.

The first two decades of the twentieth century were periods of adjustment to reservation life in now scattered allotments in the prairie-plains region for the Sioux. Some reservations even began to prosper somewhat in the 1920s. However, the terrible drought of the Dust Bowl years of the early 1930s and the Great Depression (1929–33) devastated most reser-

Figure 1.2 *Maz-zo*, a Dakota woman (Martin's Gallery photograph, 1863. Minnesota Historical Society Photograph Collection)

vations on the Plains. Still, the catastrophe provided an opportunity to introduce radical reforms. These well-intentioned if controversial reforms were introduced by John Collier of the new Roosevelt administration and were enacted as the Indian Reorganization Act of 1934. The Act was designed to improve subsistence and employment opportunities on the reservations and to ensure that tribal councils and chairmen were democratically elected. Opportunity for employment off the reservation was greatly expanded by World War II, when many young Sioux men and women volunteered for service or worked on farms or in industry in larger cities.

The second half of the twentieth century has been a time of far-reaching change and renewal for many Sioux. Reduction in mortality and high birth rates almost doubled their population, which strained employment on reservations. In response, an increased effort was made to prepare young people for urban employment. The Eisenhower administration enforced this trend with its 1952 Voluntary Relocation Program, which was designed to relocate Indians to centers of employment as private citizens. Poorly educated and discriminated against, many of these young people soon returned to the reservation. A more drastic measure was House Concurrent Resolution 108, which called for the US to unilaterally end the special status of Indian tribal reservations. In the late 1960s, as part of the "counter-culture" movement, the national American Indian Movement (AIM) was formed to combat deprivations and injustices. These demands for civil rights were supported in part by the 1964 Civil Rights Act.

By the 1970s, the once radical position that Indians should be able to follow their own cultural traditions – rather than be forced to assimilate to Euro-American ones – became more widely accepted. The publication of Dee Brown's immensely popular *Bury My Heart at Wounded Knee* in 1971 and a new confrontation at Wounded Knee in 1973 led by Russell Means, an Oglala Sioux, heightened public consciousness of the plight of the Sioux. In addition, since the 1950s powwows have become linked into circuits that bring scattered Indian people together, if only for a few days, to reaffirm their Indianness and to seek solutions to powerlessness and poverty. Also in the early 1970s, legislation and policy statements by Presidents Nixon and Ford reversed the Eisenhower initiative and recognized the right of the Sioux and other Indian people in the US to self-determination without the withdrawal of government support. The 1975 Indian Self-Determination and Education Assistance Act, which transferred many governmental and administrative powers to Indian tribes, is an example of this new direction in US Indian policy.

An increasingly articulated goal in the last three decades of the twentieth century has been sovereignty and immediate access to specific rights granted by past treaties. A series of laws has reaffirmed these rights. This effort has been immensely accelerated by the infusion of millions of dollars from gambling casinos on Indian lands. Beginning in the mid-1970s, and expanding rapidly in the 1980s and 1990s, gambling has become a source of individual and tribal funds not encumbered by US government restrictions. This new economic base has made life easier for some Sioux and allowed individual tribes to pursue their legal rights with ever-increasing vigor. Today, although transformed through decades of forced assimilation and intermixing with people from many other cultures, the Sioux nation and culture is in a vigorous, if difficult, renaissance.

Problems with Modern History and Ethnography

With rare exceptions, histories of the Sioux are written from a "modern" perspective, that is, from a view of human history rooted in Enlightenment philosophy. This is true as well of the vast majority of Sioux ethnographies, which are descriptions and interpretations of the customary behavior, beliefs, and attitudes of the Sioux at a moment in time called the "ethnographic present." Although professional historians and anthropologists have written some of these histories and ethnographies, most have been written by missionaries, Indian agents, professional writers, and people with a personal interest in the Sioux.

Most readers assume that these histories and ethnographies are accurate, authoritative accounts, and read them for their content. A more demanding and insightful approach is to focus on the myriad of issues involved in writing and reading histories and ethnographies. Some of these issues are internal to modern history and ethnography, and concern standards of scholarship developed within this perspective since the eighteenth century. Others are postmodern and question the very foundation of Enlightenment philosophy. While many of these basic issues are raised in this introduction to the Sioux, none are resolved. For reasons that will become apparent, each reader cannot help but formulate her or his own understanding of the Sioux.

The Enlightenment is a western European ideology or way of perceiving and interpreting the world that developed in the eighteenth century through the works of Voltaire, John Locke, and other philosophers.[2] Like other views of the world, it is based on assumptions about the nature of reality, of human beings and other life forms, and of ways of knowing. Among the basic assumptions of Enlightenment philosophy are the ideas that all human groups share the same basic physical and psychological make up, so there is no biological barrier to human development; that progress is the dominant characteristic of all aspects of human life, including moral, technological, and social aspects; and that progress results from the exercise of reason or rational thought. Later chapters will argue that the first two assumptions guided many Euro-American patterns of interaction with the Sioux. The third assumption has a heritage in modern history and anthropology in an emphasis on reason, truth, objectivity, rationality, consistency, accurate description, and correctness, among other features of Western social science. Because of these values, modern social scientists assume that it is possible to provide a true and adequate account of the history of the Sioux. They assume, too, that this process can and should be conducted in an objective manner with the methodology of their discipline.

Postmodern critics question these assumptions and everything else that is taken for granted by modern social scientists. They argue that the concepts of history and anthropology have to be re-conceptualized. Among their concerns are modern views of representation, truth, reality, and science. They conclude that conventional views of history and anthropology are at best inadequate and at worst illusory and exploitative. These issues have obvious implications for understanding the Sioux.

A primary target of postmodernists is the modern assumption that it is possible to reproduce or re-present a true image of a past or present cultural reality. Besides being entangled in cultural and personal perspectives, representation, according to its critics, excludes ambiguity and imposes a standpoint of interpretation by controlling the proliferation of meaning, when many diverse meanings are possible and should be explored. In addition, representation assumes that everyone understands the meaning of words, images, and symbols the same way. Postmodernists argue that because words, images, and symbols are language-dependent, representation is always indeterminate (Wittgenstein's irreducible pluralism of language).[3] If these arguments have merit, then representation necessarily distorts and possibly even creates the social world that it is supposed to re-present. This critique has implications for the concepts of reality, truth, science, history, and ethnography that must be considered in our effort to understand the Sioux.

Modern history and ethnography assume that an independent, external reality exists. That it can be discovered, and objectively described and interpreted. Western social science has generally supported a positivist, materialist notion of reality in which material things, and only material things, exist independently in a real world.[4] By assuming an independent reality of real things, modern social science is able to "discover" and "depict" its object of study "as it really is." Representations can be judged accurate or not, and can be used to confirm or falsify interpretations. However, if representation is problematic, then the ability to reproduce and duplicate external reality is called into question. Objectivity becomes an illusion and the concept of truth (in the sense of "true" knowledge claims) a potentially dangerous tool of modernity. By maintaining that there is a "truth to the matter," that there is a single best or correct answer to every question, modern social science excludes the possibility of multiple realities and of conflicting versions of the truth of a situation. Most postmodernists argue that truth claims silence the argument of "the other" – the Sioux, for example – and are products of power games "manipulated into position by those whose interests they serve."[5] The notions of "reality construction" and of different theories of reality have been proposed as less naive alternatives to the positivists' materialist notion of reality. A contextualist theory of reality, for example, maintains that knowledge claims are the result of agreement within their context, whether the context is a linguistic community, a society, or a social science profession. More extreme is the view that reality is only a linguistic convention, that language produces reality. This latter position is predicated on the view that there are indeterminate real-world referents for words, images, and symbols.

These views of reality, objectivity, and truth have implications as well for the very notion of social science. Modern social science is based upon a materialist assumption of reality; a self-correcting method, grounded in reason and rationality, that is assumed to be universal across disciplines; the idea that social realities can be understood as systems of causal relations; and the belief that conflict among interpretations can be adjudicated by reference to external reality as the ultimate arbitrator. Of course, if modern notions of truth and objectivity are questioned, then it is impossible to distinguish good and bad interpretations with any certitude. By extension, the role of reason itself in modern social science can be challenged. This is possible from a variety of perspectives. For instance, even though people can engage in "reasoned arguments," their thoughts are culturally contextual and reflect preference rather than privileged insight. In addition, from another perspective, "good reasons" have been given for a multitude of actions the consequences of which have been disastrous for the Sioux.

All of these objections call into question conventional views of history and ethnography. If there is no real, knowable past, if truth and reason are context-dependent, if no grounds exist for defensible external validation, then what are history and ethnography about? What is their purpose? Answers vary. According to the End-of-History and New History movements, they are creations of modern Western nations that innocently or sinisterly fabricate "façades" that, while claiming to be objective and scientific, serve instead to deceive, to legitimate modernity, and to reinforce Western myths and ideologies at the expense of those of "the other."[6] As meta-narratives ("Grand Narratives"), they stress, for instance, continuity, progress, closure, direct causal understanding, the search for origins, and correct interpretations, and preclude multiple interpretations, intertextuality (the existence of "infinitely complex interwoven interrelationships"), the absence of truth, and plural realities. In addition, by focusing on dramatic events, important individuals ("Great Men"), and wars and treaties, on deep, enduring, and autonomous social structures, and on the "pure" culture unadulterated by trappers and Indian agents, history and ethnography ignore the impact of external, public events on everyday experience. They ignore women, children, and old people, who are uneliminable members of Sioux society.

These are basic issues that readers of histories and ethnographies must make decisions about or at least become aware of in "reading" the Sioux. Is a history or ethnography only a story? Is it possible to describe (represent) other cultures and formulate theories about them? Is all insight of equal value? How do we distinguish "what really happened" from fictional accounts of the past? What roles do history and ethnography play in our society? Can we ignore these issues and still avoid an "innocent reading"?

The Sioux as Historical Relic, Exotica, Subject, and Text

Other fundamental issues involved in reading about people with another culture revolve around how they are perceived by authors in some global sense. Most books and articles written about the Sioux view them, for instance, as a historical relic or as exotica, or as both. For many people, the Sioux of the East are frozen forever in the 1830s and the Sioux of the West in the war years of the 1860s and 1870s. In this view, present-day Sioux are faded reminders, historical relics, of what they once were – at least in the mind of the Western observer. A related perception pictures the Sioux as an esoteric people who once lived in the distant, wild frontier, where they pierced their flesh during the Sun Dance, hunted massive bison from horseback, and had other strange but interesting customs. As exotica, they present an exciting alternative to our own humdrum lives. Basic questions should be asked about these perceptions: Whose interests do they serve? Are they paternalistic and perhaps demeaning to the Sioux? In their quest for the exotic, do authors "over-interpret" the Sioux, that is, make them appear more different and esoteric than they actually were and are?

More subtle problems concern the Sioux as subject and as text. At its simplest, the Sioux as subject refers to the Western conception of the significance of human beings. In this conception, a person is a self-aware, rational, self-conscious, autonomous, unified, and self-determining agent, who is the "preconstituted center of the experience of culture and history."[7] Furthermore, as isolatable agents they are presumed to be independent of social relations and to have the capacity to maintain or change them. As the building blocks of social processes, the actions and points of view of the subject are the focus of modern analysis.

Postmodernists regard this conception as an illusion, a fiction, and an invention of humanist philosophy. From their perspective and that of Freud and others, human beings are better characterized by self-deception, diversity, powerlessness, and contradiction.[8] What we say, do, and think cannot be taken at face value. At an extreme, a person is only a mask or a role in a drama whose scenes are not the products of anyone's plan or intention. For these and other reasons, the anthropologist Claude Lévi-Strauss once suggested that the ultimate goal of his research was not "to constitute man but to dissolve him."[9]

Postmodernists contend that the notion of the modern subject, as an ideological construct, has had a largely negative effect in Western society. As the focus of analysis in most histories and ethnographies, the notion has detracted from other avenues of understanding. An example is the investigation of the linguistic construction and symbolic meaning of large-scale social structures, and of change as manifest in their transformation. According to this latter research strategy, no human action is meaningful without being situated within the context of a structure. Others contend that the notion "fraudulently underscores the individual as a potentially effective, rational agent," when s/he is not; has been almost exclusively male-centered (the "Great Men" of history); implies an object, and thereby designates the observer (author) as subject and relegates those being studied (the Sioux) to passive object status; and leads to an objectification that encourages the reader to view individuals as mere members of a group, among other charges.[10] Although these critiques are most often aimed at the notion of the individual as subject, many apply as well to social wholes. For example, the Lakota and other Sioux social groups are often treated as if they have the characteristics of a person, as if they are self-determinant and unified.

These contentions imply that the notion of the subject should be eliminated, be de-emphasized as a focus of analysis, or be rethought and "repositioned." At the very least, they raise fundamental issues for the reader intent on learning about the Sioux. For instance, what justification is there for assuming that the subject should be the center of analysis? Does this focus detract from learning about the processes that shaped and now shape the Sioux? How has this focus been expressed in books and articles about the Sioux? Would the history/anthropology of the Sioux be more interesting without the modern subject?

It is worthwhile as well to consider what is implied by the notion that the Sioux can be read as a "text" or are a "text." For postmodernists, a society, an archaeological assemblage, a life experience, a reservation, and just about anything else is considered a text.[11] All phenomena, all events are texts. Unlike modern written texts that are assumed to have a knowable content determined by the author, postmodern "texts" – like the Lakota – have multiple interpretations no one of which is necessarily more correct or meaningful than another. In this view, the Sioux have no single meaning, since political, social, religious, and economic events encourage an infinite number of interpretations. By implication, a variety of readings is available. Rather than an objective, separable, and internally integrated social reality, they are undefined, fragmented, and enmeshed in an infinite play of intertextual relationships with other "texts." Consequently, it is fruitless to search for *the* correct meaning or description of the Sioux as text. Although interpretation is not completely arbitrary (some things happen and others do not), readers still (re)-create the text. Said another way, there is a difference between simply "seeing" (the impact of electromagnetic impulses on the retina of the eye and so forth) and "seeing as" (learning to see those impulses as, for example, a "Sioux woman"). There is a difference between the existence of "brute facts" and their interpretation.[12]

Reorienting the Reader

Considerable uncertainty exists today concerning the relationship of the author, reader, and written text. In modern history and anthropology, the author is assumed to write a text to communicate a specific message or to convey knowledge. Her or his role is to "re-present" a social reality in order to educate, to instill moral values, or to otherwise enlighten the reader (about, for example, what really happened at Wounded Knee). As a "readerly" text, a book or article is to be read for its specific message or content. The reader's role is to "passively" absorb or grasp this information. In classrooms across the country, examinations assure that students "correctly" understand what they read and are told.[13]

Postmodernists diminish the importance of the author for a variety of reasons: the modern author assumes privileged access to truth, a view that postmodernists consider naive at best; authors are not always conscious of the implications of what they are saying; by imposing a "truthful" account, the modern author discourages multiple interpretations and often becomes an unwitting instrument of the status quo; and by imposing order on events by binding them together in a rational, explanatory framework (a history or ethnography), the author-writer can mask the paradoxical, the chaotic, the ambiguous. This movement symbolizes as well a general protest against author(ity). Critics point out, too, that the modern concept of an author is not a natural idea but an idea with a social history. According to Foucault and others, the idea emerged during the Middle Ages as a means of authenticating scientific statements.[14]

The outcome of these debates is a repositioning of the reader. For the modern reader, who reads in pursuit of truth and knowledge, a more active reading is required to identify authorial bias and the distortion of meaning, to discover new sources of information, and to explore alternative explanatory frameworks. The task remains the accumulation of true knowledge through diverse and deeper readings, and the goal remains the determination with certitude of what "really happened." By contrast, postmodernists empower the reader more dramatically. Any number of readings are possible because a text does not have a "best" reading. Indeed, we should expect different readers to offer divergent interpretations of a text because there are multiple realities in a postmodern world. Likewise, some readers will share similar readings of a text because they learned to read in the same "interpretive community" (a culture, subculture, academic discipline, and so on). However, none of these readings is privileged or at best is privileged only within a certain context. In the extreme, the postmodern reader (re)-creates the text in the act of reading; the postmodern text is a "writerly" text "rewritten" (interpreted, created) by the reader with every reading. Here reading becomes textual construction, not knowledge building.

These divergent views raise other interesting questions for readers setting out to learn about the Sioux. Is any written text about the Sioux open to multiple readings? Are all readings of equal value, or is it possible to choose among incompatible interpretations? How do we evaluate divergent written texts or readings? To what extent does a written text have an objective status? Should the reading of the Sioux-as-text by Sioux "readers" be privileged? In the last instance, do readers "write the text"? Again, one's answers to these and related questions affect the nature of their encounter with the Sioux. To refuse to engage questions like these is to already embrace a point of view.[15]

An Overview of the Text

Except for chapter 2, the remaining chapters follow the pattern established in this introduction to the text. After a brief review of the content of the chapter, a "basic history" section is followed by a series of four to six topical issues that I consider important in thinking about the Sioux. Some of these issues fall within the ambit of modern social science: What additional sources of information should be explored? How do we evaluate that information in order to get at "the truth of the matter"? How has the bias or special interests of an author affected his or her interpretation of the Sioux? Others are postmodern in tenor. Who has benefited from (fraudulent) claims of truth? How have Western concepts of space and time influenced our understanding of Sioux culture? Where in the literature are the voices of women, children, and old people?

The topical issues chosen reflect my own interests. Inquisitive, "writerly" readers should prepare their own list as a guide for learning about the Sioux. The chapters progress through time in an ordered, linear sequence whose temporal divisions are largely arbitrary. Other authors – and individual Sioux – would choose different formats and highlight different events.

two

The Prehistory of the Sioux, 9500 BC–AD 1650

At the time of writing, there is no monograph-length archaeological study of the prehistory of the Sioux. The University of Minnesota's Lloyd Wilford, who established the foundation of Minnesota archaeology between the 1930s and 1950s, thought the prehistory of the Sioux could be traced back through changing styles of pottery manufacture and burial of the dead.[1] His successor at the University of Minnesota, Elden Johnson, excavated several village sites in the Mille Lacs Lake area that he thought were occupied by bands of late prehistoric and contact period Mdewakanton Dakota.[2] With the exception of these and several studies based on Johnson's Mille Lacs Lake collections, Sioux prehistory as a topic of investigation has been ignored by professional archaeologists. Because of this vacuum, chapter 2 develops a history of the Sioux before Euro-American contact.

Sections one and two summarize existing views of Sioux prehistory and introduce problems of identifying social groups in the archaeological record. Sections three through five examine the archaeological record, human skeletal biology, and historical linguistics for traces of Sioux prehistory. The final section develops an interpretation of Sioux prehistory consistent with these traces.

The Received View of Sioux Prehistory

At present, there are conflicting narratives of the origins of the Sioux. When compared, the origin narratives of native Sioux differ not only among different divisions of the Sioux, but from those of other Siouan-speaking groups.[3] Historically, the origin narratives of some bands changed, too, as they migrated out onto the northern Plains.

While oral traditions and written accounts by historians generally agree that Minnesota was the core late prehistoric homeland of the Sioux, they disagree about where the Sioux originally came from. For the sake of brevity, these contending views can be divided into three groups, each of which shares a common geographical theme. According to the most popular geographical theme, the ancestors of the Sioux came from the east.[4] In one version of this theme they landed on a peninsula on the east coast of North America and, with the guidance of the *Umketehi* ("Underwater Panthers"), followed the *c'anka duta* ("Red Road") west to Minnesota country. According to the second geographical theme, the ancestors of the Sioux came from a land of cold winters and lots of ice to the north.[5] In a version recorded by Ruth Landes, they moved southwestward into Ojibwa territory and then into the Mississippi Valley, where they made permanent villages at Winona and La Crosse.

In contrast to these directional movements, the third theme claims that the Sioux or at least some divisions of the Sioux were "in this Mid-American region for a fairly long time."[6] One version of this theme was recorded by James Walker, a physician at Pine Ridge Reservation from 1896 to 1914. According to the stories he was told, the First People were lured out of the underworld where they were living to the earth's surface, which they reached by passing through a cave. Their children are the Lakota Sioux. Some Lakota believe that the cave their ancestors passed through is Wind Cave in the Black Hills of western South Dakota. The stories also tell how and why the earth, sun, daytime, nighttime, blue waters and sky, moon, animals, birds, insects, and other features of the natural world were created.[7]

A companion problem is determining where the ancestral Sioux lived in Minnesota in the late prehistoric period. Accounts agree that the Dakota lived in the forests of east central Minnesota and northwestern Wisconsin, with at least one important village cluster near the Rum River outlet of Mille Lacs Lake.[8] The late prehistoric homeland of the western and central Sioux, the Lakota and Yankton–Yanktonai, is less secure. When mentioned in the earliest written records, they are referred to only vaguely, for they were the most distant of the Sioux from the zone of Euro-American contact. According to the most common view, they lived to the west of the Dakota in the forested headwaters region of the Mississippi River. Others think they lived in the tall-grass prairies of southwestern Minnesota and the adjoining area of South Dakota.[9]

Since these narratives are contradictory, they cannot all be true, at least for the origin of the Sioux as a population. This is not to claim that they have no historical basis. Some could refer to the history of family groups and others could serve other purposes in traditional Sioux culture, such as legitimating a claim to land. We turn now to a review of paleoanthropological sources of evidence for Sioux prehistory. Since this evidence itself is weak, it is not possible to conclusively rule out any of the three main origin themes. Consequently, our goal is the modest one of assessing how well these sources of evidence support each theme.

The Anthropology and Archaeology of Identity

A necessary first step in reviewing paleoanthropological sources of information for historic, named peoples is to ask whether their social identity changed over time. Could the ancestral Sioux have been a people, tribe, cluster of bands or tribes, ethnic group, culture, society, or some combination or sequence of these and other identities? The question is important for three reasons. First, the archaeological signatures of different patterns of social relationships are not identical. If we naively assume that the Sioux were always a cluster of tribes with a stable, enduring identity, we might not think to look for the archaeological signatures of the other identities they had in the past. Second, if we have some notion of the kinds of past social groups we are investigating, we have frameworks, if only tentative, for organizing and interpreting data. Finally, anticipating the social identities of the ancestral Sioux helps delimit the processes that might have been at work in their formation and maintenance.

A question of equal importance is the signatures of these identities in the archaeological record. What, for example, would a band, tribe, people, or culture look like in the archaeological record? Are these signatures easy or difficult to recognize? Are some of them easier to recognize than others?

Let us begin by examining the terms "band" and "tribe" in some detail. Both types of social organization are important in the model of Sioux prehistory developed later in this chapter. Bands are small-scale societies of hunters and gatherers that generally number fewer than one hundred people.[10] Their members are kinsfolk linked by descent, marriage, fictive relationships, and friendships. For at least part of the year, they live in mobile, autonomous, nuclear family groups (families consisting of a married couple and their young children) that exploit regional wild food resources. Because of their mobility, their housing usually consists of insubstantial dwellings or temporary shelters. The band itself is the aggregate of related families that comes together when food is abundant or when there is a pressing need. Although some bands have headmen, they are leaders in name only and have no formal means of enforcing their decisions. When present, leadership is nearly always based on personal status and authority. Even though there are economic differences and disparities in status and power among their members, they are not as marked as in more complexly organized societies. The size, composition, and duration of the aggregation of bands usually vary from year to year, depend-ing on social circumstances and the availability of food resources.

Like bands, tribes are generally egalitarian, functionally generalized multi-community societies linked together through kinship and friend-ship ties, a common derivation and customs, and a common language.[11] However, pan-tribal devices, such as sodalities, age-grades, secret socie-ties, ritual congregations, and crosscutting associations devoted to kin-ship affiliations, link them together. In addition, unlike band members, they tend to live for much of the year in settled homesteads or villages that might occur in clusters as a defensive measure. Most tribal people have a diet based largely on cultivated plants and domesticated animals. Typi-cally, they are settled farmers or, less often, nomads. Tribes are usually larger than bands and can be composed of thousands of people. Familiar examples of early historic tribal social networks in northeastern North America that exhibit these characteristics include the Huron, Miami, Illi-nois, and Winnebago.

Although structurally decentralized, the integrating devices of tribes are capable of creating multi-community alliances for mutual defense, non-aggression, and exchange. Pan-residential integration, when it occurs, is organized by individual villages, inter-tribal men's associations, lineages, or clans, rather than by a formal sovereign governing authority, as in chiefdoms and states. Consequently, alliances are temporary, partial, and fragile. Conflict can occur among tribal segments, and network bounda-ries remain poorly defined.

Explanations of the emergence of tribal social networks are diverse and contentious.[12] In general, the tribalization process is regarded as an ad hoc ephemeral reaction to the presence of more highly organized and of-ten aggressive societies. In this context, tribal formation results from hos-tile interaction, trade, the imposition of political form or tribute, ideological conversion, or some combination of these factors. Regardless of the spe-cific cause, the emergence of tribal social organization is not considered an internal evolutionary development but a strategy by marginal groups to cope with asymmetrical power relationships with neighboring groups. For this reason, warfare is a defining feature of tribal societies. In aggres-sive interactions, the integrative possibilities inherent in tribal social or-ganizations give tribal members a greater probability of survival than does a band level of organization.

Discussions of the tribalization process generally focus on the asym-metrical relationships that develop between bands and states or chiefdoms. However, the presence of more complexly organized, warlike neighbors with a tribal social organization might also push bands toward a tribal level of sociopolitical organization for the sake of survival. In the process of coalescing for defense, bands-cum-tribes generally adopt some of the social, political, and symbolic features of their aggressive neighbors. Further study might reveal patterns of variation in duration, intensity, and level of control in these asymmetrical relationships, depending upon whether the neighbor in the relationship is a state, chiefdom, or tribe. For all of these reasons, the causes and results of the tribalization process vary widely. The particular causes and results of the process must be determined in each case; archaeologists cannot assume, for example, that there is a uniform set of causes and results embedded in the archaeological record that can, with effort, be recognized without fail.

Tribal names vary through space and time because of the situational context of alliance formations. As the nature and geographic direction of external stimuli shift, new alliances are created under new names and the memory of older alliances are incorporated into traditional lore or forgotten. In situations where external social and political stimuli are removed, the bonds of tribalization normally weaken and dissolve, and the corporate bodies that once linked communities disintegrate.[13] Both of these situations have important implications for the reconstruction of the prehistory of tribes.

In contrast, an ethnic identity is based on a shared attitude of "we" versus "them."[14] Assuming an ethnic identity is one way of organizing interaction among groups and of maintaining social boundaries with more powerful neighboring polities. Importantly, ethnicity is not something that always existed in the past. Like a tribal social organization, it is an aspect of social organization that comes about through economic and political relationships and intergroup competition. Language is usually an important component of ethnicity, and ethnic and linguistic boundaries are often the same. This "we" versus "them" attitude is expressed in a self-appointed name and the active maintenance of cultural and territorial boundaries with the "other." Highly visible and distinctive social symbols, such as hairstyle, clothes, and decorative pottery, are developed to make social interaction easier by clearly distinguishing friend from foe. A common ethnic identity and self-awareness, while not restricted to tribal social organizations, are characteristic tribal traits.

A culture refers to a group of people who share common customs, speak a common language, and occupy a particular territory.[15] Cultures have an ideological, symbolic dimension that must be understood in order to comprehend the activities of its members. A people is a more amorphous concept. The name that bands and tribes use to refer to themselves often means in translation "the People." More generally, the word refers to people who speak a common language.

What do the archaeological signatures of these social identities look like? Are some signatures more difficult to identify than others? Because bands and tribes are defined in part by differing settlement patterns, their presence or absence can sometimes be identified archaeologically by degree of settlement agglomeration or the presence or absence of substantial buildings and large villages. Other material clues to their presence or absence include the presence or absence of the residue of domesticated plant foods.

Other social identities, such as ethnic group, culture, and people, are normally more difficult to recognize in the archaeological record. This conclusion is consistent with the results of studies of the material referents of social identities in modern societies.[16] These studies affirm that material goods, such as decorated pottery or style of spearhead, are unreliable indicators of established social boundaries. Not all material goods are used to maintain and signal tribal and ethnic membership, and those that are vary from one culture to another. There is, then, no simple one-to-one correlation between material culture patterning and the boundaries of social groups. Confusion is introduced, too, by the presence of other kinds of symbols, such as those of rank or age group, and by expressions of decorative fashion. The historic nineteenth-century Sioux had many identities, all at the same time. They were members of a nation, tribe, family, linguistic group, and gender and age groups, among other identities.

Archaeologists assumed at one time that particular features of the archaeological record, especially ceramic traditions and arrowhead styles, were the material identifiers of cultures, peoples, and language groups. An archaeological culture, for instance, was traditionally defined as a "constantly recurring assemblage of artifacts," with pottery vessels often a key diagnostic. A distribution map of the occurrence of that type of pottery was thought to establish the boundaries of the people of which it is a material manifestation. However, archaeological cultures do not necessarily represent social entities in the past and, importantly, are not intended to do so. An archaeological culture is merely a classificatory device that recognizes similarities among assemblages of artifacts and features. This means that similarities among artifact assemblages do not necessarily represent the presence of a social group. Likewise, the distribution of a pottery type does not necessarily define the boundaries of a tribe or any other cohesive social group. To equate such notional "cultures" with "people" is now seen to be extremely hazardous. These problems are particularly severe for ethnicity, which is an awareness of being one people. One solution is to search for the signatures of broad processes, such as tribalization or ethnogenesis, rather than concentrate on the isolated identifiers of the presence of a culture.

These findings do not negate the fact that such groups now exist and once existed in the past. They only mean that archaeologists have not found a reliable way to distinguish social identities in the archaeological record. Their message is that the archaeological record must be read in a more sophisticated way: the relationship between the archaeological record and social identities must be explored and established, not merely assumed.

The Archaeological Record

Three sources of paleoanthropological evidence are used here to evaluate Sioux origin narratives and to form a model of Sioux prehistory. The first source is the archaeological record.

Unlike contemporary Minnesotans, the ancestral Sioux received their food energy from local plant and animal food resources. Consequently, an appreciation of the nuances of Minnesota's archaeological record, and of subsequent Sioux history, requires some familiarity with the state's broad-scale associations of plant and animal communities and climate. These associations provide insights into the nature of the Sioux homeland and help explain why the Sioux interacted differently with their neighbors to the south and north. They also provide a background for understanding the divergent lifeways that Sioux bands adopted when they eventually moved from their forested homeland into the prairies and plains to the south and west.

Biologists have divided Minnesota's mosaic of forests, lakes, and prairies into four general habitat zones (figure 2.1).[17] The most northern zone, which covers only a narrow slice of northeastern Minnesota, is composed of boreal forest. Also called the Subarctic or Spruce–Fir–Moose–Caribou biome, it is a vast region of bogs, lakes, rivers, and coniferous forests. Among the larger animals present in the late prehistoric period were moose, caribou, black bear, beaver, and snowshoe hare. Although a popular resort area now, this recently deglaciated land with its long, cold winters, deep snow cover, and short, warm summers was a difficult environment for Indian economies due to seasonal fluctuations in local food resources.

A second habitat zone composed of deciduous forest was confined to the southeastern corner of the state and to some south-central counties. Also known as the Oak–Deer–Maple biome, the zone contained broadleaved deciduous trees that drop their leaves in winter. Compared to a boreal forest, a deciduous forest tends to have larger numbers of a wider variety of animals. White-tailed deer was the primary game animal, but black bear, elk, cottontail rabbit, beaver, and muskrat were also among the animals hunted or trapped. Badgers and an occasional bison lived in open woodland. The deciduous forest zone has shorter winters, less snowfall, and longer, hotter summers than does the boreal forest zone.

The boreal and deciduous habitat zones overlap in central and northern Minnesota to form a broad transition zone. Popularly called the

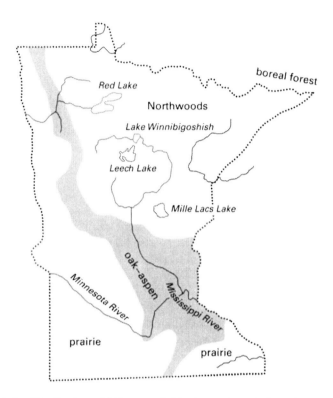

Figure 2.1   Distribution of Minnesota's biotic provinces before the spread of the Big Woods

northwoods and more technically the Lake Forest habitat zone, this zone contains both boreal and deciduous forest plants and animals. Boreal forest plants and animals increase in frequency to the north and those typical of the deciduous forest become more common to the south. The climate is intermediate as well. While winters are still long and cold, summers are somewhat longer and warmer than in the north. Like the boreal forest to the north, the land is covered with extensive lakes and bogs, a heritage, too, of Ice Age glaciation. The northwoods extends eastward across northern Wisconsin to New England.

The last habitat zone is composed of tall-grass prairie. Also known as the Grass–Oak–Bison biome, it once covered large areas of western and southern Minnesota. At historic contact, bison, elk, badgers, gophers, and coyotes were among the animals living in the prairie. Forests were present along stream valleys, around lakes, and on some plateaus and low hills, and copses of oak and hickory trees were scattered throughout the open grassland. The short-grass prairie, or Great Plains, the eventual habitat of many Sioux, begins west of Minnesota in the Dakotas between the 97th and 100th meridians.

The post-glacial prehistory of Minnesota is complex and dynamic. We concentrate here on what archaeologists call the Woodland tradition (c.200 BC–AD 1650), for the most secure associations between the ancestral Sioux and prehistoric archaeological complexes are with this tradition. Our goal is to associate the ancestral Sioux with specific Woodland archaeological complexes and natural habitat zones.

Archaeologists divide the Woodland into two sub-traditions, the Initial (c.200 BC–AD 500) and the Terminal (c. AD 500–1680).[18] A hunter-gatherer lifeway characterizes both phases in Minnesota. The Initial Woodland is marked by the first construction of conical earthen burial mounds and the appearance of pottery vessels. Archaeological complexes associated with this sub-tradition include Malmo and Brainerd in the northwoods and Howard Lake and Fox Lake in the prairies and deciduous woodlands to the south. Malmo and Howard Lake pottery, which is concentrated in the east-central section of the state, has a southern Havana–Hopewell cast, which includes dentate-stamp decoration, beveled lips, and familiar zoned patterns of decoration. Havana–Hopewell complexes developed to the south of Minnesota in Illinois, Indiana, and Ohio.

AD 500–800 was a transitional period in the northwoods between Initial Woodland and full Terminal Woodland lifeways. The Brainerd complex might have persisted in the Mississippi River headwaters region until AD 800. However, a new archaeological complex called St. Croix appeared during this period in that area of Minnesota once occupied by the Malmo complex. Stretching from the northwestern corner of Wisconsin across eastern and central Minnesota into the Red River valley, St. Croix sites, like earlier Malmo sites, seem concentrated in the Mille Lacs Lake region. The dentate-stamp decoration of St. Croix and related ceramics, such as Onamia, exhibit continuity with earlier Havana–Hopewell-related Malmo and Howard Lake ceramics.

By AD 800, a continuum of Blackduck-related Terminal Woodland complexes was present in the northwoods. Effigy Mound and other Terminal Woodland archaeological complexes occupied the southern prairies and deciduous woodlands. Although separated into three archaeological complexes – Blackduck, Kathio, and Clam River – northwoods Terminal Woodland people shared a similar appearing material culture and a mobile hunter-gatherer lifeway. Wild plant resources, especially wild rice, were gathered annually, and deer, elk, and other, smaller local mammals, including aquatic species, such as fish, turtle, mussels, and ducks, were hunted and captured within a circumscribed range. The first ricing and midden features found around Mille Lacs Lake date to this period.

Because of their size, low density, and narrow artifact content, the great majority of Blackduck–Kathio–Clam River sites appear to be ephemeral, shifting residential camps utilized by small, autonomous family groups. There might have been, however, a few larger villages. Elden Johnson excavated a rectangular, semi-subterranean house at the Mille Lacs area Petaga Point site that had a floor area roughly 6 by 11 meters (6.5 x 12 yards) with an additional 2-meter (2.1-yard) entrance passage.[19] The floor, which was depressed 50 cm (19 inches) below the original ground surface, was outlined by a line of postmolds, which are the organic stains of deteriorated wooden posts. An offset main fire pit was located toward the entrance. The structure had burned and masses of charcoal and partially burned wood were scattered over the floor.

Because a few Kathio pottery sherds were on the surface of the floor under the charcoal, Johnson thought the most likely association of the house was with the local Kathio Wahkon phase. The impressions of four other house features were also identified at the site, at least one of which was burnt, too. This association must remain suggestive, for no detailed reports exist for these excavations, and associations in these shallow, mixed Mille Lacs sites are notoriously difficult to confirm. It remains unclear whether the houses actually formed a village cluster or were occupied in sequence over the years.

Differences among these archaeological complexes consist primarily of local style preferences in the shape and decoration of pottery jars. However, all pottery jars are tempered with grit, globular in shape, cord-marked on the exterior surface, and decorated with cord-wrapped stick impressions. The east–west flow of ideas at this time resembles a pattern visible in earlier archaeological assemblages in this habitat zone. Because of this east–west stylistic and spatial continuity, these closely related archaeological complexes have been called the Blackduck–Kathio–Clam River Continuum, with the name sequence moving roughly from west to east.

Settlements of the Clam River complex, the most eastern of the complexes, are found in the Wisconsin tributaries of the St. Croix River, and in the northwoods and bordering deciduous forest zone of eastern Minnesota.[20] Clam River is the most poorly known of the three complexes. The closely related Kathio complex is situated along the southern boundary of the northwoods in central Minnesota and in the west-central Lake District, which stretches westward across the deciduous forest zone into the prairies to the west. The greatest density of Kathio settlements, however, is thought to be the east-central Mille Lacs Lake area, which is considered the core settlement area of the Kathio complex. At least a dozen archaeological sites with Kathio occupations have been found around the Rum River outlet of Mille Lacs Lake alone.

Situated in the northwoods to the west and north of Kathio, the heart-land of the early Blackduck complex is similar to that of the earlier Brainerd complex. Concentrated in the Mississippi River headwaters region around the Leech Lake basins, Lake Winnibigoshish, and other lakeshores, early Blackduck settlements have also been found to the south in the prairies of the Lake District, to the west in the Red River valley, and across the far northern forests of the state. As in the Kathio complex, Blackduck sites are scattered across the landscape. People with Kathio and Blackduck artifact assemblages appear to have moved between seasonal sources of food, such as fish runs, wild rice beds, and bison herds.

Archaeological assemblages change abruptly in the southern prairies and deciduous woodlands of Minnesota between AD 1000 and AD 1300. Besides a radical shift in the appearance of pottery vessels, clustered villages appear and evidence of maize (corn) horticulture is abundant. Palisade walls, presumably for defense, surround some villages. The archaeological complexes that date to this transformation include the Mississippian-related Cambria and Silvernale phases along the Minnesota and Mississippi rivers, and, later, several phases of the Oneota tradition. The historic Siouan-speaking Iowa and Oto Indians seem likely descendants of at least some Oneota in this region.

A parallel and equally abrupt transformation occurred in the southern portion of the northwoods at the beginning of the fourteenth century, if not earlier. Ceramic wares changed radically in appearance, people aggregated into clustered, defended villages, and the harvesting of a grain, now wild rice, seems to have been dramatically intensified, for clay-lined ricing jigs are a common feature in late components in Mille Lacs Lake sites. This new cultural expression in the northwoods has been called the Psinomani archaeological complex. In the Mille Lacs Lake area, it coincides with Elden Johnson's Shakopee phase (AD 1300–1680). The complex is composed of archaeological assemblages in the southern portion of the northwoods that contain Sandy Lake and Ogechie ceramics. Additional changes in material culture equipment include the addition, at least in the Mille Lacs Lake area, of ground stone artifacts, such as grinding slabs and ferruginous shaft straighteners, and of scapula hoes.[21] These tools appear to represent, like the ceramics, a strong southern Oneota influence.

Details of Psinomani settlement-subsistence patterns remain poorly documented due to artifact mixing in shallow sites and a lack of excavation reports. However, Elden Johnson considered these people "forest fringe dwellers" who exploited the resources of the forests and adjoining prairie. Their seasonal activities most likely included bison hunting in the prairies, wild rice harvesting, fishing, the hunting of woodland mammals, and the gathering and collecting of wild vegetal foods in both habitats.

Figure 2.2   Sandy Lake pottery vessel from the Cooper site (courtesy of the Wilford Archaeology Laboratory, University of Minnesota)

Johnson thought that they were as actively engaged in prairie maintenance using fire to maintain game levels as they were in maintaining the quality and size of their wild rice beds.

Wild rice and chenopod (a plant of the goosefoot family) are the most frequently recovered plant remains at Mille Lacs Lake sites, but corn, squash, tobacco (*Nicotiana rustica*), and morning glory, among other plants, have been recovered in smaller numbers at one or more sites. Tobacco and squash appear to have been locally cultivated in garden beds worked with scapula hoes.[22] Although poorly documented, wild rice beds might have been managed, too. The most frequently recovered animal remains are deer, elk, small mammals, domestic dogs, fish, ducks, turtles, and mussels.

Unlike the scattered settlement pattern of the earlier continuum, Psinomani villages and camps are clustered in a small number of widely separated localities. Areas between these settlement aggregates seem abandoned except by seasonal extractive groups. These out-village groups must have been fairly mobile and small, for they have left little sign in the archaeological record.

The Cooper (21ML9) and Wilford (21ML12) sites at the Rum River outlet of Mille Lacs Lake are apparent examples of year-round woodland

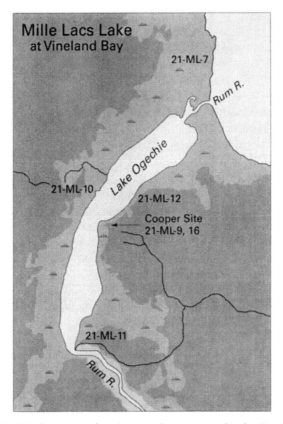

Figure 2.3   Modern map of settlement cluster around Lake Ogechie at the outlet of Mille Lacs Lake (courtesy of the Wilford Archaeology Laboratory, University of Minnesota)

villages. Large house structures are documented at both sites, but it is unclear whether they date to the Shakopee phase or to the following proto-historic phase. The structures resemble the pole-and-bark summerhouses in early historic Dakota villages along the Minnesota River. Examples of probable seasonal bison-hunting camps have been identified at the Shea and Mooney sites in the Red River region.[23] The Shea site, which is 50 meters (54.5 yards) from the Red River, covers about 16 hectares (40 acres) and was surrounded by a deep, dry moat and possibly by a palisade. Some Psinomani apparently even grew (or at least consumed) some corn at the Shea site. The ceramic assemblages at Shea and Mooney indicate that considerable interaction between eastern woodland and prairie-plains dwellers continued throughout the Terminal Woodland period. In fact, the prairies of the northern half of Minnesota and of eastern North

Dakota could have been as much Psinomani territory as were the southern two-thirds of the northwoods in Minnesota.

Sandy Lake jars are usually tempered with crushed mussel shell or with shell and finely ground grit. Shell tempering is a trait associated with the development of Mississippian cultures and the Oneota tradition to the south. Exterior vessel surfaces are nearly always cord-marked, a traditional Woodland trait, or stamped with grooved paddles, a northern Plains trait. Small amounts of locally made Oneota pottery (Ogechie ware) or northeastern Plains ware from the Red River valley area, or both, are present in most Psinomani assemblages. Elden Johnson and his colleagues were convinced that their archaeological excavations established a seventeenth-century association between Psinomani archaeological assemblages and the Mdewakanton Dakota in the Mille Lacs Lake area.[24]

This brief survey of the archaeology of the late prehistoric homeland of the Sioux raises many critical questions. When did Dakota speakers first enter the state? Where did they come from? How large was their initial population? Are the people responsible for the Malmo, Brainerd, St. Croix, Clam River–Kathio–Blackduck, and Psinomani archaeological complexes genetically related? Did they speak related languages? Does the sudden appearance of new ceramic wares represent the movement of new peoples into the region? When did Dakota speakers first consider themselves an ethnic group? A tribe? A stab at answering these questions will be made in the last section of this chapter. But first, we will examine two other sources of paleoanthropological information for clues to the origins of the Sioux.

Skeletal Biology

Information about the prehistoric Sioux is available through the study of their skeletal remains. These investigations, which are normally carried out by physical anthropologists and medical doctors, first establish a range of physical characteristics for individuals, such as sex, age at death, build (height and weight), appearance, family relationships, disease, and damage to the skeleton caused by trauma. This information is then used to answer questions about the populations of which these people were members. Typical questions are: Was the lifespan of both sexes the same or different in particular periods or archaeological complexes? Is there a correlation between malnutrition, specific diseases, violence, or types of trauma and individuals of a particular sex or age? If so, why? What was the size of the population? Were the people archaeologists associate with an archaeological complex a genetic group or composed of two or more biological populations?

A comprehensive, if pioneering, skeletal study by Nancy Ossenberg analyzed the distribution of 26 discrete, independently inherited traits of the skull in a sample of 942 individuals in 19 skeletal groups from Minnesota, the eastern Dakotas, and southern Manitoba.[25] The groups represent the three historic divisions of the Sioux, the historic Assiniboin, Cheyenne, and Blackfoot, and a range of earlier Woodland complexes. The Cheyenne and Blackfoot speak Algonquian languages, while the Sioux and Assiniboin speak dialects of Dakota.

Ossenberg concluded that, as a group, these northern samples are readily distinguishable from populations to the south in Illinois and the central Plains. She thought, however, that minor differences among the samples pointed to possible archaeological and cultural affiliations. Statistical analyses indicated that the Blackduck end of the Clam River–Kathio–Blackduck continuum was most likely ancestral Sioux, with its closest affinities to the Lakota, Yankton–Yanktonai, and Dakota, in that order. This early Blackduck sample was also closely related to the Mille Lacs Lake Kathio sample, which, interestingly, was no closer to Dakota than to the other two Sioux divisions.[26] These data support the idea that a Sioux population base was in the Mississippi headwaters region by AD 800. By implication, the Blackduck–Psinomani transition did not involve substantial population replacement.

Another relevant conclusion of Ossenberg's study was that ancestral Assiniboin were in southern Manitoba by AD 1000. Although biologically related to the Sioux, they were not, according to this analysis, offshoots of any historic Sioux band. Ossenberg thought they split instead from an earlier northern intermediary population centered on the Rainy River (the Laurel complex). Sample measurements of this early group relate them most closely with early Blackduck and to what was then called the Manitoba phase, which has strong biological affiliations with historic Assiniboin. She suggested that the oral tradition of a historic Sioux origin for the Assiniboin was a memory of a group of Yanktonai who broke away from the main body of Sioux to join the Assiniboin in the early contact period.[27]

Ossenberg also attempted to measure the biological affinity of these groups with populations that are more distant. An Illinois Havana–Hopewell skeletal sample had only a lukewarm relationship with Kathio and even more distant relationships with the other groups she examined. She concluded that it was unlikely that the Woodland peoples of the Upper Mississippi Valley, and the historic Plains tribes descended from them, originated by dispersal from southeastern Hopewell centers in Illinois and Ohio. All of the northern cranial series she examined fall into a skull form that has its closest relationships with western and northwestern populations, such as Athabascan-speaking groups. Illinois Havana Hopewell falls into another, more southern skull form. More recent skeletal studies have documented biological continuity in the prehistoric northern Plains for thousands of years, and others a close genetic relationship between the Dakota and certain northwestern Plains groups that extends back into late prehistoric times.[28] These tend to be tall individuals with large, rugged skulls that have high orbits, low cranial vaults, and large, rugged facial features.

A second study by Andrew Scherer explores the biological relationships of Western and Eastern Oneota, the Late Woodland period Effigy Mound and Kathio complexes, the Big Stone phase of the Middle Missouri tradition, and the Middle Mississippian site of Aztalan in Wisconsin.[29] Scherer's study is based on dental morphology, which has several advantages over the craniofacial skeleton as a source of biological distance data. Because of the fragmentary nature of many of the skeletal series of the Upper Midwest, studies that concentrate on teeth have a larger sample of individuals to work with. Teeth are also less environmentally plastic than bone. Scherer collected data on 120 non-metric traits from the dentition of 262 individuals from skeletal and dental cast collections in Minnesota (Western Oneota, Kathio, and Big Stone phases), Iowa (Western Oneota), and Wisconsin (Eastern Oneota, Effigy Mound, Aztalan).

Four conclusions of his study are of interest here. First, the Western and Eastern Oneota are a homogeneous, discrete biological entity. Second, the two Woodland complexes (Kathio and Effigy Mound) share an overall biological relationship that could be the result of continual east–west gene flow or a close, shared ancestry, which is considered the more likely explanation. Neither sample shares a close relationship with the Oneota samples. Third, the Big Stone phase sample is closely related to the Kathio sample. Fourth, the Kathio–Effigy Mound–Big Stone series represents a clustering of non-Chiwere/Ho-Chunk speakers, possibly the Dakota Sioux. Chiwere-Siouan speakers (Iowa, Oto, and Missouri) are generally regarded as the historic descendants of the Western Oneota and the Ho-Chunk (Winnebago) the descendants of the Eastern Oneota. Scherer's study also supports the view that the Oneota derived from a Woodland group in the southwestern Wisconsin/northwestern Illinois/ northeastern Iowa region, and repeats the conclusion of other studies that there is little biological relationship among linguistically distinct groups of Siouan speakers.[30]

Biological distance studies like these are speculative for many reasons. Four are relevant here. First, few skeletal samples are representative of the populations of which they were members. There are several reasons for this probable lack of representation: not all people in a community were necessarily buried in mounds or cemeteries, and only some of those that were have been recovered archaeologically and then studied. Second, the assignment of skeletons to archaeological complexes has been problematic in Minnesota. Both primary and intrusive burials in mounds have been lumped together, and burials lacking diagnostic artifacts have been assigned to one complex or another based on shaky ideas about complex/burial mode associations. Third, studies often assume that social groups have existed as identifiable biological populations for hundreds if not thousands of years. Disease and warfare can destroy populations, and genetic drift and population mixture can radically alter the genetic characteristics of populations over time. Therefore, studies could be attempting to associate historic groups with prehistoric populations that no longer exist. Fourth, there might be little correlation between the linguistic and biological populations of a region. Familiar modern examples are North America and England, where migration, assimilation, and cultural diffusion have produced "melting pots" of English-speaking people from diverse biological (and linguistic) backgrounds.

These examples prove the folly of naively assuming a one-to-one correlation between archaeological complexes and biological populations. Minnesota's Havana-related complexes and Late Prehistoric agriculturalists on the central Plains provide other examples where the diffusion of ideas into indigenous populations rather than the large-scale migration of new peoples seems a likely possibility. In other circumstances, gene pools remain more resistant to change than do either language or material culture. For these and other reasons, Ossenberg and Scherer consider their conclusions speculative and in need of testing by additional data analysis.[31]

Historical Linguistics

While weighed down with theoretical and methodological problems, historical linguistics is a rich, independent source of information about the Sioux before European contact. The approach is based upon the assumption that contemporary languages that show close phonological (sound patterning), morphological (patterning of sound sequences and words), and syntactic (phase and sentence patterning) similarities derive from a common ancestral language. Such a reconstructed language is called a protolanguage and the languages divergent from it daughter (or derived) languages or, together, a language family. Because of similarities and differences among contemporary derived languages, linguists can reconstruct what the ancestral language might have been like, and how and when it changed. By examining shared words, they are also able to construct numerous features of protolanguage communities, such as what they ate, where they lived, and the nature of their kinship system.[32]

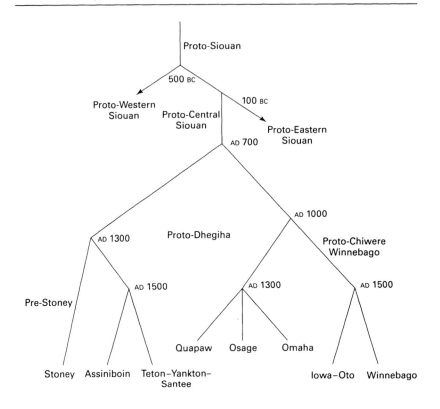

Figure 2.4   Linguistic dating of Central Siouan language (adapted from Springer and Witkowski 1982, Figure 3)

Linguistic dating provides both relative and absolute age estimates of when events or processes happened in the past. In historical linguistics, the genetic method of dating is based on the assumption that strong similarities among languages are evidence for their derivation from a common protolanguage. By measuring their degree of similarity, some notion of when daughter languages split from the protolanguage can be obtained. For example, if two related languages are more alike than either is to a third, related language, then the third language was the first to split from the language grouping. This provides a means of ordering their associated archaeological assemblages, if they can be determined, into a relative sequence established independent of the assemblages themselves. This is an important accomplishment, for reaching the same general conclusions using independent data sets is a goal of science. The reason is that consensus demonstrates that a conclusion was most likely not an effect of the methods used.

If the further assumption is made that languages change at a constant rate, then a rough date can be obtained for when two languages split.[33] Since many factors, such as loan words, the presence of a strong literary tradition, and word taboos, can influence the rate of linguistic change, these determinations are best considered hypotheses rather than firm historical evidence. Elements of the lexicon (vocabulary), phonology (sound correspondences), and grammar have been used to establish genetic relationships in both approaches to linguistic dating.

In a 1982 study of Siouan historical linguistics, James Springer and Stanley Witkowski compared lexical items from 16 Siouan languages and dialects to generate ideas about the origin of historical Siouan-speaking groups, including the Sioux.[34] The first of the two approaches they used to determine genetic relationships among these languages was degree of lexical (vocabulary) similarity. This approach measures how many items in a list of 100 (the Swadesh 100-word list) or 200 basic vocabulary words are shared by two related languages. Basic vocabulary refers to words for activities (breathe, drink, eat, dig), items (tree, sun, hand, eye), and qualities (big, dirty, white, black) that are likely to be found in all language communities. The number of words that are similar in sound and meaning (cognates) are then counted to provide a measure of the lexical similarity of the two languages. Lexical similarity is usually expressed by a percentage. For example, the Lakota word for woman, *winyan* or *wea*, is similar enough to the Hidatsa word for woman, *wia* or *mia*, to be considered a cognate. Time of divergence is determined by applying a formula, such as $T = \log C / (2 \log r)$, where T = time in years, C = percent of shared cognates, and r = a constant of .805. Again, the results should be considered only reasonable estimates rather than accurate dates because of loan words and more variable rates of language change than originally thought.[35] In their study, Springer and Witkowski compared 182 lexical items.

Their second approach was a method called counterindication, which produces scores by comparing a lexical item between pairs of languages. If one member of a pair shares an item with other related languages but not with the other member of the pair, then it is taken to indicate that the members of the pair have closer ties with other languages in the group than with each other. A large number of these comparisons provide a counterindication score. Since the products of the two approaches should be similar, they are often used together to check the reliability of the results.

The Sioux speak Dakota, which is a member of the Siouan language family. The family is composed of 14 mutually unintelligible languages distributed throughout the eastern Woodlands and northern Great Plains.[36] In the Springer and Witkowski account, all historic Siouan languages are derived from Proto-Siouan, a parent language centered in the central Mississippi Valley region before about 500 BC. Proto-Siouan divided into eastern, western, and central subgroups between 500 BC and 100 BC. Each subgroup divided several times again before historic contact.

In this scenario, Western Siouan speakers (the historic Mandan, Hidatsa, and Crow) broke from the parent root first at about 500 BC. Its speakers moved in a general northwestern and then western direction until they reached their historic location in the northern Plains. While the Mandan and Hidatsa eventually occupied agricultural villages on the Missouri River and its tributaries in North Dakota, the Crow became hunter-gatherers in the high country east of the Rockies in the central Montana–Wyoming border region. With the use of lexical similarity rates and counterindication percentages, Springer and Witkowski suggest that Proto-Western Siouan remained a linguistic unit from about 500 BC to AD 300, when Mandan split from Crow–Hidatsa. Crow diverged from Hidatsa about AD 1200.

Eastern Siouan speakers (the historic Ofo, Biloxi, and Tutelo) broke away from the parent group about 100 BC and moved south. The largest of the original subgroups was Central Siouan (the historic Dakota: the Stoney, Assiniboin, and Lakota–Yankton/Yanktonai–Dakota; the Dhegiha: Quapaw, Kansa, Osage, and Omaha–Ponca; and the Chiwere–Winnebago: Iowa, Oto, Missouri, and Winnebago). Even though this subgroup differentiated largely in place, some members spread northward through the Upper Mississippi River drainage to southern Minnesota, where Proto-Dakota split from Proto-Dhegiha and Proto-Chiwere–Winnebago in about AD 700 (figure 1). Dhegiha and Chiwere–Winnebago became distinguishable dialects further south by AD 1000. By that time, Springer and Witkowski consider the Central and Upper Mississippi River drainage "solidly Siouan."

The spatial relationships of these subgroups and their emerging divisions can be inferred after AD 1000 from borrowed words. This is accomplished by assuming that societies that share more borrowed words together are spatially closer than those that share fewer words together. While this assumption is an obvious simplification, it again provides ideas to think about. When these calculations are made, the Dhegiha at about AD 1000 are in the south, the Chiwere–Winnebago in the middle, and the Proto-Dakota, the most isolated of the subgroups, in the north.

Proto-Dakota began to split up at about AD 1300, when Pre-Assiniboin–Stoney speakers moved northwestward away from other Dakota-speaking groups. In the mid-seventeenth century, they lived north of the middle Sioux on the Minnesota border and in adjacent southern Manitoba, where they lived a hunting-gathering lifeway in both parkland–prairie country and the boreal forest to the north. Lexicostatistics helps confirm the early presence of Assiniboin speakers in the far northwestern periphery of the

Sioux homeland, as suggested by written records. Assiniboin shares more lexical items with Lakota and Yankton–Yanktonai than with Dakota, and least with the more southern Chiwere.

The remaining Dakota languages or dialects began to diverge after AD 1500, with Lakota–Yankton/Yanktonai–Dakota forming a dialect chain. Lakota and Dakota, the two ends of the chain, were, as would be expected, the furthest apart. Linguistic evidence also suggests that after a long period of separation Mandan- and Dakota-speakers came into renewed contact at about AD 1500, and that Dakota-speakers remained in contact with Chiwere-speakers to the south during this period.[37]

Linguistic divergence occurs when groups of people speaking the same language split apart and lose communication with one another. Language splits alert archaeologists to the presence of unusual social processes. While we do not know why Proto-Dakota-speaking groups split apart, the estimated time of these splits does correspond with archaeological events reviewed earlier in this chapter. For example, early Central and possibly Eastern Siouan languages could have been associated with the Havana–Hopewell culture in the Central Mississippi Valley region. As Central Siouan speakers spread northward with their Havana culture, those who eventually became Proto-Dakota speakers could have developed the Malmo complex. Likewise, the closely related ancestors of the Iowa and Oto could have been responsible for Howard Lake and other Havana complexes in the southern part of the state. In this scenario Western Siouan speakers could have been associated with the Brainerd culture, for Brainerd or related ceramics eventually spread northward through the aspen parkland in Canada and, it seems, southward to Montana. This possibility is also supported by the presence of small but significant amounts of Brainerd pottery at Mille Lacs Lake sites. The implication is that the pottery might indicate continued contact among linguistic relatives.

With the demise of the Havana tradition at about AD 250, regional adaptations in Minnesota began to coincide with major habitats, and by AD 700, with the emergence of the Clam River–Kathio–Blackduck continuum, Proto-Dakota had diverged from the Central Siouan language group. By about AD 1300–50, most Proto-Dakota speakers had become ethnic Sioux or Psinomani. Although there is archaeological evidence of at least seasonal movement into the Red River region by Clam River–Kathio–Blackduck and earlier peoples, extended movement across the valley and intensified interaction with the Missouri Valley-centered Mandan in North Dakota did not begin until about AD 1500. This reconstruction is supported by a scatter of Sandy Lake pottery across eastern North Dakota and the presence of Plains ceramic traits, such as grooved paddle marking, on Sandy Lake jars in the forests of Minnesota and northwestern Wisconsin.

As stressed earlier in this section, linguistic dating and historical linguistics in general remain controversial, for many of their underlying assumptions are based on ideal, normative situations. Nonetheless, the ideas presented in this section illustrate the potential fruitfulness of the collaboration of archaeology, historical linguistics, and other avenues of investigating the history of the Sioux before written records. Although speculative, they provide agendas for a proactive, hypothesis-testing mode of research.

A Model of Sioux Prehistory

Obviously, these disparate bits of information are capable of supporting a range of models of the prehistory of the Sioux. The model I favor is outlined here. It should be stressed that the word "model," as used in this reconstruction, refers to a hopefully logically consistent scenario that accounts for and over-interprets existing data. Its intent in the early phases of research is to more sharply delineate a problem area – here the prehistory of the Sioux – and to propose hypotheses to guide understanding and research. Because of its hypothetical, exploratory nature, a model in this sense should be distinguished from a well-confirmed history that has an ancestry of positive tests.

I associate the ancestors of the Sioux with the Clam River–Kathio–Blackduck Continuum, which was present by at least AD 800. If the linguistic data cited above are roughly correct, the ancestral Sioux moved into central Minnesota at this time or slightly earlier. In this interpretation, societies in the Continuum consisted of kin-centered bands that occasionally joined with related bands for social and religious reasons when food supplies were abundant. At other times of the year, they were dispersed across the landscape in small, autonomous family groups. Their residential camps shifted often to maximize the gathering of regional food resources.[38] As family units grew in size, subgroups "fissioned off" to establish their own family territory. The result was a similarity of material culture and way of life, with stylistic drift evident across the southern portion of the northwoods. This pattern of drift characterizes the Clam River–Kathio–Blackduck Continuum. By about AD 1100, the zone contained an apparently large and dispersed population that might have outnumbered the Indian hunter-horticulturists (Mississippian-related and Oneota groups) now living in the southern quarter of the state.

The Psinomani social–political–material complex suddenly replaced this Terminal Woodland lifeway about AD 1300, although the exact date remains unclear.[39] In contrast to the band social organization of earlier groups, the Psinomani were a tribal society consisting of thousands of people. They lived for much of the year in larger, more permanent villages that clustered together to facilitate defense and economic cooperation. There were perhaps as few as ten or eleven of these clusters.[40] This means that many counties in central Minnesota lack extensive evidence of a Psinomani presence.

These scattered village clusters with their associated mortuary facilities were integrated through kinship ties, sodalities, friendships, and temporary alliances, and could have acted as focal points for social and political activities. Smaller camps for hunting, fishing, ricing, and other specialized activities were located for the most part within several kilometers of the central villages. However, even the central villages were no more than hamlets, with Cooper an estimated 1 hectare (2.5 acres) in size and Wilford a half hectare (1.2 acres); the largest, the Vineland Bay site (21ML7), was probably only 3–4 hectares (7.5–10 acres) in size. Like the Oneota to the south, the Psinomani – the ancestral Sioux – might have intensified the harvesting of a grain (here wild rice) to feed their concentrated populations, for other local food resources would have been rapidly depleted if they were the sole source of food energy. This process of intensification might have included the adoption of some aspects of the maize roasting and storing complex of southern horticulturalists.[41]

In this scenario, Sioux ethnic identity was established with the aggrega-

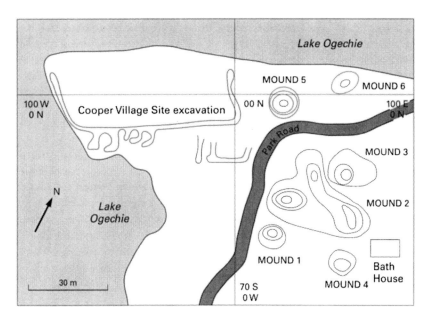

Figure 2.5   Cooper Village and Mound site, showing partial outline of a palisade wall (adapted from Lothson 1972, Vol. 2, Plate III)

tion of scattered family groups into clustered villages and the formation of tribal alliances. Psinomani camps like the Upper Rice Lake site in Clearwater County that are outside these settlement aggregations are uncommon and probably mark zones of specialized seasonal utilization or exploitation. The new Sandy Lake ceramics, which blend both Oneota (shell temper) and traditional Woodland (cord-marking and some grit as temper) elements, are one social symbol of this emerging, large-scale ethnic unity. Presumably, distinctive hairstyles, clothes, and other readily visible cues were also used to set themselves apart from the groups they were competing with. A measure of the strength of their intergroup social network and the magnitude of the external threat is the uniformity of Sandy Lake ceramics throughout the vast southern portion of the northwoods. Like other tribal societies, Psinomani tribal divisions were segmentary lineages that joined in shifting combinations in response to the magnitude and direction of external, hostile social interactions. At other times, they remained autonomous social groups that might have fought each other.

Why did the tribalization process occur at this time in the northwoods of Minnesota? What was the stimulus? The answer seems to be an escalation in trade and conflict with Oneota and other Upper Mississippian warrior cultures to the south which had developed earlier in opposition to intruding aggressive Mississippian chiefdoms.[42] Elden Johnson noted that the beginning of the Shakopee phase at Mille Lacs Lake coincided with the abandonment of Oneota villages in the Red Wing–Lake Pepin area of southeastern Minnesota and an influx of Oneota traits into north-central Minnesota. He considered this influence so pervasive that he referred to the protohistoric Mille Lacs complex as "Oneota with wild rice" or "Oneota without maize."[43]

During the Developmental horizon (AD 1150–1350) of the Oneota tradition, clusters of villages had spread to the La Crosse locality in Wisconsin, the Blue Earth River locality in south-central Minnesota, the central Des Moines River locality in Iowa, and elsewhere.[44] During the Classic horizon (AD 1350–1650), villages became larger, were occupied for longer periods of time, and were placed in increasingly defensible positions. For instance, Dixon, a Correctionville-phase site in northwest Iowa, which covers about 36 hectares (90 acres), is large for the tradition. Villages along the Little Sioux River in the same region shifted up the valley and from the floodplain to the uplands through time, presumably for defense. By about AD 1300, at least some Oneota had begun a movement westward into the lower Missouri Valley. Other Oneota gradually abandoned the Upper Mississippi River basin in the seventeenth century, when they too moved westward to join the Lower Missouri Valley Oneota. According to Dakota oral tradition, they pushed the Iowa (presumably the historic descendants of the Orr phase Oneota) out of southern Minnesota shortly after historic contact, most likely in the second half of the seventeenth century.[45] Oneota occupational activity also decreased dramatically in eastern Wisconsin in about AD 1600.

Conflict was not confined only or even primarily to Oneota groups. Milner has documented an increase in the number of palisaded sites on the northern Mississippian frontier between AD 1350 and 1500, with a further, dramatic increase between AD 1500 and 1650.[46] During the Crow Creek massacre in neighboring South Dakota in AD 1325, nearly 500 people were killed, with many bodies scalped and mutilated.[47] By the middle of the sixteenth century, what were most likely ancestral Illinois Indians entered northern Illinois, eventually ending Oneota settlement in that area.[48] The Sioux and Illinois soon became traditional enemies, for Euro-American explorers encountered war parties moving from one area to the other. All of these scattered occurrences seem to document an increase in warfare throughout the northern frontier zone after about AD 1300. The burned houses associated with Kathio pottery at the Petaga Point site at Mille Lacs could be associated with this escalation in hostility.

Other occurrences during the AD 1300–1680 period that affected the ancestral Sioux should also be mentioned. The first is the expansion of "bigwoods" trees (elm, basswood, ironwood, sugar maple, ash, hickory, butternut) over a large area of south-central Minnesota after AD 1550. Eric Grimm has suggested that this southward bulge of elm–oak forest was associated with a reduction in fire frequency due to increased precipitation and decreased temperature during the height of the Little Ice Age (AD 1550–1700). Regardless of its origins, this large-scale increase in deciduous forest significantly altered the animal community of this area and its importance to competing hunting parties.[49]

A second occurrence in the AD 800–1680 period is the development of a pattern of interaction between what were presumably ancestral Sioux and other, mostly Algonquian-speaking groups (most likely ancestral Cheyenne, Arapaho, Cree, and Ojibwa) to the north and northwest. Unlike the disjuncture between central and southern Minnesota, artifact assemblages in the central and northern parts of the state appear similar, beginning with the spread of Blackduck ceramic ware. This pattern of material assemblage similarity continues with the later spread northward of Sandy Lake ware. These artifact similarities indicate a different pattern of social interaction to the north than to the south. Exchange could have been emphasized rather than conflict. This balance might have been maintained until it was disrupted by large-scale population movements, the introduction of guns, and a growing competition for furs in the historic fur-trade period. In addition, a natural barrier might have separated the wild rice-rich lakes of the ancestral Western Sioux from the Lake of the Woods and

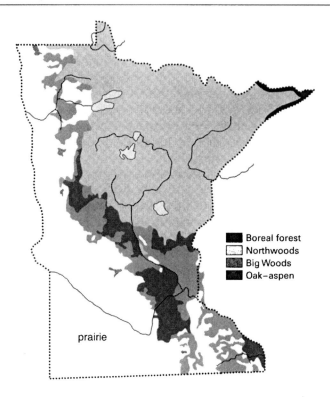

Figure 2.6   Distribution of Minnesota's biotic provinces after the spread of the
Big Woods

Rainy Lake and Rainy River in the Far North, which was the southern
homeland of what were presumably Algonquian-speaking groups. The
barrier was the "big bog," a soggy, sparsely inhabited remnant of Glacial
Lake Agassiz that covers a large portion of northwestern and north-central Minnesota.

A third, more conjectural, occurrence could have been the emergence
of the male warrior/supremacist complex that characterized the historic
Sioux until they were forced onto reservations in the late nineteenth century. This complex is commonly associated with tribal groups.[50] Warfare
provides important opportunities in tribal societies for personal advancement through the increased status and economic gains it brings. It is also
an important factor in forcing a greater degree of centralized social and
political control in egalitarian social groups. Since the male warrior/
supremacist complex is a characteristic of the historic Sioux, it seems reasonable to suppose that it emerged as part of the tribalization process that
began about AD 1300.

Evidence for trade with southern groups has not been explicitly documented, but it likely includes the "Oneotization" of Psinomani ceramics
and the presence of locally made Ogechie ware, the new ground stone
complex, and some maize (corn). Evidence for an escalation in violence or
at least the threat of violence includes: (1) the presence of a broad, uninhabited buffer zone to the south; (2) fortifications at the Cooper, Wilford,
and Shea sites; (3) signs of violence in the mortuary complex; (4) the abrupt
change to a clustered settlement pattern; (5) burned houses at Petaga Point;
and (6) an abrupt change in the cultural sequence.

The "Oneotization" of Psinomani material culture, which is seen most
clearly in the presence of rustic Oneota jars (Ogechie ware), shell-tem-
pered Sandy Lake jars with some Oneota iconographic symbols, and an
Oneota ground stone complex, indicates a pattern of emulation and conflict during the tumultuous fourteenth century that is a characteristic of
the tribalization process elsewhere. This process could also have included
the selective borrowing of aspects of Oneota mortuary customs and political and social organization. The degree of borrowing and the intensity
of the tribalization process itself most likely varied among the widely dispersed Psinomani groups in response to the intensity of localized Oneota
influences.

Despite this emulation, there were sharp material culture boundaries
between the Oneota in the south and the Psinomani in the north, with a
broad, uninhabited buffer zone in between that stretched from the Minnesota Valley northward to the southern edge of the northwoods. The
"no one's land" might have been an area of unremitting hostility, as it
was later during the Dakota–Ojibwa wars. This interpretation is supported
by the absence of all but a few sherds of Oneota and Sandy Lake pottery
in this zone. Exceptions are the Sheffield Oneota site along the St. Croix
River that dates to c. AD 1300 and an Oneota site on the north bank of the
Minnesota River at Fort Ridgely. The Minnesota River most likely served
as a considerable barrier between the two groups.

In summary, the ancestral Sioux entered the northwoods of central
Minnesota and northwestern Wisconsin from the region of the Central
Mississippi Valley shortly before AD 800. These scattered bands emerge
archaeologically as the Terminal Woodland Blackduck–Kathio–Clam River
Continuum. About AD 1300, if not earlier, they adopted the characteristics of a northern tribal society and became the People of the Seven Council Fires. Features of this transformation most likely include: (1) the
coalescence of ancestral Sioux into clusters of primary villages, at least
some of which were surrounded by wooden palisades (the Cooper and
Wilford village sites); (2) the emergence of local authoritarian leaders,
which could be reflected in the appearance of a centralized mortuary mound
complex with restricted access;[51] (3) an intensification of the wild rice

Figure 2.7   Oneota-like Ogechie pottery vessel from the Mille Lacs Lake area (courtesy of the Wilford Archaeology Laboratory, University of Minnesota)

component of the subsistence system, including, perhaps, new roasting and storage technologies; (4) the appearance of garden beds in which squash and other plants were grown; (5) the emulation and acceptance of certain Oneota-derived ceramic attributes (Sandy Lake ware) and Oneota-derived ceramics (Ogechie ware); (6) increased territorial and social boundedness, which is most clearly seen in the presence of an uninhabited buffer zone between the Minnesota River and the southern edge of the northwoods; (7) decreased residential mobility and a tendency toward year-round occupation in the emergent village clusters; and (8) an escalation in levels of violence.[52]

These features appeared rapidly throughout portions of the southern half of the northwoods, which is taken here as a sign of widespread alliance building and the adoption of a common ethnic identity. These changes must have disrupted existing kinship, social, economic, and political patterns and caused extreme intra- and inter-group stress among the ancestral Sioux. By implication, the Psinomani complex owes its unique archaeological identity to these processes of tribal and ethnic genesis.

The Psinomani tribalization process was a consequence of an intensification of trade and conflict with more complexly organized horticultural groups to the south, in particular with Orr and Blue Earth–Correctionville phase Oneota groups who were most likely ancestral Iowa and Oto Indi-

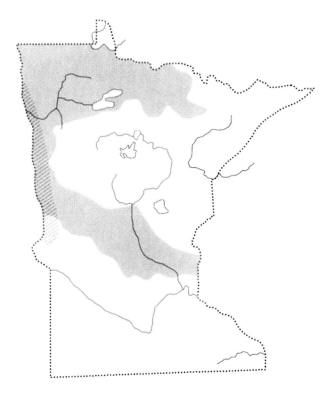

Figure 2.8   Buffer zones in late prehistoric and early historic Minnesota

ans. Violent confrontations with these and more recent arrivals, such as the ancestral Illinois, might have intensified further in the sixteenth and early seventeenth centuries. With the movement of the Oneota westward in the early to mid-seventeenth century, the alliance of the Seven Council Fires began to weaken, and by the time the Sioux began their historic movement westward and southward it had become a mythic memory.[53]

At present, the data upon which this reconstruction of the prehistory of the Sioux is based are weak. Basic reports on critical excavations at late prehistoric villages in the Mille Lacs Lake area are not completed, and glottochronology and biological relationship studies have methodological weaknesses. In addition, there have been no explicit, concerted efforts to identify other Psinomani settlement clusters except by the author in the Big Sandy Lake area of Aitkin County in the early 1980s.[54] A stronger historical sequence must be built in those areas where Psinomani settlement aggregations occur.

For these reasons, the broad outlines of Sioux prehistory presented here remain a speculative model. Nonetheless, two conclusions of general interest can be drawn from this reconstruction. First, available paleoanthropological evidence supports the "in place" geographical origin theme. The ancestral Sioux most likely lived in the Central Mississippi Valley region and later in Minnesota for at least two or three thousand years. Furthermore, if the Dakota language began to diverge into dialects after AD 1500, it is unlikely that the Western Sioux, in particular the ancestral Lakota, lived permanently in the prairies of southwestern Minnesota as early as AD 1000–1200. Their most likely late prehistoric homeland is that portion of the northwoods in the headwaters region of the Mississippi River. The second conclusion is an assessment of the broad outlines of Sioux prehistory: the prehistory of the Sioux seems as dramatic, interesting, unique, and worthy of attention as their history after Euro-American contact in the mid-seventeenth century.[55]

three
The French and English Fur Trade, 1650–1803

Histories of the Sioux between 1650 and 1803 are invariably written from a Euro-American perspective. As a result, the focus is on encounters between Sioux and Euro-Americans, on how these encounters affected Sioux life, and on what the Sioux as exotica were like. The history of this period is undoubtedly more complex and interesting, for relationships between Indian peoples in the Upper Mississippi Valley were never simple and Sioux culture has a developmental logic of its own. In addition, major, if still poorly understood, regional changes had taken place in this section of North America in the preceding century (1550–1650) that affect our understanding of the Sioux at contact in the mid-seventeenth century. Four examples illustrate the magnitude of these earlier changes.

First, native health and culture had begun to deteriorate in a broad area to the southeast of the Sioux between 1520 and 1620. Euro-African epidemic diseases, which spread rapidly into interior North America ahead of Euro-American exploration, may have contributed to this process of deterioration by altering the balance of power between neighboring groups. Second, the Iowa and Oto, the Siouan-speaking southern neighbors of the Sioux, had gradually drifted toward the western prairies and the Great Plains in the late prehistoric period. Their westward movement, which changed the balance of power in southern Minnesota, was probably due in part to accelerating indigenous warfare in the heartland of the Midwest. Third, winters had become much colder and snowier. These changes in climate, which began in the mid-sixteenth century, altered the distribution of the woodlands in the Upper Midwest and affected the nature and abundance of animal food resources. Finally, yet importantly, movement around Lakes Michigan and Superior of thousands of Fox, Pottawatomi, Huron, Sauk, Ottawa, and other eastern Indians brought new enemies and allies to the Sioux. These examples illustrate once again that there never was an unchanging, primeval Sioux way of life.[1]

Still, Euro-American fur traders did contribute to rapid changes in many aspects of Sioux culture and to a shift in the geographic location of tribal divisions. The magnitude of this transformation is comparable in retrospect to that of the formation of the Psinomani 300 years earlier, when fundamental transformations took place in subsistence and settlement patterns, and material culture. What was new was the nature of the encounter and the nature of the ensuing changes in Sioux lifeways.

The first section of chapter 3 summarizes the impact of the French and English fur trade in north-central North America. Later sections explore key issues for this period. These include the value of viewing the Sioux as a culture, the interpretation of written records and maps, the use of archaeology in historical reconstructions, the entangled meanings of exchanged items during the fur trade, problems resulting from imperfect translations from and to Dakota, and the muted voices of women.

The French and English Fur-Trade Period

In broad perspective, the early history of Minnesota and the broader western Great Lakes region to the east can be divided into three periods: the Iroquois Wars (1641–1701), the French Era (1720–61), and the British Era (1761–1819). During the long course of the Iroquois Wars, the entire area became enmeshed in military conflicts. Eastern tribes swept around the western Great Lakes to escape the wrath of the Iroquois, who had acquired guns and were intent on dominating the fur trade in the eastern Great Lakes.[2] It was within this charged environment that the first French explorers, traders, and missionaries made contact with Indian communities in the Upper Mississippi River basin.

The earliest Euro-American reports of the Sioux in their northwoods homeland were written during this period of exploration. In 1641, two enterprising Jesuit missionaries, Charles Raymbaut and Isaac Jogues, were told that the nation of the *Nadouessis* lived 18 days to the northwest or west of the Sault (Sault Ste. Marie, Michigan). Direct contact most likely began some twenty years later with the western penetration of French *coureurs de bois*.[3]

The first recorded contact between Sioux and Europeans was apparently with Pierre Radisson and his brother-in-law, the Médart Chouart de Grosseilliers, who visited Wisconsin and possibly Minnesota in the winter of 1659–60.[4] Thereafter, the general nature of French–Sioux relations are known to the end of French involvement in the early 1760s from archival sources. Later visits during this period include Father Claude Allouez's trip to Lake Superior in 1665–7, Nicolas Perrot's activities in the Lake Superior region and at Prairie du Chien between 1665–99, Daniel Greysolon Duluth's expeditions in 1678–82, Father Louis Hennepin's visit to the Mille Lacs Lake villages in 1680, and the explorations of the entrepreneur Pierre Charles Le Sueur, who spent the winter of 1700–1 with some Sioux along the Blue Earth River at Fort L'Huillier in present-day south-central Minnesota.[5] Accounts of their travels describe a dynamic intertribal environment. According to these written sources, the Eastern Sioux, the Dakota, were engaged in periodic conflicts with the Ojibwa, Nipissing, Ottawa, Huron, Illinois, Miami, and other tribes who were themselves fighting the Iroquois or their own neighbors.

By the late 1670s, the Iroquois no longer dominated the western fur trade, and by the late 1680s, the allied western Indians and the French carried the war back into Iroquois lands. After a hiatus caused by wars in Europe, French forts were reestablished in the western Great Lakes following the Peace of Utrecht in 1713. A 20-year ban on French trade caused by oversupply of furs ended in 1720, with the licensing once again of fur traders. The result was the florescence in the Upper Mississippi River drainage of the French fur trade, which lasted until 1761, when the English gained control of this region of North America. Earlier, however, French trade expanded on the western frontier, with the addition of Fort Beauharnois among the Dakota at Lake Pepin on the Upper Mississippi River in 1717, followed by Fort St. Pierre on the Rainy River west of Lake Superior in 1731, and Fort St. Charles on Lake of the Woods in 1732. After 1731, and until the renewal of French–English warfare in 1744, French fort-building activity and exploration focused on the search for a route to the Western Sea. By 1734, under the leadership of Pierre Gaultier de Varennes, Sieur de La Vérendrye, the French had penetrated the rich fur-bearing lands west of Lake Superior. By 1738, Vérendrye had visited the Mandan on the Missouri River in present-day North Dakota.[6]

Although the British entered the northern fur trade with their Hudson's Bay Company in 1670, they did not enter Sioux country, along with independent Euro-Canadian traders, until after 1763, when France ceded Canada to Britain at the conclusion of the Seven Years' War. Unlike the French, who ran official combined forts and trading posts to which Indians brought furs, the British issued licenses to traders who went to Indian villages and set up trading posts. Nonetheless, extensive illegal trade was still carried on by the French *coureurs de bois*, who circulated through winter hunting camps. In actuality, then, much of Sioux territory west of the Mississippi River continued to be unofficial French trading territory until it was transferred to Spain and subsequently sold to the US in the Louisiana Purchase of 1803. The land east of the Mississippi River was included in the Northwest Territory created by Congress in 1787.[7]

Figure 3.1   A Dakota encampment with tipi (Seth Eastman engraving, 1852. Minnesota Historical Society Photograph Collection)

Where did the Sioux live?

When first encountered by the French in the mid-seventeenth century, the Sioux occupied a vast expanse of territory that stretched from the woodlands of central Minnesota into the tall-grass prairies of the eastern Dakotas. Since no Sioux were reported living in northwestern Wisconsin, a part of the Psinomani homeland, it seems likely that the Sioux had already withdrawn westward from that area, presumably in response to the growing presence of eastern tribes.[8] Because the eastern Dakota were contacted first, the most secure information exists for the location of their villages and for their cultural practices. The further west one moves the sketchier and less reliable information becomes.

Reports from the early fur trade period generally agree that the Sioux were already divided into three divisions, each of which was composed of two or more tribes. The three divisions, which were distinguished by territory, dialect, and to some extent by customs and way of life, were, from east to west, the Dakota, the Yankton–Yanktonai (the *Wiciyela*), and the Lakota. Since the Dakota language shared by the Sioux may not have begun to separate into distinct dialects until about AD 1500, an argument can be made that they lived as a more clustered group up to this time in the southern half of the northwoods in Minnesota and northwestern Wisconsin. The Dakota were most likely located to the east around Lakes Mille Lacs and Big Sandy, and the Yankton–Yanktonai and the Lakota to the northwest, in the forested Headwaters region of the Mississippi River. According to migration legends and historical documents, the Sioux began to move southward and westward from this wooded homeland in the seventeenth century. However, the timing and nature of this drift is poorly documented well into the eighteenth century.

Some control on the timing of these movements is provided by the distribution of archaeological materials and by linguistic dating. If, as seems likely, the late prehistoric Sioux manufactured shell- and grit-tempered Sandy Lake pottery vessels, then the distribution of this type of pottery should coincide with the core territory of the Sioux before brass kettles replaced pottery in the late seventeenth century. As indicated in chapter 2, this variety of Sandy Lake ware extends from northwestern Wisconsin, across central Minnesota, and into the tall-grass prairies of western Minnesota and eastern North Dakota. Sandy Lake pottery is rare south of the northwoods. The permanent movement of Sioux villages southward occurred, then, after they no longer made pottery vessels. However, it is possible that some western Sioux began to live year-round in the northeastern Plains, where Sandy Lake ware does occur by AD 1400, if not earlier. Alternatively, the presence of the ware in the western prairies could represent seasonal bison hunting forays from their villages in the western fringes of the northwoods.

As should be obvious, the early location of the Sioux as a people remains cloudy. One conclusion that we can draw is that movements and distributions of proto-historic peoples should not be proposed without confirming archaeological evidence. The earliest written records in this area were on occasion based on hearsay, intentionally exaggerated, or distorted for other reasons. Given this caveat, it seems that the Sioux were living year-round in both the woodlands and prairies in the latter half of the seventeenth century, although the details remain vague.

The earliest maps of Sioux territory, with the names of many rivers and the location of different groups of Sioux, were drawn in the closing years of the seventeenth century. Jean-Baptiste Franquelin's map of 1678 is the earliest known map of this region. Le Sueur's geographical knowledge following his trip up the Minnesota River in 1700 to mine for copper was recorded in a map drawn by Claude Delisle in 1702. It is clear from these and other documents that the Sioux had entered the prairies of southern Minnesota and the eastern Dakotas by at least 1680.[9] Le Sueur, for instance, divided the Sioux into the Sioux of the West, who lived in the prairies and lived by the hunt, and the Sioux of the East, who lived in the woodlands in Minnesota.

In the latter part of the seventeenth century, the Yankton were living in southwestern Minnesota and northwestern Iowa. By 1720, at the latest, they entered what is now the southeastern corner of South Dakota, which became their new homeland. The Lakota, who lived for a time around Lakes Big Stone and Traverse on the Dakota–Minnesota border, also began moving westward by at least 1718, according to a map prepared in that year by Delisle. According to Lakota winter counts, the western Sioux increasingly dominated the prairie east of the Missouri River in the Dakotas after the 1720s. The Lakota crossed the Missouri River by 1750, although they apparently did not migrate out onto the Plains until after 1795.[10]

Why did the Sioux leave the northwoods?

By the date of the Louisiana Purchase and the beginning of the American period in 1803, the Sioux had moved out of the northern forests that had been their precontact homeland. Their new homeland was the prairies of southern Minnesota, northwestern Iowa, and the eastern Dakotas to and just across the Missouri River. There were many reasons for their move and, undoubtedly, the importance of these reasons varied among bands and families. An important reason is that they were pressured out of the northwoods by intruding bands of Ojibwa intent on securing new hunting grounds for the fur trade.

Before 1736, the Dakota had a temporary alliance with the Ojibwa of Lake Superior, who had no permanent villages beyond the shores of Lake Superior at the time. As part of their alliance (the Covenant of 1679), the Dakota and Ojibwa fought the Cree and Assiniboin to the north of the Dakota. In return, the Ojibwa were allowed to hunt in Sioux territory west of the St. Croix River. The Ojibwa also served as middlemen who funneled Dakota furs through Fort La Pointe in exchange for trade goods. This alliance was disrupted, however, in 1736, when the Dakota killed one of La Vérendrye's sons, Jean-Baptiste, and 20 other Frenchmen near Fort St. Charles at Lake of the Woods. The raid was purportedly in retaliation for a 1734 raid by the Cree against the "lesser Sioux of the prairies" in which Jean-Baptiste La Vérendrye had participated.[11] The raid may also have been a response to the opening of the Rainy River route by the French and the establishment of trade with the Cree and Assiniboin.

In retaliation, the Ojibwa made serious inroads into Sioux Territory in eastern Minnesota and western Wisconsin from bases at Chequamegon and Fond du Lac. According to oral tradition, Ojibwa villages replaced Dakota villages at the mouth of the St. Louis River near modern Duluth and at Big Sandy Lake during the 1740s. The Dakota were driven from Mille Lacs to the Minnesota River in about 1745. By the 1760s, the Ojibwa had secured a firm toehold in Minnesota. A differential possession of guns may have led to an imbalance of power in the early phases of this struggle. The conflict raged on into the nineteenth century, by which time the Sioux were confined to the Minnesota Valley and areas to the south and west.[12]

The documented presence of Dakota villages near Fort Beauharnois in 1728 and Fort Linctot in 1732, however, indicate that some Dakota were living near the Mississippi River–St. Croix River juncture before the onset of the Sioux–Ojibwa conflict. Comments by Hennepin, Perrot, Le Sueur, and other French visitors indicate, too, that many groups of Sioux considered southern Minnesota and adjacent parts of Iowa part of their territory before 1700. While Ojibwa pressure was surely an important part of the story, then, other processes must have been in play. These probably included the placement of French trading posts on the Minnesota and Mississippi rivers to the south of their homeland; the difficulty traders had in reaching their villages in the marshy, water-laced northwoods; the abandonment of southern Minnesota by most Oneota peoples; the Little Ice Age; declining animal populations in the eastern fringe of their territory; the appearance of the horse on the Plains; the southwestward migration of bison herds; and their increasing participation as middlemen in trade fairs with the western Lakota and other groups in the northeastern Plains.[13]

Just when and why so many Sioux migrated out of the northwoods remains unsettled. It seems likely, however, that multiple pulls and pushes were involved and that these processes affected different groups of Sioux in different ways.

Life and customs of the early Sioux

Some idea of what the Sioux looked like, how they lived, what they ate, and other dimensions of their culture before it was severely altered in the latter half of the eighteenth century can be gathered from early written sources. Unfortunately, this information is sketchy, incomplete, and often of questionable reliability, for many early Euro-American visitors had little actual contact with the Sioux. For example, Father Jacques Marquette's references to the Dakota reported in the *Jesuit Relations* of 1669–70 are based on descriptions he received from other Indians when he was at La Pointe, on Lake Superior, and Radisson and Grosseilliers may never have visited the Dakota in Minnesota, as they claimed. Descriptions of the Sioux were influenced, too, by the nature of the contact situation. Radisson first met Dakota representatives when they were away from their villages participating in a feast, and Hennepin first encountered a fast-moving raiding party that was traveling light.[14]

According to written descriptions of the Sioux during the French and the early phase of the English period, the form of their garments did not change much during the seventeenth and eighteenth centuries. The major difference was the adoption of European clothes and beads for some items, in particular by the Dakota. Pierre Radisson provides the most detailed description of Dakota clothing in the mid-seventeenth century. He describes Sioux warriors he encountered in the late 1650s as carrying bows and arrows tipped with antler. They wore a breechcloth with tobacco pouches and ornaments, such as crow skins, dangling from their belts. Their faces were dabbed with several colors, and their limbs and torso were covered with a reddish earth (hematite) mixed with very thick grease, possibly bear grease, to ward off the hordes of mosquitoes. A leather shield (buckler) decorated with symbols and feathers was worn on the left arm to deflect arrows and clubs. Men wore a kind of vest made of several layers of soft leather with sleeves that came down to their elbows when they walked or rode on horseback over the plains.[15]

Several early writers describe the seasonal settlement and subsistence round of the Dakota. They were described as mobile hunter-gatherers, who exploited resources seasonally in widely different localities. While men and boys hunted game, the primary subsistence resource, women gathered berries, nuts, and roots, tapped sugar maple, and harvested wild rice. They may have planted some crops, including maize (corn). Their basic seasonal round consisted of hunting bison on the prairies to the south and west in the summer and residence in the northern forests in the fall, winter, and spring, where they harvested wild rice and hunted deer, elk, and beaver.[16]

Their semi-permanent villages, which contained large bark-and-pole wigwams, were their largest settlements. These villages were never permanently occupied in the seventeenth and eighteenth centuries, since over-hunting depleted the game in the surrounding area. Although as many as 5,000 people are claimed to have lived in Mille Lacs Lake villages, the excavated villages at Mille Lacs, which are the largest known in the area, were in reality small hamlets. Sweat lodges were built in the villages for purification and healing, and the bones of those who died in winter were carried back to their primary villages for interment. Burial mounds were still in use during the early French contact period, for French trade goods have been found with some burials. When traveling, the Dakota used small conical Woodland tipis covered with skins or bark mats.[17]

Individual items of material culture mentioned in late seventeenth century manuscripts include bark canoes, earthen pots, bark dishes, and weapons of various kinds, including long swords and knives, tomahawks, stone-tipped arrows, and wooden war clubs. Calumet pipes, generally made of pipestone, were used on special occasions. These pipes, which

Figure 3.2   A Dakota summer planting lodge (Seth Eastman watercolor, 1846–8. Minnesota Historical Society Photograph Collection)

were decorated with feathers and other items, had a long narrow reed stem.[18]

Sioux interactions with the French and English

At Euro-American contact in the mid-seventeenth century, the Dakota wonder at the power of French technology was projected onto the French themselves, the people who brought the technology. The French were *washitchon*, powerful spirits, who must be carefully treated and respected. Nonetheless, like other Great Lakes Indians, the Dakota sought to incorporate these powerful spirits into their social world, just as they sought to incorporate French technology into their cultural practices. As guns, iron, and other trade goods became more readily available, and the Sioux became familiar with the French, the French lost their supernatural aura and became human beings like other people, though human beings that were their source of trade goods.

Since early explorers and traders lived in a Sioux world, they learned to adjust to Sioux social practices and to adopt those customs that were necessary for acceptance into Sioux communities. This often meant adoption into a Sioux family, for kinship formed the social framework of Sioux existence and regulated their relations with outsiders. These kinship ties made them relatives of the people they interacted with and gave them a place in Sioux society. Many French traders married or lived with Sioux women and took Sioux names. They were called "brother" or "father," terms that marked their incorporation into the Sioux communal world but also denoted kinship obligations. The nature of these relationships gradually changed from decade to decade as the Sioux concept of sharing resources within the community increasingly came into conflict with the demands of a rapacious European market economy.[19]

By the Louisiana Purchase in 1803, the Sioux way of life had changed dramatically. The Sioux had abandoned their northern forest-edge homeland for the prairies of southern Minnesota, northern Iowa, and the eastern Dakotas. The Lakota had crossed the Missouri River and were on the verge of a new lifeway even further away on the Great Plains. The horse and guns, and the fur trade, had drastically changed traditional annual cycles and divisions of labor between men and women. While the Dakota continued to follow a more traditional subsistence cycle, with corn horticulture supplementing the harvesting of wild rice, western groups became increasingly reliant on bison for meat and other by-products. The lifeway of the Sioux had changed forever.

Sioux Culture

From an anthropological perspective, societies are distinguished from one another by their culture, that is, by their unique set of learned behaviors and beliefs. The Sioux differ from other peoples of the world because their culture is different. A review of some of the characteristics of a culture is a necessary prelude, then, to understanding the Sioux and their interactions with Euro-Americans.[20]

First, a culture is transmitted through learning and language over the generations, rather than through the genes of ancestors. This means that people who enter a cultural tradition at birth share traditions and customs they learn as children. It also means that other people can learn to live in a culture as adults and that two cultures can share experiences and means of adaptation through borrowing or diffusion. This explains in part why those Sioux who migrated westward began to look like their neighbors in the Plains, while the Dakota in Minnesota remained more "woodland" in appearance.

Second, despite a shared cultural tradition, all cultures contain diversity. One reason is that individuals, families, villages, and other subgroups in the same cultural tradition have different as well as shared learning experiences. In addition, despite cultural constraints, like censure and ridicule, people adhere to ideal cultural patterns to different degrees. This results in further diversity. The presence of diversity in cultural traditions helps explain the divergent historical trajectories taken by different groups and families of Sioux since Euro-American contact, even though they remain members of one broad cultural tradition.

Third, a culture is generally adaptive to a physical environment and a neighboring people in the sense that those customs that enhance survival and reproductive chances are likely to persist. However, not all cultural traits are adaptive. Some, such as clothing styles and rules of etiquette, may be neutral, and different societies, such as the bison-hunting Lakota and the crop-growing Mandan, may choose different means of adapting to the same physical environment.

Fourth, cultural traits are mostly integrated for psychological and adaptive reasons. This is evident in Sioux customs, institutions, beliefs, and values, which are mostly adjusted to or consistent with one another. When the Sioux depended on hunting and gathering for food energy, they were more mobile, had smaller communities and lower population densities, and had fewer material possessions than did neighboring groups of farmers like the Mandan. Besides being integrated by their dominant economic activities and social patterns, cultures are also integrated by enduring spiritual themes and core values. By implication, if fundamental aspects of a culture change, other aspects of that culture are likely to change as well. We should anticipate finding, then, broad-scale changes in the values, gender roles, and family organization of the Sioux as their economic base shifted from wild rice harvesting, to bison hunting, to reservation dependency, to casino gaming.

Fifth, an essential element of a culture is the meanings that people ascribe to objects, behavior, persons, and events. All facets of the lives of a people, whether food acquisition and consumption, courtship, death, or the changing of the seasons, are suffused with meanings. To learn about the Sioux, then, we must penetrate behind everyday appearances – and the non-Indian meanings embedded in the products (the reports, books, movies, and so on) of their observers and interpreters – to their own world of meanings.

Finally, a culture is always changing. The impetus for change may be either internal or external, that is, it may come from within or from outside the society. Examples of internal changes are a shift in subsistence emphasis and population growth. Processes of change may also be located in networks of external relationships. An obvious example is the gradual incorporation of the Sioux in Euro-American affairs.

Adherence to the view that the human world of North America was once composed of distinct, sharply bounded, traditional, unalterable cultures has left a strong imprint on studies of the Sioux. Generally phrased in the present tense, the so-called "ethnographic present," most historical ethnographies are based on the tacit assumption that there is an ancient and genuine culture to be discovered that the contemporary Sioux have lost or are losing.

From a traditional, history-less perspective, the study of the Sioux is about Sioux culture as it was in the mid-nineteenth century, not about its past or its changes. However, the Sioux people were not isolated and their culture has changed dramatically through time. Like all tribal groups in the region, they were inextricably drawn into a growing world system of commerce and colonization.[21] Accordingly, Sioux culture was different in 1650, 1750, 1850, and 1950. This view of the Sioux calls for a different focus and for an increase in sophistication in learning about their cultural tradition. It sets a different agenda than the recapture of a primordial, traditional Sioux culture as it was before Euro-American contact.

De-scribing Historic Documents

A variety of sources are available for reconstructing (or constructing) Sioux culture in the seventeenth and eighteenth centuries. Among these are oral traditions, word clues in the Dakota language, and archaeological excavation. Nonetheless, the reconstruction of Sioux culture during this period has depended almost exclusively upon the written narratives of French and English male explorers, traders, and missionaries. Given their importance, certain questions should be asked: How reliable are they? Can we accept their content at face value? If we cannot, then what degree of confidence can we have in the historical ethnographies that are based on them? What kinds of problems require de-scribing before these accounts can be used for their ethnographic content?

Among the problems involved in de-scribing early French texts are: translation problems because of the semantic nuances of the period; missing or unavailable journals; inconsistencies between different versions of the same historical event; transcription errors; the varying social contexts in which interactions between the Sioux and the French took place; and an author's covert agenda, which may not be apparent when reading a text outside its historic context. The active reader has no choice but to weight the information in a source against all that is known about the author, the period, and the manuscript.

Classic examples of these problems occur in both Radisson's and Hennepin's narratives. Many aspects of Pierre Radisson's report remain uncertain, for the original French manuscript was either destroyed or lost. Most likely written by Radisson in French in England in 1669, it was poorly translated into English by an employee of the Hudson's Bay Company, who did not always understand what Radisson was saying. As Bruce

White has concluded, the "reader not only has to try to imagine what the French text may have said that would lead someone to translate it as the English translator did but has to decide what the English text actually says."[22] There is also uncertainty whether Radisson visited a Dakota village "seven small journeys" from the place where he celebrated the Feast of the Dead with the Dakota in Wisconsin. Did Radisson visit the village or was he merely trying to add greater authenticity to his narrative?

Hennepin's two narratives of his 1680 visit to the Dakota villages at Mille Lacs Lake introduce other problems. Translated into English as *Description of Louisiana* (1683) and *A New Discovery of a Vast Country in America* (1697), they sometimes provide inconsistent information.[23] It seems likely, too, that his *Description of Louisiana* was heavily edited to render it more effective as a subtle form of propaganda in the struggle between the Recollects and the Jesuits at the Court of Louis XIV. Was Hennepin, a Recollect Franciscan friar, actually a captive of the Dakota, as he claimed, or was he or others attempting to enhance the drama of his popular books by claiming that he was? Other popular European travel-adventure themes of the period that were used to structure his tales include a dangerous journey into unknown lands, the exploration of a newly discovered great river, encounters with strange tribes of savage Indians, and details of bizarre animals, here the bison and opossum. How have these spins to his stories affected our understanding of the early Dakota and of the nature of Dakota–French interaction during this Age of Exploration?

Many early encounters whose description is a source of ethnographic information occurred within the context of diplomatic ceremonies or other unusual circumstances. Examples are Radisson and Grosseilliers's meeting with Dakota chiefs in Wisconsin in 1659–60 and Perrot's interactions with often-hostile Dakota warriors at his trading center (Fort St. Antoine) on Lake Pepin in the late 1680s. How have these unusual circumstances affected our understanding of the Dakota? Such narratives also provide only limited glimpses of Sioux culture. Descriptions of the day-to-day activities of the Dakota as provided by Hennepin from his stay at Mille Lacs Lake are rare. An ethnography of the seventeenth-century Sioux, then, cannot just describe the Sioux as recalled by Euro-American observers. It also must be an ethnography of the process of interaction between the Sioux and the French.

Several strategies have been proposed in historical ethnography for evaluating the information contained in sources of this nature. One, called "upstreaming" by William Fenton, "proceeds from the known to the unknown, concentrating on recent sources first because they contain familiar things, and thence going to earlier sources." The danger in upstreaming is in emphasizing cultural continuity at the expense of cultural change –

of assuming, for example, that because the Dakota remained in Minnesota they represent the original culture of the Sioux. Despite claims by the Dakota that they represented the original Sioux culture, can we assume that the culture of the *Nadouessis* of the seventeenth century was the same as that of their better described nineteenth-century descendants, who now lived in the prairies of southern Minnesota? An alternative strategy is downstreaming. In downstreaming, the earliest written sources are used to construct an historical ethnography: only then are their implications for more recent sources considered.[24]

Regardless of strategy, a careful ethnography of the seventeenth-century Sioux must maintain a critical attitude toward the sources. Like an archaeologist, the reader must excavate a text to get at its buried meaning, to understand what the text is actually saying.

Reading Maps

For people with poor eyesight, the most problematic aspect of reading maps is their dense detail. Maps are otherwise considered mimetic (imitative) re-presentations of the landscape. As a result, when we compare historic maps of Sioux territory, we do so almost exclusively in terms of accuracy, with how well they capture that real past landscape. We also assume that early cartographers like Jean-Baptiste Louis Franquelin, Guillaume Delisle, and Joseph Nicollet were intent upon producing accurate representations of this region of the western Great Lakes and northeastern Plains. Historical maps that we judge inaccurate are regarded as obsolete and amusing artifacts of the Age of Exploration.

Nevertheless, the inevitable selectivity of maps imbues them with an inherent relativity that challenges the view that they are innocent inscriptions. Once we grasp "that maps are purely conventional, that convention determines perception, and that this perspective is culturally specific,"[25] we see that a map is not only a concept fraught with problems but also a wellspring of cultural information.

The westward spread of Euro-American explorers through the Great Lakes created a demand for new, accurate maps. By the late eighteenth century, systematic attempts were made to map the boundaries between three of North America's great biogeographic regions, the grasslands of the Great Plains, the northern Canadian forests, and the tundra to the north. In mapping this vast terra incognita, cartographers of the period were not just recording the expansion of European colonialism westward as a matter of exploration and discovery, but they were enabling it as well.[26]

Early Euro-American maps of Sioux territory were produced within the

Western cartographic tradition. As a result, their ways of seeing, and therefore selectivity, were predefined by that centuries-old tradition, a tradition that emphasized physical accuracy, orientation, linear scale, and utility in wayfinding. European concepts of space and assumptions about maps were based on the Euclidean and projective geometries of Renaissance and post-Renaissance cartographies.[27] In this tradition, a map was considered a mathematically generated representation of an irregular or curved space on a flat surface; by convention, geographical outlines and landscape features were drawn to scale on two-dimensional, framed surfaces.

Of paramount, if generally unacknowledged, importance in early Euro-American mapmaking was information-seeking by explorers. Peter Pond, Alexander Henry the Elder, Lewis and Clark, and other mapmakers obtained information in map form from the Sioux and their neighbors.[28] Among the information they recorded were toponyms of hydrological and other features of the regions they traveled through. Ad hoc mapmaking was also a common way to show one another where they were coming from and what the route ahead looked like.

These encounters not only demonstrate that the Sioux and other Indians made maps but that they were capable of producing exact maps of large territories. These maps displayed considerable knowledge of terrain, waterways, portages, and other landscape features.[29] Although no definite prehistoric maps are known for Sioux territory, there is extensive evidence of native map-use in all parts of the continent from the earliest Indian/non-Indian encounters. The earliest known surviving map that may have been made by a Sioux was drawn on "Stag skins" by the *Gnacsitures* for Baron La Hontan in the winter of 1688–9 somewhere in the middle of the Minnesota Valley; the La Hontan map shows the lakes at the head of the Minnesota River, the steep-sided Côteau des Prairie to the west of them, and the headwaters of the Big Sioux River.[30] Other Indian maps in Sioux territory include a 1801 map by a Blackfoot chief of the Upper Missouri region, a detailed 1837 representation of the Upper Mississippi and Missouri River basins drawn by an Iowa chief (*Non-Chi-Ning-Ga*), and a detailed map of the Cannon River region of southeastern Minnesota, which a Sioux drew for Johann Georg Kohl in 1854.[31]

Sioux and other indigenous maps differ from Western maps in certain clearly recognizable ways.[32] First, Indian maps were generally based on a principle of linear coherence rather than on the accuracy of fixed positions in space. Maps were shaped according to experience and tradition, which meant that they did not usually have consistent distances between points and that direction was not always conserved. Distances between places were given in numbers of days of travel. These conventions are understandable when we recall that the purpose of using maps in travel is to trace a continuous path from one geographic feature to another. For

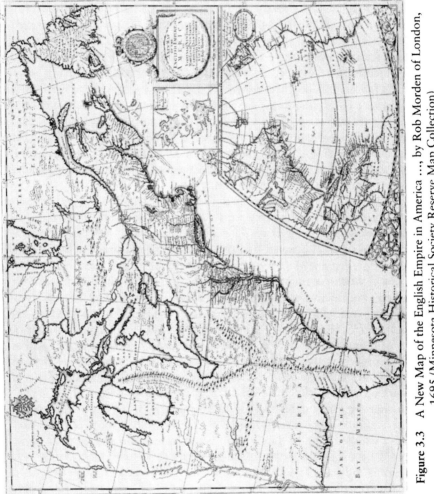

Figure 3.3 A New Map of the English Empire in America ..., by Rob Morden of London, 1695 (Minnesota Historical Society Reserve Map Collection)

this reason, quite different phenomena might be melded together for the purpose of representation, unlike more rigid Euro-American classifications. For example, Sioux maps might treat land trails and canoe routes in the same way on a map to produce an integrated route of travel. Indian conventions of map-making differed, too. Rivers tended to be represented by a straight or curved (not wavy) line, lakes were round, portages across rivers were marked by slashes, hunting grounds and habitation sites were marked by dots, and the entire network of lines was unframed.

Early Sioux maps also frequently combined aspects of both terrestrial and cosmological worlds. Indeed, some maps were solely dream maps that showed "heaven," the trail to it, mythical animals, and other features, all of which had been discovered in dreams. All of this makes sense if we recall, again, that space is experienced, represented, and symbolized differently by different groups of people, and that maps in particular are graphic representations that facilitate a spatial understanding of concepts and things. Examples of this blending of the terrestrial and cosmological are apparent in a map of the Black Hills by Bad Heart Bull and in Lakota star and earth maps painted on hides.[33] Since the sacred symbols and stories of the Lakota were written in the sky in constellations and mirrored on earth in the location of terrestrial features and the people themselves, a cartographic case could be made for the sacred destiny of a chosen people in a divinely ordained land.

Sioux maps were not crude attempts to render geometric space, then, but products of social forces that created and manipulated reality as much as they recorded it. Consequently, there are advantages to be gained in rejecting the naïve realist model of cartography if we are intent on understanding the changing world of the Sioux. Rather than passive reflections of the land, maps are windows to socially constructed worlds. As such, they are a crucial testament to the project of Empire, the nature of Sioux–Euro-American interaction, and Sioux ways of world-making.[34]

The Archaeology of Historic Sioux Culture

While the general outline of French–Sioux relations and some details of Sioux culture are known through archival sources, further details of Sioux culture and the nature of French influences can be obtained through an examination of the archaeological record. Fortunately, both proto-historic Sioux villages and French trading centers have been excavated in Minnesota and bordering states.[35]

While a professor at the University of Minnesota, Elden Johnson supervised the excavation and analysis of Mille Lacs Lake sites between 1965 and the early 1980s. These sites are on a small protected bay at the outlet of the Rum River and on the small lakes formed by the river immediately below its outlet. Many early French writers, including Radisson, mention villages at Mille Lacs Lake. Hennepin is thought to have wintered in a village on Aquipaguetin Island, now known as the Aquipaguetin Island site (21ML2). Since there are no other clusters of sites of this period located on the shores of Mille Lacs Lake, there seems little doubt that these sites represent the remains of these villages.

Johnson identified a Bradbury phase (AD 1680–1750) artifact assemblage at a number of habitation sites, including Vineland Bay (21ML7), Cooper (21ML9), and Wilford (21ML12), and at the Cooper Mound site (21ML16). All of these sites are multicomponent, have mixed components, and are generally accepted as proto-historic Mdewakanton Dakota in origin. Since only the Cooper Mound site excavation has been reported in detail, conclusions drawn from these excavations must be regarded with caution.

In contrast to French reports of large villages, the actual sites are no more than a series of hamlets. Even though site boundaries are difficult at times to determine with precision, archaeologists can gauge their general magnitude. The largest, Vineland Bay near the Rum River outlet on Mille Lacs Lake, was probably only 3–4 hectares (7.5–10 acres) in size. The

Figure 3.4   Clay-lined ricing jig from a Mille Lacs Lake site (courtesy of the Wilford Archaeology Laboratory, University of Minnesota)

Aquipaguetin Island village was probably several hectares (5 acres) in size, Cooper Village about half a hectare (2.5 acres), and Wilford about one-half hectare (1.2 acres). Wilford and Cooper were both enclosed by wooden palisades. The Cooper palisade was a rectangular enclosure measuring about 32 by 90 meters (35 by 98 yards). There is also a clear, direct association of contact-period French artifacts in both the Cooper mound and village sites. Burial feature 17 in the mound contained an Ogechie (Oneota-like) pottery vessel, several stone and bone tools, a copper ring, glass beads, and a copper knife. Fragments of European trade artifacts were scattered throughout the village with Sandy Lake and Ogechie pottery.

It seems likely that only two or three houses were occupied at a time in the Wilford village and perhaps no more than five or six houses at Cooper. The resident population at each site probably numbered no more than 50–60 people. While it seems reasonable to assume that communal hunting parties left the villages for extended periods, it appears that at least some people remained in the villages year-round.

Scattered among the houses were wild-rice threshing pits and fire pits. Deep storage pits, which were common at the time in hunter-horticultural villages in southern Minnesota, were absent. Two types of houses are thought to be associated with the Bradbury phase. One type is a rectangular summerhouse that resembles the rectangular, gabled bark houses built by the Mdewakanton Dakota along the Minnesota River in the nineteenth century. The excavated houses of this type vary in length from 6 to 12 meters (6.5 to 13 yards). The second type of house is a rectangular winter

Figure 3.5   University of Minnesota excavation of a large house structure at the Wilford site (courtesy of the Wilford Archaeology Laboratory, University of Minnesota)

house with a sunken floor, an entry ramp, a central fire pit, and a deep ash pit that may represent a cooking area. A narrow platform along one or more walls may have served as a sitting or sleeping bench.

The reconstructed Bradbury artifact assemblage includes a ceramic assemblage dominated by Sandy Lake ware. Smaller numbers of Ogechie vessels and even fewer Oneota vessels complete the assemblage. Ogechie vessels are thought to be locally made versions of Orr phase Oneota pottery. By contrast, the Oneota vessels are similar enough in appearance to Orr Phase vessels to be part of that ceramic tradition. The presence of Ogechie and Orr Oneota pottery indicates a continuation of strong southern connections, presumably with seventeenth-century Iowa Indians. The lithic (stone) industry is indistinguishable from that associated with northern Oneota sites. It includes small triangular arrowheads, trapezoidal end scrapers, double-pointed and bifacially flaked knives, sandstone arrowshaft abraders, milling stones, celts, pipestone elbow pipes, and utilized flakes. Small numbers of bone tools, including deer-ulna awls, are the most common, but bird-bone whistles or flutes, unifacially barbed points, a small round-shafted awl, and a bison scapula hoe have also been found.

Analyses of bone waste in the villages indicate that proto-historic Dakota subsistence relied primarily on large mammals and wild rice (*Zizania aquatiia*). Although bison are popularly thought to have been a Dakota food staple, only a few bison bones are present among the food refuse. Instead, deer and elk bones dominate the large mammal bone assemblage. The presumed reason is that meat was stripped from bison carcasses at kill sites in the prairies, smoked, and carried back to Dakota villages, as documented in historic records. Smaller mammals, turtles, fish, and waterfowl were present in significant numbers and an assortment of wild plant foods was eaten. Tobacco seeds (*Nicotiana rusticana*) were present in abundance. Figure 3.6 contains a list of plant remains found in a recent Mille Lacs Lake site study.

As mentioned in chapter 2, Johnson considered the proto-historic Mdewakanton lifeway a northern version of Oneota, with its uniqueness in its northwoods habitat and the substitution of wild rice for maize in the bison/maize economy of Western Oneota groups. Although reasonable and possibly correct, this model of the lifeway of the proto-historic Mdewakanton remains only suggestive, for the model has not been adequately documented or tested.[36]

Entangled Objects

Since the fur trade was the primary context in which the Sioux interacted with Euro-Americans for nearly 200 years, it seems essential to inquire

Carbonized Seeds	Total No. of Seeds	% of Total Seeds	% of Features in Which Taxa is present
Wild rice, whole (*Zizania aquatic*)	957	4.85	60.64
Wild rice, broken (*Zizania aquatica*)	10,935	55.36	88.30
Tobacco (*Nicotiana rustica*)	308	1.56	37.23
Goosefoot (*Chenopodium spp.*)	4,276	21.64	70.21
Raspberry (*Rubus sp.*)	374	1.89	43.62
Goosegrass (*Galium aparine*)	947	482	45.74
Butternut (*Juglans cinera*)	485	2.46	27.66
Blueberry (*Vaccinium spp.*)	137	.69	27.66
Smartweed (*Polygonum sp.*)	178	.89	11.70
Nightshade (*Solanum nigrum*)	4	.02	1.06
Beadruby (*Maianthemum canadense*)	672	3.40	38.30
Pincherry (*Prunus pensylvanica*)	110	.56	12.77
Skullcap (*Scutellaria parvula*)	8	.04	1.06
Cheno-ams	161	.82	4.26
Elderberry (*Sambucus pubens*)	4	.02	4.26
Bulrush (*Scirpus sp.*)	13	.07	5.32
Bayberry (*Myrica pensylvanica*)	59	.30	12.77
Hawthorn (*Crataegus pubens*)	38	.19	8.51
Bunchberry (*Cornus canadensis*)	2	.01	1.06
Mint (*Mentha canadensis*)	15	.08	5.32
Nettle (*Urtica sp.*)	9	.05	4.26
Flatsedge (*Cyperus sp.*)	12	.06	4.26
Sumac (*Rhus cf. glabra*)	18	.09	7.45
Sedge (*Carex sp.*)	4	.02	2.13
Grape (*Vitis sp.*)	3	.02	2.13
Corn (*Zea mays*)	2	.01	1.06
Chickweed (*Stellaria sp.*)	4	.02	1.06
Mint family (*Labiatae*)	5	.03	2.13
Panic Grass (*Panicum sp.*)	1	.01	1.06
Cinquefoil (*Potentilla sp.*)	8	.04	1.06
Sub-total	19,749		

Figure 3.6   Plant remains from the Wilford Village site (adapted from Bailey 1997:22)

into the nature of this interaction. Again, the range of questions that can be asked about colonial trade is truly vast. We limit our inquiry here to the material goods exchanged in the trade and the question: How did two people with radically different ways of life conceive of the objects exchanged in the fur trade?

A typical Euro-American bill of lading in the fur trade included a list of manufactured items such as kettles, axes, knives, glass beads, rings, cloth, traps, flintlocks, and armbands.[37] In return, the fur traders received animal skins and some secondary items, such as food. The objects' properties and uses thus appear to be self-evident. However, to say that kettles, axes, and glass beads were traded to the Sioux does not tell us what they received. For instance, some kettles were cut into arrowheads and knives, as well as tinkling cones and gorgets to adorn clothing. The intent of this section, then, is to explore different ways of thinking about material culture and, more specifically, to alert the reader to the importance of material culture in understanding the early historic Sioux way of life.

This domain of inquiry deserves exploration for several reasons. First, the meaning or function of an object is not inherent in it but is culturally constructed. Since fur-trade objects cannot be naively read in familiar terms, one must learn to read their meanings as the early historic Sioux might have understood them. Second, the introduction of European trade items into native societies has generally been regarded as a sign of the superiority of Euro-American material culture. The enduring image is of native people discarding their own material culture as quickly as Western substitutions become available. However, a comparative study of exchange in colonial contexts suggests that this is an overly simplistic, self-serving illusion. Societies like the Sioux had their own reasons for becoming involved with the French in trade, an involvement that developed in the absence of any physical coercion.[38]

To understand why the Sioux were willing to engage in exchange with the French, and the forms that these exchanges might have had, it is necessary to know something in general about exchange between European and tribal societies. The introduction through trade of muskets, steel knives, and brass kettles did fundamentally alter the nature of hunting, eating, working, and war among tribal societies. In addition, as European trade-networks grew, so too did the interdependence between these two different groups of people. However, the expansion of the European market system was not simply the imposition of that system on tribal communities. Each society had its own form of economic system and, for mutually fruitful trade to exist, some adjustments by both parties had to be made.

Europe during the fur-trade period was becoming a capitalist, industrial civilization. Items intended for exchange were considered commodities. Commodities are goods that become dissociated (alienated) from former owners in the sense that there is no excess social obligation that accompanies a transaction. In the enlightened views of the day, the more commodities a person owned and the greater his independence, the greater his prestige.[39]

By contrast, an exchange for a seventeenth- or eighteenth-century Sioux was not simply barter, but quite often a process during which social relationships and political alliances were negotiated in complex secular and ritualistic contexts.[40] The objects exchanged were often considered gifts, not commodities, and as gifts they came with an excess that had to be acknowledged socially beyond the exchange of the objects. As a result, groups of people became mutually entangled in webs of rights and obligations. Rather than for monetary profit, goods were exchanged not only for need but to share and to establish relationships of indebtedness. For these reasons, exchange relations were the very substance of social life among the early historic Sioux.

In tribal societies, as in any society, objects vary in rank along a scale of social value. A conch shell traded across vast stretches of land ranks higher than local foodstuffs. In general, the higher the rank of a gift, the greater the strength of social and political commitment. Traded objects vary, too, in the extent to which they retain an association with their original owners. A sacred pipe is inalienable and is kept out of circulation, for it symbolizes the immortality of a social group. Other objects have different cultural biographies and exchange possibilities. At intertribal trade fairs, some objects even assume some of the characteristics of commodities in that they are exchanged for profit or for other items without social obligation. These points are important for understanding the significance and appropriateness of an exchange in a gift economy.

Because of these differences in social value, the social arenas in which things are appropriately exchanged differ, too. Things such as shell valuables are only exchanged in a ritualized, formal context. Other items are exchanged in more casual forms of prestation. An important focus of inquiry, then, is the determination of exchange pathways and the meanings of objects in intertribal exchange.

This was the exchange context into which Euro-American traders and explorers entered in the seventeenth century. An object exchanged in a particular situation as a commodity or gift was transformed into other forms. Furs started as gifts and ended as commodities, and vice versa. Moreover, since prestation forms are specific to the nature of a social relationship, they would have varied through time as the fundamental nature of the fur trade changed. The point is that material objects and appropriations constitute a set of issues that have many ramifications for how we read early historic Sioux culture. At the very least, questions about material objects and fur-trade interactions must be situated in the early colonial cultural contexts in which they occurred.[41]

Imperfect Translations

Another pivotal problem in Sioux studies is the accuracy of translations of ideas from and to Dakota. By accurate is meant the conveying of notions rather than the precise literal translation of words. There were many reasons for miscommunication in this sense between the Sioux and Euro-Americans. A common problem was (and continues to be) a lack of competence in Dakota. Before the twentieth century, most Euro-Americans who interacted regularly with the Sioux were content to understand their language to the extent necessary to trade with them or to efficiently subjugate them. A second problem was the tension between fidelity to the original discourse and accessibility. The usual decision was to reword a discourse so that it made sense to either a Dakota or English speaker. However, in the rewording nuances of meaning were often lost. A third problem was the failure to adequately describe the specific context in which a discourse was transmitted. In a ritual or ceremonial context, for example, Sioux discourse had deep layers of meaning that were absent in conversation or in many other forms of oration. A fourth problem was the oral nature of the discourse. Since discourse was orally transmitted well into the twentieth century, the correctness of the original written recording cannot be checked.

A more serious problem was the commonly held Euro-American view that the range of thought of the Sioux, like that of other Indians, was extremely limited, for Dakota was considered a primitive language. Since complex ideas were not expected, they were not heard. Finally, many Euro-American concepts and linguistic practices were (and are) alien to traditional Sioux understanding and vice versa. The absence of equivalent key ideas resulted in confusion and misunderstanding. An example is the conjunction of the Sioux words *mitakuyase* (all of my relations) and *oyate* (nation).[42] When used together in a religious context, the word *mitakuyase* can refer not only to one's present and past relatives, but to four-legged beings and winged creatures in various combinations. *Mitakuyase oyate* refers, then, to nation groups with both physical and spiritual qualities. No adequate English synonym communicates the rich philosophical connotations of this and hundreds of other Sioux terms.

An extreme example of the problem of communication is provided by the first recording of Iron Shell's winter count, which was begun by his great-grandfather.[43] The iconograph is generally translated as "The Winter a Good White Man Came" (1807). According to oral tradition, the white man "shook hands, brought gifts and food for all, and carried with him a document." However, no one among the Sioux knew what he said, for there was no interpreter! There are also many examples of the mistranslation of names, the most prominent of which is the word "Sioux" itself. In another instance, a Yankton chief of an upper band was commonly known among Americans as "Feather in His Ear" because of a mistranslation. His real name in English meant "Feather Necklace," after his Sioux name, *Wiyaka Napin*.[44]

The translation of Sioux literature is generally considered more problematic than translation of speech or of conversations. Besides the problems of translation mentioned above, the translation of literature involves problems of transcription and recording.[45] Many of the earliest translations between English and Dakota were actually from English into Dakota, for some Euro-Americans were sure that the Sioux had need of Western text, in particular the Bible. However, by the last decades of the nineteenth century, the language and oral literature of the Sioux began to be taken seriously, and their complexity and richness fully recognized. A substantial body of translations of Sioux stories and songs has gradually accumulated.[46]

Nearly all of the earliest translations of Sioux oral literature employed the textual conventions of Western prose and poetry, for the goal was to present that literature as recognizably literary. The notion was that responsible translators should do whatever was necessary to turn Sioux pre-literature into true literature. Several examples illustrate the point. The first is James Walker's rearrangement of the pre-reservation origin stories he was told by Lakota elders into a chronological sequence to give them the familiar structure of Western origin traditions.[47] A second is a translation (or retelling) of a Brulé tale by Rufus Sage. In his retelling, elements of the romantic literary style of his time, such as "a silvery spring overhung by crags," were added to make the tale literary by the Western conventions of the time.[48] In a similar manner, poems were regularly translated into heroic couplets, which was the most popular mode of the poetry of the day. These intended improvements not only make it difficult to determine what the original Sioux vocabulary was but also mask the original form of the discourse. The translations should not be ignored, however, for, like contemporary photographs and drawings, they document earlier Euro-American attitudes to and understandings of (or uses of) the Sioux.

In the twentieth century, professional scholars became increasingly interested in how Sioux oral discourse should be translated and presented to Euro-American readers.[49] An explicit effort was made to get at those features of Sioux discourse that had been masked by their conversion through Western literary conventions. A key problem was to agree on what was permissible and what was not. For example, Sioux singers had to repeat sacred songs exactly, for they had received them from the spirits; consequently, there was little leeway in translation. In contrast, Sioux storytellers could freely improvise, and, therefore, so could translators, as long as certain verbal formulas and story lines were used. Another concern was what to do with the linguomusical utterances called vocables or nonsense syllables once a song had been removed from its musical setting.[50] The apparent purpose of these "nonsense syllables" is to modify textual materials to better fit the melody and rhythm of the song as sung in Dakota. Is a song inadequately translated from a cultural perspective if these syllables are omitted? The translation of the nuances of pronunciation and body motions during oral performances is receiving similar attention.

The problem of making Sioux discourse accessible to English speakers will always have intractable problems, of course, as long as the emphasis is on translation. Ideally, interested English speakers should learn to read Dakota, for "knowledge of any literature cannot advance without knowledge of its tone and texture."[51] Today, Dakota-language literature (both oral and written) is being studied in Dakota at community colleges on reservations and at other colleges and universities in the region.

Women's Roles/Women's Voices

Early accounts of Sioux women by explorers, missionaries, and other observers generally portray them as overworked drudges under the total domination of male relatives. Certainly, Lakota warriors were known for their flamboyant, bravado behavior, and traditional Sioux society is included among those North American Indian societies in which men dominated women. But did Sioux women have low status relative to men? If life was so wretched, why did some captured white women refuse to return to their own communities when offered the opportunity? To what extent were Sioux women able to exert control over their own lives? These are important questions, for the story of Sioux women is an essential component of the unfolding of the Sioux cultural tradition. They may never confidently be answered, however, for we rarely hear their voices or are told their stories. The issue has been muddled, too, by a tendency in more recent re-constructions of Sioux women's lives to create a flattering, utopian world that never existed except, perhaps, as a shared community ideal.[52]

What were and are Sioux women like, then? What were and are their lives? How did the fur trade, the hide trade, and conquest and partial assimilation to the culture of nineteenth- and early-twentieth-century Euro-America affect Sioux women? Was the relative power, authority, and prestige of Sioux women and men similar, unequal, or equal but different? What was the position of Sioux women in the domains of work, domestic relations, the public arena, and ritual life? How did these positions change through time and space? In these introductory explorations, it is useful to bear two notions in mind. First, the position of women was not the same in all Indian cultures. Consequently, reconstructions of the lives of Sioux women must be based on resources specific to the Sioux. Second, in traditional Sioux society gender concepts were not determined exclusively by sexuality and biology. As a result, there was a greater flexibility among

Figure 3.7   Dakota women and children guarding corn from blackbirds
(Adrian J. Ebell photograph, August 1862. Minnesota Historical Society
Photograph Collection)

the sexes in carrying out "women's" tasks than is the norm in Western
society. In other words, while gender distinctions and tasks were clearly
marked, they were tied to behavioral as opposed to biological differences.[53]

For convenience of comparison, the lives of pre-reservation Sioux women
– and the question of their status equality with men – are restricted in this
text to four topics: work, domestic relations, the public arena, and ritual
life. Women's and men's work tasks were clearly differentiated in traditional Sioux households. Women's primary tasks were domestic. Besides
gathering food and other resources, she "kept house," processed and sewed
hides, and bore and cared for children. These domestic routines were carried out for the most part in the company of other women and young girls
and boys. Men regularly left the household for long periods to hunt, trade,
fight, and gather heavier raw materials, among other allocated tasks. When
men and women were together, they ate and slept together and carried
out routine domestic chores.[54]

Because of the complementarity of work responsibilities, marriage did not involve the subjugation of women. A woman was as valued within her work roles as her husband was in his. The public standing of women rested largely on their status among the women with whom they worked and socialized with during the day. Neither set of work roles was considered superior to the other, for the efforts of both women and men were acknowledged as necessary for the well-being of the *tiyospaye*. Therefore, a woman's worth was generally couched in the language of work skills and productivity, particularly her skin work and her ability to maintain a smoothly running household, just as a man's worth was evaluated by his ability to protect and provide for his family and village.

Even though women and men were ideally equal in their different spheres of activity, then, were they equal in domestic relations? Did husbands control the conduct of domestic life and decision-making? Did a married woman exercise personal control over the allocation of her sexual and procreational capacities? Since both Sioux men and women were taught from childhood to be polite, generous, and cooperative, their relations were generally friendly. However, within families, boys tended to be somewhat more privileged than girls, and as a rule females answered to males, just as younger people answered to older. If gender dominance is measured in terms of who has the final say in decisions and by who is apt to defer to the wishes of others, men were the controlling partner within the family. Nonetheless, the wise man listened seriously to the opinions of his wife.

Traditional women were also unequal to men in the public arena of community affairs, since they were only able to exert influence indirectly through their husbands, their personal status, or by gossip. There was no direct role for women in governing the community and none held public "office." Again, however, men generally listened to the opinions of their wife or wives. Similarly, women shared unequally in community ritual life. While women could be dreamers or have other community roles, they had no leadership role in major community rituals and could not participate directly in the tribe's major annual ritual, the Sun Dance – even though the material base on which the male religious life rested was gained primarily through the labor of women.[55]

A persistent question in studies of the Sioux is the extent to which the position of women in nineteenth-century Lakota society was a consequence of the Lakota's adoption of a nomadic, bison-hunting lifeway on the northern Plains. Were the relations of production of Sioux men and women different before this transformation and among the Dakota in southern Minnesota? Students of Sioux culture who have examined the available sources have concluded that Lakota women suffered a declining presence (in the hunt, property relations, and control over goods) in Sioux society because of changes fostered by the adoption of the horse, the hide trade, and the Plains warrior lifeway. According to these interpretations, this transformation led to the emergence of male-dominated institutions and a decline in the nineteenth century of the status of Lakota women.[56]

During the reservation period, the lives of Sioux women in general became more difficult due to a decline in social status, power, and authority.[57] There were a number of reasons for this repositioning of women's roles. An early and persistent reason was a determined effort by missionaries and the US government to replace Sioux notions of gender complementarity with a Christian notion of gender hierarchy within the framework of the patriarchal nuclear family. Along with Western ideas of individualism and the distinction between public and domestic, which characterized gender relations through much of the Old World, these notions disrupted the unity of the *tiyospaye*, reduced the social status of women, and introduced the Euro-American ideal of female submission. A second reason was a dramatic change in the level of social contact between husbands and wives brought about by settled residence on reservations and the loss of many male activities, such as warfare and hunting. As men increased their presence in the local community, the autonomy of women decreased.

Other reasons for a shift in women's positions included the incorporation of labor into the larger capitalist system and external laws. Following the destruction of the Sioux native economy in the late 1870s and early 1880s, Sioux women and men were gradually incorporated into the larger national economy along new gender lines defined by outside forces. The result was a rapid change in gender roles. One reason was the greater extradomestic employment opportunities available to women. Another was a decrease in the status of women in general because of the loss of many of their traditional work activities, such as hide processing, upon which evaluations of their worth depended. External laws also redefined individual authority and rights over people and property. Based on Euro-American definitions of male household heads, these laws increased the power of men and of the importance of the nuclear family at the expense of women and the *tiyospaye*. In the process, women lost both domestic rights and their voice in official community affairs. These changes led to increased tensions between men and women.[58]

More recent trends include: a growing interest in the lives of contemporary Sioux women; a resurgence of power of Sioux women within their own communities; the appearance of the voices of Sioux women in literature; and a return to the original ideal of gender complementarity, although the nature of this complementarity is quite different today from what it was in the nineteenth century.[59]

four
The Early American Period, 1803–1850

Despite the radical changes of the French and British eras, the Sioux were still in control of their lives at the time of purchase from France by President Thomas Jefferson of the Louisiana Territory in 1803. This event began in earnest the early American period in Sioux history. At the time, the Sioux were distributed across the prairie from the Mississippi Valley in present-day southern Minnesota and northern Iowa to just across the Missouri River in the Dakotas. The Lakota had not yet adopted the Plains warrior lifeway for which they are now famous. Most of the cultural changes that had occurred in settlement location, material culture (e.g., brass kettles, guns, horses), and economic orientation (e.g., greater emphasis on hunting fur-bearing animals, gardening) had been willingly accepted by most Sioux. In fact, in 1803 the Sioux were more numerous, powerful, and widespread than they had ever been.[1] Nor in the early 1800s were the Sioux especially hostile to non-Indians. In general, they welcomed trading posts near their territory, for they wanted access to guns and other goods, and did not molest the few traders and trappers who ventured across the prairies and plains. Nonetheless, large-scale forces beyond their control were leading to qualitative changes in their traditional lifeway. Like subsequent periods, the early American period is better documented, both in written records and in oral traditions, than the periods reviewed in chapters 2 and 3.

Chapter 4 reviews significant events and processes that affected the Sioux way of life between 1803 and 1850. It then focuses on four topical issues: Sioux warfare, engendered objects and spaces, the colonial control of language, and Sioux kinship and social organization.

The Early American Period

Among the significant processes at work in Sioux territory during the Early American period were ecological adaptations to new habitats, adjustments to increasing numbers of eastern Indians and non-Indians west of the Mississippi River, tribal migrations and more widespread and complex intertribal conflict, increasing disenchantment with Euro-Americans, and land cessions. As the Lakota entered the bison-rich western prairies and the Plains, they adopted many of the subsistence and settlement customs of their neighbors and created new cultural patterns through the adoption of the horse, the hide trade, and the gun. Consequently, the western groups of Sioux came to look more like other Plains nomads, such as the Cheyenne, Arapaho, and Crow, than the Dakota, who retained many woodland features.

By the 1820s, the US government thought it had acquired enough territory to satisfy all foreseeable land needs. It seemed impossible that Americans would push beyond the fertile Mississippi Valley into the Great Plains, which was considered an uninhabitable desert. It was thus thought safe to move many thousands of eastern Indians into the Great American Desert west of the Mississippi Valley in the 1830s. Accomplished primarily through the Chicago Treaty of 1833, the eastern tribes were forced to exchange their lands for lands equivalent in size to those they had surrendered, plus expenses and compensation. In one motion the Indians would be protected from hostile settlers, they would have unencumbered lands of their own, and the "Indian Problem" would be settled.

Among the tribes dumped into Indian Territory in the central and southern Plains were the Five Civilized Tribes and the Illinois, Miami, Delaware, Ottawa, Shawnee, Pottawatomi, Sauk, and Kickapoo. Nonetheless, this attempt to establish a permanent frontier between non-Indian Americans and Indians failed miserably. First, the eastern Indians need for game and space quickly impacted Prairie people like the Osage, who had shifted to the same lands a century earlier. More drastic from the US government's perspective was the unexpected westward surge of non-Indian Americans across the Mississippi River in the 1830s. Congress soon had to amend its Indian Country act and break its promise of security to eastern tribes.

By the mid-1840s, the new rallying cry was Manifest Destiny and the extension of the country from sea to sea. In 1845, the US annexed the Republic of Texas and in 1846 the disputed Oregon country south of the 49th parallel. In 1848, a treaty with Mexico added another large section of the West that extended from present-day New Mexico through California. After the Louisiana Purchase in 1803, the federal government under Jefferson's leadership quickly sponsored expeditions to explore the new American holdings, primarily with commercial interests in mind. The most famous of these was Meriwether Lewis and William Clark's expedition up the Missouri River from St. Louis in 1804 to find a profitable trade route to the Pacific Ocean.[2] Zebulon Pike was also sent to explore newly acquired territory in the Upper Mississippi River region, as were other explorers to other areas.[3]

The opening of the American frontier after the Louisiana Purchase brought increasing numbers of Euro-Americans and trade goods to the lands of the Sioux. As the numbers of Euro-American trading posts, military forts, wagon trains, and homesteads swelled, the resources of this semiarid country became seriously strained. The strain was rapidly exacerbated by severe epidemics of smallpox, cholera, and other diseases that decimated some Indian communities, even though the total number of Indians in the Plains remained large. All of these unwanted events were occurring as intertribal warfare on the Plains was intensifying and becoming more complex.

In time, the presence of increasing numbers of Euro-Americans began to imperil the native way of life in the northern Plains. Diseases and the presence of traders did much to debilitate tribes, and the widespread use of alcohol began to undermine morale. The result was an escalation of conflict between the Sioux and Euro-Americans, and the beginning of land cessions that by 1890 restricted the nomadic peoples of the Plains to reservations. However, it was also a time of unimagined prosperity for the Lakota, with the florescence of the mounted bison-hunting lifeway.

As the western bands moved ever further out onto the plains, the culture of the Sioux nation gradually changed. Already by 1803, the three main divisions of the Sioux (the Western, Middle, and Eastern Sioux) had been living in different kinds of environments for some time. As our earlier discussion of the Sioux would lead us to expect, each division began to develop its own distinctive lifeway. Some changes resulted from adjustments to a new environment and others from interaction with new neighbors. Even though they were now speaking different dialects of Dakota, the three divisions regarded one another as relatives. Because of these emerging differences, each division is discussed separately below.

The Eastern Sioux

By 1803, most of the Eastern Sioux (Dakota) lived in the prairies between the Mississippi and Missouri rivers, south and west of their prehistoric and proto-historic forested homeland. The north-central American prairie differs from the Great Plains in amount of annual rainfall and, consequently, in its vegetation. East of the plains–prairie border, which runs approximately along the 100th meridian, there is 20–40 inches of rain a year, tall grass prairie, and many more small lakes, ponds, and swamps than in the Plains. Other prairie tribes in the region, besides the Dakota, Yankton, and Yanktonai, included the Mandan, Hidatsa, and Arikara in the Dakotas and the Osage, Omaha, Iowa, and Oto generally to the south in Iowa and Nebraska. All of the prairie tribes shared cultural traits with both Indians in the woodlands to the northeast and the Plains to the west and southwest. In general, however, there was a continuum in proportion of Woodland and Plains traits as one moved eastward or westward.

For the most part, the Dakota lived along the Minnesota Valley and along the Mississippi Valley from the confluence of the two rivers down into northern Iowa, although they continued to travel northward to their ancestral lands to gather wild rice in the fall. However, by 1830 the Ojibwa expansion into their former homeland was virtually complete. The Dakota were now being squeezed in by the Sauk and Fox to the south and east, the Ojibwa to the north, and an increasing Euro-American presence from the east. By 1839, an estimated 3,989 Dakota lived in southern Minnesota and the eastern Dakotas.[4]

The Mdewakanton was the most geographically stable of the four Dakota tribes, with Mdewakanton villages spaced out along the Mississippi and lower Minnesota rivers. In many instances, the headmen of Mdewakanton bands shared the same name with earlier bandleaders. Examples are Shakopee, Little Crow, Red Wing, and Wabasha.[5] Since some names had power, they were passed from one generation to the next. The estimated population of the Mdewakanton at the time was about 1,500 men, women, and children.

A second division, the Wapekute, lived to the west of the Mdewakanton around the headwaters of the Des Moines River near the Great Oasis and on the upper Cannon River. Sometimes referred to as renegades or vagabonds due to some of their habits, the Wapekute numbered about 800. Still further upstream were the Wahpeton, who numbered about 900. Like the Sisseton to the west, their larger encampments were along lakes formed by a broadening of the Minnesota River. Examples are Traverse des Sioux, an important river crossing, Lac Qui Parle, and Big Stone Lake, which is at the headwaters of the Minnesota River.

The 2,500 Sisseton were divided into lower and upper bands. The upper Sisseton, with some Yanktonai, had their main encampments at Big Stone Lake and at Lake Traverse, which is located along the drainage of the Red River. Although also primarily active in this border region, lower Sisseton bands under Sleepy Eye still made their rendezvous near the mouth of the Blue Earth River near present-day Mankato. This back-and-forth movement indicates that they too had most likely drifted westward after an early stop in south central Minnesota.

In the early nineteenth century, the Dakota Sioux were still living in a tense intertribal environment. A roughly northwest to southeast war zone 100 miles wide separated the Dakota and Ojibwa.[6] It stretched over 400 miles, from the forks of the Red Cedar and Chippewa rivers in Wisconsin

Figure 4.1   A Dakota hunting buffalo on the prairie near the mouth of the Minnesota River (Seth Eastman watercolor, 1846–8. Minnesota Historical Society Photograph Collection)

northwest to Pembina in the far northwestern corner of Minnesota. Lands south of the Minnesota River were the territory of the Dakota. Lands north of Mille Lacs Lake and the Crow Wing River now belonged to the Ojibwa, who by 1810 were established at Big Sandy Lake, Pokegama Lake, Cass Lake, Leech Lake, Lake Winnebigoshish, Red Lake, and the Red River of the North. All of these villages and those on the St. Croix, Red Cedar, and upper Chippewa rivers in Wisconsin were under attack by Dakota raiding parties.

A second war zone developed to the south between the Dakota and the Sauk and Mesquakie, who moved west of the Mississippi River after ceding their temporary lands in northwestern Illinois and southwestern Wisconsin. Their movement westward into the hunting grounds of the Dakota in the Minnesota–Iowa border region resulted in frequent and bloody conflicts. The most intense fighting occurred around the headwaters of the Des Moines River, which the Wapekute and Yankton had claimed for several generations.

A grand intertribal council was held at Prairie de Chien, Wisconsin, in the summer of 1825 to promote peace and to establish boundaries for tribes in the western Great Lakes region.[7] Driving the treaty was the notion by the US government that firm boundaries would reduce warfare by separating the tribes and stabilize conditions for the fur trade. However, the boundaries were generally ignored by the tribes and were soon superseded by land cessions. Consequently, the Dakota continued to be threatened from the north, south, and east throughout the 1830s and strife remained rampant in the region. Another tension was the relentless push westward of Euro-American settlement. In an area of limited resource potential for horticulturalists who relied heavily on hunting and gathering for food resources, the fighting over dwindling natural resources became intense and desperate.

Strife with the Ojibwa to the north continued unabated. New Ojibwa villages were established as far south as the mouth of the Elk River. In 1830, the estimated population of the Ojibwa in Minnesota and the border region was around 3,800.[8] As the Ojibwa, the Sauk and Fox, the Iowa, and the Omaha squeezed the Dakota's safe zone ever more tightly around the Minnesota River, more Dakota moved westward.

An American presence in Minnesota was permanently established in 1819 when American soldiers and government agents came to build Fort Snelling at the junction of the Mississippi and Minnesota rivers.[9] The land had been ceded to the US by the Dakota in 1805 in a treaty made by Lieutenant Zebulon M. Pike during his exploration of the Upper Mississippi River region. Legally US territory, Minnesota and northern Iowa both remained British Indian country for some time after the War of 1812. In fact, a final border settlement was not worked out until a further British–American treaty was signed in 1842. Pike reported British fur posts on the Rum River in Anoka County, on Big Sandy Lake, at Leech Lake, and in other areas of the state. Furthermore, the Dakota had fought alongside the British near Detroit and in western Lake Erie at the outset of the War of 1812.[10] Their loyalty was understandable, for the British fur trade was near its peak productivity at the time in the northern Great Lakes. As late as 1827, Lawrence Taliaferro, the Indian agent at Fort Snelling between 1820 and 1840, predicted that if war broke out again with Great Britain, the Dakota would support the British. As late as 1830, 18 years after the War of 1812 and almost a decade after the construction of Fort Snelling, most Dakota remained loyal to the British.

Fort Snelling's mission was to oust British fur traders from American territory, to keep non-Indian settlers out of Indian territory, and to facilitate the fur trade by keeping peace between the Dakota and Ojibwa. American fur posts were gradually established in Minnesota in the early 1800s. Before 1837, posts had been built at Mendota on Pike's Island, at Land's End a mile above the mouth of the Minnesota River, at Little Rapids in Carver County, on Grey Cloud Island, and at Oliver's Grove (Hastings), among other places.

Following the report of the starvation of 175 Dakota on the western prairies in the winter of 1828–9, Taliaferro became convinced that he

Figure 4.2   Dakota on the move along the Mississippi River, 140 miles above Prairie du Chien, Wisconsin (Seth Eastman watercolor, 1845. Minnesota Historical Society Photograph Collection)

must prepare the Dakota for integration into American society. His motives were practical ones: the fur trade was becoming less profitable, there was stress on natural resources, and the frontier would soon reach Minnesota. It seemed the most benign strategy was to turn the Dakota into American-style farmers and to teach them to speak and read English.

To accomplish his goals, Taliaferro encouraged missionary teachers to come work among the Dakota, to establish schools, and to teach farming. In 1829, he convinced one near-victim of starvation, the Mdewakanton leader Cloud Man, to try farming. Cloud Man's village at Lake Calhoun in present-day Minneapolis became an early focus of experimentation. Called Eatonville, the village had the services of teachers, farming instructors, and the missionary brothers Samuel and Gideon Pond. However, under threat of Ojibwa attack, Cloud Man and his band abandoned the village in 1839. A better known attempt to "civilize" the Dakotas took place in the 1830s at Lac Qui Parle, where the influential mixed-blood leader Joseph Renville supported the missionaries in their endeavors.[11]

The lifeway of the Dakota in the early nineteenth century was recorded in writing and pictures by many first-hand observers.[12] Their annual subsistence pattern was based on a broad-spectrum hunting and gathering strategy. The strategy revolved around the seasonal hunting and gathering of specific animals and plants. In spring, families left their winter homes and moved to maple-sugar and hunting camps. Since the Dakota had few horses, even in later times, women and dogs carried supplies from one camp to another. While earlier men hunted moose, deer, elk, and other game to supply the people, they now also hunted muskrats for the fur trade. In the summer, Dakota bands congregated in large villages along wooded river valleys, where they lived in rectangular bark-covered lodges with gabled roofs that were large enough for an extended family of a dozen or more people.

Although an idyllic-sounding picture, it was strenuous, difficult work. Artist Frank B. Mayer, who visited Kaposia in the early 1800s, described the women as modest and shy and the people in general as quiet, dignified, and courteous, but of good humor and quite open to playing jokes on each other.[13] Mayer's images are a sharp contrast to later views of the Sioux as either merciless warriors or begging drunkards.

In 1837, in response to multiple pressures, including encroaching American settlement, the Dakota sold their land east of the Mississippi River below the mouth of the Crow Wing River to the US government. It was their first major land cession – and it opened the floodgates of Euro-American settlement in Minnesota. By 1850, American farmers were pouring into Minnesota territory. Intensive Euro-American settlement soon threatened the traditional lifeway of the Dakota as described above. In addition, the US government made a concerted effort to end the Dakota way of life following the land cession. While churches were intent on converting the Dakota to Christianity, American-run Indian schools were concentrating on acculturating Dakota children to mainstream American life. Because of severe territorial constrictions and a decline in abundance of game, traditional economic pursuits became severely restricted by the 1840s. The result was an increasing dependence on the US government for goods and food.

The Middle Sioux

During the late eighteenth century, the Yankton and Yanktonai had moved swiftly into the eastern Dakotas from temporary homelands in southern Minnesota and northwestern Iowa. By 1804, when encountered by Lewis and Clark, the Yankton lived along the James, Des Moines, and Big Sioux rivers in eastern South Dakota and northwestern Iowa, and the Yanktonai roved the headwaters of the Big Sioux, James, and Red rivers in what is now North Dakota.[14]

At the time, many traders still identified the Yankton with their former homeland on the Des Moines River. In 1813, Little Dish's band was driven from the Des Moines Valley by a Sauk and Fox alliance. Following early treaties, a village was maintained on the Vermillion for joint Yankton–US government dealings. The Yankton received government services at this village from the late 1830s until they moved to a permanent reservation in the late 1850s. Other principal villages were located from the mouth of the Big Sioux River (War Eagle's village) to the northernmost part of Yankton territory near Fort Pierre. By 1834, Lawrence Taliaferro, the Minnesota Indian agent, no longer claimed jurisdiction over the Yankton because they had moved so far west.

After the death in 1823 of his brother-in-law, British agent and trader Robert Dickson, who once had a trading post on Lake Traverse, Wanaton, leader of the Upper Sisseton, and about 5,000 Yanktonai and some Eastern Sioux, spent an increasing amount of time in the upper Missouri River region. Wanaton returned on occasion to his eastern base at Lake Traverse until about 1836, but his principal headquarters became the vicinity of present Bismarck, North Dakota, about 200 miles northwest of Lake Traverse. By 1830, some 4,000 Yanktonai had moved westward, with another 1,000 remaining behind with the Upper Sisseton.[15]

Like the well-described lifeways of other Sioux tribes, the so-called traditional way of life of the Middle Sioux (the "ethnographic present") did not evolve until long after contact with Euro-Americans. It was based on the horse and Euro-American trade. Although our most common image of the Sioux is as equestrian nomads who lived in tipis year-round, the middle division of the Sioux, like the eastern, did not give up their villages or some gardening after acquiring horses. However, they did adopt many Plains traits, such as bullboats, larger tipis, and hard-soled moccasins.[16]

Their new seasonal cycle included two large-scale, multi-band bison hunts, one in spring–early summer (June–July) and the other in late fall–early winter (November–December). During other months, small groups and individuals hunted bison when the opportunity arose, as well as deer, bear, antelope, elk, and smaller game. Fish were captured by spearing with a three-pronged leister and with seines of willow built across or into the Missouri, James, and other streams near permanent villages. Women planted corn patches and vegetable gardens on the floodplains of the Missouri, James, Vermillion, and other rivers, hoed them once or twice in March–May before the spring-summer bison hunt, and harvested them upon their return from the hunt in August–October. In early spring, they tapped maple or box elder trees, although maple trees were not common and box elder is a poor source of syrup.[17]

Unlike their Sioux relatives to the east and west, the Yankton lived most of the year in permanent villages. Because there were few trees, there were no bark-covered lodges. Instead, they lived in tipis, grass-covered, dome-shaped houses, or on occasion in sizable earthlodges. Villages varied in size. A Yankton encampment encountered by Nicollet on the Upper

Figure 4.3   A buffalo hunt on the Plains (George Catlin lithograph, 1840.
Minnesota Historical Society Photograph Collection)

Snake River near present-day Faulkton, South Dakota, contained 11 lodges
and about 110 persons. A Yankton band of 80 lodges was reported by
Lewis and Clark in 1806 on Plum Creek, a few miles north of the Niobrara
River. Although the exact date is uncertain, the village of Drifting Goose,
a Yanktonai, located about 10 miles north and four miles northeast of
Mellette, South Dakota, was composed of 15 earthlodges surrounding a
plaza.[18]

Like other Sioux tribes, they held large assemblies in the summer, when
councils of the bands met to decide matters governing the tribe. Midsum-
mer religious ceremonies, such as the Sun Dance, feasts, and celebrations
were held at that time, too. Sports, like lacrosse, races, and handball, took
place alongside these other activities. As among other western Sioux, young
Yankton and Yanktonai men ranged far on war excursions.

The Yankton's trade with Euro-Americans increased steadily throughout the first half of the nineteenth century. Lewis and Clark encountered
both the remains of a trading post and traders en route upstream to trade
with the Yankton at the mouth of the James River. Manuel Lisa, the famous Spanish trader who operated out of St. Louis, established a trading
post in 1812 on the north bank of the Missouri near Chamberlain, South
Dakota to trade with the Yankton and some Lakota bands (the Brulés,
Oglalas, and "Saones,"a conglomerate of northern bands that included

the Hunkpapas and Sihasapas), which further documents the magnitude of their westward movement.

The Upper Missouri Agency was created in 1814 at least in part to encourage the neighboring tribes to engage in offensive operations against the enemies of the US, in particular the British. Manuel Lisa, the first agent, was able to keep the Lakota and Yankton neutral or on the side at times of the Americans. Like some Dakota bands, some Yanktonai fought on the British side. By 1820, the Missouri Fur Company had two trading houses for trading with the Yankton and Lakota, one above and one below the Big Bend of the Missouri. Their locations indicate that the Yankton had easy access at that time to the west bank above and below the Big Bend.

In the 1830 Treaty of Prairie de Chien, the Yankton ceded title to their land in the Des Moines River region to the US in return for a $3,000 annuity and services. The treaty reserved the right of the tribe to any lands not included in the cession. By the Treaty of October 15, 1836, the Yankton and other tribes who participated in the 1830 treaty agreed to give up all right to some of this area, and, by the Treaty of October 21, 1837, the Yankton ceded their interest in all lands involved in the 1830 treaty (2.2 million acres). Pressure for their confinement to a reservation grew. Like other Sioux, they were generally scattered, which made it difficult for US agents to negotiate with them or to deliver annuities except when they were in their permanent villages.

At the time of the 1830 treaty, the Yankton had been joined by a small group of dissident Wahpekute Dakota. Even though they retained their identity for many years, the Wahpekutes operated politically as part of the Yankton tribe. Interaction between members of the Middle and Eastern Sioux was not unusual. For example, War-Eagle, though a Dakota by birth, was a Yankton in terms of band allegiance. His village, which was located just west of present Sioux City, Iowa, was composed largely of Yankton.[19] Unlike the territory of the Osage and Kansa to the south, the land of the Middle Sioux was not as heavily impacted by the forced migration of eastern tribes into prairie zones west of the Mississippi Valley.

The Western Sioux

When encountered just west of the Missouri River by Lewis and Clark in 1804, the westernmost tribes of the Sioux, the seven Lakota tribes, were already migrating out onto the Plains.[20] In time they would dominate most of the northern Plains as the Shoshones had in the 1700s. The northern Plains extend from the southward stretch of the Missouri River on the east to the massive Rocky Mountains on the west, and from the Platte River in the south to the Saskatchewan River in the north. Major tributaries of the Missouri, such as the Cannonball, Heart, Knife, Little Missouri, and Yellowstone (Elk), flow in a generally eastward direction. With water and wood for fires, they provided excellent east–west routes of travel for bison hunts and war parties.

Although a seemingly monotonous rolling, treeless grassland that stretched hundreds of miles west from the tall grass prairie, this northern portion of the Great Plains was interrupted in places by highlands (plateaus, hills, and buttes) dotted by pine trees, such as the Black Hills of South Dakota and Wyoming, and the Badlands of South Dakota. Other features include the rolling Nebraska sand hills and in places stands of trees, especially willows and cottonwoods, along the many rivers. A long series of hills and buttes thrusting out from the western mountains was a reliable source of wood and water; they also served, when needed, as a place of refuge for Sioux pursued by superior forces. Drier than the prairie region, the northern Plains receives only about 10 to 20 inches of rain a year. Many kinds of large and small animals were present in the early nineteenth century, including bison, elk, pronghorn antelope, beaver, and fish.

By 1811 or earlier, the Lakota Sioux were well supplied with British guns. With the greater mobility provided by horses, they were sending hunting and war parties west and south of their lands near the Missouri River. In the 1830s and 1840s, the westward migration of the seven Lakota tribes gathered momentum. They began to war with the Crow for control of the Powder River country south of the Yellowstone River, in eastern Wyoming and southeastern Montana. A main impetus for their movements was the continued westward migration of the bison herds. As the Lakota moved westward, they visited the Black Hills to hunt and secure tipi poles of lodgepole pine.

By the early nineteenth century, the nomadic Lakota had separated into seven subdivisions, the Brulé, Oglala, Blackfoot (not to be confused with the major Algonquian-speaking tribe of that name), Minneconjou, Sans Arc, Two Kettle, and Hunkpapa. As these tribes moved westward across the northern Plains, they spread out from north to south. Three tribes made up the northern Lakota, the Hunkpapa, Blackfoot Sioux, and Sans Arc, and two the southern Lakota, the Oglala and the Brulé, now the two largest Sioux tribes. The Miniconjous and the small Two Kettles tribe lived between these northern and southern divisions. In the 1830s and 1840s, the Brulés and Oglalas each numbered around 3,000 people, and the Miniconjou about 1,800.[21] Probably the last of the western Sioux to migrate across the Missouri, the northern tribes lived separately but in camps close to one another along the Moreau, Grand, Cannonball, and Heart rivers in the region where North and South Dakota now meet. By the late 1840s, the northern tribes were moving into new hunting lands in Little Missouri River country near the border between North Dakota and Montana.

As they moved westward, the Lakota quickly became the major threat to neighboring tribes and to American domination of the region. Among the reasons for their success were their wealth in horses and their overwhelming numbers, for the Lakota now outnumbered the combined divisions of Dakota and Yankton–Yanktonai. Their large horse herds allowed them to choose and train only the finest horses for battle and hunting. Horses were also used to transport their growing possessions, which included stores of hides, pemmican, and food. Many of these possessions were now intended for trade. The westward surge of the Western Sioux in the early nineteenth century seized territory from the Iowa, Ponca, Pawnee, Arikara, Mandan, Hidatsa, Assiniboin, Kiowa, Crow, and Cheyenne.[22]

The northern High Plains were relatively unknown to Euro-Americans until the trading and exploration expeditions of the late 1700s and early 1800s. The earliest traders and explorers found the northern tribes engaged in constant warfare, which was a traditional practice that had been given a large technological boost by the introduction of horses and guns. By the 1820s, intertribal warfare had intensified further and become more sophisticated as all tribes acquired more horses. As raiding intensified on both sides of the Missouri during the late 1830s and 1840s, the attrition rate gradually depleted the force of warriors of some combatants. Eventually some groups were threatened with extinction, such as the vulnerable farming peoples living along the banks of the major rivers. Among these were the Omaha, Ponca, and allied Oto and Missouri tribes, who lived in what is now eastern Nebraska near the mouth of the Platte River.

The sedentary horticultural river tribes became the increasing target of raids by the powerful force of the Sioux Alliance, the combined force of the southern Lakota (Oglalas and Brulés), their Miniconjou relatives to the north, Yankton and Yanktonai from east of the Missouri River, and the Northern Cheyenne and Northern Arapaho. The Alliance formed in the 1820s and 1830s for several interrelated reasons. The first was a rapid decline in numbers of bison in the northeastern Plains just when the Lakota and Yanktonai were flooding the area. The result was an intensification of warfare among regional groups for access to the dwindling herds. A second reason was the southward movement of the Oglalas, Brulés, and Miniconjous into the still rich hunting grounds of the Platte River valley. This movement expanded the numbers of opponents these Western Sioux had to fight.

Besides this southeastern arena of conflict, the three river tribes (Mandan,

Hidatsa, Arikara) centered on the mouth of the Knife River in North Dakota were raided from the west and south in the 1830s and 1840s by the warlike northern Lakota (the Hunkpapas, Blackfoot Sioux, and Sans Arcs), often with the aid of the Miniconjous, Two Kettles, and Yanktonai, who attacked from the east and north. Raids became so intense by the 1830s and 1840s that they often continued for days.

Sioux conquests were aided at the time by the devastating impact of infectious diseases, particularly among the more sedentary tribes.[23] An especially virulent outbreak of smallpox practically wiped out the three river tribes (Mandan, Hidatsa, and Arikara) and killed half the Assiniboins and Blackfeet upstream, especially those near Fort Union. The population of the Crow declined by almost half in the 1830s and 1840s, too, due to smallpox, influenza, cholera, and other diseases. This shift in population balance greatly increased the power of the Western Sioux, for their population base had been partially protected by inoculation and by their nomadic way of life.

Intertribal warfare did not respect an enemy's age or sex, and the grisly mutilation of dead bodies was a common practice that was participated in by women and children. Corpses were scalped and skinned and their limbs hacked off. The belief was that the dead enemy would arrive in the hunting grounds in this grotesque form. Although captives were commonly beaten and mistreated, northern Plains warfare did not generally involve torture, which was more common among Eastern Woodland groups like the Iroquois and a few western groups, such as the Apache. After a successful raid, warriors celebrated their exploits by feasting and dancing. In a practice that seemed incongruous to Euro-American observers, raiding was periodically stopped to establish a truce or for the nomadic bands to trade hides and horses with sedentary tribes for agricultural produce and firearms. However, peace never lasted long because of the social and economic importance of warfare, competition over the dwindling herds of bison, and the colonizing pressures that were forcing the tribes westward.

Because of their location in the Plains, the lifeway of the Lakota differed from that of the Middle and Eastern Sioux. The Lakota acquired horses, followed the great bison herds, lived in tipis, and became the prototype of all Plains Indians in popular imagination. They were associated with war bonnets, bison robes, the hide trade, medicine bundles, sacred shields, horse gear and horsemanship, military societies, sign language, guns, the military complex and coup counting, the Sun Dance, and the vision quest. This was the classic Plains complex that existed among one group or another from about 1800 to 1880.

Lakota life changed qualitatively in the early nineteenth century, and especially after 1820, as they moved closer to the best bison country, de-

Figure 4.4   A Western Sioux camp, Dakota Territory, 1865 (Minnesota
Historical Society Photograph Collection)

creased their trade in small animal pelts, and became increasingly involved
in the bison-hide trade.[24] What was changing in the nineteenth century
was access to and ownership over wealth (in either a crude state (hides) or
a finished state, such as horses and trade goods), especially among males.

Nineteenth-century bison hunting among the Lakota bore little resem-
blance to the eighteenth-century form. By now, the horse-and-chase method
of bison hunting, which emphasized individual hunters rather than groups,
had supplanted the earlier pound-and-cliff drive as the paramount form
of hunting. Changes in labor resulted that ruptured eighteenth-century
relations of production. Since it was rooted in individual merit and ownership of horses and of slain bison, as indicated by the arrow as property
marker (where arrows were used), wealth differentials grew between families and the gender balance shifted noticeably in favor of male institutions
with an erosion of the position of women. Raiding and hunting rose in
importance and were the backbone of male ascendancy. The root of these
changes was an economic shift from a preoccupation with subsistence to
production-for-exchange, as their enjoyment of trade goods (metal pots,
knives, axes, metal arrowheads, guns, cosmetic products, etc.) demanded
a shift to an economy geared for exchange, although they remained a kin-
based society. These changes resulted in shifts in task differentiation between men and women. Other changes were the rise of individualism and
military sodalities, and an increase in ceremonies that occasioned wealth
distribution to provision people who no longer had an active role in crucial economic spheres. It was an era of unprecedented prosperity for the
Lakota.

The Lakota moved on horseback from winter camps in the spring to hunt and find fresh grass for horses. Goods were carried on packhorses or tied on travois. Large bison hunts were held in the summer. The great herds of bison provided most of their needs, and they lived almost entirely off these animals, which gave them a special way of life. Except in winter, they were usually on the move, following the herds. Although they planted few if any crops in this dry climate, women and children did gather wild plants on the plains, such as wild onion and peas, a white, starchy root (pomme blanche), and fruits and berries like grapes, plums, gooseberries, strawberries, and prickly pear.[25] Important events in the summer were tribal get-togethers and trade with the Eastern and Middle Sioux, among other groups. The tribal gathering was a time for feasts, games, council meetings, horse races for high stakes, and religious ceremonies, the most important of which was the Sun Dance.

Many bands hunted bison again in the late fall to add to their store of dried meat for the winter. In winter, they split into small groups of a few families and withdrew into sheltered areas, such as wooded strips along rivers or the woodlands of the Black Hills, where there was wood for fuel, fresh water, shelter, and bushes and shrubs to provide fodder for horses. Since it was dangerous to roam far in deep snow, the Lakota preferred to live a quiet life during the winter.

Even though the Lakota had engaged in trade with Euro-Americans along the Missouri River for many years, it was the Lewis and Clark expedition in 1804 that brought the Sioux to the attention of the American public. Since intertribal peace was essential to the development and control of the new territory, Lewis and Clark were charged with attempting to end the wars between the tribes. Jefferson's idea to curtail Plains tribal warfare was the first specific US policy to apply to the northern Plains. It remained government policy throughout the nineteenth century and took most of the nineteenth century to carry out, for it proved difficult to enforce.

After 1800, British traders moved south from Canada to include tribes of the Missouri River and beyond in their trade network. Between 1810 and 1830, even more American and British entered the northern Plains, even though the Treaty of Ghent, which ended the War of 1812, had excluded the British from the Missouri River region. Most visitors were engaged in the fur trade. Others were government officials, soldiers, and travelers.

In the 1820s, the US government sent additional exploration parties into the northern Plains and established Indian agencies at important locations.[26] The intent was to protect Americans from attack and to maintain peace among the tribes in the interests of economic progress, which at the time meant the protection of the fur trade. As American immigration increased in the 1830s, a swelling stream of fur traders, missionaries, travelers, and settlers flowed westward across the Plains. Many took the South Pass in Wyoming through the mountains. Inevitably, tribal warfare became mixed up with this sizable migration, and clashes between troops and warriors grew in frequency. This swell in migration was occurring as intertribal conflict entered its golden age.

In 1832, the steamboat *Yellowstone* arrived on the Missouri River, opening the northern Plains to the most advanced form of transportation of the day. It was also in the 1830s and 1840s that the fur trade, dominated by the American Fur Company, reached its peak. Hundreds of fur traders ascended the Missouri River and observed Indian life. By the 1840s, as expansionism seized the imagination, numerous pioneers bound for Oregon or California crossed the northern Plains. Traffic swelled to a torrent after James Marshall found gold on the American River in California in 1848. In 1849 alone, some 55,000 prospectors crossed Indian Country, though in general south of Sioux territory.

A series of forts were built to protect traders and to pacify the country. In 1828–9, the American Fur Company constructed Fort Union at the fork of the Missouri and Yellowstone rivers. At the time, it was the best-built fort on the northern Plains. In the 1830s and 1840s, the US army built Fort Leavenworth, Fort Atkinson, and other forts on the Missouri River, and eventually Fort Kearny and Fort Laramie on the Platte River. As more Americans moved westward, a crisis developed by mid-century that led to the first large-scale council on the northern Plains at Fort Laramie in 1851. In 1850, the US population was more than twenty million, compared to a number of tens of thousands of Indians on the Plains. The end of one era and the beginning of another was about to begin for the Lakota.

Explaining Sioux Warfare

Dime novels, Wild West shows, the cinema, and dozens of books and articles portray the Western Sioux as aggressive, nomadic warriors. These images are supported by scholarly studies that focus on Plains warfare in the eighteenth and nineteenth centuries.[27] In fact, the Lakota were widely recognized for their prowess in warfare among Plains Indians.

As in other Plains Indian nomadic societies, Sioux warfare was essentially an individual enterprise, with small-scale war parties organized without the sanction of larger social units. Conflicts tended to be brief, indecisive surprise attacks, fought more for glory and horses than to exterminate the foe. Counting coup and other valorous deeds usually took precedence over slaying enemies. Few large-scale battles were fought, formally organized fighting units were rare, and long campaigns by large forces were seldom engaged in for logistical reasons. Horse-raiding parties, in which membership was voluntary, generally ranged in size from about five to ten men. Because revenge raids tended to be much larger, they were usually organized shortly after the summer tribal bison hunt and Sun Dance, when large numbers of Sioux camped together.

Since bravery was the primary avenue for young men to achieve social status and a position of leadership, an elaborate system of scoring and recounting brave deeds was developed. One could gauge the magnitude of a warrior's heroic exploits by the feathers he wore in his headdress. Women rarely participated directly in warfare, but they actively urged their warriors to be fierce and to avenge the death of relations. The Sioux considered these acts to be moral and proper and to be sanctioned by the legend of the Pipe as given to them by the White Buffalo Calf Woman.

Why were the nomadic, bison-hunting Lakota the scourge of the northern Plains? How did they justify collective violence? What were their cultural patterns of warfare? Did violent conflict serve some useful purpose? These questions identify three factors that need to be separated in discussions of western Sioux warfare: (1) the causes of warfare; (2) the cultural patterns and practices of warfare; and (3) the motives of individual warriors.[28] Cultural patterns and practices of warfare relate to types of war parties, how war parties are organized, how warfare is conducted, appropriate behavior during military activities, the ranking of deeds of bravery, and the nature of victory celebrations, among other features specific to a culture. This aspect of Sioux warfare is the most extensively described in the literature.[29] The Lakota fought for a variety of immediate, personal reasons. These included the achievement of social and political status through demonstrations of bravery, the acquirement or protection of resources, revenge, the capture of women and children, and the support of political and economic allies. Undoubtedly, the reasons the Lakota fought depended on the man and the situation.

Anthropologists generally separate the reasons why individuals fight (the psychological aspect of warfare) from the broader economic, political, and social causes of warfare.[30] The assumption is that war is an aspect of culture rather than an innate human propensity for violence. If this methodological principle is accepted – that war is a struggle between systems, not individuals – then its explanation must be sought in deeper, long-term sociocultural forces, not psychological ones that make warfare look attractive to the individual.

Among the complex of historic causes thought to be responsible for Sioux warfare and Plains Indian warfare more generally are: (1) the migration into the Plains of Indian groups from both east and west, and the displacement of resident tribes; (2) the westward movement of the Euro-American frontier, which forced eastern tribes into the Plains; (3) the unequal possession of firearms among tribes, which led to an imbalance of power; (4) the desire for horses;[31] (5) competition for good hunting grounds; (6) the territorial shrinkage of the bison herds;[32] (7) protection of markets; (8) the machinations of traders and government agents;[33] (9) epidemics, which weakened some once powerful tribes and made them easy prey for the Sioux and other less affected foe; (10) the warfare–revenge cycle; (11) the importance of warfare to young men as an avenue to sociopolitical position; and (12) tribal ethnocentrism, which resulted in feelings of hostility toward outsiders ("aliens").

If cultures are mostly integrated, as argued in chapter 3, we would expect warfare to have affected Sioux social organization and culture. Suggested effects of warfare on the nineteenth-century Lakota include: (1) the socialization of male children to be aggressive and hostile; (2) a deficit for males in the male/female ratio;[34] (3) increased segregation of men and women (because of men's long absences in war); (4) promotion of the centralization of authority; (5) the formation of alliances or confederacies (here with the northern Cheyenne and Arapahos, i.e., the Great Sioux Alliance); (6) an increase in aggressive sports (a trait correlated with war[35]); and (7) increased differentials of wealth among individuals, families, and extra-familial social units.[36]

Warfare is a prime example of the dynamic, ephemeral nature of the sociocultural landscape of the Great Plains before the reservation period. The Great Plains was a region of dynamic social interaction during the seventeenth, eighteenth, and nineteenth centuries, as well as during the prehistoric period. As stressed in chapter 2, Sioux culture was never unchanging and homogeneous. By the time Lewis and Clark encountered the Lakota along the Missouri River, their culture had been revolutionized by the horse and was on the verge of further momentous changes caused by the packing of peoples into the Plains, the increasing scarcity of bison, and the push westward of the Euro-American frontier, among other intertwined factors. The study of Sioux warfare provides a window into the effects of these large-scale historic events.

Engendered Objects and Spaces

Another useful concept in understanding the Sioux cultural tradition is gender, for the culturally produced roles and attributes of women and men must have changed, and sometimes significantly, as the Sioux adapted to new environments, economies, living arrangements, and neighbors. Western cultures generally derive gender from sex by fusing sex and gender together in the categories "female" and "male." However, cross-cultural studies demonstrate that an analytical distinction must be made between sex and gender. Sex has a genetic basis and is manifest in biologi-

Figure 4.5   Bull's Ghost (*Tah-tun-ka-we-nah-hi*), a Yanktonai warrior (Science
Museum of Minnesota Photograph Collection)

cal markers such as genitalia.[37]

Gender, by contrast, refers to learned ideas and behavior, and is manifest in culturally proper ways of acting, dressing, moving, and speaking.
By implication, like race and culture, gender and sex are independent categories. Furthermore, even if we recognize only two sexes, there could be
more than two formally defined genders. For example, many societies,
including many North American Indian societies, recognize three gender
categories: female, male, and transvestite/transsexual/hermaphrodite.

Gender studies will help the reader understand more deeply how Sioux
culture worked at various times in different places. Investigations of gender systems generally focus on (1) sensitizing the reader to gender issues;
(2) the gender categories in a culture; (3) the gender roles within a cat-

egory; (4) rules for gender relations among categories; (5) gender stratification; and (6) the gender ideology that legitimates the entire structure of the system.[38] Gender studies are a rapidly growing and vigorously debated research area, too, in material culture studies and historical archaeology.[39] This section reviews four issues in the study of gender divisions among the early historic Dakota.

The first issue is the reconstruction of past gender systems through historic documents. A fundamental insight in Sioux scholarship has been that early written documents provide a white, male, colonial perspective on early historic Sioux lifeways. A parallel androcentric bias affects archaeological interpretations. Besides privileging the public "male" sphere, they have for the most part imposed Western male and female gender identities, roles, and relations on the Sioux. A contributing reason is that Sioux gender identities and roles were not clearly grasped. These biases and misconceptions affect how the early post-contact Sioux are represented to the public.

Because of the permeating bias in early historic texts, anthropologists have begun to search the archaeological record for critical information about past gender systems. Since it is normally important to recognize another person's gender, gender categories tend to be highly visible materially, spatially, and behaviorally in all societies. Gender demarcations usually include differences in dress and ornamentation, male/female facilities and spaces, and the possession and use of gender-related material objects. Because of the material imprint of these practices, gender demarcations should be visible in the archaeological sites of ancestral Sioux.[40] Archaeological remains and historic descriptions, including documents, paintings, and ethnographic descriptions, provide crosschecking references that could together provide more reliable reconstructions of earlier Sioux gender systems than can historic documents alone.

A second issue is the problem of recognizing the gender categories present in early Sioux communities. Like many Indian cultures, traditional Sioux culture recognizes three gender categories, female, male, and Two Spirits person (berdache).[41] A Two Spirits person is usually a biological male who wears female clothing, adopts a female personality, and engages in female tasks, such as pottery-making and basket-weaving. Did the same three gender categories exist among the early nineteenth-century Dakota?

Burial sites are a particularly good context for gender studies in archaeology, for a skeleton's sex can often be reliably determined and burials are normally associated with discrete clusters of artifacts and modes of interment. In an innovative study, Mary Whelan explored gender identities at a nineteenth-century (c.1835–55) Dakota cemetery associated with a summer planting encampment known as Blackdog's village. The village was one of seven contemporary Dakota summer villages along the Upper

Mississippi and lower Minnesota rivers.[42] The Blackdog cemetery is on a river terrace about five miles up the Minnesota Valley.

Excavations found what were probably 40 people interred in 25 different burials. Twenty of the burials were coffin burials; two were traditional burials containing individuals apparently wrapped in birch bark or cloth and then buried. European mortuary customs included coffin burial and possibly a linear pattern of grave placement along the terrace; no Christian artifacts were found. Dakota mortuary customs included scaffold exposure and multiple interments in a single coffin. Whelan concluded that the cemetery was "a traditional 19th-century cemetery illustrating the inclusion of selected Euroamerican items and customs."[43]

In Whelan's study, simple sex-to-artifact correlations did not reveal a strict association. The "male" gender may have included at least one woman based on the presence of "male" items like pipestone pipes, mirrors, and pouches with a skeleton sexed as female. This suggests the presence of the more fluid system of gender identity characteristic of the more thoroughly studied historic Lakota. An association of different colors of beads with "males" and "females" also hints at the presence of distinctive "male" and "female" decorative patterns on clothing.

A third issue is how to identify the tasks and activities traditionally assigned to "females" and "males." A division of labor linked to gender is common to all cultures and tends to vary with environment, economy, adaptive strategy, level of social complexity, and degree of

Figure 4.6 Dakota graves at the mouth of the Minnesota River (Seth Eastman watercolor, 1847. Minnesota Historical Society Photograph Collection)

participation in the capitalist world economy. Cross-culturally, gender roles range from mostly overlapping to sharply differentiated. Gender attribution research is concerned with identifying the activities and resources under the control of women or men. The driving questions are: Who did what, when, and where? How frequently were the activities carried out? What objects, facilities, and spaces were associated with each activity?

Gendered divisions of labor were present and important among the Sioux.[44] In another study of the early nineteenth-century Dakota, Janet Spector searched historic documents for female and male activities on a task-by-task basis as they were associated with acquiring and processing food, and making and repairing tools, clothing, and structures, among other activities.[45] She then constructed a richly textured picture of women's and men's work throughout the year as they moved from wild-ricing and harvesting sites, to deer-hunting encampments, to winter camps and summer planting villages, and on to other locations and activities. Women's work included small-game hunting, hide-working, cooking, wood collecting, farming, sugar mapling, clearing around short-term camps, and collecting wild vegetables, nuts, and fruits. Men hunted and trapped larger animals, cleared large tracts of land, and performed most ceremonies. Spector then excavated a portion of a 1830s Wahpeton summer planting village (the Little Rapids site) near Jordan, Minnesota, to explore the expression of these activities in the archaeological record.

A fourth issue is explaining the presence of one kind of gender system or another. A related issue is tracing the change of gender systems through time. How, for example, did the gender roles of Dakota men and women in southern Minnesota in the 1840s come about? How did gender function as a system-wide structuring agency at the time? How did the Sioux gender system differ in the 1740s, 1540s, 1340s, and 1140s? Questions like these are concerned with the explication of the processes of making, using, and empowering, more generally.

Cross-cultural studies indicate that gender roles, relations, and ideologies most likely adjusted among the ancestral Dakota as they shifted from being generalized hunter-gatherers to intensive wild-rice harvesters, and later to hunter–maize horticulturalists in an increasingly close colonial context. In traditional hunting-gathering cultures, egalitarianism extends to gender relations, and the activities, rights, status, and social spheres of men and women tend to be equal, even though a well-developed division of labor is present. For instance, gathering may be predominantly women's work, while men hunt and both men and women fish. In the absence of warfare, intensive politicking, and developed interregional trade, the domestic–public dichotomy among women and men tends, too, to be less well developed than among food producers.

By contrast, female status is generally lower among patrilineal horticulturalists who are associated with warfare, a male supremacy complex, and polygyny. Warfare tends to devalue women and favor the localization of related men, who dominate the allocation of prestige. As a rule, women are the main subsistence workers, with polygyny increasing household production by bringing women together. The result is gender stratification, with women having unequal access to power, prestige, personal freedom, and access to socially valued resources.

The turmoil of the fourteenth century that resulted in widespread cultural changes among the ancestral Sioux must have restructured gender relations along this trajectory. For instance, the agglomeration of settlements at the time would have led to greater concentrations of and cooperation among women. If Neolithic Europe and ethnoarchaeological studies are a guide, this may have allowed greater control over women as it did descent.[46] The appearance of large summer bark lodges suggests that women may have been controlled through a new organization of house space. Other aspects of material culture from pottery to settlement organization may have been used to "naturalize" and "mark out" the place of women in the domestic sphere. From one perspective, these changes emphasized the central importance and power of women as links among lineages and as the biological producers of children. From another, they segregated and controlled women. Although speculative and only intended to make a point, this scenario provides some notion of the specificity of the changes in the Sioux gender system that must have taken place in local historical contexts.

As a fundamental social agent and structuring principle that necessarily embraces women and men, gender cannot be neglected when examining Sioux social structure and social change. A gendered approach to comprehending the lifeways of the early Sioux has failed yet to realize its potential, despite the promising early work of Janet Spector and Mary Whelan.

Kinship and Social Organization

In human societies, patterns of kinship and social organization are based on two shared features, the prohibition of sexual relations within the primary family and with some relatives outside the family. This prohibition necessitates the establishment of "marriage" relationships between unrelated or at least distantly related groups of people. In modern industrial nations, additional elements of social organization include formal governmental agencies, business organizations, and a wide variety of voluntary associations, from fraternal organizations to youth groups. In tribal societies, the social structure is largely defined by the kinship system, which is that network of people related through marriage and descent, and by voluntary associations of various kinds.[47]

Given the centrality of kinship and social organization in traditional Sioux society, these aspects of Sioux culture require special attention. We begin by looking at functional correlations of kinship systems, for comparative studies show that systems of kinship and social organization are not random. We then look at interpretations of Sioux kinship during its most intensely studied period, the mid- to late nineteenth century. We then ask how Sioux kinship may have been different during earlier centuries and how and why it has changed in the twentieth century. Our goal is not to describe Sioux kinship and social organization in any comprehensive sense, but to alert readers to the importance of the issues.

Statistical studies demonstrate significant associations between particular types of kinship and social organization and types of economic, technological, social, and cultural conditions.[48] In general, these studies offer functional explanations for these associations based on the assumption that social behavior is shaped most fundamentally by material conditions. According to the logic of this assumption, human groups of different size and composition, and social organization, are selected under certain conditions. The rule of postmarital residence (who shall move where when marriage takes place) is sensitive to these conditions and is likely to be among the first aspects of social organization to adjust when the economic, technological, social, and cultural conditions under which a people live change. Rapid alterations in these conditions may lead to a time lag in adjustment of some other aspects of kinship and social organization.

All Sioux groups are thought to have shared a common system of kin relationship during the nineteenth century. This system of kin relationship is well documented for the Lakota and has served as a prototype in general kinship studies.[49] Most basically, the Lakota were organized in loose, bilateral bands. Their kinship system was of the Iroquois (bifurcate-merging) type, with Dakota-type cousin terms (in which parallel cousins are classified with siblings and differentiated from cross cousins). Parallel cousins are related through kin of like sex, while cross cousins are related through kin of the opposite sex. The term "bifurcate merging" refers to the fact that some uncles and aunts are terminologically equated to (or merged) with parents. Iroquois terminology is by far the most common form of bifurcate-merging terminology and is found throughout the world.

The traditional Lakota system of kin classification also emphasizes generations, differentiating relatives in five generational groupings, two above and two below a person ("ego" in kinship terminology). It has been suggested, too, that the lévirate and sororate were once regular components of the Lakota kinship system.[50] Together they form one system for selecting potential spouses for parents, should one die. Under the sororate, the preferred spouse of a mother is a "brother" of her husband, and the reverse for the lévirate.

Lakota loyalties moved outward from the family to the nation in a series of concentric circles. In the innermost circle was the family, which was composed of one or more tipi households, for polygynous marriage, where a man has more than one wife simultaneously, was an accepted practice among the Sioux before the reservation period. A camp was composed of two or more husbanded tipi households, and one or more camps formed a band (a *tiospaye*). A band generally camped together during the winter. A group of related bands formed a tribe, such as the Oglala, and groups of related tribes formed a division of the Sioux Nation, here the Lakota. In theory at least, the Sioux Nation was composed originally of seven tribes (the Seven Council Fires). However, there seems to be no consensus on how these terms should be applied (for instance, the Oglala have been considered a tribe, subtribe, and division). Likewise, the Sioux Nation is frequently referred to as the Sioux tribe.[51]

For the Sioux, kinship was not confined to the classification of relationship through links of descent and marriage, which is broadly defined in anthropology as a relationship established between a woman and one or more other persons. While the biological basis for procreation was apparently recognized, it was only one of a number of ways of becoming related in Sioux society. Since strangers were considered potentially dangerous, outsiders could be made relatives through ritual adoption. Social or fictive kinship of this sort was considered no less legitimate than other bases of kinship, and the adopted person was expected to behave in a culturally appropriate manner to his or her new kin. The expression "my relatives" included most individuals, then, with whom one interacted. All other persons were "aliens," people outside the circle of kinship.

Using kinship as the basis for organizing social action had several consequences in traditional Sioux society. First, everyone stood in a mutually recognized and accepted relationship with just about everyone else. Second, individuals addressed each other by kin terms (it was considered rude to use personal names too freely, for it emphasized a person's uniqueness). Third, kinship relationships entailed attitudinal and behavioral patterns of interaction that provided structure and organization in daily life. Like other fundamentals of Lakota society, kinship was the gift of *wakan tanka* (the "power of the universe" or the Great Unknown) and was brought by the White Buffalo Calf Woman, the Great Spirit's messenger.

The traditional Lakota, like the majority of described hunting and gathering people, had a bilateral residence pattern, which means that a married couple took up residence with or near either parental group, for it provided flexible group membership. Residential fluidity was an efficient adaptation for nomadic hunting tribes of the High Plains, for they shifted residence between winter and summer, and in response to threats from neighboring tribes and changes in bison herd distribution.[52] Depending on the situation, the composition, size, leadership, and location of social groups could change. Furthermore, the flexibility of the system allowed disgruntled factions to simply move to another band.

Although an efficient adaptation to life on the High Plains, this system of kinship and social organization may not have been an equally efficient adaptation for the Dakota in the tall-grass prairies to the east or for the ancestral Psinomani in the forested northwoods. In thinking about kinship and social organization, Fred Eggan stressed the need to look at societies "in terms of the problems of adjustment or adaptation which they faced."[53] Did Sioux kinship and social organization as described above extend throughout Sioux territory in the nineteenth century and deeply into Sioux prehistory or was it an adaptation to new conditions as the Lakota spread westward across the northern Plains? How and why might Sioux kinship and social organization have been different to the east and in earlier periods?

If our reconstruction of Sioux prehistory in chapter 2 is even approximately correct, the ancestral Sioux before about ad 1300 lived in hunting-gathering bands in the mixed hardwood forest of central Minnesota and northwestern Wisconsin. Hunting-gathering groups tend to be small, flexible in organization, and physically mobile. They also lack a clearly defined and powerful leadership. Cross-cultural studies show that in such societies the main form of family is the nuclear family, several of which make up a camp. A camp is a multifamily grouping that is adaptive because it is useful in locating food, in warning and defending against dangers, and in the effective sharing of food resources.[54] Few incentives encourage the formation of enduring social ties at any societal level except cross-cousin alliances where necessary. Since a majority of hunting-gathering peoples are bilateral, then early ancestral Sioux may have been bilateral, and may have favored cross-cousin marriage, as did the Ojibwa who replaced them.

The postulated shift to a tribal-level social organization at about ad 1300 was characterized by, among other things, the emergence of new integrating mechanisms. These may have included non-kin associations with military, social, and ceremonial functions, and nonresidential kin groups, such as clans or lineages, which are based on real or presumed descent from a common ancestor.[55] The assumption is that patrilineal descent groups and extended family residential groups, or something like them, would have been necessary to provide the larger labor force required to support the more clustered, semi-sedentary populations of the Psinomani.

Contact with Euro-Americans also resulted in subtle changes in Sioux social organization before the reservation period. For the most part, these changes involved a concentration of power, influence, and wealth. For instance, while government agents were looking for Indians they thought represented other Indians, fur traders were looking for strong, friendly leaders who would give them access to furs. These concerns led to the rise of "chiefs" with more power and influence than usual. Likewise, through the introduction of new wealth, a few leaders acquired some of the characteristics of Big Men, which led to imbalances in traditional giveaways.[56]

Sioux kinship and social organization were later modified, too, to accommodate new conditions on reservations. Among the Western Sioux, a *tiospaye* organization continued throughout the 1870s and 1880s, if not later.[57] In the early to mid-nineteenth century, government agents and missionaries worked through traditional bandleaders, whose bands still followed a seasonal round and retained their fluid composition. By 1869, some Indian agents began to interfere with the social organization of the Western Sioux by appointing chiefs for the bands. By the 1870s, there was growing pressure to end the easy movement from one band to another, especially by young men. This mounting pressure was aimed at controlling conflict, forcing young people to attend missionary schools, and forcing people to farm, all of which required permanent settlement. These trends were abetted by further land reductions, forced changes in subsistence following the extermination of the bison, and by the concentration of useful services, such as those of a blacksmith or doctor, at agency centers.

Allotment policy, one aim of which was to abolish the power of chiefs, also worked against the band structure, which began to deteriorate in the twentieth century. By the 1950s, only older Lakota understood the term *tiospaye*, and in one study only one small settlement was found to resemble the old organization.[58] Besides allotment policy, an ever-increasing number of marriages between Sioux and non-Indian Americans in the early twentieth century further eroded traditional patterns of kinship and social organization. Other changes were introduced by the Bureau of Indian Affairs (BIA), which imposed a system of inheritance based on genealogy that became an important focus of reservation life. This emphasis on genealogy was bolstered by the introduction of standardized surnames by the BIA around the turn of the century.

Still another pull away from traditional Sioux patterns of kinship and social organization was the introduction of a cash economy, which led to individualization of land tenure and hence to a weakening of kin terms. Since the rise of commercial exchange makes it possible for individuals to

Figure 4.7 Wah-ba-sha Village on the Mississippi River, 650 miles above St. Louis (Seth Eastman watercolor, 1845. Minnesota Historical Society Photograph Collection)

sell their labor and the products of their labor to support themselves, nuclear families become economically independent and residence becomes neolocal (in neolocal residence a newly married couple normally establish a domicile separate and apart from either parental home). Not unsurprisingly, then, by the 1960s a dual system had developed in which individuals were conversant with both traditional and modern kinship systems and terms.[59]

Sioux kinship and social organization provide fruitful insights into the nature of Sioux culture and its change through space and time. Kinship terminology can reflect and reveal many aspects of social behavior and social organization, while a cultural approach to kinship provides insight into how the Sioux understood that system. The study of Sioux kinship and social organization is a large-scale undertaking, however, for it seems possible that the pre-ad 1300 ancestral Sioux, the late prehistoric Psinomani, the traditional Plains Lakota, and other identifiable groups of Sioux did not share the same kinship system and social organization, at least in detail.

five
Fighting for Survival, 1850–1889

By mid-century, the US population numbered more than 20 million people, compared to a number of tens of thousands of Indians on the Plains who stood as a barrier to Euro-American westward movement. By 1860, there were 1.4 million Euro-Americans in the Trans-Mississippi west and by 1890 an estimated 8.5 million. Their travel across prairie and plains, the military posts established to protect them, and the eastern Indian nations forced westward a generation or so earlier stressed the limited resources of the environment. By 1854, the US army had 52 forts in the West, although few had garrisons of more than 100 men or any real fortifications. As the Euro-American colonization front washed westward, the US again demanded land cessions. Some bands chose to move westward away from colonists. Others chose to stay and fight for their homelands and hunting grounds, which initiated one of the epic tragedies of American history.

The first section of chapter 5 summarizes the participation of the Sioux in the "Sioux Wars" between 1850 and 1889. Subsequent sections introduce four topics for reflection: the reading of drawings and photographs, Custer's Last Stand, men's voluntary associations, and traditional Sioux religion.

The Fight for Survival

The ongoing pattern of raids and counter-raids on the northern Plains that lasted from about 1850 to 1889 is collectively known as the Sioux Wars.[1] Important phases of the Sioux Wars are the Grattan affair in 1854–5, the Dakota Conflict (or Little Crow's War) in 1862–4, the War for the Bozeman Trail (or Red Cloud's War) in 1866–8, and the War for the Black Hills (or Sitting Bull's and Crazy Horse's War) in 1876–7. The Massacre at Wounded Knee in 1890 marked the end of the Indian wars and the beginning of a new era. Because of their fierce resistance to Euro-American expansion and mistreatment at this time, the Lakota Sioux became the most famous of Plains Indians.

By mid-century, the prevailing attitude among Euro-Americans was that the traditional Sioux lifeway, like that of all Indians, was doomed to extinction before the onrush of settlers. Consequently, Commissioner of Indian Affairs Luke Lea outlined to Congress a new federal program in 1850 for the assimilation of all American Indians. This policy was to be carried out through American-style agriculture practiced on Indian reservations. Some 360,000 Indians were living on 441 reservations across 21 states and territories by 1880. Indian agents were placed in charge of each reservation. Besides enforcing regulations designed to erase all aspects of Sioux culture, they were responsible for the "proper" education of Sioux children, who were considered the hope of the future if Indian people were to survive. In general, well-intentioned Americans considered this policy humane and enlightened. After all, what other feasible option did the US government have besides extermination?

In exchange for their lands, the Sioux were promised money, goods, and services. Goods and services generally took the form of tools, seed, livestock, and help from agency farmers. The goal was to start them on what was called the Corn Road. Weekly rations of food, clothing, and staples were also provided (or promised) to tide the Sioux over until they could grow crops to replace bison meat and the goods obtained from their trade in hides.

There were many obstacles to transforming Sioux hunters into farmers: agricultural work was traditionally women's work; most reservations had poor growing conditions; and small individual land allotments were inadequate for ranching cattle. In addition, the Sioux were generally expected to use tableware, cut their hair, wear American-style clothes, learn English, and become Christians. While the Sioux Wars have captured the Western imagination, the gradual and painful adjustment to reservation life and the Corn Road is a more heart-rending, complex, and, in many ways, interesting story. At the height of the Sioux Wars in the 1870s, less than one-third of all Sioux remained free-roaming bison hunters.

While the Western Sioux were initially content to extract tolls from non-Indian travelers moving through their territory, hostilities escalated as the volume of travelers increased and non-Indians began taking shots at them. By 1851, the federal government convened a major peace council at Fort Laramie in Wyoming with the Western Sioux, their Northern Cheyenne and Northern Arapaho allies, and other northern Plains tribes. Primary aims of the council were to create peace among the Indians and to assure safe passage for travelers along the Oregon Trail, which ran from Missouri to Oregon. One of the largest ever assemblies of Plains Indians, some 10,000 native people attended the council. Chiefs agreed to stop harassing travelers on the Trail and to allow the US government to build roads and forts in Indian territory. An attempt was made, too, to discourage intertribal conflict by defining the hunting territory of each group. Afterward, a delegation of 11 chiefs, including some Sioux, was taken to the White House to call on President Millard Fillmore, the "Great Father."

Violence erupted only three years later near Fort Laramie when Lt. John Grattan attempted to arrest a Brulé Sioux, High Forehead. High Forehead had killed a straying cow belonging to a Mormon party bound for Utah. In a fatal miscalculation, Grattan and his detachment of about thirty men attacked the Indian camp for this and other incidents; the US forces were wiped out and their bodies mutilated. Conquering Bear, a chief, and other Western Sioux who were awaiting their annuities were killed as well. An expeditionary force of 600 soldiers led by General William Harney set out to punish the Sioux. Traveling up the Platte River, they attacked a Brulé camp at Blue Water in Nebraska, where 85 Brulé were killed or wounded and dozens taken captive.

Figure 5.1 Eastern Sioux treaty delegation to Washington, DC, 1858: *Akepa, Anpetu-tokeca*, Charles R. Crawford, *Hakutanai, Ma-za-sha, Maza Kutemani, Mazzomanee, Ojupi, Upiyahidejaw, Wamdupidutah* (Charles D. Fredericks photograph. Minnesota Historical Society Photograph Collection)

By the 1850s, the US army had adopted the concept of total war. In this strategy, an entire tribe was held responsible for the misdeeds of a few. General Harney and other US commanders championed the new, stringent policy. Although the policy succeeded on the battlefield, it brought war to the northern Plains. Passions were enflamed and distrust grew on both sides.

Strife swept the central Plains in the 1850s, too – as they had long been a corridor for settlement and a planned rail link between East and West, the government wanted to keep them free of roaming Indians. Kansas and Nebraska were opened to colonization in 1854. By 1859, the Southern Cheyenne and Arapaho faced a grave threat to their livelihood. While the Fort Laramie Treaty of 1851 had acknowledged their right to hunt bison in certain areas of the plains, those hunting grounds were now being crossed by thousands of American prospectors bound for the gold fields beyond. The traffic and debris scared away the bison, depriving the Indians of not only meat and hides but also of the trade goods they had come to rely on. The Sioux to the north were well aware of the plight of their southern neighbors.

These events affected all three branches of the Sioux, but in different ways. The dire consequences were, however, the same.

The Middle Sioux

A US military expedition on the Missouri River under the command of General Harney noted in 1855 that the Yankton still maintained their traditional annual economic cycle.[2] During the summer, the Yankton hunted bison; in the winter, they lived in lodges along the wooded banks of the lakes and streams in their territory. However, many streams were being thinned and entirely stripped of their timber during the winter snows. Not only were the trees being used as firewood, but the bark of cottonwoods was being used as feed for horses. By 1857, some Yankton were living in scattered villages of log cabins and, apparently in at least one instance, in earthlodges, where they were raising corn and vegetables, and awaiting their annuities.

By the mid-1850s, American settlers began to reach the Yankton territory in large numbers, with many living as squatters along the eastern edge. In 1857–9, the Yankton and members of several other Sioux bands attempted to drive the settlers eastward. However, the Treaty of April 19, 1858, signed by a number of Yankton chiefs, including Struck-by-the-Ree and Charles F. Picote, a mixed-blood, ceded the major portion of their lands in return for guaranteed annuities from the federal government, assignment to a reservation, and unrestricted use of the pipestone quarry in southwestern Minnesota. Most Yankton still live on or near this South Dakota reservation, with concentrations in the towns of Yankton, Wagner, Greenwood, Marty, Ravinia, and Lake Andes.[3]

The Eastern Sioux

In 1851, the second treaty of Traverse des Sioux and the Treaty of Mendota resulted in the cession of all Dakota land between the Mississippi and Big Sioux rivers, from central Minnesota south into northern Iowa.[4] These treaties reflect the desperation and pragmatism of the Dakota following the failure of the fur trade, the growing pressure of non-Indian settlement, and continuing conflict with the Ojibwa. There new reservation was a 10-mile-wide corridor on both sides of the upper Minnesota River. The reservation ran from Lake Traverse in the west to Little Rock Creek in western Nicollet County in the east, a linear distance of about 150 miles.

Western Dakota groups, the Sisseton and Wahpeton (the "Upper Sioux"), were settled above the Yellow Medicine River around an Upper Agency (Granite Falls). Eastern groups, the Mdewakonton and Wahpekute (the "Lower Sioux"), were placed below the river around a Lower Agency (Morton). About 6,000 Dakota occupied the reservation at this time. Each pair of bands was grouped around an Indian agency, an Upper Agency at Yellow Medicine and a Lower Agency at Redwood. The bands received their annuities and dealt with traders at the agencies. Confinement to the reservation also gave government officials and missionaries the opportunity to prepare the Dakota for assimilation into American life.

In 1858, the year Minnesota achieved statehood, officials asked the Dakota to give up the north side of the Minnesota River for settlement or risk seeing all of their land claimed by the newly organized state. Despite warnings of inevitable violence by the Episcopal bishop of Minnesota, Henry Benjamin Whipple, and others, conditions for the Dakota became worse in the early 1860s.[5] Among the festering sources of resentment were: the handling of their annuities, which were often late or insufficient (due at least in part to the diversion of the federal government's focus at the outbreak of the Civil War in 1861); shabby treatment by some traders and government agents, who cheated them; the effort to turn them into farmers; intermarriage, which blurred the line between Dakota and non-Dakota (people of mixed blood now made up about 15 percent of the reservation population); confinement to the reservation, where they could no longer follow their traditional economic cycle; the decline of the fur trade; continual disappearance of game; growing settlement pressure by non-Indians; the aloofness of their new northern European neighbors, who had little interest in interacting with the Dakota; and growing tension between those Dakota, called "Cut Hairs," who were adopting American customs and traditional "Blanket Dakota" who were not. In addition, the absence of many non-Indian men, who were away fighting the Civil War, and the traditional bravado of young Sioux men led to an increase in tension throughout southern Minnesota.

On August 17, 1862, Dakota frustration over their situation erupted in open conflict under the reluctant leadership of Little Crow, their most respected chief.[6] The war, which lasted six weeks, resulted in the death of about 500, mostly civilian, non-Indian people and eventually numerous Dakota. The Dakota took over the Upper and Lower agencies, chased many settlers from their farms, and attacked the town of New Ulm, which was near the reservation. Soldiers from Fort Snelling and Fort Ridgely eventually moved up the Minnesota Valley and, after an important victory near Wood Lake, forced the Dakota to surrender at Camp Release

Figure 5.2   Little Crow (Joel E. Whitney photograph, 1862. Minnesota Historical Society Photograph Collection)

on September 26. At least 3,000 Dakota, many of whom had not partici-pated in the conflict but feared retribution, fled westward. About 1,700, both "friendlies" and "hostiles," were held prisoner at Fort Snelling dur-ing the cold winter of 1862–3; 38 Dakota men were hanged at Mankato for killing civilians or assaulting women.

To discourage a wholesale uprising by the Sioux, the US army mounted punitive expeditions against the Dakota who had fled westward to settle among Lakota and Yanktonai in what is now North Dakota. The army, which was led by Generals Henry Sibley and Alfred Sully, fought mixed forces of Sioux at Big Mound, Dead Buffalo Lake, and Stoney Lake in 1863 and at Whitestone Hill and Killdeer Mountain in 1864. The Dakota and those Sioux who had helped them paid a high price in suffering for their Minnesota conflict. Little Crow himself, who had fled to Canada, was shot and killed by settlers, when he returned to Minnesota in 1863 on a horse-stealing expedition. His scalp was turned in for the posted bounty. Successful from a military perspective, this campaign fueled the resentment of all Sioux and set the stage for wider conflict across the northern Plains.

Because of this conflict, the government negated all Dakota treaty rights, confiscated their land, and banished the Lower Sioux from Minnesota with the Forfeiture Act of February 16, 1863. Although the Upper Sioux were allowed to remain, few did so due to rampant anti-Indian sentiment and for fear of reprisals. As few as 50 Dakota remained in Minnesota in 1867 from a population estimated at 4,370 in 1805 and 6,000 in 1850. Most who left the state were placed on reservations or homestead settle-ments in the Dakotas and Canada.[7]

By the 1870s, small groups of Dakota were filtering back into Minne-sota to rejoin their relatives who had stayed in the state. The 1870 census indicates that there were 175 Indians and about 440,000 non-Indians then living in southern Minnesota. Most of the Indians were probably Dakota. A special census in 1883 counted 237 Dakota living at 13 localities (Shakopee, Wabasha, Grey Cloud Island, Mendota, Bloomington, Faribault, Hastings, Redwood Falls, Red Wing, Prior Lake, St. Paul, West St. Paul, St. Peter). The largest community was at Shakopee (47 people from 11 families). By the late 1880s, government appropriations were being used to buy parcels of land at Prairie Island, Lower Sioux (Birch Coulee), and Prior Lake, where the Dakota had to rely on the govern-ment, local hunting, gathering, and fishing, and their gardens for food. These lands became core properties for twentieth-century Dakota com-munities. The exception was the Upper Sioux community. Made up mainly of Sisseton, it was not formally established until 1939.

The aftermath of the Dakota conflict of 1862 reverberated across the prairies and northern Plains for many years. Horrified by the massacre

Figure 5.3 Captured Eastern Sioux in a fenced enclosure on the Minnesota River flats below Fort Snelling (Benjamin F. Upton photograph, November 1862. Minnesota Historical Society Photograph Collection)

and mutilation of civilians, an intransigent anti-Indian mood gripped the region and many non-Indians were determined to get rid of the Dakota by moving them to camps far from Minnesota. This heritage of bitterness between non-Indians and Dakotas lasted well into the twentieth century.

The Western Sioux

To the west, the Lakota and their allies increased their pressure on the three village tribes to their north (the Mandan, Hidatsa, and Arikara) throughout the 1850s. They also attacked with renewed intensity the village tribes to the southeast, especially the Omaha and Pawnee. At times, fighting became so intense that it threatened the very lifeway of these village tribes. As the power of the village tribes declined, the power of the nomadic Lakota rose to new heights.

A primary cause of Lakota migration and intensified tribal warfare in the 1850s was the declining size of bison herds in the eastern Plains. Contributing factors in the decline of the herds were an intensification of the hide trade, an increase in the numbers of Indians who were hunting bison for subsistence, and the hunting of bison by ever-increasing numbers of American travelers along the Oregon Trail. In addition, mixed bloods from Canada began penetrating the territory of the Yanktonai in the 1840s to hunt bison for the hide trade. Their livelihood threatened, the Yanktonai and Yankton struck back. Eventually, many Yanktonai followed the retreating bison herds westward.

To the west, the Lakota and their allies filtered up the Missouri River and into southeastern Saskatchewan. They encroached on the Platte River hunting grounds in Nebraska, Colorado, and Wyoming, pushed the Crows from their land along the Powder River and around the Black Hills of northwestern Wyoming, and moved into the mountain country of the Shoshone. The Western Sioux and their allies, who were now able to field as many as 8,000 warriors at a time, raided every nook of this vast territory.

Leading the fight against the engulfing American frontier were Red Cloud and Crazy Horse of the Oglala, Spotted Tail of the Brulés, and Sitting Bull, the most famous of the chiefs, of the Hunkpapa. Their allies the Northern Cheyenne were lead by Dull Knife and Little Wolf, and the Northern Arapaho by Black Bear. Trained in intertribal conflicts in the 1850s and early 1860s, they were the leaders during the climax of northern Plains warfare in the late 1860s and the 1870s. Although some saw non-Indian Americans as simply an alternative tribal enemy, others were well aware of their superiority in numbers and technology. Nonetheless, the Sioux and their allies knew that they stood to lose more than their land if they conceded without a struggle. They trusted, too, in the strength of their spiritual relationship with sacred powers to guide and protect them in their struggle to preserve their way of life.

Threats to the lifeway of the Western Sioux and to all Plains Indians worsened with the end of the Civil War in April 1865 for a series of interrelated reasons. First, fresh waves of Americans surging westward on the overland trails were competing for the same habitat as the Western Sioux. Some were moving westward because of new legislation, such as the Homestead Act, which granted land to veterans and settlers, and others because of congressional charters that licensed the construction of railroads across the West. The westering wave of migration was swelled, too, by the rush to the Rocky Mountains following the gold strikes of the 1860s, which resulted in the forging of new trails, such as the Bozeman Trail to Montana. The swell in the number of travelers moving through the northwestern Plains angered those members of the Sioux Alliance who hunted there.

A second reason was the increasing destruction of the bison herds. From 1850 to 1883, the hide trade rose meteorically.[8] After completion of the transcontinental railroad in 1869 made bulk shipment out of the Plains profitable, the wholesale slaughter of bison for boxcar loads of hides began in earnest. By about 1870, non-Indian hunters armed with high-powered rifles were ranging southward from central Kansas into the Texas Panhandle. From 1872 to 1874, just three years, non-Indian hunters on the southern Plains alone killed more than three million bison. The slaughter contributed to the intolerable strain on nomadic Lakota communities. By the mid-1870s, bison were nearly extinct on the central Plains. Unable to maintain their food stores, many bands in this region of the central Plains made their final move to a reservation in Oklahoma. The northern Plains remained the final arena of widespread Plains warfare.

A third reason was the new "peace" initiative developed under President Grant in the late 1860s. The policy was based on a humanitarian idealism that considered confinement to reservations the key to protecting Indians from the corrupting influences of frontier Americans. In addition, their sedentary setting would provide the federal government the opportunity to teach the Indians the benefits of farming, Christianity, and the other, positively valued aspects of the American way of life.

The olive branch of peace was to be offered first. If that failed, a more severe approach to forcing the free-roaming bands back to their allotted reservations was to be applied without hesitation. Anxious to clear the Lakota and other Plains Indians from the path of US progress, the federal government placed William Tecumseh Sherman in charge of overseeing the army's efforts in the West. Major General Philip Sheridan, the new commander of the Department of the Missouri, was directed to adapt the tactics of a new kind of total warfare, which Sherman had effectively applied against the Confederacy during the Civil War, to Plains Indian warfare.

The goal of the strategy was to break the will of the renegades by attacking their villages when they were at their most vulnerable, in the winter. During the winter, the Lakota lived in smaller, more scattered villages and were less mobile than in the summer because of the snow and cold. Warfare between Plains Indians was fought, therefore, mainly during the warmer months of the year. Sherman aimed to destroy the shelter, food, and horses of "renegade" Sioux, and to capture the families of fighting men. No peace was to be made with a tribe until it admitted defeat. In practice, the military side of the peace policy led to the occasional overzealous massacre of peaceful Indian villages. Perhaps not unexpectedly, the launch of the new policy coincided with a rise in Sioux hostility toward non-Indian Americans.

In the late 1860s and 1870s, which was the height of the Sioux Alliance's military glory, the Sioux Alliance (Lakota, Yanktonai, Northern Cheyenne, and Northern Arapaho) continued to move westward across the northern Plains. Aided by a smallpox epidemic in 1869 and the massacre of Blackfoot Chief Heavy Runner's village by US forces in 1870, the Alliance ended the Blackfoot's long domination of the northwestern Plains in 1869–70. In the 1870s, the Sioux came into regular conflict with the Blackfeet. Already by 1865, the Alliance totaled some 20,000 people, 5,000 of whom were warriors. Because of its size, the Alliance was able to mount large war parties of 1,000 men or more that overwhelmed smaller groups. The size of these aggregations of warriors was unprecedented on the northern Plains. The Alliance itself was the result in part of the continuing encroachment of non-Indian immigrants, for the tribal bands were forced to combine for defense and offense.

The traditional Sioux way of life was affected, too, by the determination of some bands and individuals to live on reservations. They thought it better to live off government annuities than to hunt ever-rarer bison. Although a small trickle at the time, this shift marked the real beginning in the decline of intertribal conflict. Therefore, while some chiefs continued to fight, others rode into Fort Laramie in 1868 to sign a treaty. Most "renegade" leaders knew that armed resistance had to collapse. However, they also knew that the cessation of hostilities would bring no respite, for the subsistence agriculture taught by government agents was an Eastern ideal unsuited to the Plains. The only alternative was bare survival on meager, often wormy, imported government handouts of flour, lard, salt pork, and some beef. Droughts of the 1870s were the final problem, for they caused the failure of the crops planted by many Indian people.

In what is known as Red Cloud's War (1866–8) or the Powder River War (1865–8), the Lakota and their allies fought fiercely in defense of their newly conquered Powder River hunting grounds in southeastern Montana. Tension ratcheted up, too, when the federal government sought to fortify the Bozeman Trail in 1866 by building or rebuilding forts Fetterman, Reno, Phil Kearney, and C. F. Smith along the trail. Led by the Oglala chief Red Cloud, warriors of the Sioux Alliance successfully battled Montana-bound miners and their military protection, just as they had successfully taken the land earlier from other tribes, in particular the Crows and Shoshones.

Concerned that warfare throughout the northwestern Plains would hinder westward expansion, Congress decided to negotiate a peace settlement with Red Cloud and his co-leaders. In 1867, President Grant formed a Peace Commission whose task was to assure the safety of Americans and to bestow the benefits of civilization on the western Sioux and their allies. To accomplish this peace, the Commission was to establish boundaries for each of the Plains tribes. The Treaty of Fort Laramie in 1868 closed the Bozeman Trail and defined the boundaries of a Great Sioux Reservation, which covered the western half of present-day South Dakota (west of the Missouri River).[9] The treaty drove a wedge through the Lakota community. Red Cloud and about two-thirds of the Lakota honored the treaty. The remaining one-third ignored the treaty, including the Lakota led by Crazy Horse and Sitting Bull.

New threats emerged soon after the Fort Laramie Treaty of 1868. By the summer of 1871, surveyors for the Northern Pacific Railroad and their military escorts were moving westward through Lakota hunting grounds along the Yellowstone River. In 1874, Lt. Col. George Armstrong Custer led a federal expedition into the Black Hills of Wyoming and South Dakota and found gold. Soon prospectors were encroaching on ground set aside for the Sioux by treaty. The government did not attempt to remove them. In 1875, President Ulysses S. Grant decided the government would withhold meat rations if hostility was resorted to by reservation Indians. He then approved military action against those "hostiles" who were still roaming free.

Again, the objective was total war. Messages were sent to the hunting bands to report to the agencies by January 31, 1876, or face the consequences. None of the bands complied. With the help of Indians hostile to the Sioux and Cheyenne, including Crows, Pawnees, and Shoshones, the army set out in the spring of 1876 to destroy the camps of the bands and force them onto reservations. Some of the most famous battles on the Great Plains took place at this time. The resulting battles, variously called the War for the Black Hills or Sitting Bull and Crazy Horse's War (1876–7), culminated in the annihilation of Custer and 210 men of the 5 companies he led at the Battle of the Little Bighorn. The battle has been described in detail from many perspectives in many publications.[10] At its height, Sitting Bull's encampment had nearly 1,000 lodges, at least 1,800 warriors, and thousands of horses. Never before had so many Indian fighting men joined forces on the Plains. The Battle of the Little Bighorn was the greatest of all Indian victories during the course of the Plains wars and the last great Indian military victory on the Plains.

While the first three battles in the war for the Black Hills were great victories for the Sioux Alliance, the final five were victories for the US army and brought the resistance of the Sioux, Northern Cheyenne, and Northern Arapaho to a virtual close. The defeat at Little Bighorn infuriated federal authorities. In July, General Sherman persuaded Congress to place the northern reservations under the absolute control of the army. Indian agents in the troubled region were replaced with army officers, who tended to treat all Indians on reservations as potentially hostile. Weapons, ammunition, and horses were confiscated, and some men were held as prisoners of war.

The final blows against Sitting Bull, Crazy Horse, and others came from the US army in a brutally effective winter campaign under the direction of colonels Randall Mackenzie and Nelson Miles. Indians recently recruited on Sioux reservations aided the army. During the 1877 campaign, Miles was responsible for forcing most of the remaining hostiles onto reservations or into Canada. On May 6, 1887, Crazy Horse acknowledged defeat and surrendered at Fort Robinson, Nebraska. He was killed by a soldier while submitting to arrest later that year.[11]

Although the power of the Sioux Alliance was broken, sporadic raiding by the Sioux continued on through the 1880s. Sitting Bull, who had fled across the Canadian border into Alberta, eventually led his followers back into the US, where he surrendered on July 19, 1881, at Fort Buford at the juncture of the Missouri and Yellowstone rivers in what is now North Dakota. He was eventually shot, too, while resisting arrest. The last "formal" war party recorded on the northern Plains involved five Yanktonai warriors who were raiding out of the Fort Peck Reservation, which had been a source of raids throughout the 1880s.[12]

By about 1880, large bison herds were no longer encountered on the Plains, and, by the early 1880s, only a few hundred bison survived.[13] Two additional problems in the 1880s added to the Lakota's gradual loss of full autonomy. The first was a great influx of settlers into the Dakotas, and the second the passage of railroads through their territory. The coming of railroads was a final blow to a people who had suffered every other imaginable misfortune in their lives.

Because the US army had won the war for the northern Plains, the Lakota were regarded as a conquered people. As a conquered people,

Figure 5.4 Cattle to be shot and the carcasses divided for beef rations, Dakota Territory, 1880 (Gilbert photograph. Minnesota Historical Society Photograph Collection)

their land was regarded as obtained by conquest rather than through purchase or treaty negotiations. The tribes were forced to negotiate and were required to accept what was offered them, which generally was land poorly suited to farming. Well-intentioned people generally believed, too, that the establishment of reservations would provide an opportunity for the Lakota to learn American ways. As a result, the decisions made by Congress during this period contain not only provisions for reservations but also for agents, education, tools, health benefits, clothing, foods, and so forth. Agents and their missionary colleagues strongly urged the Western Sioux to give up their holy symbols and rituals, break up long-standing polygynous marriages, and work long, backbreaking hours on farms plagued by lack of rain and by grasshoppers. With the annihilation of the bison herds, this branch of the Sioux had no choice but to hunt other game and to live on the annuities distributed at their agencies. The reservations established during this later treaty-making period are lands reserved by the federal government, then, for use by certain Plains Indians.

Besides attempting to farm, raise cattle, and tame horses, few options were left to Sioux warriors. In 1878, Congress authorized the recruitment of paid Indian police forces at the agencies. Some tribesmen were subsequently able to affirm their warrior heritage by serving as reservation police or as troopers in all Indian cavalry units. Camp police were commonly drawn from the ranks of warrior societies, such as the Kit Foxes and the Big Dogs. Many Sioux warriors, especially Lakota, joined William F. "Buffalo Bill" Cody's highly successful Wild West Show and similar shows between 1883 and 1933. While the popular image of the Lakota is as Plains bison hunters and warriors, hundreds of Sioux traveled extensively for years throughout North America and Europe with such shows. Sitting Bull himself joined Buffalo Bill's show for a few months in 1885.[14]

Prompted by western cattlemen and others in the mid-1880s, Congress passed the General Allotment Act (or the Dawes Severalty Act) in 1887. Many well-meaning individuals believed that the law, by forcing American Indians to live like other Americans, would help speed the Sioux assimilation into mainstream American culture. Of course, others were mainly interested in obtaining Sioux lands. Under the Dawes Act, certain reservations were to be divided and allotted to heads of Indian families and individuals. The remaining land was to be sold to non-Indians. Many of the same people advocated eradicating Sioux culture and religion and sending Sioux children to American-run boarding schools for the same purpose. This serious threat to Sioux culture – the breaking up of tribal land and the dissolution of tribalism – is generally called the Assimilation and Allotment period (1887–1934) in US Indian policy.

Change came slowly on the reservations in the late 1880s, for the men found farming and ranching no replacement for the prosperous old bison-

Figure 5.5   Western Sioux watermelon feast at a county fair, 1885 (Minnesota
Historical Society Photograph Collection)

hunting days. For an experienced warrior, nothing replaced the exhilara-
tion and material success of horse stealing, counting coup, and bison hunting. Since these activities were the very base of male social life in traditional
Western Sioux culture, their culture began to radically change, too. This
radical shift was hastened by the forceful and deliberate suppression of
many other traditional practices of Western Sioux culture. For example, in
1887 Indian Affairs prohibited intertribal trading and celebration, for fear
that intertribal interaction would foment revolt. Also as important, these
activities, which included storytelling and general visiting among relatives,
were considered counterproductive to the adoption of the American ideal
of hard work. Individuals would wander from their reservation tasks at
odd times and often for extended periods. The Sioux would never become
mainstream Americans unless they were made to change their customs. Increasingly, the warriors realized that their traditional way of life was over.

With no way to gain war honor by showing the people how brave they
were, some men, with nothing to replace their old activities, turned to
dissolute lives of uselessness and drunkenness. Some tried to show how
brave they were by getting into trouble with their non-Indian neighbors.
It seemed that nothing would ever be the same again.

Looking Through Pictures

A picture is a visual representation painted, drawn, photographed, or otherwise rendered on a flat surface. The earliest Euro-American pictures of

the Sioux are sketches and paintings, most of which were drawn before the westward spread of the camera and photographs in the 1860s. These sketches and paintings are of two general types. The first type is composed of portraits of members of delegations who traveled to Washington, DC to call on the "Great White Father." Drawn in the artist's studio, the subjects were usually in a sitting position, wearing their ceremonial best. Commissioned by the Indian Office, the portraits were intended as records of the likeness of principal leaders for identification purposes and as a record for posterity of a vanishing race. Charles Bird King, Washington's resident Indian portraitist from 1822 to 1842, drew many of these group pictures.[15]

The second type of sketch and painting was of Sioux life in Minnesota and on the northern Plains. In Minnesota, Seth Eastman drew dozens of pencil sketches, watercolor drawings, and oil paintings of the daily life of the area's Dakota while stationed at Fort Snelling as an officer in 1830–1 and again from 1841 to 1848.[16] John Mix Stanley, Robert O. Sweeney, Peter Rindisbacher, Paul Kane, Frank B. Mayer, and others drew pictures, too, of pre-Dakota Conflict life and personalities, such as Little Crow, in the Minnesota region. George Catlin, Carl Bodmer, Alfred J. Miller, Charles Schreyvogel, Frederic Remington, and other painters traveled westward to the northern Plains to draw the Western Sioux and other tribes in their natural setting. Some, like Bodmer and Miller, were commissioned to make paintings, while the intention of others, like Catlin, was the creation of a moneymaking Indian Gallery back east and in Europe.

Photography was invented in 1839. English photographers in Great Britain took the first-known photograph of an American Indian in 1843. By the early 1850s, photographs had replaced paintings in recording Indian visitors to Washington, DC. Charles Bell, Mathew B. Brady, Alexander Gardner, and A. Zeno Schindler photographed Indian delegations to the nation's capitol in the second half of the nineteenth century, including most Sioux delegations. Joel Emmons Whitney, B. F. Upton, Adrian Ebell, and others photographed Little Crow and scenes of the Dakota Conflict in Minnesota in the early 1860s. Following the conclusion of the Civil War and the return of the nation's attention to the West, young photographers like William Henry Jackson, John K. Hillers, and Timothy O'Sullivan were hired by railroad survey and Army exploration teams to photograph the Western Sioux and other tribes in the American West.[17]

The heavy and cumbersome photographic apparatus and slow development process limited photography to professional use until the 1880s. In 1888, George Eastman introduced the Kodak ("You push the button, we do the rest"), the first mass-market handheld camera. Besides being lighter and easier to use, the Kodak made photographing moving people much

Figure 5.6   General Seth Eastman in army uniform, 1860 (Minnesota Historical Society Photograph Collection)

more efficient than the older wet-photo process. James Mooney, an early anthropologist, used a Kodak to photograph the action of the Ghost Dance in the early 1890s. The extraordinary simplicity of Eastman's handheld Kodak quickly revolutionized photography and led to a rapidly accelerating number of photographs of the Sioux by the turn of the century.

Since few people owned and used cameras before the mid-1920s, most photographs of the Sioux were printed and distributed through public media, especially postcards.[18] Because the invention of photography was linked to the development of journalism and advances in transportation, visual images of the Sioux became increasingly included, too, in newspapers and available to people everywhere. This incidental series of events in conjunction with the public's fascination with Plains warfare helped make the Sioux the quintessential American Indian.

Nineteenth- and early-twentieth-century photographs of the Sioux were taken by a variety of people, including government agents, commercial photographers, tourists, missionaries, and settlers. Together, these photographs and earlier drawings would seem to provide a rich source of cultural historical information about the Sioux. However, visual images cannot be read uncritically. Because the photographic process is mechanical, it is perhaps natural to believe that photographs provide objective presentations of real scenes, unlike drawings and paintings, which are obviously an artist's interpretation. The general notion is that had we been there, this is what we would have seen – that photographs provide unproblematic "raw data." However, while cameras may operate mechanically, just what is photographed and what one sees in a photograph are culturally conditioned. Photographers select scenes and pose their subject in conventional ways, and viewers consider photographs realistic because they have learned to see them as such.

In anthropology, the interpretive process of culturally decoding historic images is one facet of the subdiscipline of visual anthropology.[19] From the perspective of visual anthropology, historic photographs are social documents. Besides comprehending the photographer's intention, visual anthropologists must also try to understand the viewer's interpretation of a photograph. The ultimate goal is the excavation of information from the photograph about past cultures and people.

Visual ethnohistorical research requires a variety of skills. For photographs, these include: (1) locating historical photographs, which can be an arduous and frustrating undertaking; (2) documenting the images (e.g., determining the provenance, photographer, and date); (3) becoming intimately acquainted with the history of photographic technology and of the peculiarities of particular photographers; (4) understanding the sociocultural background of the photographer and the intended audience; and (5) becoming familiar with the culture portrayed in the photographs.[20] For instance, the wooden stare of pre-1880s photographs was due in large part to the technological limitations of early photographic equipment, for subjects had to sit in an unmoving position during the long exposure process. In the field, photographs were generally of still scenes shot outdoors because of long exposure times and the potentially incendiary nature of indoor flash.

Early pictures of the Sioux are problematic in other ways, too. Pictorial representations of the Sioux were framed at the time in conventional Western ways of seeing "Indians." Dominant nineteenth-century tropes include the "noble savage," the "chief," the "vanishing American," the "princess," and the "warrior." Photographers imposed their vision of what a bloody savage of frontier legend should look like by posing Sioux men in war bonnets and fringed buckskin clothing grasping a tomahawk, bow and arrow, spear, or rifle. Their dark skin, long hair, stern look, and "primitive" equipment confirmed their representation as the "other" and as exotica. Many photographs explicitly called attention to these tropes with captions like "Brave," "Chief," "Warrior," "Squaw," and "Primitive Methods." The photographs were intended to amuse, often to make money, and to illustrate, if only subliminally, the triumphant march of Western civilization.[21]

Other images documented the assimilation of the Sioux to Western civilization as one aspect of the US government's commitment to the policy of assimilation. Post-Civil War examples include the "before-and-after" photographs of Carlisle Indian School students taken by J. N. Choate and "tamed" warriors placed out of context. Red Cloud, the most photographed American Indian of all, was posed in most pictures as a Plains Indian with flowing hair, feathers, and warrior clothing. His "transformation" is evident, however, in many other photographs in which he is wearing a suit coat, a white shirt, and a tie. Other poses were Victorian, with women standing next to their seated husband, or classical, with "warriors" reclining on animal skins or draped with robes (blankets). These pictures record the transformation of a cultural Indian to a cultural White person, although one with dark skin.[22] By the turn of the century, the dominant image of the American Indian was that of the Plains Indian, especially that of the Sioux.

Of course, stereotypes like these appropriated the "reality" of the Sioux and of their culture. They were tools of misrepresentation by a colonial ideology intent upon bringing about and documenting the decline and extinction of Sioux culture. Nonetheless, when contexualized and viewed as ethnographic documents, the value of these visual images for ethnohistorical investigation is apparent. Early photographs have proven of value, too, to tribal historians and Native educators in helping revive traditional dance costumes and other aspects of indigenous ceremonies.

The Sioux themselves also drew numerous pictures. Chroniclers recorded historic events, such as the annihilation by allied Sioux and Cheyenne forces of Custer's troops at the Battle of the Little Bighorn, in pictograph form. Since many of these pictures were drawn on the pages of ledger books, they are known collectively as ledger drawings. Other pictures were drawn on skins to record something significant that happened during the year, such as a meteor shower or the death of an important person.[23] Sitting Bull may have been the first Sioux to take a photograph when he pressed the shutter of a loaded camera in 1882. Since Sioux pictures record historic events from the "inside," they are important, if neglected, social documents in the history of Sioux culture. In recent years, the Sioux have become their own drawer and photographer.[24]

Figure 5.7   Red Cloud in fashionable Western dress (Science Museum of Minnesota Photograph Collection)

Despite their rich potential as ethnohistorical documents, photographs and other images remain a neglected resource for understanding the history of the Sioux. There are good reasons for studying pictures of the Sioux: (1) they expose Western perceptions of the "other" (who in this case are the Sioux); (2) it is possible to look into and through pictures to gain insights about the Sioux; and (3) changing trends in Western perceptions of the Sioux can be tracked through pictures. Pictures freeze stereotypes in time for deconstruction. The promise is that readers will work their way toward more accurate, or at least varied, understandings of the Sioux through this process of critical reading. None of these endeavors should proceed, though, without an understanding of the ethical issues involved in photographing the Sioux or other American Indians.[25]

Custer's Last Stand?

Custer's Last Stand is one of the most widely recognized historical events in US history. Although Custer and his troops lost, they were widely reported at the time to have gone out fearlessly in a "blaze of glory" against insuperable odds. Almost instantly, Custer's Last Stand became an enduring national myth. The basic facts of the battle seem clear. In spring 1876, the Seventh US Calvary under Lieutenant Colonel George Custer was ordered to force "renegade" Sioux and Northern Cheyenne onto reservations. The plan called for a coordinated pincers movement of several armies on an unknown number of Indian people in what is now southeastern Montana. The Seventh Calvary reached the banks of the Little Bighorn River on June 25 and immediately engaged in battle with a force of perhaps 2,000 to 3,000 warriors. Custer and the men in the five companies under his immediate command at the battle were killed. The men of seven other companies under his second in command, Major Marcus Reno, fought for two days until additional US forces arrived. In all, 268 of the nearly 600 men under Custer's overall command died. An estimated 150 men on the Indian side were killed during the battle.

Because of incomplete and conflicting information, many issues about the battle remain hotly debated. What happened on the battlefield? Did Custer disobey orders by not waiting for support forces? Were the actions or inactions of his fellow officers responsible for his defeat? Was Custer a fool or a hero? Custer buffs have generated a surprisingly large literature in attempting to answer these and other questions.[26]

Custer's Last Stand is important to students of the Sioux for several reasons. Since this was a seminal encounter between the Sioux and American forces, it is important from an historical perspective to understand the details of the battle. From a Sioux perspective, what happened at the Little Bighorn? What kinds of arms did the Sioux and their allies have? What tactics did they employ? Since the mid-1980s, archaeological surveys and excavations have provided physical clues in the form of artifacts and their contextual relationships that tell us a great deal about these activities. By recording the precise location of cartridge cases with their distinguishing marks, for instance, the movements of individuals can be traced. In combination with Indian accounts of the battle, a more balanced account of the battle is beginning to emerge. One interpretation of the archaeological evidence even suggests that there was no "last stand" at all.[27]

More important here is the second reason for an interest in Custer's Last Stand. From shortly after the battle until the present, the battle has been cloaked in myth.[28] Furthermore, the nature of the myth has changed through time under pressure from Sioux/Cheyenne "activists" and through a shift in American values. These changes track changing national attitudes toward the Sioux and Indian people in general. In its own time, the battle symbolized the winning of the West "fairly and squarely." Even though Custer was defeated, the battle was emblematic of fair play in the triumph of civilization over the forces of savagery. Custer, the buckskin-clad hero with flowing hair, was a martyr to progress, for his death marked a new beginning as the frontier era ended. This concept of Custer's Last Stand is obviously a creation of popular culture and an American national myth. It has through time been retold and reinvented in films, novels, and other media.

Since the mid-1980s, the federal government has been actively reinterpreting the meaning of the battle – and now from an Indian point of view. This shift was symbolized in 1989 and 1990 by the appointment of an Indian woman as battlefield superintendent and by a change in name from the Custer Battlefield National Monument to the Little Bighorn Battlefield National Monument. The shifting significance of the battlefield is reflected, too, in changing interpretative programs at the monument and in documentary films like Paul Steckler's *Last Stand at Little Bighorn* (1992).[29] Today, there is an ongoing struggle over the cultural meaning of the Battle at Little Bighorn. The issue is not so much who won and how in 1876, but who will control the interpretation of the battle in the future. For this reason, the Battle at Little Bighorn and "Custer's Last Stand" are both of pivotal interest in gaining some understanding of Sioux culture and its context in contemporary America.

Men's Clubs (Associations)

Men's clubs (associations, sodalities, fraternities) refer to "formally constituted groups bound primarily by ties of shared interest rather than kinship or coresidence."[30] Non-kin and non-territorial groups share a number of characteristics: (1) they crisscross the bonds of local political and family ties; (2) they have some kind of formal, institutionalized structure; (3) they exclude some people; (4) members share a common purpose or interest; and (5) members generally have a sense of pride and feeling of belonging. Where they occur, voluntary associations play a significant role in the functioning of society.

Societies differ considerably in the degree to which they have voluntary associations and the kind they have. Voluntary associations are less common among nomadic hunter-gatherers, where social activities are generally individual, family, or band matters.[31] Likewise, they are less common in chiefdoms and pre-industrial states, where the ruling political structure imposes its own authority in their place; historically, perhaps as much as 90 percent of the total population of such societies had no personal involvement in voluntary associations of any kind. However, voluntary associations do have important social and cultural functions among tribal peoples and in industrial states.[32] Of these types of societies, voluntary associations play their most institutionally important roles in tribal societies, where they are primary integrative devices for social solidarity. In industrial states, other political, economic, and social institutions play this integrative role.

Voluntary associations in tribal and industrial societies share several features: (1) they are more commonly all-male rather than all-female; (2) they have a magico-religious aspect (e.g., ritual induction or initiation, rites and ceremonies, a system of mythological justification); (3) they are a focus of political power; and (4) they may cloak their activities in secrecy (as a means of controlling non-members and of maintaining internal solidarity). Besides reducing factionalism in the tribe by uniting people with different kinship loyalties, voluntary associations often supervise political and economic affairs, punish tribesmen for transgressions against the tribe, train warriors, perform religious rituals, educate the young, and provide entertainment and recreation, among other services to the tribe. In some societies, voluntary associations supersede kinship as the most important organizational principle.

Two basic kinds of fraternal groups existed among pre-reservation nineteenth-century male Lakota: policing or military societies known as *akicitas*, which were open to young men by invitation, and civil or leadership societies whose members formed the political authority of the camp (*tiyospaye*) and tribe.[33] The number of civil and police societies varied among the divisions of the Lakota, fluctuated in importance over the years, and varied in degree of localization. While some were pan-tribal, others were confined to a single band. New societies were also created from time to time. Together, these associations provided a tribe (e.g., the Oglala) with a strong and effective political organization, if by political organization is meant "groups that exist for purposes of public decision making and leadership, maintaining social cohesion and order, protecting group rights, and ensuring safety from external threats."[34] While the emphasis here is on the more visible and dominant men's groups, women might join the White Buffalo Calf society or other voluntary associations.[35]

Lakota policing or military societies (*akicitas*) included the Kit Foxes (*Tokalas*), Badgers (*Irukas*), Plain Lance Owners (*Sotka Yuhas*), Brave Hearts (*Cante Tinzas*), Crow Owners (*Kangi Yuhas*), and White-Marked Ones (*Wicinskas*). *Akicitas* maintained civil order during camp movements and communal bison hunts, organized raids, and protected the camp. They also provided a full social life for their members, with feasts, dances, and competitive games throughout the year. Though ostensibly policing societies, they had a strong military emphasis that was expressed through formal songs (which typically refer to matters of death on the battlefield), origin stories, requirements for leadership (leaders had to exhibit extreme valor to the point of death), and rituals, which celebrated militarism. Competition between societies in games (e.g., the Moccasin game) and military accomplishments was a key element in fostering militarism.

Individuals signaled their membership in an *akicitas* by wearing or carrying official paraphernalia, painting their face with a particular color or design, and styling their hair in a special manner (e.g., a roach). Individuals with political aspirations had to prove in a policing society that they were worthy of a position of leadership. Therefore, membership in an *akicitas* was a necessary step toward acquiring and maintaining leader status.

Lakota civil or leadership societies included the Big Bellies (*Naca Ominicias*), White Horse Owners (*Ska Yuhas*), Tall Ones (*Miwatanis*), and Owl Feather Headdresses (*Iyuptalas*). The *Naca Ominicia* was among the most eminent of these voluntary associations. Its members were patriarchs past their prime, such as former headmen, famous retired hunters and warriors, and distinguished spiritual leaders. Also called the Chief's society, the *Naca Ominicia* provided the real council of the tribe and held a true legislative responsibility. During tribal gatherings, its members would meet at the red-colored Council Lodge at the center of the camp circle to hear reports and make decisions. Because they appointed tribal administrators and executives (the Shirt Wearers), they had some control over tribal administration. Since the rituals associated with some of these appointed positions were expensive, the positions tended to be hereditary within prominent families. Like the *akicitas*, they displayed badges of office. Restraining the younger men in the *akicitas* was a continuing problem for these older leaders, who were more inclined to seek peaceful resolutions of external problems. However, because war was the main route to becoming a leader and an important man, younger men were difficult to restrain, for they were eager to display their bravery in war.

Voluntary associations are generally assumed to be a characteristic feature of traditional Lakota society, at least as it is represented in the "ethnographic present." When the dimension of time is added, however, it seems likely that these kinds of associations developed within the Sioux cultural tradition for particular reasons and changed through time.

Since formal voluntary associations tend to be rare in band-level societies and are especially likely to develop when there is warfare between tribes, they may first have developed in strength among the ancestral Sioux (the Psinomani) in the fourteenth century. Like segmentary lineage organizations, pan-tribal voluntary associations (sodalities) have military value because they can mobilize allies in many local groups for attack or retaliation against other tribes. This is particularly the case with local groups that change in size and composition throughout the year. Since kinsmen are not always nearby for cooperation in warfare, military associations provide allies wherever one happens to be. In this interpretation, military societies arose in addition to, rather than as an alternative to, kin-based (a lineage system) and politically based (a tribal form of organization) forms of integration.[36]

Some scholars have suggested, alternatively, that Lakota pan-tribal voluntary associations, like those of other Plains tribes, developed out of simpler antecedents during the late eighteenth and early nineteenth centuries as an adaptation to the economic changes that followed the spread of the horse.[37] According to this interpretation, as the Lakota spread across the northern Plains, two activities in their new adaptive strategy required strong leadership. The first was organizing and carrying out raids on enemy camps to capture horses. The second was managing the summer bison hunt. Given the absence of other integrative devices, the development of military and civil voluntary associations was an effective response to these needs.

The Lakota's traditional military and civil voluntary associations atrophied under the impact of reservation life. However, new kinds of voluntary associations have proliferated at all levels of Sioux life. As in modern urban–industrial nations in general, many voluntary associations among the Sioux today possess a legally recognized corporate identity and operate under electoral and bureaucratic norms and procedures. Men and women participate more equally in their membership, and many more voluntary associations for women are in existence. Many are mutual-aid societies that help individuals adjust to life under American rule, that supplement traditional family functions (e.g., youth associations), that provide support for migrants as they adjust to life in a city, and that enhance the integrity of traditional social institutions and mores, among many other functions.

A majority of books and articles today continue to concentrate on the flamboyant military societies of the bison-hunting Sioux. In the meantime, the Sioux themselves have developed new kinds of voluntary associations that are playing increasingly important functions in their society. Besides facilitating social change and adjustment to life in the twenty-first century, many of these associations have been effectively integrating traditional Sioux values into this process to create the unique society that is Sioux culture today.[38]

Traditional Religion

A religion is a set of beliefs concerning the cause, nature, and purpose of the universe. These beliefs answer questions about existence, provide moral guidance, and help people cope with typical problems of the human condition, such as death, illness, and natural catastrophes, among other functions. Most basically, a religion gives life meaning and provides individuals security in an unpredictable world. All known peoples have or have had a religion in this basic sense. This section introduces a few of the characteristics of the traditional, richly textured religion of the Sioux.

The Lakota, Yankton–Yanktonai, and Dakota share basic, traditional religious beliefs with some variation in details. At its most fundamental level, traditional Sioux religion was (and continues to be) based upon concepts held in common with other North American tribes.[39] These include the beliefs that: (1) the universe is filled with a power (*wakan*) that can be used for good or evil; (2) everything in the universe is related and interdependent; (3) every day must be filled with sacred worship (prayers, rituals, songs, dances, ceremonies, etc.) to ensure the continuing care and attention of the spiritual powers; (4) sacred knowledge and persons knowledgeable in it are responsible for teaching morals and ethics; (5) some individuals (medicine men, spiritual leaders) have a special aptitude (calling) for sacred knowledge and are responsible for passing sacred knowledge and practices on from generation to generation; and (6) humor is a necessary part of religion, for human weaknesses often lead to foolish behavior.

In traditional Sioux society, the universe was created and is controlled by – or at least consists of – *wakan tanka*, "the Great Unknown" ("the Great Holy").[40] Human beings and nature (animals, plants, rocks, and all other things) are not competing but interrelated and interdependent elements in the universe, which is *wakan tanka*. The life force, which is also *wakan tanka*, is distributed everywhere in a cosmic hierarchy. Since the life force (the power) of many animals and other natural beings is greater than that of humans, these animals and other beings have some control over human lives and, consequently, must be respected. To survive, people have to persuade them to share their power. Praying, dancing, chanting, and smoking a holy pipe are some of the means used to send messages to the spirits. The spirits might provide them aid, too, if they make themselves pitiable through fasting, weeping, or other signs of humility.

The spirits might also be persuaded to act as guardians for individuals or as intermediaries between people and still more powerful sacred beings or spirits. Among the most powerful sacred beings are the Sun, the Sky, the Earth, and the Rock, with the Moon, the Wind, the Falling Star, and the Thunderbird at a somewhat less powerful level; lesser beings (e.g., the bison, the bear, and human beings) and the four winds are at still less powerful levels in the hierarchy. Another key idea is the necessity of keeping a proper balance in the universe, for too much of any good thing is considered bad. This notion is fueled by the certain knowledge that sacred beings are as likely to harm humans as to protect them, depending on their mood and the good or bad behavior of The People.

A major religious figure in traditional Lakota religion is the White Buffalo Calf Woman, who, as the messenger of the Great Unknown, brought The People the gift of the pipe and the seven ceremonies that were the foundation of the Lakota way of life.[41] The seven major ceremonies – sun dancing, the sweat lodge, seeking a vision, keeping the ghost, making relatives, throwing the ball, and preparing a girl for womanhood (along with individual rituals) – are the means by which the Lakota receive spiritual benefits and maintain balance in the universe. All ceremonies and rituals are based on the holy pipe, the conduit through which prayers are sent to the Great Spirits.

During the nineteenth century, the Sun Dance was the major religious ceremony of the Lakota.[42] Normally a four-day ceremony in summer, the personal sacrifices to the Sun of young men, who often had skewers thrust through their flesh, was especially intended to secure the protection of the holy beings for all Lakota people. The ritual intensity of the Lakota's version of the Sun Dance attracted intense Euro-American attention.

Because many Dakota fled Minnesota after the Conflict of 1862, the religious practices of some Dakota came to resemble more closely those of their western relatives. In general, however, the Dakota held two major religious ceremonies: the Sun Dance and the Medicine Dance.[43] Since the Dakota did not believe in self-sacrifice, their Sun Dance was more informal and less popular than the Lakota ceremony. The Medicine Ceremony introduced people to the sacred mysteries of medicine men and to the ability to cure.

Although less well known, the religious practices of the traditional Middle Sioux seem to have reflected their intermediary geographical position.[44] While some practices were like those of the Dakota, others were apparently borrowed from neighboring Missouri River tribes. Of their dances, the Sun Dance, Snowshoe Dance, Yuwipi, Medicine Lodge Dance, and Soul Keeping Dance were similar to those of Woodland tribes. For instance, a single man without a lodge and crowd of celebrants could perform a Sun Dance, and, at least among the Yanktonai, some dancers used sacred bundles.

A characteristic of Native American religions or sacred ways is their adaptability. Although core concepts might remain stable for long periods, particular rites and customs were altered when necessary to adjust to changing circumstances. A persistent focus on reconstructing (or "recording") traditional ways in the "ethnographic present" has detracted from the nature of this flow through time. For example, if, as seems likely, the Lakota did not move permanently out of Minnesota until the 1700s, then the bison not only rapidly became the mainstay of their diet but also rapidly assumed a greater religious emphasis than it most likely had in the northwoods of Minnesota.

In a similar manner, while the gift of the holy pipe to the Lakota by the White Buffalo Calf Woman may have deep prehistoric origins in its fundamentals, it may have adjusted in detail to the Plains environment as the Lakota drifted westward. It is interesting in this context that the use of red catlinite to make pipes (and the platform pipe itself) does not appear to have become widespread in the northeastern Plains and adjoining prairies until after AD 1300.[45]

As a final example, even though it is commonly implied that the three major divisions of the Sioux shared a common religion, it seems that this is true only at a high level of abstraction. Their religious practices differed in detail, with "Woodland" practices more prevalent eastward and Plains practices more prevalent westward. While much has been written about specific Sioux religious practices (and especially Lakota practices) at particular times and places, or as understood by particular individuals, then, the global picture of the development of Sioux religion through time and space remains to be investigated.

six
Assimilation and Allotment, 1889–1934

By the late 1880s, the Sioux were a devastated people who lived in fragmented, mixed communities on reservations. They had suffered total military defeat, most of their territory had been taken from them, many of their children had been forcibly sent to distant boarding schools to be educated in the American way, and they were expected to learn farming and English. All of these consequences were the result of a combination of government policies. They were now the impoverished wards of a reservation system intent on suppressing their beliefs and ways of living. Many young men, apparently overwhelmed by the new emptiness of their lives, surrendered to alcoholism, ennui, and even suicide.[1]

Chapter 6 reviews some of the events and processes that affected Sioux culture during the ensuing period, which is known as the Assimilation and Allotment period. Subsequent sections focus on four topical issues: storytelling, prophecy narratives, time, and the use of language as a tool of colonialism.

Reservation Dependency

South Dakota became a state in November 1889. Since much of the state was part of the Great Sioux Reservation as defined in the treaty of 1868, there was a clamor by settlers to open a large portion of the land for sale. Some settlers even moved onto the reservation illegally. Rather than protect the Lakota from intruders, the federal government broke the Great Sioux Reservation into four separate reservations that same year. Each of the seven Lakota branches became identified with one or more of these reservations.[2] The populations living on these diminished lands were but a portion of what they had been decades earlier, for their numbers had been decimated by warfare, inadequate annuity supplies, starvation, poverty, and disease. To the east and north, the other Sioux bands had already been settled on their small reservations for many years.

A powerful new movement, called the Ghost Dance, which was flourishing throughout the West, gave some Western Sioux brief hope that the old ways would be restored. The Ghost Dance movement, which had originated about 1870 among the Northern Paiutes of Nevada, taught peace and accommodation to Euro-American ways and promised a world without disease and pain.[3] The movement also included a prophecy that there would be a great apocalypse, possibly in the spring of 1891, after which all white people would disappear and the ghosts of their own now-dead relatives would be resurrected. The old Indian life would be restored and vast herds of bison would roam the grasslands once again.

A militant version of the religion spread rapidly to all Lakota communities in April 1890. Many angry and dispirited Western Sioux fervently embraced the new doctrines, for, as Red Cloud later recalled, "There was no hope on earth, and God seemed to have forgotten us. The people snatched at the hope."[4] Alarmed by the intensity of the movement, the prophecy of their imminent demise, and the belief by some Lakota that the power of its visionaries could be used in battle, nervous government agents ordered a stop to Ghost Dancing on Sioux reservations and attempted to jail its leaders. On December 14, James McLaughlin, the agent at Standing Rock, sent Sioux police to arrest Sitting Bull, who he thought was inciting the Ghost Dancers to rebellion. In the scuffle that broke out Sitting Bull was shot and killed by Red Tomahawk, an Indian policeman. Alarmed, a group of armed Minneconjou dancers led by Big Foot fled from their Cheyenne River reservation. On December 29, many of his band of 350 Minneconjou were massacred at Wounded Knee by soldiers of the 7th Calvary, Custer's old unit.[5]

Could the plight of the Sioux get worse? It could and it did. Following the end of the Indian wars in the 1870s, the federal government turned to assimilating those Sioux who had survived forced subjugation. Congress acted quickly and forcibly in implementing a new, broadened assimilation policy toward American Indians. One new policy was the extension of US criminal jurisdiction over reservations through the Major Crimes Act of 1885. However, the hallmark of their broadened initiative was the passage in 1887 of the General Allotment Act, which is more commonly known as the Dawes Act for its writer, Senator Henry L. Dawes of Massachusetts. The intent of the law was to break up the tribes by replacing their traditional communal "ownership" of the land by the Anglo-Saxon system of individuated property.[6]

According to the General Allotment Act of 1887, most reservations were to be divided into small allotments ("farms") of about 160 acres per individual family. The land left over after every family had received its allot-

ment would be opened up to corporate use, sold to non-Indian homesteaders, or placed in federal trust status for later development of military posts,
national parks and forests, and other federal endeavors. In passing the law,
Congress planned to turn tribal people into self-sufficient, American-style
farmers and to break the grip of traditionalism, which it thought was im-
peding the necessary assimilation of Indians into American society.

Many Sioux were opposed to accepting allotments, for they wanted to
maintain their traditional ways of living. However, federal officials threatened to cut off supplies of rations to those Sioux who resisted accepting
allotments. This was a severe threat, for the amount of rations issued in
the late 1880s and early 1890s had already been reduced by half. Many
Sioux were living on the brink of starvation and a severe drought had
resulted in a loss of crops by some families. By the 1920s most Sioux had
received an allotment, and through political machinations a good portion
of it was soon leased or sold to non-Indian farmers, businessmen, and
bankers, for to many families the lease or sale of their land was their main
source of income.

The federal government's allotment policy was disastrous for the Sioux
for many reasons: (1) the policy itself resulted in the loss of thousands of
acres that were declared "surplus" after allotment; (2) still more land was
lost when many Sioux opted to sell their allotment; (3) after Congress
amended the Dawes Act in 1891 to permit Indians to lease their allotment, many Sioux quit farming and lived off the small income they received for leasing their land, which eventually contributed further to their
poverty; (4) many Sioux were too old, too young, or too physically disa-
bled to farm; (5) the pattern of small, scattered allotments was unsuitable
for ranching or for the large-scale cultivation that was necessary in the
grasslands of the Great Plains; (6) few Sioux had the capital to buy the
extra land, plows, seed, and draft animals necessary to make farming
productive, and government appropriations were insufficient to meet this
need; (7) because of patterns of inheritance, most of the original allotments were eventually jointly owned by as many as 100 people, who either could not agree on how to use the land or who sold it because none
of them could make a living on the small portion they owned; (8) since the
Sioux were now supposedly on their way to economic self-sufficiency, the
federal government reduced or ended some appropriations that were guaranteed by treaty; (9) the Act undermined traditional concepts of commu-
nally owned land; and (10) the scattered allotments discouraged the
traditional practice of living in larger, often extended family households
(the assumption was that the Sioux would become self-sufficient more
quickly if they lived in nuclear families like other Americans). In retrospect, the allotment policy actually decreased the economic potential of
farming and reduced the number of acres under cultivation.

Numbers illustrate the staggering amount of land lost. Between 1904 and 1916, Pine Ridge reservation, originally 2,721,597 acres, was split into 8,275 plots that together totaled 2,380,195 acres. The remaining land was either assigned to the tribe as a whole (about 147,000 acres) or bought by the federal government. More than half of the land in allotments was eventually sold or leased to non-Indians. By 1934, 2,195,905 acres of the original Rosebud reservation had been sold to outsiders or ceded to the US government. Likewise, Dakota and Yankton–Yanktonai reservations lost hundreds of thousands of acres to homesteaders and other outsiders.[7]

By the late 1920s, increasing poverty among the Sioux was leading to higher rates of hunger and malnutrition, and long-lasting diseases like tuberculosis, malaria, and venereal diseases were on the rise. Pollution in neighboring streams contributed to poor health, as did unsanitary conditions in cabins. In 1926, Edgar Howard, a Nebraska member of the US House of Representatives, described the living conditions at the Santee reservation as "deplorable beyond words."[8] Furthermore, settlers were forming new towns on reservations, such as Wagner and Lake Andes on the Yankton reservation, and railroads were being laid through reservations where concentrations of white settlers were now living.

Due in large part to the allotment policy, where the Sioux lived and how they lived changed dramatically during this period. To reduce mobil-

Figure 6.1   A Sioux woman fleshing a hide in North Dakota, 1913 (Science Museum of Minnesota Photograph Collection)

ity and improve living conditions, federal officials introduced several types of frame houses in the 1890s. The most commonly built house was a two-room, 18-by-24-foot frame structure that was issued to new allottees by the Bureau of Indian Affairs so that they could live on their new farm allotments. Because these "issued houses" were poorly built and let the cold in, they were difficult to heat in winter. Many were eventually abandoned or used as sheds, although some continued in use with additions into the mid-1900s. Small cabins were also built near agency and mission centers for the elderly or for other people who needed help. Some Sioux built their own house or lived in a log cabin. A few even erected a tipi outside their Euro-American style home because of its relative coolness during the hot summers, and perhaps to signal their traditionalism.

Some Dakota and Yankton immigrated from reservations in Nebraska and the Dakotas back to Minnesota toward the end of the nineteenth century, where they joined their relatives who had remained in the state. While some family groups lived at Grey Cloud Island, Bloomington, Mendota, Granite Falls, Wabasha, and other locations during this period, most were concentrated at Prairie Island, Prior Lake, and Birch Coulee (the Lower Sioux community) by the early 1930s. The Prairie Island Reservation, whose name was officially changed to the Prairie Island Indian

Figure 6.2   A typical 12'-×-14' house built for the Prairie Island Dakota in the 1930s (photographed in July, 1960. Minnesota Historical Society Photograph Collection)

Community in the 1960s, was established under federal acts of 1888, 1889, 1890, and 1934, when land was purchased for this branch of Mdewakanton Sioux. At the beginning of the Great Depression, Dakota holdings in Minnesota included 258 acres at Prior Lake, 120 acres at Prairie Island, and 470 acres at Lower Sioux. In a 1929 census, 554 Dakota were counted in Minnesota. An unknown number of mixed-bloods who lived in the Twin Cities of Minneapolis and St. Paul were not included in the count.[9]

To prepare the Sioux for assimilation into American society, the federal government became increasingly determined by the end of the nineteenth century to undermine their traditional values, which were considered antithetical to this transformation. This policy was carried out in various ways. For instance, the Sun Dance was made illegal and alternative, non-traditional activities were promoted. Frequently, only Sioux men who wore American-style clothing and had their hair cut short would be hired for government jobs. Even Canada adopted a strong assimilationist policy in the 1890s when Hayter Reed, then Commissioner of the Department of Indian Affairs, outlawed some traditional religious and secular ceremonies and attempted to force Indian peoples to abandon other ancestral customs. Those who disobeyed were threatened with fines and prison sentences.[10]

By the early 1900s, the Sioux were economically depressed and only half-assimilated. In contrast to the growing prosperity of American and Canadian farmers and ranchers around them, the economic and living conditions of the Sioux deteriorated. There were numerous reasons for this. For instance, their crops were continually plagued by infestations of insects, cold weather, and droughts that made farming very difficult. Federal policies inhibited their ability to compete fairly in expanding regional labor and product markets or to make farming decisions on their own. The situation was exacerbated in the early twentieth century when the government withdrew benefits and closed some Indian agencies because it thought the Sioux were ready to become self-supporting citizens. For all of these reasons, farming eventually failed for many Sioux between 1889 and 1934.

Those Sioux who turned to cattle ranching in the early twentieth century to support their families did not fare any better. Again, US and Canadian government policies proved counter-productive. Up to World War I, some Lakota were able to develop large herds of cattle and to breed quality horses. However, after the US entered the war, most of these cattle were forcibly sold "for the war effort" and their rangeland leased to non-Indians. Large American agricultural companies succeeded in leasing more land on the reservation after the war ended. Canadian Dakota were eventually forced, too, to give up successful herding enterprises because of government intervention.

Figure 6.3   Good Earth Woman (*Makawastewwin*), Prairie Island Community, 1930 (Minnesota Historical Society Photograph Collection)

While some Sioux groups were awarded small amounts of money around the turn of the century for lands taken illegally from them in the nineteenth century, this money did not last long. Consequently, many Sioux began to turn to sources of income other than farming or ranching. Some supplied nearby settlements and military posts with timber or bison bones that could be sold to manufacture bone-china dishware. Others worked as lumbermen, construction workers, or seasonal farm laborers. Some women were employed as domestic workers. And both men and women began manufacturing souvenirs and handcrafts for sale to nearby settlements. Where possible, especially in some of the Canadian reservations, people hunted, fished, and gathered wild foods away from their settle-

Figure 6.4 Lace-makers at the Redwood Falls Mission, Lower Sioux Community, Morton, Minnesota (Edward A. Bromley photograph, 1897. Minnesota Historical Society Photograph Collection)

ments. A few Sioux even moved to Michigan to work in the emerging automobile industry. In general, most people survived the difficult late-nineteenth- and early-twentieth-century period by doing odd jobs to earn a bit of cash.

Despite the relative prosperity of the 1920s, most Sioux people entered the 1930s surrounded by poverty and failure. The farming lifeway, which was still suffering from a 1920s recession, was further damaged by the Great Depression and by the terrible droughts and dust storms of the early 1930s. Besides the failure of their own crops and herds, the need for farm labor was steadily declining because of the gradual increase in the mechanization of farm work. There were fewer jobs in town, too, because everyone was experiencing hard times.

During this same period, concerted efforts were made to replace traditional tribal governments headed by hereditary chiefs by an American-style elected government. On most Sioux reservations, this meant replacing traditional governments with an elected assembly of community representatives, some form of business commission, and a man "made chief" by a Bureau of Indian Affairs agent when the old hereditary chief died. However, by the 1920s even these organizations were being neglected by US officials. The notion was that a people on their way to self-sufficiency no longer needed a government of their own.

As they had many times in the past, the Sioux adjusted to these new circumstances. Again, as in the past, it was a difficult transformation. They now lived in two cultures whose core values and ways of world-making were incompatible. While the old nomadic lifeway was gone forever, many Sioux maintained faith in the values of their own traditions. However, they had been forced to abandon most of their traditional social and religious practices under threat of censure. When they objected to how they were being treated, their protests were ignored and they were punished for their complaints. Both the US and Canadian governments and their agencies were forcing, instead, unwanted economic and political changes upon them. Nonetheless, their basic values and some of their traditional customs remained. It was in this environment that they began to develop a way of life at the end of the nineteenth century that incorporated change but remained true to their core cultural beliefs.

The continuation of their customs and beliefs was expressed in many different ways. As in the past, they continued to rely on extended-family relationships to work their way through difficult times. Resources of all kinds, including cash and labor, were pooled and giveaways were used to redistribute food, blankets, clothing, and other items. Despite censure and attempts at control, dancing and feasting continued, often on the American holidays they were expected to observe as part of the assimilation process. Likewise, although most Sioux participated in some Christian

Figure 6.5   A Sioux woman jerking meat in Dakota Territory in the early 1900s (Science Museum of Minnesota Photograph Collection)

activities, such as church services, many continued to believe in the spirit world of their ancestors. They also adopted some of the new Indian movements that were sweeping through Plains reservations. Two of the most widely adopted of these were Peyotism and the Grass Dance.

Peyotism, which was first adopted by some Western Sioux in about 1900, is a blend of traditional Indian and Christian elements that is based on the sacramental use of the peyote plant, a hallucinogen. The ingestation of the peyote button, which is compared to the eucharistic use of bread and wine, produces personal revelations that are not unlike the traditional visions that underlie prophesy, the acquisition of spirit power, and healing. The Peyote Road advocated Western values, such as self-reliance, hard work, and monogamy, but also the revival of elements of traditional dress and other institutions, and values like kindly charity and morality. It also prescribed strict sobriety.[11]

Although Peyotism's appeal was never 100 percent on a single reservation (it was closer to 35–50 percent), it soon became a significant force much opposed by Christian churches, the Bureau of Indian Affairs, and many other groups and individuals. The argument was that peyote was an addictive drug whose use harmed Peyotists mentally and physically. Every effort was made to suppress the new religion, including a strenuous effort begun in 1912 to pass federal legislation against peyote. Consequently, Peyotism was forced underground and did not emerge forcefully until passage of the Indian Reorganization Act in the 1930s.

The Grass Dance, which is an ancestor of the modern powwow, had a different history. According to Lakota tradition, it was a warrior dance learned from the Omaha in about 1860. This Omaha Dance, which became known as the Grass Dance among the Lakota, was a lively, energetic dance. Its popularity grew in the 1890s, for, with the demise of warfare, it was one of the few means young men had of retaining some semblance of a warrior identity. Since it was secular, not religious in nature, it was not attacked, like the Ghost Dance, as a pagan religion. Furthermore, the showiness of the dance and the deer-hair head roaches and feathered bustles of the dancers began to attract tourists, who with the passage of time now considered it an entertaining "war dance."[12]

During this same period, traditional Sioux art not only flourished but also continued to find new avenues of expression, despite the predicted demise of traditional Sioux culture by authorities. Many of these innovations reflected modern influences and reservation life. While sunbonnets and parasols were decorated in traditional ways, new materials like coins and pieces of tin can were used to decorate clothing, just like beads, tinklers (rolled cones made from thin sheet metal), and porcupine quills had in the past. New design motifs, such as the American flag, were used in beadwork, basketry, and other traditional crafts. In addition, new Western skills, such as quilting and lace-making, were incorporated into their art repertoire. Their flourishing art was given a boost, too, by non-Indians, who began to collect their products, giving many impoverished Sioux a new source of needed income.

Reform movements also grew with great vigor between 1889 and 1934. One effect of the official investigation of the Wounded Knee massacre was the first public hearing into living conditions on Lakota reservations. Still, despite obvious problems, many federal agents thought that the government's assimilation policy was successful, for many Sioux spoke English, dressed like non-Indians, and were practicing Christians. Official inspections of life on Sioux reservations between 1912 and 1915 added to this optimistic picture by focusing their reports on the most successful farmers and ranchers.

Nonetheless, national reform movements were growing and Sioux men and women were prominent members of many of these movements. Both Charles Eastman, a Dakota, and Gertrude Simmons Bonnin, a Yankton, were founding members of the Society of American Indians, the first national pan-Indian association dedicated to promoting the cause of all Indians.[13] Its members, who became known as the red progressives, established their headquarters in Washington, DC, began publishing the

Figure 6.6 A Western Sioux village near the turn of the nineteenth century (Science Museum of Minnesota Photograph Collection)

American Indian Magazine, and adopted an agenda of social and political change. Other reform movements had different, often opposing, interests and agendas. Nonetheless, the movement coalesced around the scandal to cheat Indians of allotments, land claims monies, and, in some areas, royalties for oil and mineral rights. John Collier, often described as an idealistic social worker, formed a new lobbying group, the American Indian Defense Association, that mounted a campaign to protect Indians' constitutionally guaranteed freedom of worship and to stress the concepts of cultural pluralism and self-determination, among many other issues.[14] By the 1920s, these combined efforts had once again brought the plight of the Sioux and other American Indians to public attention.

The Sioux were also active reformers within their own reservations.

Figure 6.7   Dr. Charles A. Eastman, 1920 (Minnesota Historical Society Photograph Collection)

Chief Red Hawk and a group of Oglala reenacted the Little Bighorn battle in 1907, and a peace council was held at the battle site in 1909 by a group of horsemen wearing war bonnets. A diverse group of Lakota launched the first of many legal offenses at the Cheyenne River Reservation in 1911, when they formed the Black Hills Treaty Council to pursue their claim that the US government took the Black Hills illegally in 1876.[15] The Council drafted a bill in 1915 for consideration by Congress that would give the US Court of Claims the jurisdiction to hear their grievances. When the measure passed Congress in 1921, the Council filed lawsuits against the federal government seeking compensation for the taking of the Black Hills and as yet unsettled claims.

In 1922, the Commissioner of Indian Affairs ordered a survey of most Indian families on reservations in the West in preparation for the drafting of a new five-year plan. The survey reports were unsettling, even shocking. After spending hundreds of millions of dollars to hasten assimilation and self-reliance through farming or ranching, the Sioux, like many other Indian nations, had lost most of their land, only a few families were able to support themselves by farming or ranching, alcoholism was rampant, most families were chronically short of food and other necessities, and most families were discouraged and living in dire poverty. The reports generated a wave of criticism that resulted in the launching of a new comprehensive study in 1926 by a privately-endowed research group, the Institute for Government Research. Its report, *The Problem of Indian Administration*, which was published in 1928, is more popularly known as the Meriam Report after the staff director, Lewis Meriam.[16] In stark, accusing terms, the report itemized a range of "deplorable conditions" on Indian reservations, including Sioux reservations. Among these were: (1) an infant mortality rate twice that of the general population; (2) a grossly inadequate medical budget (about 50¢ a person per year for field treatment); (3) high illiteracy rates; (4) overcrowded and "grossly inadequate" boarding schools; (5) a per capita income among many Indians five times less than the national average of nearly $1,350; and (6) a death rate from tuberculosis more than 17 times the national average.

The Meriam Report blamed the practice of allotment on the failure of assimilation and the impoverishment and demoralization of Indian peoples. A number of suggestions were made. Among these were to: (1) greatly increase funding for education and health; (2) end allotment; (3) send all children to day schools near their home rather than to distant boarding schools; (4) increase Indian cooperation wherever possible; and (5) allow those who wanted to remain Indian to do so. The report set the stage for the enactment of the Indian Reorganization Act and the radical reforms of the 1930s.

By the early 1930s, non-Indian farmsteads and communities surrounded most Sioux families, their traditional cultural practices were discouraged, and many had lost access to their own land. As a result, friction between the factions that had always existed among Sioux communities was gradually exacerbated. Among the factions were full-bloods and mixed-breeds, progressives and conservatives, and those able to make their living from farming or ranching and those who had lost their land. Many of the latter had moved to agency towns, where they became dependent on BIA agents and other officials for jobs. Other tensions existed between those who vigorously resisted confinement to reservations, those who thought the reservation was a haven within which traditional culture could be preserved, and those who considered a reservation an oasis between an old and a new way of life. Some of these groups accepted while others rejected American authority. Factions formed around almost every disputed issue, with the composition of factions varying depending on the issue. Although Sioux leaders had pleaded with authorities for the right to be Sioux, factions on most communities disagreed, often vigorously, about what that meant.

And the situation was becoming worse. The farming recession of the 1920s and the Great Depression of the 1930s brought most reservations to a low point in their history. Many Sioux came close to starvation and reservation agents warned of disaster without federal intervention. Yet, forced allotment and assimilation had not erased that part of Sioux culture that made them distinct. Although their culture was dramatically altered between 1889 and 1934, its core themes had survived the traumas of the period.

Storytelling

Like a Walt Disney movie, Sioux stories seem intended to amuse rather than to educate. Consider the story of "The Man and the Oak." There once lived a Sioux couple that had two children, a boy and a girl. A strange girl who had no relatives came to live with the family, who addressed her as daughter or sister. The girl fell desperately in love with the boy, but because she was considered his sister, she could not openly show her feelings. Disguising herself, she sat in his tent at night. Curious to find out who this mysterious woman was, the boy accidentally burnt the strange girl on the cheek with his torch. Feeling remorse, the young man lay down under an oak tree, a shoot of which grew up through his body, pinning him to the ground. His sister promised to marry the one who released him. Revealing that the strange girl was actually a sorceress who had bewitched the young man because he would not love her, the all-powerful god of lightning and thunder freed the boy and took his sister away as his bride.

In the story "The Boy and the Turtles," a great many turtles at a lake, seeing a boy come to hunt them, jump into the lake with a great splash and turn into hundreds of little men, who splash water up into the air to a great height. When the boy's village learns of what he saw, they place him in the seat of honor (opposite the door) in the council and rename him *Wankan Wanyanka* ("sees holy"). The lake was renamed *Wicasabde*, "Man Lake."

These and many other stories were passed down to the present generation by Sioux elders and appear in collections of traditional Sioux oral literature. Among the most widely read of these collections are James R. Walker's *Lakota Myth*, John Neihardt's *Black Elk Speaks*, Joseph Epes Brown's *The Sacred Pipe*, and Ella Deloria's *Dakota Texts*, a bilingual collection of 64 narratives.[17]

Black Elk, an Oglala *wicasa wakan* ("holy man") and Catholic catechist, told his great vision in full for the first time through Neihardt in 1931 and again to Brown in the late 1940s. Among his best-known stories are "The Gift of the Sacred Pipe" and accounts of the seven rites of the Oglala Sioux. The now familiar story of the gift of the pipe is a foundational narrative in Lakota culture. In the story, "The White Buffalo Calf Woman," the sacred messenger of the Great Spirit, brings the People the peace pipe, tobacco, and seven rites. After instructing them in their proper use, she leaves the village and, in their sight, changes into a bison calf.

Students of American literature are increasingly considering this story and other traditional oral narratives stimulating subjects for interpretation. Besides revealing the many layers of meaning of an oral narrative, a goal of these studies is to get at and share the specific Lakota meanings of the text, meanings that make this literature Lakota rather than Euro-American or Navaho. Other scholars are attempting to clarify Black Elk's purpose in relating his vision, to determine the extent of the recorders' "enhancement" of the vision, to provide a postcolonial reading of Black Elk, and to provide a "foreign-language" criticism of Black Elk's original Lakota text, among many other, often contentious, issues. A popular current trend is to devalue Black Elk's teachings because they seem compromised by Christianity.[18]

What was (and is) the purpose of storytelling among the Sioux? Are the stories of "The Man and the Oak" and "The Boy and the Turtles" merely intended to amuse? Was Black Elk unconsciously distorting traditional Lakota stories by mixing in elements of Christianity, or did he have a different, more conscious intent in mind? What should we make of discrepancies in narrations of what appear to be the same story? These and similar questions hint at a different use of storytelling among the Sioux than mere amusement.

Among people without written history, such as the pre-reservation Sioux, the narratives of the skilled storyteller interweave information, culturally appropriate behavior, and philosophical guidance, and frame the unfamiliar and unexpected within a larger context of shared meanings.[19] Even seemingly simple narratives like "The Man and the Oak" and "The Boy and the Turtles" do more than entertain. They are a source of accumulated wisdom and order, as we will see, that provide guidance in an uncertain and changing world. Narrative storytelling is an active way of engaging the world, then, that reproduces and shapes culture and gives it its integrity.[20]

Some Lakota stories are *ohunkakan* ("made-up stories") that, while fairytale-like, give people "a perspective on contemporary struggles so that they might think of them as the same ordeals that are always the precondition of wisdom and fulfilled consciousness."[21] Others are *wicowoyake* ("true stories") that, while they usually contain supernatural characters and events, indicate how the People survived and coped in the past. Lakota oral narratives are full of sorcerers, monsters, and varied incarnations of *Iktomi*, "the Trickster." The principal figures often must distinguish between a relative and a trickster who may be disguised as a relative. The stories of "The Man and the Oak" and "The Boy and the Turtles" illustrate these themes in Lakota storytelling. The first underscores the importance of kinship for survival in Lakota society. In this theme, caring kinship relationships are often represented by the devotion of brother and sister, as in the story. The second story calls attention to the importance of the individual who is able to establish connections with the divine, for the People must maintain and renew alliances with protective spirits to survive.

Black Elk's most forceful stories are *hanbloglaka* ("dream-" or "vision-talks") and *waktogloka* ("kill-talks"). *Hanbloglaka* are told to maintain or renew "the people's confidence in their traditional methods of obtaining spiritual protection," and *Waktogloka* relate "accomplishments which make the people confident of their future on the basis of their past."[22] When Black Elk said, "Our hoop is broken," he was not referring to the imminent extinction of his people, but to a fading during a period of devastating oppression of those understandings that gave significance and integrity to the life of his people. As mentioned earlier in the chapter, the Lakota were forbidden to follow many of their most important traditional practices during the early reservation period.

Narrative storytelling among the Lakota loses much of its puzzling nature when it is viewed in this manner, that is, as a social activity that creates and re-creates Lakota culture. Rather than being disconcerted by shifts in the meanings and some of the details of stories when storytellers address difference audiences in different situations in different historical contexts, the intent of these differences should be explored. A single story can be used to convey a range of messages to different audiences. The story of "The White Buffalo Calf Woman" and "The Gift of the Sacred Pipe," for instance, is a powerful, foundational narrative in Lakota culture. No singular interpretation can adequately convey all the meanings that have emerged in its telling by different narrators since it was first told (and dreamed) hundreds of years ago. Nor should it be surprising that interpretations of oral narratives are regularly and often bitterly contested and debated, even within a single community.

As a cultural strategy of communication and as a social activity, then, Sioux stories are not to be judged on how "authentic" they are in some traditional sense, but on performance, intent, appropriateness, and effectiveness. Rather than focusing on rediscovering *the* authentic version of a story, it is far more rewarding to view the story as a text whose meanings are not fixed but emerge in practice through time.[23] On this reading, there is no one primeval meaning embedded within the text that awaits rediscovery through "proper" textual analysis. Nor is one version of the story truer than any other version.

In this reading, oral tradition actively reinterprets history to accommodate new events. It is this flexibility that allows a gifted storyteller to make sense of a confusing situation by incorporating it within a shared framework of metaphors and understandings.[24] This perspective provides a different reading of Black Elk's amalgamation of older Lakota beliefs and Christianity than does a reading intent on recovering the authentic Lakota voice. Gifted storytellers always creatively reinterpret their cultural understandings. A shift in location of the cave in the ground from which the People first emerged – from Minnesota to the Black Hills of South Dakota – is just one of many examples of this process of creative reinterpretation. Ultimately, oral narratives may tell us less about "what really happened" in the past than about long-term social processes.

Today, some traditional Sioux regard English as just another Native language and writing as just one more way of telling a story. Increasingly, the Sioux are making oral tradition and material objects central to their definition of Lakota and Dakota culture. Storytelling, dancing, and the display of ceremonial regalia have become standard ways of socially reproducing their culture, of demonstrating ethnographic authority, and of countering narrative erasure by the dominant society. Claims to aboriginality, collective rights, and indigenous justice increasingly confront Western narratives of the Euro-American encounter with the Sioux. Whether the Dakota Conflict of 1862, the Battle of the Little Bighorn, or the Confrontation at Wounded Knee in 1973, Sioux stories of these events confront and compete with Western forms of understanding. In this context, traditional narrative is increasingly competing with Western discourse as an authoritative explanation of contemporary events. There are many

Figure 6.8   A Western Sioux man in ceremonial dress near the turn of the
nineteenth century at Cannon Ball, North Dakota (Science Museum of
Minnesota Photograph Collection)

opportunities today, from powwows to national Indian conventions, to
observe the unfolding of this movement.

Although only briefly introduced here, it should be apparent that close
attention to oral narrative can contribute deeply to our understanding of

the Sioux people and their culture. Sioux stories must not be marginalized in the face of Western discourse or dismissed as merely amusing. As an ongoing social activity, oral tradition has sustained Sioux social life throughout the difficult twentieth century.[25]

Prophetic Movements

A revitalization movement is a "deliberate, organized, conscious effort by members of a society to construct a more satisfying culture."[26] Revitalization movements, which are a common worldwide phenomenon, share a number of defining features: (1) they appear in the presence of extreme cultural stress during periods of rapid cultural change; (2) they originate in one or more hallucinatory visions by a single individual; (3) during the visions, one or more supernatural beings (God, the Great Spirit) appear to the prophet-to-be and outline a new way of life; (4) the new way of life is considered divinely sanctioned; (5) the prophet may show evidence of a rapid transformation of personality soon after the vision experience; (6) in an evangelistic or messianic spirit, the prophet reveals his revelations to other people; and (7) as a revolutionary act, the revitalization movement encounters some resistance from the dominant regional power.

Revitalization movements vary in some features, too. Among these are: (1) whether they profess to revise a traditional culture, to import a foreign cultural system, or to create for the first time a new Utopia; (2) in their relative degrees of secular and religious action, with religious action involving communication with supernatural beings; (3) to the extent that they are intended to expel the person or customs of foreign invaders ("nativistic movements"); and (4) in their degree of success or failure. The purpose of revitalization movements is to reduce cultural stress by helping people adapt to and make sense of their rapidly changing world and their place in it.

Examples of revitalization movements include the Delaware Prophet (associated with Pontiac, 1762–5), the Handsome Lake Revival (Seneca, 1799–1815), and the Shawnee Prophet (associated with Tecumseh, 1805–14) in North America; John Wesley and early Methodism (1738–1800) in Europe; the Xosa Revival (South Africa, 1856–7) and the Sudanese Mahdi (the Sudan, 1880–98) in Africa; the recent "Islamic Revolution" in the Middle East; and the Taiping Rebellion (China, 1843–64) and the Vailala Madness (New Guinea, c.1919–c.1930) in Asia.[27] Both Christianity and Mohammedanism originated in revitalization movements.

New pan-tribal religions appeared on the Great Plains in the 1880s and 1890s as Indian peoples felt the despair of reservation life. As these religions spread from tribe to tribe, they incorporated local styles and interpretations. One of these religions, the Ghost Dance, is a classic example of a nativistic revitalization movement.[28] While in a trance when the "sun died," probably during the solar eclipse of January 1, 1889, the Paiute Wovoka (Jack Wilson) was instructed by God to tell the people to stop fighting and quarreling, to love one another, and to accommodate to Euro-Americans. If God's commands were obeyed and enough Indians prayed and danced together, the people's despair would turn to joy and they would be reunited with their loved ones in the Above World.

To carry out his commands, God told Wovoka to dance the traditional Paiute Round Dance. Moving in a circle, like the life-giving sun, the dancers shuffled hand-in-hand from right to left, praying and chanting for four consecutive nights. Exhausted dancers entered trances during which some reported seeing their ancestors. Following their vision, they admonished the people to conduct themselves in such a manner that they, too, would attract spiritual power.

In 1890, the Lakota adopted a version of the Ghost Dance under the guidance of the Oglala holy men Short Bull and Kicking Bear.[29] Less interested in accommodation than other tribes, the Lakota hoped that the Ghost Dance would bring back their days of glory when they were bison-hunting warriors. Some dance leaders taught that if the Lakota obeyed God's commands, as they interpreted them, then God would wipe all white men from the face of the earth. In the meantime, to protect themselves from harm, the Ghost Dancers cut decorated garments called Ghost Shirts from trade muslin as if it were hide. The shirts were sewn together with animal sinew using traditional methods and decorated with power symbols, especially stars and eagle feathers. Ghost Shirt power was thought impenetrable to bullets.

In 1890, hundreds of Lakota fervently danced the Round Dance with their eyes focused hypnotically upon eagle feathers, which were to waft their soul to heaven. While in trances they saw their ancestors in heaven and were told by the spirits to revive neglected traditional institutions. Government agents entrusted with civilizing the Lakota were angered by the strengthening of traditional Lakota culture, the abandonment of farms while people gathered to dance, and by prayers that were directed at their imminent destruction at the hands of God. Ghost Dancing was banned and its leaders jailed. The movement then went underground.

The Ghost Dance did not die at Wounded Knee. The Round Dance and its accompanying Ghost Dance songs continue to be a part of the eclectic religious life of some reservations today. In the first decade of the twentieth century, the Ghost Dance became a religion for guiding one's life, as Wovoka intended, rather than the magical act for restoring Eden that some Lakota groups had briefly made it. Congregations continued to gather to sing the beautiful Ghost Dance prayers, exhort one another to respect the teachings of their tradition, to cooperate, and to enjoy celebrating meals (feasting) together. By 1900, however, the threat that allotment into severalty posed to the cohesiveness of their society spurred many Lakota to adopt a religious practice that more clearly emphasized the importance of the community as a congregation and as a support for the distressed than did the heaven-directed Ghost Dance. When the last of the original converts to the Ghost Dance died in the early 1960s, the religion seemed gone. However, the revival of militant pride in traditional Plains Indian beliefs during the 1970s renewed interest in the Ghost Dance religion. It remains, in modified form, a part of the religious life of some reservations today, although it has almost disappeared.

In broader perspective, prophecy narratives and revitalization movements are just one facet of the larger phenomenon of prophetic movements.[30] In North American ethnohistory, a central question is whether prophetic movements were indigenous or a response to Euro-American contact. One position grounded in Max Weber's analysis of Old Testament prophets views prophecy as exceptional behavior that arises in reaction to external events, such as population decimation or dislocation. These events are so severe that they threaten the continued existence of a cultural lifeway. As an exceptional event, prophetic behavior needs analysis and interpretation. These analyses normally focus on the social context of the movement and on the success or failure of specific prophets in transforming their cultural milieu.

An alternative view increasingly shared by ethnohistorians is that prophecy is a routine narrative framework used to explain the present. Furthermore, prophecy is consistent with the expected behavior of spiritual leaders. Prophecy narratives are serious representations of the world that attempt to maintain order in a disruptive world through the use of conventional explanations that make sense of unsettling disruptions in familiar ways. At a more mundane level, prophecy and visions were relied upon to gain detailed foreknowledge of future states of affairs. Typical examples include decisions about where to hunt deer, when and where to find bison herds, and when and where to raid.[31] In one form or another, then, prophecy permeated the very infrastructure of Sioux society.

If prophecy narratives provide a conventional way of making sense of dislocating changes, then prophecy must have been more widespread in the history of the Sioux than we recognize. All kinds of externally induced changes could have resulted in the appearance of prophets and revitalization movements. Examples include: the postulated AD 1300 tribalization movement; the Little Ice Age, not only because of deteriorating climatic conditions but because of shifting habitat boundaries; the sudden influx of vast numbers of Eastern Indians during the Iroquois wars; the arrival of fur traders and the rise in competition among Indian groups for access to furs; the constant conflict between neighboring groups in the eighteenth and nineteenth centuries for space; the presence of competing Roman Catholic and Anglican missionaries in the nineteenth and twentieth centuries; the Black Hills gold rush in the mid-nineteenth century that brought hundreds of would-be prospectors to Sioux territory; the expansion of the US through Sioux territory in the nineteenth century, with its serious long-term consequences for the Sioux; the imposition of reservation life; the forcing of Sioux children to attend residential schools; the construction of the continental railroad through Sioux territory in the late nineteenth century; and the mass destruction of wildlife, especially bison. Prophets could have arisen in response to all of these externally induced stresses. The legend of the pipe itself most likely has its roots in a vision-dream of a new way of life by individuals under extreme stress in the late prehistoric period. The Ghost Dance revitalization movement has received the most attention, undoubtedly, because it occurred at a time and place where there were many observers who not only wrote accounts of the movement but also were intent on suppressing it.

Rather than signs of failure to cope with stressful, external events, prophecy narratives are better viewed as successful engagements with change. Prophecy narratives represent an alternative and competing discursive framework that continues to provide authoritative explanations of disruptive events. Increasingly, too, prophecy is being invoked by some traditional Sioux elders to claim authoritative interpretations of the past.[32] There are many opportunities today to observe this emergent interplay between Western and indigenous discursive frameworks.

Colonizing Time

When stripped to its core, the notion of time is concerned with the comparative occurrence of events. To compare the occurrence of events, a system of reference for specifying when they occurred is needed. Any phenomenon that involves change with time can be used as a scale. Examples are the rotation of the earth, the swing of a pendulum, and a shift in the quantum states of atoms. In most cultures of the world, the reference scale is based on some aspect of the earth's rotation about its axis.

In spite of this shared foundation, conceptions of time vary widely from one culture to another. For some cultures, time is linear, for others, circular or spiraling.[33] Some cultures believe time is a vitally important objective and quantifiable aspect of the real world that can and should be measured with precision and accuracy. For others, it is qualitative, relational, and useful primarily for measuring significant intervals in social life. These differences are important, for they dramatically affect how people think about concepts like history, work, and the future. A clash of different notions of time, work, and history took place during the colonization of the Americas, when North American governments tried to assimilate Indian people into the rhythm of American life.

Traditional Dakota–Lakota concepts of time are known only in broad outline, for early reporters of their lifeway failed to grasp the underlying complexities of their notion of time. Assuming that it was simple and primitive, their cursory reports most often concentrate on comparing fragmented Sioux notions of time to Western notions of time.[34]

However, we know from these reports that for pre-reservation Sioux, significant time units were based on natural phenomena, especially the seasons, the sun, and the moon. They were also qualitative and relational, rather than quantitative. Since their world was made in fours, time was composed of four parts (the day, night, month, and year), just as there were four classes of animals (crawling, flying, four-legged, and two-legged (people)). Time was measured by night and by moons. The year began with the first month (most likely April) of the first season (spring), whose arrival was marked by the return of flocks of ducks or crows. Each year was divided into four seasons (spring, summer, autumn, and winter) and thirteen months, whose names differed among groups but referred to a characteristic of a local season, such as Snow-exists-time.

Since the winter season completed the year, the Sioux divided the past into winters instead of years. Each winter was designated by a pictograph that recorded an unusual event that took place that year, such as the death of a famous man or the arrival of a stranger. This made a chronicle, called a winter count.[35] Because significant events differed among the bands and tribes, winter counts record a variety of historical events, depending on who was keeping the count. While some Sioux, especially the Lakota, kept winter counts, they had little interest in the notion of a year as such, that is, as an objective stretch of quantitative time with an arbitrary beginning and end.

Days and nights were not given numbers or names, such as Tuesday, and, although there was no name for time alone, the Sioux had words for daytime and nighttime, as well as moon time (a month), world time (a year), and earth-changing time (seasons). Days were divided into periods that referred to the position of the sun, such as the rising sun or the setting sun. Some groups kept a count of months and days using a moon-counting stick.[36] A night was recorded by making a notch on one side of the stick and the passing of a month by a notch on the other side of the stick. Although the counter did record the passing of objective, linear time, its real purpose was to jog the memory of a group's storytellers, for their stories were more important than the precise, accurate measurement of time.

In a culture without clocks and factories, there was no need for seconds, minutes, or hours, for time was elastic rather than invariable. An appointment was for the morning or afternoon, rather than for 10:10 AM or 2:45 PM. If asked to specify a particular time, the moon of a season of a winter was good enough. Nonetheless, as keen observers of their surroundings, they could tell the general time of year by the appearance of vegetation and features of animals, such as the size of a fetus in a slain deer and by star positions.

The Sioux had two main units of historical time, the year and the generation, which was understood to be the lifespan of an old man (about seventy years). Past events, such as when a person was born, were located in time using the winter count. Most Oglala, for example, knew the pictograph representing the year they were born. A member of a band might refer to his age by saying, "I was born the year Crow Eagle was lanced." The date of an event might be remembered as far back as three or four generations, but it was said of older events, "That happened long ago."

Time in Western culture is conceived of as a thoroughly objective, invariant, and precisely quantifiable feature of nature. Time is measured by clocks in hours and minutes, and progresses linearly from a beginning to eternity. Like a beaver pelt, it is a commodity that can be measured, saved, spent, and wasted. These notions, which underlie the work rhythms of industrial Europe ("clock time"), are historical consequences of the rise of wage labor and the insistence by capitalists that they get "a full day's work."[37]

This Western notion of time is vastly different from an attitude toward time and work-discipline shared by hunter-gatherers and many pre-industrial farmers, including earlier European cultivators and peasants. These people are not necessarily less motivated or work less. Rather, their notions of work-discipline are rooted in the notion of "task time." When something has to be done, it is, so effort varies seasonally and in other ways, and work rhythms are more closely integrated into patterns of social life.

Since Euro-Americans thought they knew what kind of economic work structure (i.e., farming) would lead to progress among Indians, they tried to induce the Sioux to adopt Western notions of time and the work rhythms of industrial capitalism and the agrarian West. This endeavor stressed that work should be steady and regular and carefully controlled. To assimilate the Sioux, then, the governments of North America had to change Sioux concepts of time. This attempted transformation was carried out by vigorously insinuating the notion of "clock time" into the daily life of the Sioux. Precise meeting times ("be here at 10:10 AM") were set, children were subjected to the regular rhythms of school periods, and workers had to "clock in" and "clock out" at factory and office jobs.

The colonization of time by North American governments has had several undesirable effects on the public's understanding of the Sioux. First, although late-nineteenth-century Sioux had an identifiable work culture, it was not the work culture of their employers or the government. Non-Indian commentators blamed the lack of "progress" in Sioux communities on laziness. Thus, the "laziness" factor contributed to the resolve of government officials to expose Sioux children to Western values and knowledge in Western-style schools.

Second, as employers began to demand a regular, full-time commitment from workers (or they would be given the sack) and the rewards of a job made it too valuable for some to give up, Sioux communities began to fragment between those willing to accept Western-style work and those who were not. This fragmentation helped shape a discourse on Sioux society that separated progressives from traditionalists, the productive working portion of the population who had adopted Western concepts of time and work from a "backward" portion without jobs who had not. On reservations, the "progressives" were more often than not "half-breeds" who worked for the government or a business in town, while the "traditionalists" were "full-bloods" who lived in the backcountry.

A culture's concept of time also affects its concept of history. At its simplest, history is merely an organization of past time. How it is thought of beyond this shared base varies widely from culture to culture. In Western cultures, it is important to place truthful historical facts in a temporal grid composed of precise units of time, whether hours and days, or years and centuries. By contrast, history in traditional Sioux culture is a sacred endeavor that integrates stories of all kinds to amuse and relate mundane events, but also to teach proper social behavior and to convey an understanding of the place of the Sioux in the cosmos.[38]

The contestation over time in reservation-era Sioux culture has been a long one, then, for a number of reasons. First, since there is more than one way of organizing the working day and the working life, some Sioux are exploring, both individually and collectively, a series of new forms that are a compromise between traditional notions and the exigencies of living and working in North America today. As federal governments once sought to remake time in one direction, they are attempting to remake it in another. Whether working in crop production, urban casual labor, or as a professional nurse or doctor, they are engaged in the complex process of testing these notions. Second, while many Sioux have adapted to Western concepts of time in the workplace, the rhythms of family and community life have stayed more elastic and traditional; the result has been the creation of a dichotomy between work and non-work, and the coexistence of multiple rhythms in Sioux communities. In a sense, the colonization of time has succeeded only in the narrow social sphere of "working." Third, discourses of the late twentieth century are marked by their silences concerning the actual lives of Sioux workers. If the idea is that performance in the workplace is shaped by how children and young people are socialized and acculturated, then one would anticipate that this milieu would be probed for avenues of accommodation.

As students of Sioux culture, we must consider the multiple ways in which colonialism has affected the Sioux cultural tradition. Time is a critical aspect of this process, for how it is conceived and reconceived affects cultural concepts of daily life, work, history, and the very meaning of life itself.[39]

Language and Colonial Power

Since the Sioux and Euro-Americans spoke different languages, means of communicating had to be established. Translators served this function into the early twentieth century. However, many fur traders learned to speak some Dakota and many Sioux learned to speak French or English. With the movement into Sioux territory of increasing numbers of Euro-American soldiers, missionaries, administrators, travelers, settlers, and scholars in the early nineteenth century, English was promoted as a lingua franca. It also became an ideological tool of the US government's policy to assimilate the Sioux into American life. The need to communicate and the intent to control were inseparable motives for the government's policy. Nonetheless, they need unpacking in the study of the history of the Sioux.

The control of verbal means of communication has been a foundation of Western colonial expansion throughout the world.[40] Just because it is a more subtle use of power than economic constraints or brute force, language control is one of the most insidious means of colonial penetration, for a language communicates more than simple verbal exchanges. As a product of culture, a language represents the world of the "other" in a culturally distinctive manner. Every language contains its own concepts of time, space, land, leadership, gender, and so on, and categorizes aspects of "reality" like foodstuffs, plants and animals, and types of trade goods in its own way. Consequently, colonizers were not only imposing a foreign language on native peoples, but a foreign way of world-making. It should come as no surprise, then, that American expansion westward and the use of English as an ideological tool followed each other closely.

The US government had two primary rationales for promoting the use of English as a lingua franca in the Great Plains. First, in the process of extending one administration over the whole country, the government sought a common means to communicate that would bridge the linguistic diversity among native peoples. Given the large number of languages spoken by native peoples, it was impractical to expect government agents to learn all or even several native languages. As an instrument of government, then, English became the language of treaties and other official documents, and the Sioux were given English names. A process of inscription also began in which rivers, lakes, and other prominent landscape features in Sioux territory were assigned official English names. A consequence of this policy was that few US agents mastered Dakota to the extent that the service of interpreters was not needed. No one seriously doubted that the government had to impose order and control on the means of communication with native peoples.

The second rationale for promoting English as a lingua franca was to prepare the Sioux for their transformation into Americans.[41] This requirement seemed a reasonable, even generous one, for numerous European immigrant groups had learned to speak English for the same reason. This linguistic transformation was to take place through the formal education of Sioux children, a task entrusted in the nineteenth century primarily to missionaries. By the early 1800s, missionaries had begun to set up educational institutions in Sioux territory in which, as a matter of US government policy, English was to serve as the medium of instruction. Americans were convinced that to become an American one had to speak English, whether one was German or Sioux. As a matter of assimilation policy, an attempt was made to suppress the Dakota language, too.

Eventually many Sioux became bilingual, as English was added as a second language. In general, Dakota was used in the home and among Sioux, while English was used in public with non-Dakota speakers. When Sioux men and women moved to towns and cities to work, English generally became their primary language. Even though some traditional Sioux actively resisted American language policies, only a small percentage of Sioux were able to speak fluent Dakota at the end of the twentieth century. Today, English has become the lingua franca of the Sioux and for many the only medium of verbal communication.

In the 1980s and more recently, with a new self-determination and independence, Sioux leaders began to restore traditional names and, in many cases, to introduce other linguistic innovations to symbolize their renewal. Resurgence is occurring too in the use of the Dakota language, especially in Indian-controlled schools and colleges. These changes recognize the close interconnection between language and self-determination. At the same time, scholars interested in colonialism began to explore how language is used to express, reinforce, or resist power, and the deep connection between politics and language policy. Just how English was used and even imposed on the Sioux remains at the time of writing an underexplored issue.

seven

Restoration and Reorganization, 1934–1975

The Restoration and Reorganization period began in 1934 with the enactment of the Indian Reorganization Act (or the Wheeler–Howard Act). The act ended the government's long-standing policies of assimilation and allotment. Sponsored by President Franklin D. Roosevelt and vigorously implemented by his Commissioner of Indian Affairs, John Collier, the IRA, as it is familiarly called, radically altered the government's position toward Indians by promoting limited self-government and the renewal rather than erasure of Indian culture. However, the IRA could not solve problems endemic to Plains reservations, such as poor farming land and devastating droughts. As a result, many Sioux, like other Plains Indians, moved off reservations to find work in towns and cities in the West and Midwest, where they were often the last to be hired and where they were surrounded by prejudice, misunderstanding, and poverty.

Although by the mid-1930s some elements of pre-reservation Sioux culture were forgotten or imperfectly remembered, and much of their land had been lost through allotment policies, the core of their heritage lived on in tribal memories. Some rituals, once suppressed, such as Peyotism and the Sun Dance, emerged from hiding, and knowledge of their language had not faded. Still, freedom to revive a culture is not the same as its revival. Not everyone agreed on the details of traditional practices, on how to create an effective, functional tribal government, or even on whether their energies were best spent reviving a past way of life. Nonetheless, small steps toward self-determination were begun that became giant strides in later decades.

Chapter 7 reviews this period of restoration and reorganization among the Sioux. It also reviews four issues of topical interest: health and disease, shifting household composition, formal education, and the Dakota language.

The Re-emergence of Sioux Culture

The years leading up to the Great Depression of the 1930s became increasingly difficult for the Sioux and for most Americans. Throughout Sioux territory, the Lakota–Dakota were dispirited, angry, and dependent on the government and local charities for support, as were many of their non-Indian neighbors.

Following the inauguration of President Roosevelt in 1933, John Collier, the new Commissioner of Indian Affairs, promised an Indian New Deal for reservations modeled after Roosevelt's promise of a New Deal for other needy Americans. Following recommendations in the 1928 Meriam Report, Collier proposed new policies designed to aid Indian communities and a new relationship between the federal government and those communities. Many of these ideas were quickly approved, though in altered form, by Congress, which passed the Indian Reorganization Act (IRA), the driving force of the Indian New Deal, in 1934.[1]

Among other initiatives, the IRA halted the practice of forced allotment; provided funds for economic enterprises, education, and new hospitals; provided funds for the purchase of non-Indian owned land in and around reservations; and encouraged people to maintain and use their traditional language, to revive traditional dances and ceremonies, and to otherwise recover traditional customs "as they saw fit." It also provided guidelines for the establishment of limited self-government on reservations in the form of tribal constitutions and elected tribal councils. To signal the seriousness of the New Deal, tribal councils were given the task of developing economic resources as tribal enterprises and of managing federal and local programs on reservations. The enactment of the IRA in 1934 was, in principle at least, a stunning reversal of government policy that affected every Sioux community in some way.

In an attempt to be democratic, the act gave each tribe the right to decide whether the act would apply to them. Some Sioux were bitterly opposed to the act, for while it did give them a degree of self-government through elected tribal councils and some power to manage their own finances and affairs, the ultimate power to make decisions remained with the BIA in Washington, DC. Nonetheless, most Sioux reservations and communities voted to accept the IRA, for a provision of the act provided for the expansion of their landholdings, and it was a well-intended step toward self-reliance.[2]

Even though the Sioux in Minnesota did not live on reservations, the IRA, when accepted, officially recognized their communities as Indian Communities. They were then permitted to purchase additional land and to benefit from the provisions of the act. The process did not proceed, however, in a straightforward manner. Serious internal bickering over the act among the Sisseton, Wahpeton, and some Yankton and Mdewakanton at the Upper Sioux Agency at Granite Falls, and indecision caused by the rejection of the IRA by the main Sisseton Reservation in South Dakota, delayed their establishment as a Community until 1939. There was also a brief, unsuccessful attempt to merge the Mdewakanton communities into one unit. Eventually, each community was able to retain its independence and to establish its own tribal council.

The creation of the Prairie Island Community exemplifies the ensuing process. A corporate charter, constitution, and bylaws were drawn up. According to the provisions of the constitution, the Community was to be governed by a council of five elected officers with two-year terms; additional committees were to be appointed by the council to address tribal needs. The Prairie Island Community was approved on June 30, 1936 and an additional 414 acres were purchased through the IRA. At the Lower Sioux Agency at Birch Coulee, an additional 1,200 acres were purchased, and in 1938, 745 acres were purchased for the Upper Sioux Community.

In Nebraska, the Santee Reservation, which had lost more than 68,000 acres, added 3,368 acres to the 3,132 they still retained. The Sioux at Sisseton and Devil's Lake (Spirit Lake) purchased additional land, too, as did the Santee living in Flandreau, South Dakota, who bought 2,100 acres. The Flandreau Santee also successfully petitioned to have their Indian colony officially changed to a federal reservation to protect their land

Figure 7.1 The Prairie Island Community Hall in 1960 (Minnesota Historical Society Photograph Collection)

from taxation and sale. By 1935, all but one Lakota reservation had adopted a constitution and established a tribal council in accordance with IRA provisions.

Besides becoming eligible for relief through the Indian New Deal, the Sioux became eligible for assistance from a host of New Deal programs that were available to all citizens, for the reservations, like the rest of the country, were in the grip of the Great Depression. One of Collier's first moves was to bring direct economic relief to the reservations, which he did in a variety of ways. Roosevelt's Emergency Relief Administration (ERA) purchased livestock for slaughter for food and to subsidize ranchers.[3] Another form of direct economic relief was emergency packages of surplus food that had been purchased by the US Department of Agriculture to take excess farm products off the market and provide income for producers. The packages contained flour, cheese, sugar, canned meat, and other staples, as well as surplus army clothing. These emergency shipments, which continued for nearly ten years, saved many Sioux and other Americans from starvation in the 1930s.

Like other Americans across the country, Sioux men and women were eligible to participate in federal New Deal employment programs, such as the Works Progress Administration (WPA), Civilian Conservation Corps (CCC), Civil Works Administration (CWA), Public Works Administration (PWA), and the National Youth Administration (NYA). During the duration of these programs, they built roads and dams, constructed schools and recreational facilities, drilled wells, planted trees, terraced pasture land on the Missouri Hills to prevent erosion, pooled water for livestock, and installed telephone systems to assure communication for fire control, among other special projects intended to improve reservations. Some of these crews were integrated, while others were composed of only Sioux.

Other federal funds were provided at this time to purchase materials to repair allotment buildings and to upgrade government buildings and offices. For instance, Indian artists were hired through the WPA to make rugs and pottery for offices and to paint murals on buildings. About three out of every four men on the Rosebud Reservation worked for a time during this period for the CCC, which allowed them to move, in the words of one Sioux writer, "from absolute deprivation to mere poverty."[4] Despite more opportunities for employment than in earlier decades, life was grim for most Americans during the Great Depression and even more so for those living in the Dust Bowl on the Great Plains. Nonetheless, IRA and other federal programs did help ease poverty on Sioux reservations during the 1930s.

A cornerstone of Collier's New Deal vision for improving life for the neediest Indians was the creation of colonies with free housing and their own dairy, horse barn, canning kitchen, and community garden. Funds for the development of the colonies came primarily from the Indian Relief and Rehabilitation program. Additional agricultural land near the colonies was purchased through the authority of the IRA and given to the tribes for their colonies. Special tribal committees appointed by reservation superintendents were given the authority to manage the colonies. More than a dozen colonies were established on Sioux reservations, including four alone on the Yankton Reservation. Behind Collier's vision was a well-intended desire to give those Indian peoples who cared to the opportunity to live once again in their traditional extended-family communities.

Although living conditions for the Sioux began to improve during the 1930s, not all planned changes worked out as smoothly as Collier had intended. He encountered dissent from a multitude of conflicting positions everywhere he went. By the mid-1930s, some Sioux, now attached to their personal allotments, worried that they would forfeit ownership of their land if they moved to a colony. Others, who had never lived in a communal setting, found sharing difficult and soon became disillusioned with communal life. Because of pulls, pushes, and community quarrels, few families remained in a Collier colony for more than a year. By 1950, only one family lived in a cabin in a Collier community on the Yankton reservation.

One of the strongest pulls was a swell in off-reservation employment opportunities during World War II in the early 1940s. Given the opportunity, many Sioux left the reservation and its problems when the opportunity became available. By the late 1940s, those Sioux who had remained on their reservation were living for the most part in allotment housing. Repairs and improvements during the Indian New Deal had made them habitable once again, if only to a degree.

Once reservation tribal groups voted to come under the IRA, they were faced with the task of drafting or redrafting Western-style constitutions and bylaws according to terms in the IRA.[5] This proved a contentious task for some groups, for their traditional political organization had been smaller-scale bands that, while governed by a hereditary leader and a councils of elders, were bound together by kinship and friendship. Furthermore, community adults, if usually men, had the right to participate in decision-making until a consensus was reached – in contrast to the Anglo-Saxon concept of majority rule. Nonetheless, the provision that caused the most concern was the continuing legal authority of the Secretary of the Interior to reject tribal decisions he did not favor. While they were being given the right to draft a constitution, hold elections, and organize councils, then, the act inherently limited their powers of self-government. For many this was a real sham, for self-government without final authority is not true sovereignty.

Other tribal members were concerned with the shift of power from a few BIA officials to a few council members. They forecast abuse, and many tribal councils did become powerful and often controversial. Rather than BIA agents, many landless people would depend for their jobs on a few tribal members whose loyalties would be to their own kin. IRA tribal councils would be able to wield power in other ways, too. For instance, they could control their constituency by setting criteria for tribal membership. In some instances, this was eventually accomplished by requiring reservation residency or a high blood quantum for tribal membership.

Opposition to the IRA arose from a myriad of other directions, too. Some communities felt they had been tricked into accepting the IRA by the ulterior motives of a few opportunitsts.[6] Members of the American Indian Federation, the "major voice of Native American criticism of federal Indian policies during the New Deal," vigorously argued against Collier's policies in Congressional committees, for they were opposed to all federal control of Indian communities.[7] On Sioux reservations, factionalism broke out between New Dealers, who eagerly looked forward to new opportunities for leadership on IRA tribal councils, and Old Dealers, who were usually older, full-blooded traditionalists who had established positions as elders. Since disgruntled community members could no longer simply move to a more compatible community, as in earlier times, factionalism grew on all reservations. Given such problems and the severe changes that Congress had made in Collier's original proposal, the IRA was never as successful as he had envisioned.

Other problems faced by Sioux people in the 1930s were not directly associated with the IRA. On reservations, a schism was growing between those Sioux who lived in reservation towns and those who remained rural dwellers. Townspeople were more likely to look like other Americans in terms of hairstyle, clothes, and mannerisms, and to speak English. Rural residents were more likely to continue the old ways. That is, they were more likely to wear their hair long, to wear some "traditional" items of clothing, to speak Dakota, and to participate in giveaways and other traditional cultural practices. Another schism, which often paralleled the rural–town split, grew between "full-bloods" and "mixed-bloods," with the latter generally having a better grasp of contemporary American political and business proceedings.

Tension was developing once again, too, over land and its control. Although guaranteed by treaty, their land base was being eroded by large-scale federal water-control projects. Between the 1930s and the 1960s, the Army Corps of Engineers built a series of large dams along the Missouri River. While the projects were expected to bring irrigation water and electricity to Western Sioux reservations, they also flooded parts of some reservations. The most severe loss occurred on the Standing Rock and Cheyenne River reservations in the late 1940s and early 1950s, when dam waters covered most of their best-wooded bottomland. The Oahe Dam alone flooded 160,889 acres on the two reservations. Besides destroying wild food resources and their timber source, the rising water inundated their most productive farms and best ranchland. Many Sioux were especially incensed by this federal action, over which they had no control, for the resulting reservoirs were planned as recreation areas for a mostly non-Indian public.[8]

Despite the infusion of IRA funds and materials, the economic situation of many Western Sioux improved only slightly for a variety of reasons. The arid conditions and small size of most farms on Western reservations made it difficult to grow the crops needed to obtain a living income. And although the IRA provided funds for additional land purchases, these funds – like the IRA itself – evaporated in the early 1940s with the outbreak of World War II. Townspeople, too, found it increasingly difficult to obtain wage work, for there were few industries or other opportunities for non-government employment near Western Sioux reservations. This was in contrast to the Dakota in Minnesota, whose communities were near sizable towns and cities. Nonetheless, while the Minnesota Sioux were relatively prosperous compared to their relatives in Nebraska and the Dakotas, their standard of living was still poor compared to their non-Indian neighbors. Furthermore, because of their proximity to large numbers of non-Indians, they were more likely to experience daily discrimination.

In Canada, the Great Depression of the 1930s also brought hard times to those Sioux living on reservations. At Oak River and Oak Lake in southern Manitoba, only the largest, most profitable farms were able to purchase the increasingly expensive farm machinery that was needed to survive and thrive during the Depression. Shortages of land and money gradually resulted in a schism, as in the Dakotas and Nebraska, between those with profitable farms or ranches and those without the funds they needed to compete. Misfortune bred misfortune. Although reservation land could not be sold to outsiders, its use could be transferred to other reservation residents. Consequently, those Sioux with sufficient capital bought up the use rights to good agricultural land, which, with the use of the modern farming equipment they had purchased, increased their crop yield and income. The less fortunate either abandoned farming or tried to eke out a living on their small, remaining parcels. Of those who abandoned farming, some sought employment as farm laborers, but the mechanization of farming had reduced even those traditional jobs. Consequently, most men, if they worked at all, found employment in local manufacturing plants, lumber mills, and railroad yards. The women worked as domestics in non-Indian Canadian homes or in local factories.

In the US, this downward spiral was interrupted, if only temporarily, by the outbreak of World War II. During the course of the war (1941–5), over 25,000 Indian men and women served in the armed forces. Another estimated 40,000 left reservations each year for work in war industries in distant towns and cities. Sioux men and women participated eagerly and in large numbers in the war effort. Others found work near their reservations, for the surge of young people into the armed forces had left many local businesses understaffed. Still others found employment as construction workers at nearby military facilities, such as the military base near Rapid City, South Dakota. When the war ended in 1945, many Sioux chose to remain in the towns and cities to which they had become accustomed, despite the fact that they were forced to live in poorer neighborhoods and were still subject to discrimination.

After Collier's retirement in 1945, the federal government readopted its pre-1930s policy of assimilation. Federal administrators, with the backing of Congress, began to search for new ways to bring Indians into the mainstream of American life. The strategy they adopted was to end all responsibilities to federally recognized tribes and to terminate their status as wards of the government. In 1946, Congress established an Indian Claims Commission (ICC) to settle cases where federal employees had mismanaged tribal funds or where the government had bought tribal treaty land at inadequate prices. Although the ICC later played an unanticipated role in federal–Indian relationships, the notion at the time was to rid the government of any last monetary obligation it might have to federally recognized tribes.[9]

In the 1950s, with the backing of the Eisenhower administration, vigorous attempts were made to implement the new termination policy. Among the major efforts were the passage of Public Law 280, which shifted the obligation for social and other services to Indian peoples from federal to state government, and the passage of House Concurrent Resolution 108, which gave the federal government the authority to unilaterally end the special status of Indian tribal reservations. The argument was that Indian peoples no longer had to rely on federal programs, as they had clearly demonstrated through their war effort. For some officials, Jefferson's vision of the integration of Indian people into American life had been fulfilled.

The Eisenhower administration's termination policy resulted in the withdrawal of federal social services and responsibility for aging facilities from many reservations.[10] As for other Americans, these services and obligations were now the responsibility of state and local governments. The most dramatic action taken under the authority of House Concurrent Resolution 108 was the termination of the recognition of some tribes. For these tribes, the result was cultural and economic disaster. Their communal tribal land was allotted among its residents or sold off, and all land became taxable. Government Indian agencies were shut down, services were withdrawn, and status as an Indian ward of the government ended. From the federal government's perspective, the rights and obligations of these Indian peoples were no different – and certainly no more – than those of any other US citizen. Tribes not yet scheduled for termination were dismayed, for the government's action meant that it assumed it could unilaterally disregard the obligations of treaties and other legal agreements.

Another far-reaching attempt by the federal government to abdicate its responsibilities for tribes at the time was the policy of relocation. Many Sioux and other Indians were persuaded to move to industrial centers, such as Minneapolis–St. Paul, Denver, Chicago, Dallas, Seattle, and Los Angeles, by government "relocation" programs, especially the Voluntary Relocation Program in the 1950s and the Employment Assistance Program in the 1960s. Many others moved to local towns, such as Green Bay in Wisconsin and Rapid City in South Dakota. The notion was that Indian people would become fully integrated into American life once they received the education and training they needed to find long-term employment. Government officials justified their relocation policy by pointing to the poverty and dependency of Indian people on overcrowded reservations, despite extensive government efforts to improve their way of life for nearly a century.[11]

In addition to the "pull" of promised jobs and educational opportunities, living conditions on reservations provided a "push" for many Sioux as well. Among these were chronic substandard housing; a deterioration of employment possibilities after the war effort; inadequate income from farming, in part because of the inheritance problem; and inadequate opportunities for the level and type of education needed to obtain and keep jobs.

The government added several other "pulls" and "pushes" to spur relocation. To add to the "push," funding levels for all kinds of programs on reservations were slashed to the bare minimum. And to add to the "pull," relocation officers on reservations painted overly rosy pictures of the employment possibilities that awaited Indians in cities; some individuals were also given token, inducement payments, provided one-way funds for transportation, and, in some cases, funds for job-training instruction. And many young people, hoping to find jobs in towns and cities in the Midwest and elsewhere in the US, did leave their reservations.

Some Sioux reservations lost substantial numbers of people. For instance, the Santee reservation lost 60 percent of its population by 1960; by 1962, only 2,999, mostly elderly, people remained. In the 1950s, the population of the Yankton Reservation fell to about 1,000 people, and the Prairie Island Community in Minnesota lost most of its younger people. In general, those who remained were the most traditional and the infirm, and older, retired folks who preferred the lower cost of living and the social support of family and friends that the reservation provided.[12]

In the late 1960s and 1970s, funding opportunities comparable in magnitude and diversity to Roosevelt's New Deal became available once again on reservations through President Johnson's War on Poverty. Antipoverty programs provided federal funds for new schools, health clinics, community centers, roads, and housing, and other public facilities; other programs provided welfare assistance and food, and Head Start helped young children get ready for school.[13] These programs not only provided better facilities and housing on Sioux reservations but, like the New Deal, they created a range of jobs for reservation residents. With improved living conditions and the emergence of new employment opportunities, urban Sioux began to return to their communities and reservations. This gradual increase in population initiated a trend that continued throughout the last quarter of the twentieth century. As might be expected from past experiences, not all developments were positive for the Sioux people. Since the new funds flowed through the tribal council, the power of the council increased during Johnson's War on Poverty. This occurred primarily through a strengthening of the old patronage system, for council members controlled access to most War on Poverty jobs.

By the late 1960s and early 1970s, most Sioux had electrical power and some had telephones. Some had jobs in nearby towns and cities or worked as farm laborers, while others still farmed or grazed cattle where it was difficult to grow crops. The main crops were now wheat, corn, and millet. Many worked for government associations. In spite of these improvements, housing and schooling remained inadequate and the Sioux population remained disgruntled and mistrustful of the government.[14]

Although the entrance of the US into World War II effectively ended Collier's Indian New Deal, his initiatives provided an atmosphere that encouraged the growth of overt Indian activism. Even though the Sioux and other Indian people often vilified him, he did encourage an attitude of pride in being Indian. To provide an Indian voice in the changes initiated by the IRA, the National Congress of American Indians (NCAI) was founded in 1944. More radical, younger Indians organized the National Youth Council in 1961. In the 1960s, too, the Indian Claims Commission, which had been created in 1946 to speed the termination of the government's obligation to Indian tribes, now unexpectedly drew Indian activists and their lawyers into national politics "to beat the system." Many prominent activist Indian writers of this period, such as Vine Deloria, Jr., and Luther Standing Bear, were Sioux.[15]

More radical action was taken by other Sioux with the aid of members

Figure 7.2 The Noah White residence on Prairie Island, July 1960 (Minnesota
Historical Society Photograph Collection)

of other tribes and non-Indian sympathizers. One of earliest actions to
draw national attention was taken by a mixed group of activists that included Sioux in San Francisco. In 1964, after the federal prison on Alcatraz
Island in San Francisco Bay closed, the activists filed suit claiming the
island for Indian peoples according to treaty rights. A delegation that
included Allen Cottier, Richard McKenzie, Mark Martinez, Walter Means,
and other Sioux briefly occupied the island in March of that year. Even
though only a symbolic gesture of self-determination, their action focused
the nation's attention, if only for a brief moment, on Indian land issues.
While their lawsuit was eventually dismissed, their occupation of Alcatraz
Island prepared the way for a major occupation of the island five years
later in 1969. Beginning in November of that year, more than a hundred
Indians from across North America held the island for 19 months.[16]

The protests of the 1960s, which were extensions in part of the Black
Power movement and the anti-Vietnam riots of the times, marked a radical departure in US–Indian relationships. For a brief period through the
mid-1970s, protests aimed at exposing the lethal effects of colonization
and the depredations of North American governments became a central
focus of some Sioux and other activists. Once again, North Americans
heard the unmistakable call for sovereignty for all Indian nations.

One of the most militant American Indian rights groups in the late 1960s
and early 1970s was the American Indian Movement (AIM). Two Lakota
men, Russell Means and Dennis Banks, and two Ojibwa brothers, Vernon
and Clyde Bellancourt, founded AIM in Minneapolis in 1968.[17] Raised in
urban settings, they were familiar with political process in modern America.
As experienced Vietnam veterans, too, they had learned their civil rights
in the service, where there was little overt discrimination against Indians.

Their strategy was direct confrontation with anyone with political power who they thought was responsible for Indian rights violations, whether in federal or state government or on reservations. To attract widespread local and national media attention to Indian issues, AIM members dramatically staged these confrontations wherever and whenever possible.

As AIM attracted increasing attention and new recruits, its male members began, for several reasons, to creatively adopt a stereotypic Lakota "warrior" appearance. The image, which had been popularized in Wild West shows by Buffalo Bill Cody and his Lakota collaborators and later in films, was a familiar public stereotype that people could identify with. Furthermore, the image provided AIM members a shared, simplified "look" that they could easily adopt and that provided the members of the movement some unity.

The two most visible media-event confrontations sponsored by AIM at the time were the seizure of the Bureau of Indian Affairs headquarters in Washington, DC, in 1972 and the siege at Wounded Knee in 1973.[18] The occupants of the BIA headquarters in 1972 were part of a national demonstration called the Trail of Broken Treaties. The goal of the demonstration, as the name implies, was to use media attention to raise public awareness of the US government's long history of treaty violations. After caravans of activists had brought the message of the demonstration to local attention at stops across the country, the activists converged on the nation's capital. Within a few days they had barricaded themselves inside the headquarters of their most oppressive agency, the BIA. For six days, they searched files for documentation of the government's mishandling of their affairs.

The occupation at Wounded Knee followed a series of events in South Dakota, including the lightly dismissed murder of Raymond Yellow Thunder, an Oglala man from Pine Ridge, and the founding in 1972 of the Oglala Sioux Civil Rights Organization on the Pine Ridge reservation. The instigation for the formation of the organization was what one tribal faction saw as corruption and abuse of power by tribal officials, especially Richard Wilson, president of the Tribal Council. Wilson, who had won election over a traditionalist for the position that same year, was aligned with the more acculturated, mixed-blood, town-dwelling faction on the reservation. Following his election, Wilson had immediately formed an Oglala police force (the "goons") to enforce his policies, attempted to block the political activities of opposing factions, and banned AIM members from the reservation.

Russell Means and other AIM members were invited by several traditional leaders to come to the reservation and support their cause. On February 27, 1973, the mix of protesters occupied the small community of Wounded Knee, which was widely considered the nation's most tragic symbol of the oppression of the Lakota and all other American Indians. The result was a confrontation between about 300 activists barricaded in the village and a large force of well-armed FBI agents, federal marshals, and local police officers. By the end of the 71-day occupation, two Indians, Frank Clearwater and Buddy Lamant, a Lakota, had been killed by federal agents and several other Indians and one federal marshal wounded.

While Wounded Knee was the most dramatic and publicized protest by members of the Sioux nation for Natives' rights during this period, it was not an isolated incident. In the 1960s, for instance, the tribal chairman of the Prairie Island Community, Amos Owen, initiated an annual observance to honor the Dakota men executed in Mankato after the Conflict in 1862. The ritual became formalized in 1975 as the Day of Reconciliation. At the rite that year, traditional songs were song in honor of the 38 executed warriors and Norman Blue, then chairman of the Lower Sioux Community, read their names in Dakota. While many of these protests of the 1960s and early 1970s were largely symbolic, they helped foster a revival of cultural pride in Sioux history and beliefs.

Under the provisions and encouragement of the IRA, traditional Sioux religious practices began to reappear, if at first in an atmosphere of caution. Rather than eradication under policies of forced assimilation and Christianization, they had quietly slipped underground for protection. The most ancient of traditions, the Way of the Pipe, was the first traditional practice to resurface among some Sioux in the 1930s, although in a form appropriate to the period. As in the past, the purpose of the activities that accompanied these ceremonies was to convey traditional spiritual values and to establish community social standards. By the 1960s, Peyotism and the Sun Dance began to be practiced with increasing intensity, and the Ghost Dance religion was revived by a small number of Sioux in the 1970s. However, Christianity remained an important part of the belief system of most Sioux.

A parallel revival that accommodated change occurred throughout many other areas of Sioux culture. For instance, since Indians could now hold and attend traditional dances at any time, the powwow gradually developed into a unifying social institution. Powwows became gathering-places where problems could be discussed. They also provided an opportunity for Sioux who no longer spoke Dakota, lived and worked off-reservation, and had received a non-Indian education to become acquainted with their Indian heritage. Wearing modern versions of nineteenth-century costumes, they joined with traditionalists in the dances of their ancestors. As powwows became linked into circuits after the 1950s, the old male Grass Dance became secularized into the popular and competitive "War Dance," and semiprofessional performers began to wear increasingly spectacular outfits.[19] A new innovation, dance contests with prizes, soon appeared.

Alternative men's dances, such as the Gourd Dance, also gained popularity during the 1970s among the Lakota and other northern Plains Indians.

A long-term vision of AIM members and other activists was the creation of Indian schools that had an Indian heritage focus. Indian teacher-training programs were started at several public universities and colleges in Sioux territory and new Sioux-focused curricula were developed. Soon a number of Indian schools appeared that were staffed with Indian administrators and teachers. A small number of Indian-run community colleges were established on reservations, too, to better provide Sioux youths college-level, job-related skills.

However, not all trends at the time led to the revival of Sioux cultural traditions. Many Sioux only spoke English, had married members of other tribes or even non-Indians, were increasingly of mixed blood, and had formed friendships with non-Sioux in boarding schools, in the armed services, and in the towns and cities in which they lived. Furthermore, most reservations and some communities were composed of a mixture of Indians from different nations. The result was a growing pan-Indian movement and further diversification of the Sioux Nation.

With other Indian nations, the Sioux had taken bold steps toward sovereignty between 1934 and 1975. Most Sioux had refused to abandon their cultural heritage and their unity as a nation. Instead, they had continued to build on the initiatives begun during the period of Restoration and Reorganization. In the 1960s, government policy under presidents Kennedy and Johnson swung back once again to tribal self-determination, which at the time meant a strong tribal identity and greater Indian self-government than allowed in the IRA passed by Congress. By the mid-1960s, termination as a federal policy had failed. Along the way, Sioux activists had learned how to effectively express tribal issues in a national forum, while other Sioux had begun to more actively explore Western art forms, such as formal dance groups, novels, and the theater, as expressions for their own tribal traditions.

Still, in the mid-1970s, many Sioux remained in low-paid jobs or were unemployed. As a result, they continued to live, as in the past, below the poverty level. Their suicide rate in the US was twice that of other North Americans, and, in both Canada and the US, their mortality rate was well above that of non-Indians. In spite of these hardships, Sioux culture was being revived. Hope and self-determination were on the horizon.

Health and Disease

It is common knowledge that Indian peoples, including the Sioux, were tragically affected by Old World diseases, such as smallpox and measles, and by inadequate nutrition and living conditions on reservations well into the twentieth century.[20] However, many specific issues about Sioux health and disease remain inadequately investigated and understood. What, for instance, were the main sources of health problems among the Sioux before historic contact? How do these problems compare in type and severity with their health problems in the eighteenth and nineteenth centuries? How have activity-level alterations, reduced nutritional quality, physiological stress, and population nucleation on reservations influenced their health? What was the impact on Sioux health of settlement aggregation and increased conflict in the fourteenth century? How did the restructuring of diet that must have accompanied the movement of Sioux out of the northwoods affect their health? How did participation in the fur trade influence their health? How many Sioux were there in the late prehistoric period, and how does that number compare to Sioux population sizes in 1800, 1900, and 2000?

A study of Sioux health provides insights into many aspects of their history. For instance, a comparison of the health of the Sioux in precontact and post-contact times is one means of judging the impact of Euro-American contact and settlement; population size fluctuations track the adaptive success of a people; and the health of the Sioux in the twenty-first century will increasingly be a measure of the success of their drive toward self-determination. As we move back in time, issues concerning Sioux health become more difficult to resolve because of inadequate information. Still, skeletal studies, ethnohistorical sources, computer simulations, and epidemiological theory provide some insight into Sioux health before the availability of extensive written records.

To assess the historical impact of Euro-American contact and colonization on the health of the Sioux, health patterns endemic to their populations before contact must be understood. This is because nutritional stress, population decline, and the impacts of infectious diseases after contact are a result in part of a people's adaptation and health before contact. Unfortunately, there is little evidence for the precontact health of the Sioux. What there is comes mainly from a small number of skeletal remains. In a study by Arthur Aufderheide and his colleagues of what were assumed to be late prehistoric and protohistoric Dakota in the Mille Lacs cluster of sites, individuals were found to be in good health.[21] However, in addition to the small size of the sample, the situation is complicated by other sampling problems, for few Psinomani (late prehistoric Sioux) seem to have been buried in the ground. Most of the dead were apparently left exposed on platforms or in other above-ground settings. As a result, there is little surviving trace of these populations.

In other areas of the mid-continent, increasing late prehistoric settlement aggregation and density created suitable environments for the development and spread of new diseases, such as smallpox and tuberculosis. European epidemic diseases may have reached the Midwest by 1520 and the northern Plains by 1600.[22] In the Midwest, Oneota population clusters along the Mississippi and Fox rivers in Wisconsin, Iowa, and Minnesota may have been devastated. If population losses of this magnitude occurred this early, they would have influenced the relationship between the Oneota and Psinomani, and may have contributed, because of population imbalances, to the movement of the Sioux out of the northwoods.

In spite of increased warfare and violence, and a deterioration of the health of some populations to the south, the Sioux seem to have remained a healthy population through the protohistoric period. This conclusion is implied by Aufderheide's bioanthropological study of 70 individuals from the early seventeenth century Mille Lacs area Cooper Village and Cooper Mound sites.[23] People between the ages of 45 and 60 tended to have a mild degree of degenerative joint or disc disease in the lower back, and about 50 percent of the 70 Dakota died before the age of 36. However, both males and females were robust, healthy, and well nourished, and most of those who lived past childhood died in their fourth or fifth decade, with a few living into their sixties. Furthermore, dental caries were absent, as was dental hypoplasia. The only evidence of aggression was associated with a male in his mid-forties, who was buried at the center of the Cooper Mound. He seems to have died from arrow wounds, for a stone point was stuck in his knee and several others may have been in his soft tissues.

Developing a secure demographic profile for the protohistoric Sioux is problematic, too, because of biases in skeletal recovery, differential preservation of types of skeletons, and the practice of above-ground burial. Present skeletal and site evidence is too thin and patchy to determine whether there was a significant shift in Sioux population between AD 1300 and European contact. On the other hand, this evidence does not support a population base for the Sioux of more than 12,000 to 15,000 people in AD 1600.[24]

To the west along the Missouri Trench, crowded villages of Mandan, Hidatsa, and Arikara suffered a series of staggering population losses from acute infectious diseases, including smallpox, measles, cholera, and whooping cough, beginning in the mid- to late seventeenth century.[25] According to one estimate, the Arikara population shrank from 15,000 in AD 1700, to 2,600 in 1804, to 500 in 1888 due to disease, malnutrition, and intertribal warfare. A particularly deadly smallpox epidemic in 1837, which was spread by the river steamboat *St. Peters*, reportedly killed half the Hidatsa and reduced the Mandan population from about 1,600 to 125 people. At the same time, some nomadic groups, especially those Western Sioux who had received vaccinations, increased in numbers. Treaty negotiation sessions, such as the gathering at Prairie du Chien in Wisconsin in 1825, were also responsible for the spread of disease.[26]

The western migration of the Sioux across the northern Plains took place within this large-scale trend of population decline. Because of their nomadic lifeway and heavy vaccination, the Sioux suffered the lowest mortality of major Plains tribes. The impact on tribal relations was enormous. Among the effects were: (1) a shift in tribal allegiances and a realignment of tribal boundaries; (2) destruction of the intertribal trading system on the upper Missouri River, which led to greater dependence on Euro-American traders and their goods; (3) the loss of food-obtaining capabilities by some bands due to a reduction in size of cooperative work groups, which led to a greater dependence on government annuities and assistance; and (4) the emergence of nomadic groups, in particular the Lakota, to a position of power on the northern Plains. While the less nomadic Dakota and Yankton, who had become dependent on doles and assistance, were among the first "reservation Indians" of the area, the numbers, strength, and reputation of the Lakota all greatly expanded in the nineteenth century. Subdivisions of the Yanktonai ranged between these two extremes.

During the mid-nineteenth century, treaties with the Sioux promised medical care if they moved to a reservation or to a smaller reservation. As with other services, the medical facilities and reservation doctors were to be paid for from money the Sioux received for land cessions. In cases where these funds ran out, Congress continued to provide medical care, if for no other reason than a fear that disease-infested Indian villages would infect neighboring non-Indian settlements, which were growing in number.

As groups of Sioux moved onto reservations, they entered an unhealthy environment with poor sanitation, frequent water contamination, and overcrowded conditions, all of which favored the spread of infectious diseases. Other problems included: (1) an increase in inactivity and carbohydrate consumption that led to gains in body weight and size; (2) poor housing and overcrowding in communities that were larger than the small extended family groups they were used to; (3) a government-supplied diet that was extremely high in fats, sugar, and salt, and low in protein and vitamins (to paraphrase a sentiment on reservations, "Flour, salt, and sugar, all sources of health problems, all white"); and (4) increased alcoholism. Although the federal government prohibited the sale of alcohol to the Sioux and other Indian people between 1832 and 1953, alcohol abuse was a major problem for many Sioux.[27]

Since the mid-1950s, there have been renewed efforts by tribal leaders and state and federal governments to improve the health of the Sioux and other Indians. Among these initiatives have been: (1) the transfer of the Indian Health Service (HIS) from the BIA to the US Public Health Service within the Department of Health, Education, and Welfare (now Health and Human Services) in 1955; (2) the Indian Health Care Improvement Act of 1976, which upgraded reservation facilities and services and provided some funds for urban Indian health care; and (3) a self-imposed prohibition by most tribes against drinking alcoholic beverages at certain functions or in certain facilities, such as at some casinos. Minnesota was one of the first states (in 1923) to assign public health nurses to work with Indians, and the Indian Health Board in Minneapolis, which was developed by local Indians to meet local needs, remains a national model for urban Indian health programs.[28]

While improvements have been made, especially where health care through the Indian Health Service or other health-care providers is available, the health of the Sioux as a people remains far below the national average. The Sioux still have higher annual death rates per 1,000 population, higher birthrates, higher infant mortality rates, and more severe alcohol problems than does the general, non-Indian public. In addition, incidences of depression, violent death, school and job adjustment problems, and families in crisis remain high.

If the health of a people is a gauge of their adaptive success, then the Sioux have not fully recovered from their period of colonial subjugation on reservations. Nonetheless, if their health problems are a result of poverty, oppression, and a lack of education, there should be continual improvement in their health during the twenty-first century. The reasons are many, including a rising standard of living, strengthened self-government, bold new tribal initiatives in reviving their distinctive cultural tradition, and the incorporation of traditional Sioux medical practices into some Western health care systems.[29]

Sioux Households

Households are task-oriented residence units whose members may or may not be related by kinship, although most households around the world are made up of family members related through kinship.[30] Multiple studies have demonstrated that there is a relationship, in general, between the structure and function of households. For example, the size and composition of households usually shifts to meet the labor requirements of new production tasks. Regularities have been suggested for some of these relationships.[31] An instance in hypothesis form is, "The more diverse and simultaneous the productive tasks within a yearly cycle, the greater the tendency for large households to exist." Given these regularities, we can anticipate that Sioux households changed considerably over time in size, composition, and function, for Sioux culture has changed and diversified through time and space.

Among the pre-reservation Lakota, the camp or "lodge-group" (the *tiyospaye*) was the core of society. Each was an autonomous economic unit composed mainly of the members of one or more extended families.[32] Since an isolated conjugal family of a man, his wife or wives, and small children was not capable of maintaining an adequate food supply or of defending itself, its activities were carried out as part of the extended family arrangement of the *tiyospaye*. As Royal Hassrick has phrased it, home "was not so much one's own lodge but rather one's village, and the tiyospe, the assembled tipis of one's family, might be likened to an airy dwelling with many rooms."[33] This arrangement exemplifies the close integration of kinship and societal functions, such as production, consumption, and protection, among the prereservation Sioux. Still, households did exist within the *tiyospaye*.

During the summer Sun Dance camp, families were arranged by prestige in a circle, with the order prescribed by the four pipe owners (*wakincuzas*) in charge of the movements of the camp. A household consisted of one of these ordered positions around the circle. At other times of the year, household location was more informal, with tipi locations determined by family relationships and customary positions.[34] In principle, a new household could be placed wherever one chose. While generally a single tipi, a household might consist of a cluster of tipis. In most cases, this occurred where a man had multiple wives, when a young married couple lived with one of their parents, or an older, attached relative had her or his own tipi. When more than one tipi was present, the lodge of the primary couple or person was the center of the household. The composition of a household might consist, then, of a man and his wife or wives, their younger children, an older relative or two, perhaps a slave, and occasionally a young married couple.

There was a definite division of labor within the pre-reservation Lakota household that has been described in general terms many times.[35] There were also proper ways to enter a tipi, places to sit, and arrangements of furnishings. Although the Lakota moved frequently throughout the year, the household seems to have retained its integrity during these moves. In spite of this general knowledge, the range in size and composition of pre-reservation Lakota households has not been worked out in detail.

Traditional Dakota villages or lodge groups (*tiyospayes*) and households were similar to those of the Lakota with allowances for their different annual subsistence cycles.[36] Among the Dakota, the *tiyospaye* was also an economically self-sufficient social unit that acted together throughout the year, and its members consisted for the most part of the members of a number of interrelated families. Households were tightly integrated into all aspects of village life. Each household had a fixed or customary position within the *tiyospaye* as it moved from one location to another. While the Dakota lived in tipis made from hides during the winter, they stayed, however, in large, peaked elm-bark houses in the summer.

The nature of the household in late prehistoric Sioux societies can only be tenuously modeled at present. Our main sources of information are cross-cultural patterns and the characteristics of the Psinomani lifeway outlined in chapter 2. The structure and function of households among most band-level hunters and gatherers is closely related to variations in economic and reproductive tasks and activities. Among these societies, households are generally an autonomous unit composed primarily of a nuclear family, for this type of household maximizes mobility and flexibility in making a living. Consequently, if Blackduck–Kathio–Clam River Continuum societies were mobile band-level hunting-gathering groups, as proposed in chapter 2, then they may also have had nuclear household units.

In contrast, households among the Psinomani were more likely organized principally as production groups with an emphasis upon exchange among households, as within the historic *tiyospaye*. The production of resources was increased and surplus provided by the development of larger, more efficient domestic labor units. These most likely included large polygynous households in some instances. Production was increased by expanding, or rearranging, the workforce along age, sex, and group lines to meet the demands of cooperative procurement activities, such as intensive wild rice-harvesting and mass animal hunts and drives. The goal was to gather food surpluses for new kinds of intergroup feasts, festivals, and ceremonies. Due to their larger size, such households were also relatively sedentary.[37] From this perspective, the traditional Sioux *tiyospaye* originated among the Psinomani with the development of village life. One would expect, however, that Psinomani and later Dakota households were somewhat dissimilar in detail because of their different geographic settings and historic contexts.

In the early reservation period, the importance of the Sioux household in intra-community production and sharing declined in response to a change in the activity spheres that underlay household form. Because of the allotment system, families and individual adults were dispersed to live on separately allotted parcels of land. In addition, plural marriages were banned. As a result, the consanguine family of the *tiyospaye* fragmented. The imposed model was the nuclear farming family of white society. Since the conjugal family frequently lacked the stability to sustain itself in a period of cultural and economic stress, the rate of divorce and number of broken homes rose sharply.[38] Nonetheless, grandparents (and especially grandmothers) continued to play (and still play) the role of guardian for the children of these marriages.

Figure 7.3 House built for an Eastern Sioux family at the Redwood Falls
Mission, Lower Sioux Community, Morton, Minnesota, 1938 (Minnesota
Historical Society Photograph Collection)

In recent decades, changing economic and educational opportunities
have led to a rapid change in Sioux household structure and dynamics.
Among the forces at work are: outmigration to work in towns and cities;
a more prominent role for women in income generation, which has led to
greater independence for women; and increased access to a liberal education and the women's movement, which together have encouraged changes
in internal family dynamics, such as shared decision-making and budget
control. In parallel with American society in general, household form in
Sioux society should increase in diversity in the future. For instance, we
should expect to see among the Sioux, as in American society in general,
an increase in numbers of intergenerational households in which "adult
children" return to live with their parents.[39]

Formal Education

In pre-reservation days, Sioux children learned by doing within their social hierarchy of family, band, and tribal grouping. All adults shared responsibility for educating the young. Storytelling, respect for elders, a sense
of community, and stress on traditional values – especially sharing, generosity, hospitality, and kinship with all living things – played prominent

roles in their education. Youths were considered educated or mature when they grasped the basics of their cultural and spiritual heritage and had become proficient in carrying out the economic tasks on which their survival depended.[40]

Education of Indian children according to emerging European models was a significant component of the colonization of North America almost from the beginning. For well-intended reformers, a pragmatic Western-style education was the most efficient means of helping Indians become productive, accepted members of the larger society. From the passage of the Dawes Act in 1887 to the IRA in 1934, assimilation and Western-style education were intimate companions, for the aim of both was the civilization through acculturation of American Indians. Belief that Indians had to undergo cultural and religious conversion was very strong in American society into the 1930s and continues today among some segments of society.

Rather than deal with each tribe separately, Congress passed the Civilization Fund Bill in 1819. The purpose of the bill was to provide American Indians an education equivalent to that of other frontier children; that is, they should learn to read, especially the Bible, and to farm, for most rural Americans were expected to be pious, settled farmers. As Indian people were moved in ever-larger numbers to reservations in the Great Plains after the Civil War, it became clear that special programs would be needed to hasten the assimilation of Indian children into American society. The strategy selected was the creation of non-denominational schools. In 1873, the Civilization Fund Bill was repealed and a government school system developed under the direction of the Bureau of Indian Affairs. During the transition, the government contracted with existing mission schools, which now were called contract schools because of the structure of their support. Although Congress later decided in its Appropriations Act of 1895 that it would no longer fund religious schools, mission schools continued to receive ever-dwindling funds into the middle of the twentieth century.[41]

By 1880, a number of federally operated schools had appeared. While some were day schools, others were boarding schools either on or off reservations, whose intent in part was to segregate children from the supposed retarding influence of traditional reservation life. Between the late 1880s and 1900, during the early assimilation period, the favored model was an off-reservation boarding school based on the coeducational Carlisle Indian Industrial school founded by Richard Henry Pratt at Carlisle, Pennsylvania in 1879.[42] At the core of Pratt's educational philosophy were two notions: (1) the idea that the eventual assimilation of Indians into American society depended on the destruction of their traditional culture; and (2) the idea that this was best achieved through military-style discipline.

Sioux children attended Carlisle as well as many other boarding schools, such as St. Benedict's Agricultural Boarding School for Boys built outside Fort Yates, North Dakota, in 1878. Federal boarding schools were also set up at Wahpeton and Bismarck, North Dakota. During the allotment period, the idea grew that only by getting children away from the influence of their parents could changes be made. By 1890, some 153 federal Indian schools of various types were in operation. By 1900, there were 25 off-reservation boarding schools, 81 reservation boarding schools, 147 day schools, and 32 contract-supported day schools in the US.

By 1900, federal policy had shifted to a focus on reservation schools and a curriculum designed to train Indian children for contemporary life on reservations. Under the direction of Thomas J. Morgan, who became Indian Commissioner in 1889, BIA schools were restructured to better resemble American public schools. By 1891, the BIA was also encouraging Indian students to enroll in public schools. The curriculum at BIA schools offered both vocational training (in domestic skills for girls and manual labor for boys) and some competence in the academic skills of reading, writing, and arithmetic. Training in religious schools was similar, though academic work was often based on the Bible and some students were trained for future mission work on reservations. All teaching was in English. While well intentioned, the Morgan system, which operated until the 1930s, continued to disregard Indian culture and language.[43]

Figure 7.4   Santee Normal Training School, The Dakota Home, Nebraska, 1890 (Minnesota Historical Society Photograph Collection)

By the 1920s, significant problems in the federal Indian education system became the rallying point of educational reformers. Among these problems were: overcrowding in schools, which caused significant health problems in some areas; deterioration of buildings; too constricting a focus on industrial training; classes that stopped at the eight or tenth grade, which precluded most Indian children from obtaining a college education; strong objections by many parents to having their children taken from them and placed in distant boarding schools; and dwindling budgets. Most significantly, BIA schools were not achieving their primary goal, which was the acculturation of the Sioux and other Indians into American society. When most students completed their boarding-school education, they found it easiest to return to their reservation. Since many were inadequately prepared for work in non-Indian communities and had not received a traditional tribal education, they lived estranged lives. Despite these drawbacks, pan-tribal relationships developed at boarding schools and many students developed friendships with teachers.

One result of the reform movement's attack on federal Indian policy in the 1920s was the 1928 Meriam Report. Among its educational policy recommendations were a shift to reservation or local day schools for all children so that they could live with their parents or relatives, and a curriculum that recognized that they were Indian children living difficult multicultural lives. Among the many trends in Indian education that have taken place since the call for reform are: (1) the appearance of Indian-controlled grade schools whose curriculum emphasizes traditional culture and acculturation from an Indian perspective; (2) the development of tribally controlled community colleges and an increase in the number of Indians attending college; (3) increasing graduation rates at all levels; (4) increasing numbers of Indian children attending public rather than BIA-managed schools; (5) a proliferation of enrichment programs; (6) greater accountability for Indian education funds (to ensure, for example, that it is being spent directly on the education of Indian children rather than being dumped into a general fund); (7) a shift to and strengthening of Indian community and parental control in all aspects of Indian formal education (a movement toward Indian involvement and control of the schooling of their children); (8) a sharp decline in the number of boarding schools; (9) a conscious emphasis in reservation schools and colleges to prepare students for a productive life on the reservation and for tribal needs; (10) a move to integrate traditional and western educational models in the classroom; (11) an increase in numbers of native Americans attaining college degrees; (12) a weakening of BIA control over Indian education with the creation of an Office of Indian Education within the US Department of Education, which is now responsible for administering the various Congressional acts that provide assistance to Indian educa-

Figure 7.5   The Four Winds School, Minneapolis

tion); (13) increasing numbers of professional Indian educators; and (14) increasing numbers of Indians going on to law school, medical school, and business school, and so on.[44]

These trends have been the result of pressure from advocacy groups,[45] such as the Committee of One Hundred, the Society of American Indians (founded in 1911), the American Indian Higher Education Consortium (created in 1973), and the National Indian Education Association (founded in 1970), recommendations in investigative studies and reports,[46] and legislation designed to improve the quality of Indian education.[47] Among the acts are the Johnson–O'Malley Act of 1934, the Indian Education Act of 1972, the Indian Self-Determination and Education Assistance Act of 1975, Title XI of the Education Amendments of 1978, and the Tribally Controlled Community College Assistance Act of 1978.

Although the growth of positive educational experiences for Sioux people has accelerated since the 1930s, the path has not always been smooth. Among the many problems have been a loss in progress and funding during the Great Depression and World War II, the destruction wrought to Indian communities during the termination era of the 1950s, and a slowdown of support during the Reagan presidency. The growth and development of innovative educational programs was slowed, too, by the

Bureau of Indian Affairs, which tried unsuccessfully to defund the Johnson–O'Malley Bill (as amended) in 1986.

Studies of the effort to educate Sioux children within Western systems of learning have repeatedly demonstrated that these systems have failed to effectively acculturated Sioux children into American society, and that they have been psychologically damaging to many students.[48] These conclusions have been the spur for the development of more traditional settings for the schooling of the Sioux and other American Indians. Today, Indian-controlled schools on reservations are the norm rather than the exception. Opportunities exist, too, for attending schools with a traditional Indian focus in larger cities like Minneapolis.

The Dakota Language: Dictionaries, Grammars, Texts, and the Ethnography of Speaking

Dakota is an unevenly studied dialect complex, even though it became the largest speech community of the five Siouan languages spoken on the Plains. Since some dialects are not well studied, in particular Yankton and Yanktonai, the Dakota dialect complex has been divided in various ways by linguists. Some linguists recognize five divisions (Assiniboin, Stoney, Yankton–Yanktonai, Santee (Dakota), and Lakota) and many others only four divisions (Santee (Dakota), Lakota, Yanktonai, and Assiniboin). In general usage, the language is broken down into three dialects, Dakota (Santee and Yankton), Nakota (Assiniboin and Yanktonai), and Lakota (Teton).[49] Although they are sometimes referred to as separate languages, even spatially distant dialects like Santee (Dakota) and Lakota are so close that their speakers can understand each other in the same way that people from England and Texas can understand each other. Statistics published in 1980 estimate that there were at the time 6,000 Sioux who spoke Lakota (Teton), 2,000 who spoke Santee (Dakota), 2,000 who spoke Assiniboin-Stoney, and 1,000 who spoke Yankton–Yanktonai.[50]

Early linguistic work on Dakota dialects and other Plains Indian languages was generally part of broader, usually haphazard, studies of the natural history of the region by missionaries, army officers, traders, and other interested individuals. For the most part, they wrote down lists of words phonetically, which often makes it difficult today to determine how the word or expression was actually spoken. However, many serious attempts were made during the latter half of the nineteenth century to describe particular dialects in some detail, especially by missionaries intent on spreading the word of the Gospel. Since these individuals were not trained linguists, the dictionaries and grammatical sketches they compiled often suffer from technical problems. Nonetheless, they remain invaluable sources of information for the study of and resurrection of Dakota dialects.

In general, "adequate descriptive material" means a dictionary, a grammar, and a set of texts for a language. In contrast to Yankton, Yanktonai, Assiniboin, and Stoney, which are poorly documented, Santee (Dakota) and Lakota are adequately described according to these criteria. Both have been the subject of intensive, if sporadic, investigation. Santee (Dakota) was recorded over a century ago through the efforts of two Presbyterian missionaries, Stephen R. Riggs and Thomas S. Williamson, and Lakota is one of the most richly documented Indian language dialects in North America, with a dictionary, grammars, and texts. Today, Dakota is a stable language, with many of the dialects taught at universities, colleges, and in the lower grades. With the help of older living speakers, a vigorous effort is being made to pass on these dialects to future generations.[51]

Besides the structure of Dakota dialects and their time of derivation from protolanguages, linguistic anthropologists are interested in the social and cultural context of Dakota. Among other pursuits, ethnolinguists make inferences about earlier cultural practices based on words retained in a contemporary language. Dakota and the Siouan language family in general have been the focus of only limited ethnolinguistic research of this sort. Frequently cited examples are Gilmore's early ethnobotanical work and Matthews's attempted reconstruction of the proto-Siouan kinship system.[52]

Ethnolinguists are also concerned with the ethnography of speaking, that is, with linguistic performance or with how people actually use language when speaking in different social contexts. In this focus, they are interested in questions like: What was nineteenth-century Sioux "small talk" about? How did Sioux speech vary with social position and situation? Were phonetic variations involved? Were there gender, ethnic, and status differences in speech? What did pre-reservation Sioux ask as a greeting ("Where are you going?" "What are you cooking?," and so on)? Did they expect a detailed answer or only vague answers? Did terms of address reflect social relationships, such as kin and age relationships? How did the formality of the occasion influence address? How were personal names determined, and why and when did they change during one's lifetime?

Sociolinguists are interested in contrasting patterns of conversation, for they are a common source of misunderstanding. For instance, American English speakers generally try to get to know a stranger by rattling on about the weather or where one comes from (rather than about other topics, such as how much money they make). Since "traditional" Sioux consider it impolite to interrupt, they do not respond with equally idle chatter; additionally, since English speakers have traditionally been more politically powerful, it is generally thought best not to respond until one has some idea of what the person wants. Misunderstandings occur when English speakers interpret the lack of immediate response as a sign that they are being snubbed. On the other hand, Dakota speakers conclude that English speakers talk too much about nothing and are not interested in what he/she has to say.

Language is a rich source of information about still other aspects of Sioux culture. The Dakota language lexicon (or vocabulary) is the set of Sioux names for things, events, and ideas. As in other languages, the Dakota lexicon is a window through which one can explore how the Sioux perceive the world and what kinds of things are important to them. Such specialized sets of terms and distinctions are known as a focal vocabulary. Compared to the slow-changing structure of the Dakota language, its focal vocabulary and its lexical distinctions have been dynamic in the historic period as the Sioux shifted from northwoods wild-rice harvester, to prairie hunter-horticulturalist, and, for many, to Plains bison hunter. As new words and lexical distinctions were added as needed, others gradually faded from use.

As this brief review demonstrates, a people's language is the soul of their culture, of their way of life. This is why Sioux scholars insist that non-Sioux intent on learning the ways of their culture must first immerse themselves in their language.[53]

eight
The Sioux Today: Self-Determination, 1975–2000

During the last quarter of the twentieth century, new federal legislation continued the direction in US Indian policy initiated by the IRA in the 1930s. Included in the new legislation were: the 1975 Indian Self-Determination and Education Assistance Act, which transferred greater government and administrative powers to federally recognized tribes; the 1978 Indian Child Welfare Act, which gave Indian people the right to retain custody of their children; the 1978 American Indian Freedom of Religion Act, which stated that it was federal policy to protect and preserve the right of Indian peoples to practice religious traditions of their choice; the 1990 Native American Grave Protection and Repatriation Act (NAGPRA), which required museums and other institutions that received federal funds to return human remains, and funerary and sacred objects, to tribes; and the 1990 Act for the Protection of American Indian Arts and Crafts, which made it a criminal offense to falsely identify oneself as an Indian in order to sell artwork.[1] Nonetheless, these government actions did not resolve all controversies between the Sioux and the federal government.

This final chapter reviews these controversies and three topical issues: Sioux humor, stereotypes of the Sioux, and contemporary problems of Sioux self-identity.

A New Independence

A continuing concern of the Lakota in the last quarter of the twentieth century has been the illegal seizure of the Black Hills in South Dakota by Congress in 1877. Besides representing an illegal action against the Lakota people, many Lakota consider the Black Hills sacred land inhabited by powerful spirits. Even though the Court of Claims awarded the tribe $105 million for the land in 1980, an award upheld on appeal by the Supreme Court, the Lakota have refused to accept forced payment for land they consider theirs. A second controversy is the life sentence given Leonard Peltier, an Oglala activist who was involved in a gunfight with FBI agents in Custer, South Dakota, in 1975. Peltier's supporters claim he was framed by the government and Amnesty International considers him a political prisoner of conscience. Neither controversy has been settled.[2]

In recent decades, groups of Sioux have also exercised their right to perform rituals that "mend the broken hoop." Examples are the retracing of Big Foot's tragic path to Wounded Knee in 1990 (the hundredth anniversary of the massacre) by the Big Foot Memorial Riders, and the Mah-Kato Powwow in Minnesota, which annually honors the Dakota warriors executed at Mankato in 1862. In 1986, then governor Rudy Perpich declared a Year of Reconciliation for the State of Minnesota modeled after the 1975 Day of Reconciliation, a precursor to the Mah-Kato Powwow. By formally mourning for their ancestors killed by the federal government, the Sioux are looking toward the future and the flourishing of a distinctive Dakota–Lakota culture.[3]

Since the mid-1970s, economic opportunities have expanded for the Sioux. On most Sioux reservations, small businesses have opened that employ community members. Examples are (1) a 2,400-acre ranch on the Santee Reservation; (2) the Sioux Manufacturing Company and Dakota Tribal Industries, both factories among the Spirit Lake Nation (formerly

Figure 8.1   Dancers at the 2001 Mankato Powwow (courtesy of the *Native American Press/Ojibwe News*)

the Devil's Lake Reservation) that manufacture equipment for the US Department of Defense; (3) Dakota Western, a plant on the Lake Traverse Reservation that manufactures plastic bags; and (4) the Cheyenne River Telephone Authority and Lakota Technologies, Inc., a data-processing corporation, on the Cheyenne River Reservation. Many other Sioux in both Canada and the US have found a wide range of public or private employment either on reservations or in nearby towns and cities, such as Prince Albert in Saskatchewan and Watertown in South Dakota. Sioux men and women employed in the public sector generally work in the offices of tribal governments, for the Public Health Service, for the local branch of the Bureau of Indian Affairs, in social services and schools, or in day-care centers, among other areas.

Nonetheless, many Sioux still find it difficult to obtain employment on or near their reservation. Despite the government's early efforts to transform the Sioux into farmers, few Sioux now earn their living farming. The main reasons are the high cost of equipment and the poor quality or amount of available land.[4]

Undoubtedly, the most successful economic enterprise initiated by the Sioux since the mid-1970s has been legalized gambling, for gambling on tribal lands is not subject to government interference, a right confirmed by the US Supreme Court and by the 1988 Indian Gaming Regulatory Act. The first Sioux to take advantage of this highly profitable business was the Shakopee Mdewakanton Community, which opened the Little Six Bingo Palace in 1982. Other Minnesota Dakota communities soon followed. When high-stakes casino gambling was added in 1985, profits soared. In 1986, gross income from Little Six alone was $18 million. Although profits are divided in different ways by different groups of Sioux, all reserve some funds for the tribe and distribute payments to individuals. The largest present facilities are Mystic Lake Casino, operated by the Shakopee Mdewakanton since 1992, and Treasure Island Casino on Prairie Island, both near the large Twin Cities metropolitan area. At Prior Lake, tribal funds from gambling profits have been used to build the Dakotah Sport and Fitness Center, which was completed in late 1994, and the Playworks, a state-of-the-art child-care center that opened in January 1995, among other facilities. By April 1994, every member of the Shakopee Mdewakanton Dakota – man, woman, and child – had received $500,000.[5]

Legalized gambling on tribal lands west of Minnesota, while less successful because of their more rural locations, has still proven to be a bonanza for some reservations. As with Minnesota Sioux communities, most of these ventures began as bingo halls. An example is the Yankton Sioux Tribal Bingo Hall in the Missouri Hills above Fort Randall, which opened in the early 1980s. When transformed into the Fort Randall Casino in 1991, employment surged from 75-percent unemployment to full employment and a $3 million profit was made in the first eight months. While not as profitable as the casinos in Minnesota, they do provide tribal members jobs and a salary. Still, through an accident of non-Indian population concentrations, a disparity in wealth has developed between the Eastern Sioux and their Western Sioux relatives.[6]

Since the mid-twentieth century, Sioux leaders have become increasingly aware of the inextricable link between their goal of self-government (sovereignty) and economic independence. Besides motivating the development of gaming parlors, this same awareness has spurred the development of improved educational opportunities for younger Sioux. Many larger communities now have their own primary and secondary schools in which the Dakota language and Dakota–Lakota culture and history are taught as part of a comprehensive curriculum. Many Sioux reservations also have accredited colleges. Examples are the Santee campus of the Nebraska Indian Community College at Santee, the Sisseton–Wahpeton Community College at Lake Traverse, the Little Hoop Community College among the Spirit Lake Nation, and Sitting Bull Community College at Standing Rock. Ironically, some of these institutions occupy facilities once built to eradicate Indian culture.

Indian Studies' programs or departments that teach Dakota–Lakota language and culture have opened at a number of regional public colleges and universities, such as the Department of American Indian Studies at the University of Minnesota. Efforts are being made in some states, such as South Dakota, to ensure that the teachers of non-Indian children are trained in Indian studies so that they may sensitize their students to Indian history and the debilitating effects of negative stereotypes.[7]

The cultural revival begun among Sioux people in the 1960s grew with new vigor during the last quarter of the twentieth century. This revival has been characterized by an increasing ability by greater numbers of Sioux to merge new ways of doing things with age-old traditions. Among those traditional customs reemphasized are the use of the Dakota language, a growing sense of community responsibility, especially within the extended family, and participation in ceremonies and social festivals in which giveaways and dancing play a role.

For many Sioux, the revival and expanded use of the Dakota language is an integral part of their drive toward renewal and self-government. Today, many Canadian Santee and Sioux in the US speak somewhat fluent Dakota, especially in more traditional, rural communities. Dakota is also spoken at religious ceremonies (both traditional and Christian) and in important social contexts, such as a powwow. To ensure the continuation of the language, it is taught, as mentioned above, in schools at all levels on reservations and in some universities. Most Sioux, however, speak a modern dialect of Dakota that incorporates loan words from English and other Indian languages. Nevertheless, the use of the language preserves the unique way of world-making encapsulated in the language, provides a degree of privacy, and promotes the feeling of being Dakota–Lakota.

The giveaway is one of several community events in Sioux society in which traditional values – generosity, sacrifice, harmony, respect, and cooperation – are expressed. Traditionally, a giveaway took place at the end of a year of mourning after a death. This period of mourning, called Keeping of the Soul, was one of the Seven Sacred Rites given to the Sioux by the White Buffalo Calf Woman, according to Black Elk. Today, giveaways more likely commemorate an important occasion, such as a marriage, a birth, or a graduation. During pre-1890s giveaways, bison robes, horses, blankets, bear teeth, furs, hides, and other items were given by the relatives of the deceased to everyone in attendance, which usually meant the people in their community. Today, distributed items tend to be blankets, beadwork, colorful star quilts, bolts of cloth, clothing, and household goods. For blankets and cloth, favorite colors remain those of the four directions (green, red, yellow, and white), or blue for the eagle. While the context of the giveaway and the items distributed have changed, its original purpose – to maintain family bonds to community and friends – remains. After the gifts are distributed, speeches laden with moral lessons for the community (and in particular for the young) may be given and a traditional feast held.[8]

A greater proportion of Sioux are also practicing traditional arts and crafts, and participating, if occasionally, in traditional ceremonies. Sun Dances are held on a number of reservations, especially in rural communities, and some individuals go on vision quests. Others seek the care of traditional tribal healers and perform ceremonies in the ways of the holy pipe. An effort is being made by many to celebrate special occasions in a more traditional way. This usually means the use of traditional objects, some modified items of traditional clothing, and the use of the Dakota language, if only for part of an occasion. In artwork, an important traditional medium that is being revived is the creation of jewelry and other items of adornment from colored beads. For example, these and other pieces of artwork are on display each year at the Tribal Arts Fair in Sioux Falls, South Dakota.

Some practices, whether in religion or art, continue to combine traditional and Western non-Indian motifs and concepts. An instructive example is the picture above the altar at St. Paul's Church at Marty on the Yankton Sioux Reservation. As in other Christian churches, the picture contains images of the Virgin Mary, baby Jesus, and a choir of angels – but all are Indians. Mass at the church is an expression of the same mix of cultures: the Christian liturgy, written in the Dakota language, is performed to an Indian drumbeat, and both Christ and the ways of the holy pipe are honored.[9]

Figure 8.2   A quilt giveaway, Dakota women, Poplar, Montana, 1934
(Minnesota Historical Society Photograph Collection)

Throughout the last quarter-century, no other action has signaled the revival of the Sioux so strongly as their growing and enthusiastic attendance at powwows (and *wacipis*). International powwows are held each year at Fort Totten and Rosebud, and most reservations or communities have powwows and powwow grounds. Examples are the grounds in Lake Andes and Greenwood, and at Chouteau Creek Community Hall, among the Yankton, and the Shakopee Mdewakanton Dakota Community powwow. Like today's rodeos, contemporary powwows are a complex blend of myth and reality, whose mythic portion has grown stronger through the years. And like the Western dress of the rodeo cowboy, the outfits of powwow dancers are largely a twentieth-century creation. Regardless, for many Sioux the powwow is more than a dance; it is a reaffirmation of their identity as a Sioux and, more broadly, as an Indian.[10]

Another measure of the revival of the Sioux since the mid-1970s is the growth of their landholdings. An unanticipated, unintended consequence of allotment policy was the "heirship problem." In the 1890s and early 1900s, land was allotted according to the number of eligible tribal members on a reservation. However, tribal membership did not remain stable. Between 1900 and 1950 alone, the number of recognized Indians recorded in the US census increased by about 50 percent. This surge in population left many Sioux without land or with only a small fraction of a lot that they shared with other tribal members.

To help ease the problem, Congress passed legislation (the heirship bill) in 1984 regulating inheritance of land on Indian reservations. Under federal law, tribes have the right of eminent domain on their lands. Inheritance of land is limited to close relatives and shares must be at least 2.5 acres in size or the land reverts to tribal ownership. It is current federal policy, too, to give tribal officials or individual tribal members the first option on buying land on reservations that comes up for sale. These shifts in policy have resulted in the consolidation of tribal land and in the repurchase of thousands of acres of land on Sioux reservations once lost through the allotment policy. As one example, tribal land among the Spirit Lake Nation (the former Devil's Lake Reservation) increased from 650 acres in 1960 to about 27,000 acres in 1993.[11]

Modern housing has also been built on Sioux reservations in recent decades. As one would anticipate for this period, this housing displays the mix of cultures found in other dimensions of Sioux culture. An example is the retirement facilities built for elders at Marty, Wagner, and Lake Andes on the Yankton Reservation. While Western in appearance, the facilities are located near cluster housing in order to enhance a sense of community among relatives and friends. Another difference is the general absence of flowerbeds, trees, and lawns around reservation homes. Rather than adopting the Euro-American symbol of success of a "neat yard," reservation Sioux find other expressions for their tribal cultural values.[12]

In spite of these clear signs of cultural revival, the Sioux continue to face difficult problems. One is a burgeoning population. High birth rates, a reduction in mortality, and the positive imagery of Indians in the 1960s and 1970s, which increased the willingness of some individuals to identify as Sioux, have led to a steady increase in numbers of Sioux on recent censuses. Even though about half of all enrolled Sioux live off-reservation, the dramatic rise in their numbers has caused severe strain on young adults seeking employment on reservations.

In the 2000 census, the following American Indian populations were recorded for Sioux reservations in the US: Lake Traverse (formerly called Sisseton) 3,453, Spirit Lake (formerly called Devil's Lake) 3,317, Santee 563, Flandreau 326, Lower Sioux (formerly called Birch Coulee) 294, Shakopee Mdewakanton Community (formerly called Prior Lake) 175, Prairie Island 166, Upper Sioux (formerly called Granite Falls) 47, Pine Ridge 12,985, Rosebud 7,747, Cheyenne River 6,249, Standing Rock 5,964, Crow Creek 1,936, Lower Brulé 1,237, and Yankton 2,633. The numbers of Sioux in Canada remain much lower. According to the 1992 Canadian census, for example, the populations of the four Manitoba reservations were: Long Prairie Sioux 903, Oak Lake 373, Birdtail Sioux 336, and Dakota Tipi 141, and the population of the Wahpeton Reservation in Saskatchewan was 146. These often dramatic increases in numbers of enrolled tribal members living on reservations have added to the pressure to prepare young people for urban employment.[13]

Tension between factions continues to be a problem on Sioux reservations. A long-term tension exists between progressives who accommodate to American life to varying degrees and traditionalists who attempt to closely follow tribal traditions as they understand them. Traditionalists argue that those Sioux who actively participate in American culture are perpetuating colonial rule. Progressives counter by maintaining that it is important to obtain a good education and career for their children in modern America – and, in some cases, that much of what is considered traditional practice is either a mythic ideal or fabricated. Among those many Sioux who live in communities away from their reservation, there is a continuum between those who maintain strong ties, return often to visit, and participate in family and community events and those with little connection to their tribal culture.

Tension exists, too, between "full-bloods" and "mixed bloods," even though the difference is often more a matter of attitude than genetics. During the twentieth century, increasing numbers of Sioux married people from other tribes or non-Indians. Consequently, the proportion of mixed-bloods on tribal rolls has climbed dramatically. In fact, much of the increase in Sioux population over the decades has been among the mixed-blood portion of the nation. A few traditionalists have argued that the purity of Sioux "blood" or at least Indian "blood" should be protected. One of their reasons is the belief that mixed-bloods are historically responsible for the loss of Sioux land and other onslaughts on Sioux culture. Others argue that the notion of pure Sioux "blood" is mythic nonsense; what matters is, as in the past, commitment to cultural tradition.[14]

Because of these pulls and pushes, every Sioux must make a choice today in how she or he will live. Their choices vary along a continuum from very traditional to very progressive. Typically, the very traditional live on a reservation, participate in powwows and the Sun Dance, pray with the pipe or peyote, speak Dakota as a first language, sponsor giveaways, send their children to Indian schools, avoid higher education, and maintain firm ties with their extended family (their *tiospaye*). Those who opt for the progressive end of the continuum live in cities or towns and do none of these things. Those who opt for a middle course try to live active lives in both cultures.

The reasons for making one choice or another vary, but geography plays a role. Those Sioux living near urban centers in Minnesota, such as St. Paul, Minneapolis, and Hastings, cannot avoid making some accommodations to urban non-Indian society. Those living to the west on Pine Ridge and other reservations in rural settings are less pressured to conform to the norms of non-Indian American society. The divide is roughly between the Dakota to the east and the Lakota and Yanktonai to the west, with the Yankton in the middle.

Like other Indians, the Sioux live off-reservation for many reasons. One important reason is tension with tribal leadership. Some tribal leaders and councils continue to follow a patronage system that favors family and close friends for tribal jobs. Leaders also sometimes shifted the rules for tribal membership to increase their voting faction and distribute annuities in what might be considered a biased manner by outsiders. Individuals out of favor with the current leadership, who are successful by non-Indian American standards, or who are subjected to other tensions, may find it easier to distance themselves from reservation life. Examples of being too successful have included the accumulation of personal wealth or the completion of a university degree.[15]

Other contemporary problems include high unemployment, pathological gambling, disputes over mineral, water, or health rights, and continuing prejudice and misinformation. Despite remarkable gains on some reservations, especially among the "casino" Sioux, rates of unemployment and underemployment remain high, and economic enterprises continue to fail in part because of insufficient funds on some reservations. The construction of a regional power plant beside the Prairie Island Community in Minnesota has introduced new health hazards. Studies have demonstrated that radioactive gases from the plant increased the risk of cancer in the area six times the state standard. A later attempt to construct a storage facility for spent nuclear fuel at the plant and a leak of emissions resulted in lawsuits to bar the storage facility.[16]

Finally, prejudice against and misinformation about Sioux culture continue to exist in Sioux territory and more widely. Job discrimination against the Sioux and other Indians continues in part because of differing notions of "work." Perhaps the majority of Americans believe, too, that tribal members are welfare loafers and cheats who use reservations as a dodge to avoid paying their share of taxes. Actually, reservation Sioux pay most of the same taxes as other Americans, with some exceptions, just as other Americans enjoy some exceptions. The "free" government benefits they have received over the decades have been deducted from land claims and other awards. Likewise, welfare and other benefits provided the Sioux are available in one form or another to their non-Indian neighbors.

Religious persecution has continued, too, at times. Examples are government stings to apprehend individuals selling parts of endangered species, such as eagle feathers and claws, to ornament pipes or to include in medicine bundles. These cases remain complex, for while it is lawful to possess these items for religious purposes, it is against the law to sell them.[17]

Today, ties among the Sioux remain strong, even though they are divided by attitudes, tribal policies, and territory. The majority are attempting to maintain a balance between their own cultural traditions and participation in a rapidly changing global market. Since most tribes are scattered through different, occasionally multi-tribal, reservations and in towns and cities, their integrity as a distinctive people has gradually faded. Today, Wapekute on a reservation in Canada, for instance, are likely to have more in common with their Yanktonai neighbors than with other Dakota in Minnesota or Nebraska. As a result, it is difficult to distinguish one group of Sioux from another or from their non-Sioux Indian neighbors, although some dialectical differences persist. Because of intermarriage, shared educational experiences, and interaction together in cities and on reservations, some Sioux have a stronger sense of "Indianness" than of band or tribal identity. This homogenizing process is being vigorously crosscut in some Sioux communities, however, by the creation of annual celebrations that bring members of tribes or divisions together for feasts, giveaways, traditional ceremonies, and powwows. How the interplay between these opposing forces will play out will be a major theme in Sioux history in the twenty-first century.[18]

Another trend in the last quarter of the twenty-first century has been a revolutionary movement toward sovereignty by Sioux and other Indian communities. Looking to the courts for fairness, they have had a number of successes, including the Boldt decision in 1974 and the Voigt decision of 1987, which acknowledge the prior existence of Indian sovereignty. They acknowledge, too, that treaties only ceded certain accommodations, not the surrender of their rights as a people. Today, the Sioux and other Indian nations are continuing to push for their rights and privileges as citizens of the US or Canada and as nations as provided in the treaties their ancestors signed.[19]

Although reservations were created as temporary refuges for Indians until they became "civilized," they will not disappear in the near future. One might ask why, for many remain the center of poverty, substandard housing and living conditions, factional dispute, and what appear to outsiders to be wasted lives. For some Sioux, the reservation is their home, as it was the home of their parents and grandparents. For others, it remains a retreat from the competitiveness and prejudice of non-Indian society. But for many others, a reservation is valued as a sanctuary where Sioux religion and culture have been preserved and nurtured.[20]

During the nineteenth century, the Sioux people were devastated by war, their numbers reduced by disease and exploitation, and their land confiscated by the federal government. In the twentieth century, repeated efforts were made to suppress their culture and to undermine their unity as a people. Still, the Sioux have survived as an amalgam of related, conscious ethnic groups. At the end of the twentieth century, they are emerging again as a political force in the heartland of North America. While

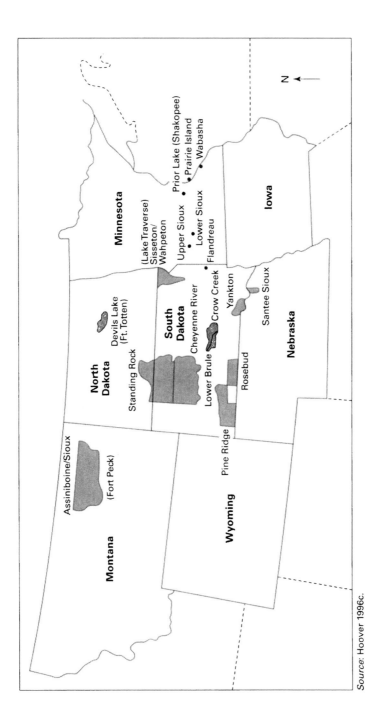

Figure 8.3 Location of Sioux reservations in the United States (adapted from Hoover 1996c)

Source: Hoover 1996c.

many are still poor, they are in the middle of an economic and cultural renaissance in which tradition and modern global culture are finding a unique expression. Their numbers are growing, their leaders have become skilled at legal maneuvering and media manipulation, their living conditions are improving, and the potential of continued growth is good. Today, the Sioux Nation is alive and healthier than it has been since the early nineteenth century.

Sioux Humor

While myth, ritual, language, and other aspects of culture help people make sense of the world, none guarantee escape from the fickleness of fate. Even though we might act properly according to religious and social norms, bad things can happen and normally do to everyone of us. While in myth the Trickster is discovered and the brother saved, real-life solutions are not so neat. Both magical rituals and modern-day medicines can fail. We may even be skeptical about our beliefs and myths. A universal outlet for these doubts and uncertainties is humor.[21]

The word "humor" is used today to denote anything that makes us laugh or that we find amusing.[22] Examples are a pun, a quip, a jesting or amusing remark, a witticism, and a joke. A joke is often a story that depends for its humor on seeing a situation, experience, or another person from an unexpected and often incongruous but amusing perspective. When Charlie Hill, the well-known Indian comic, quips that the first English immigrants were illegal aliens ("Whitebacks, we call 'em"), that is humor.[23] A joke can also be an act that is amusing or incongruous, as when Guy Dull Knife Sr. hid dozens of cans of sardines under other groceries in his wife's shopping cart so that she would have a bit of a surprise at the checkout counter.[24] The word "humor" is applied, too, to the ability to perceive or appreciate the comic in an experience or situation. Regardless, humor is not something to be taken seriously, at least at first laugh.

Humor has many uses besides amusement, for jokes more deeply can be expressions of contradictions, anxieties, ambiguities, and doubts. For instance, humor can draw our attention to the very real ambiguities and problems in our everyday lives. In doing so, it sharpens our cultural awareness and clarifies our problems. By drawing attention to the ambiguities and contradictions in our lives, it also helps us find meaning in the world by helping us decode or "read" our experience.[25] And, among many other uses, humor can act as a social control by clarifying the split between proper and improper behavior and can ease tension among family members and within other close social groups.

Humor also has therapeutic value. By drawing attention to problems, it makes them seem nonsensical or at least less threatening. Humor, whether verbal wit or comic inversion, can comically diffuse fear and anxiety, identify and take the sting out of injustices, acknowledge complexity, subvert the oppression of hegemonic ideologies, and decenter the certainties of stifling, imposed social structures. It does this by having us laugh at the problems and contradictions of life, and, as a consequence, by making them a source of pleasure. From this perspective, humor is an art for survival. According to John (Fire) Lame Deer, a Minneconjou Sioux leader and holy clown, for people who have suffered as much as the Lakota, "laughter is a precious gift."[26]

In worldwide perspective, humor occurs in culture-specific contexts. If humor is in part an expression of fears, anxieties, and ambiguities, then one can expect the focus and thrust of humor to vary among cultures, for few share the same strains and stresses. A cultural setting is needed, then, to understand humor. As the Lakota wit Vine Deloria, Jr. has phrased it, "One of the best ways to understand a people is to know what makes them laugh."[27] What, then, makes the Sioux laugh?

The Sioux do laugh a lot and many are and have been great jokesters.[28] They laugh among themselves at all levels of society and at the odd behavior of those around them. Much of their humor is rooted in traditional "contrary" wit, Trickster reversals, deadpan joking, and the tall tale. Humor is one of the defining features of Sioux literature and is central to the actual, deeper meaning of their stories.

The Sioux and other Indians have used humor in multiple ways in response to Euro-American colonization. As an example, Deloria and others have used humor in a positive manner to negotiate the Euro-American history of genocide, removal, and oppression. Rather than reverse racism and warfare, humor has been their best and sharpest weapon. Ironic "rez" (reservation) jokes have replaced arrows and bullets, and remain a way of counting coup.[29] This use of humor has been the "cement" of the pan-Indian movement. Shared Columbus and Custer jokes alone have bound together Indian groups who agree on little else except resistance to Euro-American colonization. Humor is also increasingly being used by the Sioux to dispel misconceptions about their lifeway and as an important form of cultural resistance to domination by white American society. The *locus classicus* of these uses of Sioux humor is Vine Deloria, Jr.'s *Custer Died For Your Sins* (1969).[30] Deloria is a master at taking comic potshots at anthropologists, bureaucrats, clerics, the BIA, and many others to raise Indian–White issues.

Another use of humor as a weapon of resistance is the humor of inversion. Here the white world is turned upside down and inside out. It may be expressed in a simple but effective way by wearing a Western shirt backward as if one did not know how to wear it. More seriously, one may invert white ways by rejecting what are perceived to be white values, such as the accumulation of wealth, the adoption of the Protestant work ethic, and driving a new, expensive car. In a more self-defeating manner, inversion may be expressed through tragic self-addiction to fats, sugar, drugs, and alcohol.

Much humor in Sioux culture draws on ancient traditions of the anti-hero Trickster who as comic teacher, fooled and two-faced them, as in the story of "The Boy and the Oak" in chapter 6. A favorite trickster among the Lakota is *Iktome*, the wily spider. *Iktome* represents a no-good, comic know-it-all, who fools the people whenever given an opportunity (thus his name, "One Fools the People"). Trickster tales turn on a comic mistake that teaches valuable lessons, such as a tolerance for deviance, the knowledge that we can mistake circumstances, that we must securely identify our friends and enemies, and so on. These are important teachings, for survival may depend on being alert to the illusions of reality.

The Sioux also, like most societies, have clowns who poke fun, in one way or another, at what others might regard as very serious things. Among the Sioux, the *heyoka* is a sacred clown, a holy fool, whose "sacred play or holy laugher in some ritual performances cleanses wounds, reinforces social norms, and relaxes rules so that people can live with them."[31] Through sacred clowning, the *heyoka* mediates between all things spiritual and worldly (according to Lame Deer, the two are one). As Joseph Epes Brown has commented in reference to Nick Black Elk as a *heyoka*, by fooling around, the sacred clown "shatters the structure of the rite in order to get at the essence of the rite."[32] By comic inversion, the "fool impersonator" teaches the people that nothing is fixed, that all is potentially "contrary," and that the sacred and profane, the funny and the serious, are the twin faces of the cosmos. These are deep-seated principles of Sioux culture rooted in their concept of a balanced world.[33]

Sioux culture is seriously humorous to its core, then. Many Sioux are comic deconstructionists who use humor as serious play in mediating the ambiguities and contradictions of the human condition. Rather than the sullen victim, a better image of the Sioux is the comic artist who draws upon tribal "comic" wisdom to heal and survive. In historical perspective, the Sioux must always have bonded and revitalized, exorcized and healed, and survived through laughter.[34]

The Stereotypes We Know Them By

Stereotypes are conventional, usually oversimplified conceptions or beliefs about a people or a type of person. In novels, films, and American popular culture, images of the Sioux are usually stereotypes. As with other

Indian peoples, these stereotypes are often negative and of males, for images of males have dominated Wild West shows and western films and
videos. Among the most common of these stereotypes are the war-bonneted
"chief," the near-naked "warrior" with face-paint, the "drunken Indian,"
and the Red Power "militant." Because facelessness characterizes Sioux
women and North American Indian women in general, stereotypes of
women, while more varied, are less frequently encountered. The most
popular stereotype of Indian women since World War II is the "princess"
or "maiden." A current variant of this stereotype is the "Pocahontas"
image, which portrays lovely, Barbie-shaped Indian girls sacrificing themselves to save handsome white males. Alternatively, Sioux women are stere-
otyped as drudge-like "squaws."[35]

These stereotypes were originally popularized in the Wild West shows
of the late nineteenth and early twentieth centuries, and later in Hollywood movies and videos, postcards, advertisements, photographs, and
newspapers. Because these were for-profit enterprises, the exotic and "romantic" in Indian life were emphasized rather than the commonplace.
Since few non-Indian Americans had close contact with Indian people,
these stereotypes became widely accepted as fact in popular culture. Many
of these same images have been perpetuated in museum exhibits and scholarly writings, where the Sioux are depicted as either lingering, archaic
remnants of a bygone era or as "primitives" struggling unsuccessfully to
fit into modern American life.[36]

Overly positive, romantic, even utopian stereotypes are as problematic
and often as harmful as are negative images. Positive imagery of the Sioux
increased dramatically in the 1960s and 1970s with the anti-war movement, the environmental movement, and the civil rights movement. The
upswing continued through the last three decades of the twentieth century with New Age religious movements, feminist movements, gay rights
movements, alternative health movements, and New Ecology movements.
Among these "positive" stereotypes are the spiritual "guide" (either male
or female), the mystical environmentalist (the "genuinely natural" Sioux)
in harmony with nature, the Two Spirits person (berdache) free to explore her or his sexuality, and the skillful hunter or valiant warrior who
communes with nature and forest spirits in a world free of politics, grief,
and the strains of daily communal life.

Although positive and even anti-Euro-American, these utopian fanta-
sies are misleading because they portray perfect people unencumbered by
"the complexity of the true human condition."[37] From a non-Indian perspective these images portray Indians as idealized others. From an anthropological perspective, they are as much Euro-American cultural products
as are notions of Sioux women as drudge-like squaws or princesses. They
can be harmful to Indian self-conceptions, for being positive they are more

Figure 8.4   Standing Eagle demonstrating the craft of pipe-making to visitors at Pipestone National Monument in 1980 (postcard published by Northern Minnesota Novelties, Crosslake. Minnesota Historical Society Photograph Collection)

seductive. One frequent result is a painful discordance between who one is and who others think she or he is. Another is the danger of expecting too much of oneself by trying to live up to a past that never really was.

Of course, negative stereotyping was and is not confined to non-Indian Americans. The Sioux once characterized their intimidated Arikara neighbors as "women" and some Sioux refer to tribal members they believe have "sold out" to the federal government as "Uncle Tomahawks." Stereotypes of the other are used by all societies to help define themselves and to differentiate themselves (usually positively) from the "other." Nor can stereotypes be eradicated by simply exposing the problem, for people with vested economic and social interests, whether white American or Sioux, will rarely acknowledge the other as an equal.[38]

Nonetheless, readers intent on forging a multicultural American society must work diligently to discredit popular stereotypes of the Sioux and of all "others" in general. The reasons are many and varied. These caricatures continue to exert powerful, negative effects on how some Sioux see themselves; inhibit Sioux in situations of discrimination from rightfully pursuing their cultural identity; misrepresent social realities and cultural processes; set a (false) standard of cultural authenticity against which the Sioux-ness or Indian-ness of some individuals are evaluated (even within Sioux society itself); belittle the lives of Sioux men and women by stereotyping them as "squaw" or "chief"; deflect attention from the lives of real Sioux women and men, who today may be teachers, factory workers, lawyers, casino employees, and business owners; and inhibit an understanding of what life was like in Sioux society in the nineteenth century and earlier (for instance, most Sioux men in the nine-

Figure 8.5   A typical postcard portrait of a Western Sioux family in 1940
(Minnesota Historical Society Photograph Collection)

teenth century never attacked a wagon train or were attacked by the US cavalry).

As part of their struggle for self-determination, a few Sioux began to aggressively respond to these images in the 1960s.[39] With difficulty, they have managed to exert some influence on how images of their people are portrayed in film, video, and other popular media. Anthropologists have become more actively involved, too, in countering the distorting stereotypes of the Sioux, both negative and positive, that permeate popular culture both here in America and overseas. It is an obligation of the profession to engage in critical interpretations of stereotypes, repair misinterpretations of cultural differences, and help provide new concepts of the Sioux and of other American Indians. For the Sioux, this understanding may not be as utopian or as flattering as their positive stereotypes, but it will be more realistic and show them to be a part, along with all other peoples, of the human condition.[40] The goal is to help affect the way future generations perceive Sioux culture, values, and historical actions.

From an ethnohistorical perspective, stereotypes are a critical focus of study, for they are not static but shift in form and emphasis depending on historical and local circumstances.[41] As ever-present psychological components of self-identity, they were and are one means by which groups of people define themselves and define each other. An exploration of the history and range of stereotypes imposed on the Sioux and used by the Sioux would provide insight into how the Sioux have been constituted by others and have constituted themselves through time.

Who is a Sioux?

One of the most contentious and vexing issues facing the Sioux today is the question, Who is a Sioux? More precisely, what does it mean to say that someone does or does not have a legitimate right to say she or he is a Sioux? By whose definition or criteria should this be true? The question of Sioux identity is important for many reasons: (1) There are different definitions of what it means to be a Sioux or more generally an Indian both among Indians and non-Indians. Whose definition should be followed and why? (2) Who is considered a Sioux will influence the course of Sioux self-determination in the twenty-first century; (3) the ability to decide who is a member of a nation is a measure of that nation's sovereign standing; (4) some individuals fraudulently identify themselves as Sioux or more broadly as Indian for economic gain. Definitional criteria are obviously needed here; (5) identity conflicts are a source of anxiety for multicultural and mixed-blood individuals, and for individuals both on and off reservations; and (6) the criteria for who is a Sioux have changed through time with shifting social, economic, and political environments. How will these criteria change in the future and why?[42]

A common, false assumption is that all Sioux shared a common identity until forced onto reservations and "assimilated" after 1890. It seems more likely that the personal identity of Sioux individuals was always diverse and shifting. In the past, as today, an individual's identity was multilayered, with the layers composed of such institutions as the immediate family, the extended family, the *tiospaye*, a men's or women's association, the band, the tribe, and the nation. As the composition and nature of these institutions changed, one's identity would have changed, too. Indeed, before the occurrence of the late prehistoric tribalization process one's identity as a Sioux and even as a Lakota, Dakota, or Yankton–Yanktonai may have been non-existent or at best only weakly developed. As the domain of the Sioux stretched ever outward from northwestern Wisconsin to the Rocky Mountains, the outer layers of Sioux identity would have become ever more diverse. Consequently, by the reservation period the Sioux were a collection of ethnic groups bound together by historic tradition and a common language.

Today, Sioux communities are even more complex and diverse than they were in the late nineteenth century. The primary reasons are assimilation, acculturation, and intermarriage with non-Indians, and the multi-ethnic composition of most reservations.[43] For these and other reasons, most contemporary Sioux are multicultural and of mixed-blood ancestry. This diversity is reflected in the variety of references that the Sioux use to describe themselves. Examples are mixed-blood, long-hair, full-blood, traditional, multicultural, progressive, and enrolled or unenrolled.

Individuals and communities manage this diversity in different ways. Some Sioux who live on or near reservations are English-speaking Christians. Like many other Americans, they would like their children to have a good education and a professional career. Other Sioux are primarily interested in restoring traditional practices and preserving the Dakota language. In general, a variety of religious orientations are present in Sioux communities, including Peyotism, the traditional Sun Dance, and several Christian sects; individuals are likely to participate at times in two or more of these orientations. Like other Americans, some individuals have abandoned, if only temporarily, religious practice of any kind. Many other Sioux live away from reservations in towns and cities, and are subject to additional tugs and pulls on their personal identity.

As should be clear, individuals who identify themselves as Sioux are taking a wider variety of paths in their lives today than at any time in the past. As a result, there is no easy answer to the question, "Who is a Sioux?" Rather than opt for one among many answers, this discussion focuses on some of the issues involved in understanding what is involved in working toward an answer to the question.

The answer to the question "Who is a Sioux?" was much clearer and definite in Sioux communities before the twentieth century. In the past, tribal membership was determined by family and community membership. Even then, a person's identity as a Sioux might be somewhat fuzzy, for people were adopted and introduced into a family for a variety of reasons, as mentioned earlier in the text. Many others married into a Sioux tribe. Besides Indians from other tribes, these new "Sioux" included French, English, and other Europeans, and Afro-Americans. Their children were "mixed-bloods" who in turn married other Sioux. The notion of a full-blooded Lakota or Dakota people, then, is largely a myth. Nor was degree of blood quantum a measure of loyalty to Sioux interests. Consequently, by the early nineteenth century the idea of defining a Sioux purely by genetic makeup was nonsensical.[44] What made a person a Sioux was language, customs, clothes – in a word, culture. Sioux identity was fracturing, however, along geographical lines as some bands moved increasingly westward and adopted new customs.

Sioux identity was subjected to increasing stress for several reasons during the early reservation period. First, government agents and missionaries attempted to alienate Sioux from the places and communities, and the traditional daily activities, of their youth. Second, as important was the practice initiated by the US government to determine who was eligible for treaty benefits and, later, the allotment process. Formal rolls were compiled that listed the members of each reservation group. Generally, one-quarter degree of blood was required of the group into which one wished to be enrolled to be accepted by the government as a member. Besides excluding some people who might be Sioux culturally, this federally imposed criterion for Sioux identity usurped the right of the Sioux as sovereign nations to determine their own membership. The process resulted in "rifts" between groups with different blood quanta, who thought the federal government was giving preferential treatment to one group or another as a matter of policy.[45] Finally, the attempt to assimilate Sioux children between the 1880s and the 1930s by indoctrinating them in Western values, and by denying them access to traditional beliefs and practices, addled further the issue of Sioux identity.[46]

As important as these early problems are, space allows only a listing of issues of Sioux identity after the 1930s. As will become apparent, contemporary Sioux identity involves a complex interplay between family histories, educational background, tribal associations, governmental policy, and personality, among other dimensions. Importantly, the identities of individual Sioux are necessarily being worked out not in a vacuum but in interaction with and in opposition to other identities that exist in the world today. Seven of these issues are mentioned here.

The first issue is the difficulty many multi-heritage individuals have in establishing a satisfactory and acceptable ethnic identity. Some individuals who are biologically Sioux (by tribal standards) know little about traditional Sioux culture because no one taught them, they have no interest in being a Sioux, or have decided not to identify themselves as Sioux or an Indian in a largely non-Indian social and work environment. Many of these individuals were not born into a tribal environment and are not active in their tribe. Are they Sioux? Bi-racial individuals may have difficulty reconciling their non-Indian European or African ancestry with their Sioux ancestry. Those who live in cities might prefer to hide their Sioux ancestry because of racism, prejudice, and stereotypes. Others would like to adopt a Sioux identity but do not look like a Sioux. Because of the Euro-American-introduced concept of race, there may be attempts to exclude them from Sioux membership to protect tribal purity, benefits, or both. The result has been an identity crisis among some individuals and some degree of divisiveness about who is a Sioux.[47]

A second issue is the criterion by which the federal government is willing to recognize a person as Sioux or more broadly as an Indian. Because some criterion was and is necessary to determine who qualifies for services, the notion of a blood quantum was an initial requirement. Such a notion, for instance, was contained in the language of the IRA of 1934. IRA councils then had the task of setting a specific criterion for tribal membership. As a rule, the BIA provided services to all individuals who had 25 percent or more Indian blood. These policies replaced traditional criteria of kinship and culture with Euro-American concepts of race. Since the 1960s, tribal communities have increasingly used political action and court cases to win the right to determine their own membership. The somewhat confusing direction the US government has taken since is reflected in the various definitions of "Indian" in subsequent legislation. The Indian Education Act of 1972 includes an all-inclusive definition of "Indian." By contrast, the Self-determination Act of 1975 defines an "Indian" as a person who is a member of an Indian tribe. Today, the primary means used by the US government to identify an individual as a member of a Sioux tribe is by enrollment. Is this a fair criterion? According to this definition, who is being included and who is being excluded?

A third issue is tribal criteria for membership. Different Sioux tribes or communities have adopted different criteria for determining tribal membership at times because of shifting cultural circumstances and economic fortunes, such as the development of a successful tribal casino. The rationale is that a sovereign nation has the right to decide its own rules of membership. The most common membership criteria among Sioux tribes is one-quarter blood quantum and descent from a tribal member; children do not have to be born on the reservation.[48] This means that one of a person's four grandparents was a tribal member and that this grandparent was descended from four tribal members. In practice, these calculations may be difficult to determine and verify for a variety of reasons.

While allowing tribes to set their own membership criteria is a means of recognizing their cultural differences, the practice has resulted in a number of problems: (1) some tribes have applied membership criteria that other Americans might consider unfair, even though the tribe is guaranteed that right as a sovereign nation; (2) some people who consider themselves Sioux, who grew up on a reservation, and who have a strong Sioux identity may not have the legal right to be considered a Sioux; (3) for one reason or another, tribal leaders may dictate how tribal membership is defined; and (4) not everyone who claims to be a Sioux agrees that they need to be tribally enrolled or even recognized by their tribe to be a Sioux. While the issue of tribally defined criteria for membership may be contentious at times, the tribal right to determine its own membership is a mark of tribal sovereignty.

A fourth issue of Sioux identity is the tension between traditionalists and progressives.[49] During the last half-century, groups of American Indians have increasingly argued among and between themselves over who has the right to be called an Indian. Traditionalists worry that the inclusion of people who are not culturally Sioux will dilute the identity of the Sioux as a people. They work to preserve and resurrect the "old ways." On the other hand, at least some progressives find traditionalists amusing relics of the past and uncivilized. They support Euro-American style economic development or other values. Progressives might see the removal of burial mounds that stand in the way of casino expansion more important to the future of their community than the preservation of a sacred place of uncertain tribal affiliation. Because of these contrasting attitudes, some individuals, especially those who do not speak the language, live on the reservation, or look "Indian," do not enjoy the "cultural entirety of being Lakota" (or Dakota).[50] Must a person who is Sioux by blood quantum share traditional customs, values, and beliefs to be a welcome member of a Sioux tribe? Should people who are not culturally Sioux be excluded from tribal membership so that others may maintain a sense of community belonging and a unique, historic Sioux identity?

A fifth issue is just how or even should an identity as a Sioux be expressed. Typical symbols and expressions of Indianness are hairstyle, items of "Indian" costume, and the use of slang words, such as "rez," "Indian time," and *wasichus* (the Lakota word for Whites), that function to create an "in-group" identity. Other expressions of belonging include the use of the Dakota language, the adoption of "Sioux" attitudes toward other Indian groups and non-Indians, shared patterns of joking and teasing, and participation in powwows and tribal and Indian community-center activities in general.

A sixth issue touched on earlier is the identity of urban versus reservation Sioux. In a cost-cutting maneuver in the 1950s, the US government initiated a program that moved large numbers of Indians away from reservations. Many of these individuals ended up in major urban areas.[51] At the same time, Congress cut back on the amount of money it gave reservations. In response to the financial squeeze, some reservations encouraged people to leave so there would be more funds and services for those who stayed. Some of these reservations also began to require reservation residency to maintain tribal membership, access to federal funds, or both.[52]

Currently, most Sioux live off reservations and within urban communities. Many of these individuals have maintained lifelong ties to their tribal community but others have not. Some of the latter continue to identify themselves as Sioux and some do not. Urban Sioux intent on preserving their tribal identity attend intertribal powwows or sweats, urban community centers, and other pan-Indian tribal institutions and organizations. A few enter university Indian studies centers or send their children to an urban Indian school. By the nature of these activities, they have less direct contact with their relatives on reservations than Sioux who make other decisions. By the year 2000, an increasing number of Sioux are the third generation of their family to live off-reservation in a town or city. More likely than not, they live in mixed Indian communities that not only lack the problems of reservation tribal government but have a strong pan-Indian, rather than specifically tribal, cultural identity. This group, too, is developing its own cultural symbols and understanding of what it is to be an Indian in America today.

A seventh issue is ethnic differences between Sioux tribes or bands and the continued, long-term separation of distinct tribal communities on different reservations. Do the Lakota, Dakota, Yankton, and Yanktonai consider each other equally "Sioux" today? Do the dispersed communities within these divisions consider themselves members of the same ethnic group?

In spite of 100 years of attempted assimilation, the Sioux have maintained a form of self-identification. Nonetheless, these Native American people are continually exposed to globally homogenizing forces, such as the radio, newspapers, television, and even the World Wide Web, that make the preservation of tribal identities and culture difficult. Because of growing wealth disparities due to casinos and a large urban population, the question "Who is a Sioux?" will remain a contemporary issue that will be negotiated and renegotiated in the context of shifting economic, institutional, and cultural relations. Since population size makes a difference in income, will internecine bickering over identity increase as competition for casino funds accelerate? How does a nation accommodate internal sovereign peoples within its borders? How will the politics of blood quantum play itself out? Who will be a Sioux in the year 2100?

The Sioux people were and continue to be a loose alliance of native North American nations. While many continue to live in poverty and misery, many others are actively engaged in recovering and practicing their own cultural traditions. For all of the reasons mentioned above, their road to true sovereignty will not be easy, straightforward, or uncomplicated. Nonetheless, spirit, determination, and vision burn brightly. In my view, the following story captures the passionate expectancy of this return to cultural pride and independence as the Sioux enter the twenty-first century.[53]

Come On and Soar, We Are Eagles!

By accident, two eagle eggs were placed among chicken eggs on a farm. When they hatched, the newborn eaglets copied the behavior of the chickens around them. They spent their days pecking and scratching, pecking and scratching. One day one turned to the other and said, "I don't feel like a chicken. I think I'm something else." The other eaglet replied, "No, no. We're chickens. We're supposed to peck and scratch. That is what chickens do." So the eaglets went back to pecking and scratching, pecking and scratching – and months passed.

Eventually, a more mature eagle flying overhead looked down and saw them pecking and scratching, pecking and scratching. The eagle flew down and said, "What are you doing? You're eagles." "No, no," said the eaglets, "We're chickens. We're supposed to peck and scratch." "Nonsense," said the eagle, "you're eagles. Let me carry you high up into the air and show you how to soar." "No, no," said the eaglets, who were afraid, "We're chickens and chickens are not supposed to soar." However, with encouragement from the eagle, the more adventurous of the two eaglets agreed to be carried high up into the air to learn to soar. At first, after the eagle had let go, the eaglet tumbled and fell through the air, even though it wildly flapped its wings. At the last moment, it righted itself and began to soar through the air. It soared and soared through the sky, first in one direction and then in another. Finally, it swooped down toward the other eaglet and said, "Come on and soar, we are eagles!"

Notes

1 Reading the Sioux

1. There is disagreement over the origin and meaning of the word "Sioux" (Treuer 1994:27–9). I follow Parks and DeMallie (1992:234), who find little support for the now popular, pejorative etymologies "snake-like-ones" or "lesser adders." The Ojibwa word for the Sioux, spelt here as *Nadouessis* or *Naudoweissious*, has alternative spellings, such as *Nadouesioux*, *Nadonessiou*, and *Nadoweisiw-eg*. Most Indian tribes are known today by a Euro-American mashing of another group's name for them; the name generally means "speaker of a foreign tongue." For instance, the word Cheyenne comes from the Lakota word *sha-hi'ye-la*, meaning "people of an alien speech." Some ethnologists prefer the terms Santee, Yankton–Yanktonai, and Teton to Dakota, Yankton–Yanktonai, and Lakota, as used in this text.
2. For the Enlightenment, see Williams (1999) and Munck (2000).
3. Rosenau 1992:93.
4. For an introduction to logical positivism as a research program, see Gibbon 1989.
5. Rosenau 1992:77-91.
6. Rosenau 1992:62–7.
7. Giddens 1984:2.
8. For Freud's concept of the decentered, fragmented, and heterogeneous subject, see Flax 1990:59.
9. Lévi-Strauss 1966:247–55.
10. Rosenau 1992:42–61.
11. Rosenau 1992:34–41.
12. Searle 1995.
13. The distinction between writerly and readerly texts was developed by Roland Barthes (1974, which is an English translation of the original 1970 French publication).
14. Foucault 1979; Barthes 1977.
15. Some readers may consider the above three sections "too negative." A few words should be said, then, about my view of historical ethnography. In my view, acknowledging that there has been a loss of innocence in understand-

ing other peoples is not the same as acknowledging that nothing truthful about them can be learned. While unavoidably biased in one manner or another, ethnographies and early historic reports are not the same as fictional texts. There was a logic to traditional Sioux culture, as there is to the way of life of the Sioux today. Either certain events happened in the past or they did not. What is problematic is the interpretation – the reading or understanding – of that logic and of those events. Simply denying the existence of these problems of understanding is poor scholarship and lax thinking; the issues must be grappled with and resolved (which is not the same as solved!). Our present understanding of historical ethnography empowers and challenges readers; their diverse readings promise to enrich our understanding of the peoples of the world. Rather than "too negative," then, there is optimism in this view – or so I believe.

2 .   The Prehistory of the Sioux, 9500 bc–ad 1650

1. Wilford 1937, 1944.
2. Johnson 1984, 1985; Birk and Johnson 1992; Aufderheide et al. 1994.
3. Schneider 1994:27–35. Origin beliefs among contemporary Sioux are as varied as they are among non-Indian Americans. Many twentieth-century Sioux are Christians and believe in some version of the biblical origin story. Others have adopted an evolutionary, scientific viewpoint. Still others, like many non-Indian Americans, prefer a traditional answer to the question of their origins. This section focuses upon the latter in the expectation that traditional origin beliefs may provide insightful interpretations of the archaeological record.
4. Mooney 1991 [1896]:1058; Kellogg 1925:172–3; Swanton 1943; Thwaites 1959 [1896–1901]:64:279–80; Hassrick 1964:62 (n.1); Robinson 1967 [1904]:19; Treuer 1994:17–18; Powers 1996a:299. Treuer (1994:17) captures the tone of these claims: it "is fairly certain that the Dakota had lived for many years east and south of the Minnesota–Wisconsin lake area" and did not fully occupy the Upper Mississippi watershed until the seventeenth century. In general, the Dakota's original homeland was thought to be the Appalachian Mountains or somewhere further to the north and east. See Howard (1984:37-41) for the version referred to here.
5. Landes 1968:22–5; Pond 1986 [1908]:174.
6. Blegen 1975:20. There are other proposed homelands for the Sioux besides the three mentioned here. For instance, Lund (1980:7) believes the Dakota entered Minnesota from a southwesterly direction in the late prehistoric period.
7. For Lakota genesis themes recorded by Walker, see Walker (1983:206–7) and Jahner (1987). For a nineteenth-century photograph of the Black Hills, see Bonvillain 1994:18.
8. Winchell 1911:68; Little 1985; Hoover 1996a:161; Howard 1980 [1966]:2–3.
9. Hurt (1974:43) concludes from a study of "a large body of historical records"

that these "documents all indicate that the Sioux, when they first came to the attention of the French, lived in the general area of the headwaters of the Mississippi." According to Schoolcraft (1853–7:2:172), Dakota (Lakota?) tradition identified the region near Leech Lake in the northwoods as their ancestral homeland. However, others favor a prairie homeland for the Western Sioux (Michlovic 1985; Gregg 1994:93; Picha 1996:24–5, 50). Picha (1996:24) proposes an association between "ancestral Dakota" (presumably ancestral Lakota or at least Western Sioux) and the Late Woodland Lake Benton ceramic series. Lake Benton ceramics occur throughout the prairie-lakes region of southwestern Minnesota between c. ad 700–1200 (Anfinson 1997:75–85).

10. Service 1979; Fried 1967; Kottak 1991:103–5. It should be stressed that hunter-gatherer societies and bands are not coterminous kinds of social organizations, and that hunter-gatherer societies display a wide range of sociocultural complexity (Lourandos 1997:8–31).

11. Sahlins 1968; Fried 1967, 1968, 1975; Helm 1968; Upham 1990; Gregg 1991; Kottak 1991:105–21.

12. For a sampling of the literature on the tribalization process, see Sahlins 1968; Service 1971; Fried 1975:95–105; Bender 1985; Dincauze and Hasenstab 1989; Ferguson and Whitehead 1992; Keeley 1996.

13. Eder 1987.

14. For a sample of the literature on ethnicity from an archaeological/historical perspective, see Shennan 1989, 1991; Friedman 1992; Graves-Brown et al. 1996; Jones 1997:56–105.

15. See chapter 3 for the value of viewing the Sioux from a cultural perspective.

16. For the archaeological signatures of social identities, see Haarland 1977; Kimes et al. 1982; Shennan 1989, 1991; Graves-Brown et al. 1996; Jones 1997:107–27; Lourandos 1997:29–30. For examples of contemporary studies, see Hodder 1982 and Roberts et al. 1995. .

17. For the animal and plant biomes of the northwoods, see Benyus (1989) and Daniel and Sullivan (1981); for Minnesota more generally, see Tester 1995.

18. Johnson 1984, 1985; Gibbon 1994; Mather and Abel 2000; Mather 2000. Johnson (1984) divided the early Terminal (Late) Woodland tradition in the Mille Lacs region into two phases, Vineland (c. ad 800–1000) and Wahkon (c. ad 1000–1300). Archaeological complexes refer to similar appearing sets of artifacts (e.g., pieces of pottery, bone, and stone); phases add the dimension of time to a complex. Although the welter of archaeological complexes listed in the text (e.g., Brainerd, Malmo, Howard Lake) might seen confusing (and they are), they are mentioned here to point the way for further study by the reader of the prehistory of the Sioux.

19. Johnson 1971:17–19, 1984; Mather 2000:60. Two particularly large house floors excavated at the Wilford site (21ML12) are reasonable precursors for the historic Mdewakanton summer bark house (Johnson 1962; Mather 2000:70).

20. McKern 1963; Ritzenthaler 1966; Van Dyke and Oerichbauer 1988; Meer et al. 1994.

21. Johnson 1984. In contrast to their abundance on Minnesota Oneota sites,

only one bison scapula hoe has been found in Mille Lacs habitation sites (Birk and Johnson 1992:209).

22. Mather 2000:69; Bailey 1997; Thompson 2000; Valppu 2000. For animal remains at Mille Lacs sites, see Johnson 1985:158–9; Whelan 1990; Mather et al. 2000.

23. Michlovic 1987; Michlovic and Schneider 1993. Along the Red River, Sandy Lake assemblages seem concentrated between Fargo–Moorhead and Grand Forks–Crookston (Michlovic 1985:134–5).

24. The scarcity of French and English trade goods in these sites may be due to the difficulty traders had in reaching the Mille Lacs Lake area by canoe (Blair 1996 [1911]:2, 32, 117; Birk and Johnson 1992:233; also see Birk 1994). Although the Psinomani are technically hunter-gathers, they were a complex hunting and gathering group for this area.

25. Ossenberg 1974. For a recent study of prehistoric biological populations in the Upper Mississippi River basin that, while informative for other aspects of this model, does not include a Psinomani sample, see Myster (2001). For criticism of Ossenberg's sampling categories, see Syms 1985:90–2 and Saylor 1980.

26. The important Mille Lacs area Cooper Mound skeletal sample, which seems associated with emergent Mdewakanton Dakota, was not included in Ossenberg's study.

27. On the timing of the separation of the Assiniboin, see Treuer 1994:37–8. Linguistic studies support an earlier, prehistoric (c. ad 1300) separation (Springer and Witkowski 1982; Syms 1985:75–7; also see Parks 1988:177). The fact that the Assiniboin are already listed as a separate nation by Nicollet in 1634–5 adds support to this suggestion (Winchell 1911:519).

28. Skeletal studies indicate a long-term biological continuity in the northern Plains, with some in-migration in the late prehistoric period (Key 1994:186; Myster 2001:210, 230). Also see Owsley and Rose 1997; Benchley et al. 1997.

29. Scherer 1998.

30. See Overstreet (1995) for a discussion of the homeland of the Oneota. Glenn (1974) and Key (1983) compare populations of Siouan speakers; also see Sullivan 1919.

31. Rapid advances in determining biological relationships are being made through the direct analysis of genetic material, which can be extracted from bones, teeth, and hair. Although DNA studies that involve the Sioux (e.g., Smith et al. 1999) are rare at the time of writing, they provide the best available means for assessing ancestor/descendant relationships between living populations and prehistoric skeletal populations.

32. For the fundamentals of historical linguistics, see Campbell 1997, 1998; for a short overview with a focus on Siouan speakers, see Schneider 1994:45–54.

33. Swadesh 1952; Lees 1953.

34. Springer and Witkowski 1982. For other accounts, see Hollow and Parks 1980:80; Syms 1985; T. Grimm 1985. There are significant differences between these accounts. For example, while Springer and Witkowski date the

split between Dakota, Chiwere, and Dhegiha at about ad 700, Hollow and Parks (1980:Table 3, Fig. 1) place the same split at c. ad 1200. The results of a quantitative study of Siouan linguistic relationships by Richard Carter are generally similar to those of Springer and Witkowski (Syms 1985:86–8).

35. For the formula, see Gudschinsky 1956. For cautions, see Bergsland and Vogt 1962; Hollow and Parks 1980.

36. For studies of the Siouan language family, see references in the topical review of the Dakota language in chapter 7.

37. The Yankton and Yanktonai are generally referred to as the Yankton–Yanktonai in socio-political divisions of the Sioux because they speak the same dialect. This implies that they split apart from the same ancestral tribe more recently than ad 1500 and lived in adjacent areas, as they have in the historic period, during their migrations from the northwoods.

38. In terms proposed by Binford (1980) and Lourandos (1997), these band societies most likely had a fluid group structure, with an emphasis upon mobility, rather "open" social networks, relatively "immediate-return" economic strategies, and a "residential" strategy in which the community moved to spatially dispersed resources. Compared to tribal social networks, there was less emphasis upon polygyny, ceremony, exchange, feasting, and boundary maintenance.

39. The dating of the emergence of the Psinomani complex remains unsettled and unsettling. Snortland (1994:66) reports a radiocarbon date of ad 890–1260 for a Sandy Lake pottery vessel associated with a human interment at the Jamestown Mounds (32SN22) in eastern North Dakota, and Rose and David Kluth have obtained several radiocarbon dates that place Sandy Lake ware in the Headwaters region of Minnesota during the twelfth century. However, Sandy Lake radiocarbon dates in other areas generally postdate ad 1300 (Justin and Schuster 1994:82–3). I suspend judgment on pre-ad 1300 radiocarbon dates for two reasons. First, unusually early radiocarbon dates have been obtained in both of these areas for other archaeological complexes. Second, there are much larger amounts of Blackduck–Kathio pottery throughout central Minnesota than Sandy Lake pottery. If Blackduck–Kathio pottery dates to ad 800–1000 and Sandy Lake pottery to ad 1000–1650, then Sandy Lake pottery should be about three times more abundant. The reverse proportion seems to be the case. On the other end of the timescale, it is possible that the eastern end of the Blackduck–Clam River–Kathio continuum continued to flourish in northwestern Wisconsin for some time after its demise at the Mille Lacs Locality (Mather 2000:61). The possibility remains, then, that the timing of the emergence of the Psinomani complex may have varied from one region to another. The date of ad 1300 adopted here for the emergence of the Psinomani complex, at least in the Mille Lacs area, follows Johnson's (1984) suggested cultural chronology and available radiocarbon dates (Mather 2000:24). If the emergence of the Psinomani complex is related to the movement of Oneota from the Red Wing area of Minnesota, as suggested by Johnson, then the date may be somewhere in the ad 1250–1300 range, for some archaeologists have suggested that Oneota from that area entered the Central Illinois River valley in the late thirteenth century.

Some confirmation of the nature of this structural transformation comes from the transformation of historic Minnesota Ojibwa populations. According to Eggan (1966:94): "The Chippewa, as the Ojibwa south of the (Canadian) border are generally called, had better weapons, but the Dakota had larger villages and were better organized. The struggle was over hunting grounds, and, in order to succeed, the Chippewa had to develop the village as the permanent unit and to organize village alliances and warrior organizations, which were unknown in the north."

40. The determination of the number and location of these settlement clusters remains a primary objective of prehistoric Sioux studies. Besides Mille Lacs Lake, settlements were probably located at Big Sandy Lake, Knife Lake, Red Lake, Leech Lake, Lake Winnibigoshish, Yellow Lake (Wisconsin), Pokegama Lake, and Bay Lake. However, given the frequent movement of settlements in the early historic period (as judged by their location on maps of the time), the presence of a settlement in the early historic period is not sufficient evidence for the presence of a prehistoric Psinomani settlement. In 1695, Tioscaté, a Dakota who went east with Pierre Le Sueur, asked the governor-general of New France for protection for 22 villages, but his frame of reference (e.g., settlement clusters? only Dakota villages?) is unclear (Brodhead 1853–87:9:610).

41. Again, in terms suggested by Binford (1980) and Lourandos (1997), these later, more complex hunter-gatherer tribal societies are characterized by "bounded, discrete groups"; more formal leadership; "delayed-return" economic strategies; a "logistical" strategy (including storage), where resources are obtained and brought back to a central base camp; a strong emphasis upon territorial and boundary maintenance, feasting, ceremony, and exchange; higher levels of sedentism (decreased mobility); and an increased use of fixed economic facilities (weirs, traps, garden beds, fields, and the like).

42. Emerson 1999.

43. Johnson 1984, 1991:5. Birk and Johnson (1992:211) refer to it as "a unique version of Oneota, in which wild rice is a substitute for maize."

44. Gibbon 2001.

45. Pond 1986 [1908]:174. According to oral tradition, the Iowa and Oto moved westward to join the Omaha along the Big Sioux or Missouri River (Hurt 1974:63–4). According to Winchell (1911:535), the Iowa were expelled from Minnesota by the Dakota sometime after 1679, for the Iowa were living " on the west side of the Mississippi at and below Lake Pepin" at that time.

46. Milner 1999; also see Milner et al. 1991.

47. Willey 1990.

48. Emerson and Brown 1992.

49. E. Grimm 1985. Archaeologists have not explored the impact of the expansion of the Big Woods on Minnesota's late prehistoric societies (but see Birk 1991:243–4). Denser woods may have decreased the size of the habitat preferred by both bison and deer.

50. Divale and Harris 1976.

51. Birk (1977) suggests that the small number of known burials under mounds

may mean that they represent a form of status burial. He also refers to un-published data that indicate that the usual burial track was inhumation in shallow pits on or close to habitation sites.

52.   Resource productivity may have been manipulated in other ways besides the use of garden beds. Among the possibilities are: (1) the fire management of adjacent prairie ecosystems and their plant and animal communities (Johnson 1985:162); (2) the water management of wild rice beds; (3) the more inten-sive use of "marginal" environments; and (4) shifts in procurement strate-gies toward procedures and devices that captured prey or gathered plant foods en masse, thus maximizing the use of time, energy, and people power (more labor-intensive collecting, processing, and storage of plant foods; more communal hunting, in particular for bison; and more communal fishing, with the use of weirs, traps, artificial drainage systems, and the like). It should be noted, however, that fixed fishing equipment, such as weirs, was not normal Dakota gear in the nineteenth century (Landes 1968:192; Pond 1986 [1908]:30, 40), although the Yankton (most likely) did build large weirs in South Dakota (Haberman 1983). The accumulation of stored surpluses of food would have been necessary to support the elaborate systems of intergroup feasting, ceremony, and exchange that cement tribal alliances together. The complexity of the Psinomani socio-economic-religious system has been masked, I would argue, by the societal dislocations and demands of the fur trade of the seventeenth century. For the position of the buffer/war zone, see Hickerson 1965:54–7 and Watrall 1968.

53.   DeMallie's (1982a:11) claim that early historical documents do not support the existence of a confederation known as the Seven Council Fires does not weaken this view, for these documents are based as they must be on the memory of informants. According to the position adopted here, the Seven Council Fires had begun to break up by the early sixteenth century. As Hurt (1974:14) em-phasizes, the "fact that they referred to seven fires ... and not a single one indi-cates that they viewed themselves more as a confederacy of tribes" (than as a single tribe). Today, the word "alliance" rather than "confederacy" is preferred.

54.   Gibbon 1987.

55.   The model sketched in this chapter provides a spatial–temporal series of events and a set of processes that together re-construct Sioux prehistory. However, because of the fragile nature of the evidence, many issues remain open to question. For instance, when *did* the ancestral Sioux enter Minne-sota? Did the proposed Psinomani alliance form at about ad 1300, as sug-gested here, or earlier? Who *were* the competitors of the alliance? Do the material culture differences between the Blackduck–Kathio–Clam River Continuum and the Psinomani complex *really* represent a shift from a band-level to a tribal-level social organization? What *is* the degree of biological distance among communities of Sioux, and how can these differences be explained? When *did* northern Siouan languages and dialects emerge? What *were* the socio-economic pathways actually taken by Psinomani settlement clusters? The range of unresolved issues that awaits further investigation is truly immense. As stressed in the introduction to this chapter, the explicit archaeological study of Sioux prehistory is in its infancy.

3.   The French and English Fur Trade, 1650–1803

1. For the possible impact of Euro-African epidemic diseases, see Green 1993. For Oneota movements, see Gibbon 2001. For the impact of the Little Ice Age, see Baerreis et al. 1976; E. Grimm 1985; Grove 1988. For the movement of eastern Indians around the Great Lakes, see White (1991) and Tanner (1987).

2. For an overview of the Iroquois Wars, see Richter and Merrell 1987; Tanner 1987:29–35; White 1991:1–49. The period of the Iroquois Wars was a time of increasing threat, disruption, technological imbalance, and shifting alliances for the Eastern Sioux.

3. For the first mention of the Sioux, see Kellogg 1925:89; Thwaites 1959 [1896–1901]:18:231–3 and 23:225; Hurt 1974:43–5. Jean Nicollet, a French explorer, may have recorded the first reference to the Dakota Sioux when he visited Green Bay, Wisconsin, in 1634–5 (Winchell 1911:519). For the *coureurs de bois*, see Adams (1961:142) and Nute (1978 [1943]:64n, 184).

4. Adams 1961; Nute 1978 [1943]:58–69; Upham 1905.

5. For general overviews of the French period in the western Great Lakes, and French explorers and traders, see Anderson 1984:29–57; Blair 1996 [1911]; Blegen 1975:31–62; Folwell 1956:I:1–52; Little 1985; Nute 1978 [1943]; Gilman 1992; Gilman 1974; Kellogg 1967 [1917], 1925; Peterson and Anfinson 1984; Tanner 1987; Thwaites 1959 [1896–1901], 1902–8; White 1991:1–268; Wedel 1974; Hickerson 1974c:13–69. Hurt (1974:43–66) provides a documentary history of encounters with the Sioux for the seventeenth century.

6. Burpee 1968 [1927]; Hurt 1974:71–83. For French forts in the Minnesota area, see Birk 1982, 1991, 1992; Kellogg 1925, 1927; Nute 1930; Hickerson 1974c:23–47. These French posts were built in areas that were easily accessible by waterway, such as Prairie Island, Lake Pepin, Mankato (the juncture of the Minnesota and Blue Earth rivers), and the juncture of the Little Elk and Mississippi rivers, which is 50 kilometers southwest of the Mille Lacs sites (Birk and Johnson 1992:219).

7. For the English period in the western Great Lakes, see Allen 1976; Anderson 1984:58–102; Folwell 1956:I:53–72; Gilman 1992; Kellogg 1935; Tanner 1987; White 1991:269–516. For English period travelers and traders, see Abel 1939; Ekberg and Foley 1989; Gates 1965; Gelb 1993; Nasatir 1931, 1990; Hickerson 1974c:70–82; Parker 1976; Ronda 1994.

8. Nicolas Perrot remarked that in the 1680s some Huron and Ottawa had encroached onto the eastern tributaries of the St. Croix River, including the Namakagan, with Dakota permission (Hickerson 1974c:13–14). The Dakota apparently received their first French merchandise from this group in about 1656, when the Huron and Ottawa lived at the northern end of Lake Pepin (White 1994:381–2). Among the items they received from Radisson and Grosseilliers in 1659–60 were "a kettle, six hatchets, two dozen knives, six files, two dozen awls, two dozen needles, six dozen looking glasses made of tin, a dozen little bells, six ivory combs, and some vermilion" (White 1994:384).

9. Ehrenberg 1987a:5. Franquelin's map was based on Joliet's 1674 "lost" map of the Mississippi (Warkentin and Ruggles 1970:37, 39; Delanglez 1943, 1946; Wood 1987:28). For reviews of early maps, see Wedel 1974; Picha 1996:29–46; Ehrenberg 1987a; Wood 1983, 1987; Warkentin and Ruggles 1970; Tucker 1942; Temple 1975; Wheat 1957; Hurt 1974:43–93. For Delisle's 1702 map, see Wheat 1957:Map 82. The printing of Delisle's 1718 map symbolically marks the withdrawal of French interest from the Upper Missouri. The result was an information gap that lasted until about 1790. For the location of eastern Sioux groups prior to 1700, see Howard 1960a:257, 1980 [1966]:11, 20; Hickerson 1974c:13–22; Anderson 1984:22–8; Upham 1908:I:232–6; Johnson 1985:154; Birk and Johnson 1992:216. Some authors believe the Dakota began their westward shift as early as 1650 (Meyer 1993:13; Danzinger 1979:37; Warren 1984 [1885]:157). In the 1685 Minet map, the *les Sciou* appear in the Upper Mississippi region and the *nadossiou* to the southwest (Tucker 1942:3–4, Plate VII). Minet, an engineer, had accompanied René Robert Cavelier, Sieur de la Salle, on his 1682 exploration of the Mississippi Valley from the Illinois River to the Gulf of Mexico. However, a note on the 1688 Coronelli map places the People of the Prairies (*Tinthonha o' Gens des Prairies*) near the headwaters of the Mississippi, which could mean that they were seasonal bison hunters whose semi-permanent villages were in the forests (Ehrenberg 1987b:179; Wheat 1957:Map 70; Temple 1975:Plate 60). Similar interpretive problems exist with the 1701 Moll map, which places the *Tinthonha* northwest of the head of the Minnesota River (Wheat 1957:Map 81) and the 1702 Delisle map, which also places the "Nation des Tintons" near Lakes Big Stone and Traverse (Wheat 1957:Map 82). At best, cartographic information indicates that the western Sioux were using the prairies in the Lake Traverse–Big Stone region along the modern-day Minnesota–South Dakota border by the mid-1680s, though, according to Radisson and Grosseilliers, they moved back into the northern woods in winter for protection (Upham 1905:504–5, 1908:I:184; also see Hennepin 1938:91, 1974 [1903]:253). Robinson (1967 [1904]:23) says the Mdewakanton left their woodland home in c. 1760 to settle about the falls of St. Anthony.

   The complexity of the 1600–1750 period likely resulted in distinct changes in the distribution and nature, and the name, of Sioux divisions; the implications of these probable socio-political transformations merit greater attention than they have received (it is usually assumed that an early, unfamiliar name for some group of Sioux is an alternative label for a division known from a later period rather than the name of a socio-political grouping that later became extinct, perhaps through dissolution).

10. For overviews of early western Sioux movements and divisions, see Mekeel 1943; Howard 1972:281–3; Hyde 1937:3–32; Hurt 1974:67–223; Woolworth 1974:25–31; Champe 1974; DeMallie 1975; Anderson 1956; Jacobson 1980; Henning 1982:58–9; McGinnis 1990:2, 18; Birk and Johnson 1992:218; Pickering 1994:59–60; Picha 1996:47–66. According to an Omaha migration legend, the Yankton preceded the Teton out onto the tall-grass prairies of eastern South Dakota (DeMallie 1975:348).

11. For an account of this series of events, see Burpee 1968 [1927]:175–211. Holzkamm (1983:226–7) maintains that the relationship between the Dakota and Ojibwa was intermittently hostile throughout this period, not just after 1736.

12. For accounts of the long eastern Sioux–Ojibwa conflict (1736–1863), see Treuer 1994; Tanner 1987:43; Gilman 1992; Warren 1984 [1885]; Danzinger 1979; Burpee 1968 [1927]; Hickerson 1974a, 1974b, 1988 [1970]; Kellogg 1925. Landes (1968:15) suggests that because of Ojibwa pressure some Sioux groups began to return less often to their winter woodland homes after their summer prairie bison hunts, a point also made by Winchell (1911:534).

13. For mention of these other "pulls" and "pushes," see White 1978; Anderson 1980a; Holzkamm 1983; Pond 1986 [1908]:174; Neill 1902:211; Birk 1991:245. For the use of trade fairs to trace the westward movement of the Lakota, see Hyde 1937:8. White (1978) proposes a three-phase westward advance of the western Sioux across the Plains.

14. For Radisson and Grosseilliers's possible visit to Minnesota, see Nute 1978 [1943]:33, 65–6; Meyer 1993:4. See Hennepin (1938:97) for his own first encounter with the Dakota.

15. For descriptions of arm shields, see Blair 1996 [1911]:I:126). Similar shields were worn by later Sioux warriors, too (Pond 1986 [1908]:125; Wissler 1907:22–3; Howard 1980 [1966]:Pls. 5, 7). According to Wissler, the designs and medicine objects tied to the shields protected the user from harm during battle. For descriptions of early Sioux dress and ornamentation, see Carver 1956:226–7; Abel 1939:177; Hennepin 1938:100; Perrot in Blair 1996 [1911], I:78; Pond 1986 [1908]:31-37; Gelb 1993; Adams 1961:137. For a description of the French merchandise the Dakota may have been using at this time, see Birk and Johnson 1992:219–32.

16. For Dakota settlement and subsistence during the period, see Parker 1976:95; Perrot in Blair 1996 [1911]:I:160–2; Hennepin 1938:104–23; Hickerson 1974c:13–39; Whelan 1990. The Sioux Allouez (Thwaites 1959 [1901]:L1, p. 53) described in 1666–7 hunted, gathered wild rice, and cultivated only tobacco; he does not stress the importance of bison hunting in their economy. According to Lalemant in 1642 and Grosseilliers and Radisson in about 1660, the Sioux raised both corn and tobacco (Thwaites 1959 [1898]:23:224–5; Upham 1905:491–3). Archaeological studies of plant remains in Mille Lacs villages indicate that corn was present but rare (Bailey 1997).

17. For Hennepin's description of life in a Dakota woodland village at Mille Lacs, see Hennepin (1938:104–13) and White (1988). Both Allouez and Radisson and Grosseilliers state that the Sioux lived in cabins covered with skins; the latter reference also mentions mats (Thwaites 1959 [1898]:23:224–5; Upham 1905:504). For the early use of sweat lodges, see Carver (1956:390) and Hennepin (1938:108). For the proto-historic Dakota use of burial mounds, see Lothson (1972) and Birk and Johnson (1992). For tipi, see Pond (1986 [1908]:38–9, 46–7). Based on trade items, Cooper Mound One was constructed sometime between 1670 and 1740 (Lothson 1972:1:21).

18. For war clubs, see Carver 1956:295–6; Parker 1976:97; Hennepin 1938:118; Pond 1986 [1908]:41. On the presence and use of the calumet, see Blair

1996 [1911]:208; Hennepin 1938:99-107; Pond 1986 [1908]:122–3. Pipe stems were occasionally as long as 1.5 m (5 feet).

19. For the importance of kinship ties in Sioux society, see Deloria 1998 [1944]; Anderson 1984; DeMallie 1994:130–3; and the section on kinship in Chapter 4 of this text. The British never married or adopted into Sioux groups to the degree the French did, which helps explain why the transition from British to American influence was met with less Indian resistance than the traumatic transition from French to British influence.

20. For the concept of culture, see Ember and Ember 1990:13–30; Kottak 1991:35–48; Carrithers 1992. Cultural beliefs include values, attitudes, ideals, and views of the supernatural. The symbolic, ideal, and non-objectified nature of these aspects of culture makes it impossible to recapture the fullness of a culture from the archaeological record alone.

21. Wolf 1982. Among the many questions that a cultural perspective raises are: How did Sioux culture differ in 1650, 1750, 1850, and 1950? How and when did the integration of Sioux culture loosen as the westernmost groups drifted westward across the northern Plains? Because of the present geographical and historical distance between groups of Sioux, does it make sense to talk about a contemporary Sioux culture?

22. White 1988:3. For similar examples, see Wedel 1974:157–8, Fig. 3; Stipe 1971:1033–4; Nute 1978 [1943]:30; Holzkamm 1983:227.

23. Hennepin 1974 [1903], 1938. See Nute (1938) for a critical discussion of the writing of *Description of Louisiana*.

24. For Fenton's quote, see Fenton 1952:335. For arguments against the hypothesis that the Dakota represent the original culture of the Sioux, see DeMallie 1971:15–16 and White 1988. For downstreaming, see White 1988. Other problems occur as well. For instance, not all texts or parts of texts are equally accurate, and not all questions can be answered with the same degree of assurance. Besides these problems, the most common danger remains reading into the text what we expect it to say. These same cautions apply, too, of course, to texts that are more recent. A classic example is William Warren's (1984 [1885]) oft-quoted description of the Battle of Kathio; there is no evidence of earthlodges at Mille Lacs Lake sites and the battle itself may never have taken place (Anderson 1980a; Butcher-Youngans 1981; Johnson 1985:157); also see Anderson (1984:47) and Mather (2000:70).

25. Belyea 1998:140. On reading maps, see Gell 1985.

26. Kaufman 1989; Ruggles 1991. For maps of Sioux territory in general, see Wood 1981, 1983, 1987, 1993; Picha 1996; Allen 1987; Delanglez 1943, 1946; Hurt 1974; Tanner 1987; Ehrenberg 1987a; Wedel 1974; Wheat 1957; Warkentin and Ruggles 1970. The first map reference to the Sioux is on Jean Boisseu's map of 1643 (Hurt 1974:45). For maps as enablers of colonialism, see Cosgrove and Daniels 1988; Ryan 1994; but see Belyea 1992a.

27. Harley and Woodward 1987.

28. Howard 1972:292–302; Lewis 1987, 1998; Ruggles 1991.

29. Lewis (1998) remains the single best source on Indian mapmaking and map use.

30. Lewis 1998:51; La Hontan 1905 [1703]. There were undoubtedly earlier

maps that have not survived. Hennepin (1938:125), for example, mentions that in 1680 the "great chief of the Issati or Nadouessioux ... marked with a pencil on a paper I gave him the route we should follow for four hundred leagues of the way."

31. Ruggles 1991, Plate 19; Lewis 1987; Kohl 1857. A Cree drew a map of the route to the Western Sea on birch bark for La Vérendrye. Also see Belyea 1992b.

32. Indian maps were produced on hide, blazed on the trunk of trees and birch bark, and pecked in stone, among other media. The earliest of these maps appear to have been drawn using indigenous pictographic methods. In general, efforts by explorers and government cartographers to translate these maps into conventional Western forms have erased American Indian cartographic conventions and culturally specific views of the world.

33. Bad Heart Bull and Blish 1967; Goodman 1992. A vision of what may have been a representation of the Lakota cosmos was painted around a tipi cover in a German collection destroyed by allied bombing in World War II (Corum 1975). For other aspects of dreaming and maps, see Brody 1981. Sioux maps and accounts of mapmaking more recent than about 1925 are considered too acculturated by formal education to provide accurate information about traditional forms of mapmaking and interpretation. It should be noted that the earliest maps are now being used for a new purpose, to legitimate land claims.

34. Viewed from the perspective developed here, maps of Sioux territory should stimulate our curiosity. What role did maps play in inscribing the wilderness, the emptiness, during the early missionary (Jesuit) project and French–English fur trade? Did maps play a role in the creation of the western Great Lakes as a place of great and readily accessible riches (as they later played a role in portraying the Great Plains as a vast and barren desert)? Why did the rhetoric of cartography change in Sioux territory in the nineteenth and twentieth centuries? Since naming is one of the prime aspects of cartography, whose names for rivers, lakes, and other elements of the landscape were used on early maps and why? Why were the locations of Sioux settlements included in early maps, when in other parts of the world, such as Australia, native peoples were erased from maps?

35. For proto-historic/historic period archaeology in the Mille Lacs area, see Johnson 1984, 1985; Dickson 1968; Birk and Johnson 1992; Little 1985:151; Lothson 1972; Butcher-Youngans 1980; Anfinson 1980; Mather and Abel 2000; Mather 2000. The Aquipaguetin site (21ML2) remains unexcavated except for brief tests (Wilford 1937, 1944:329–30, 1949; Mather 2000:63). Douglas A. Birk, a senior archaeologist at the Institute for Minnesota Archaeology, has carried out the most sustained and productive archaeological work on the French presence in Minnesota (see Birk 1982, 1991, 1992; Birk and Johnson 1992). For the archaeology of western Sioux historic sites, see Picha 1996:67–82; Warren 1986a; Haberman 1981, 1983; Lees 1985; Keller and Keller 1982 (Fig. 4); Hurt 1974:37–8; Howard 1972:296, 303.

36. Historical archaeology offers numerous fruitful avenues of investigation for persons interested in the early historic Sioux. How different in appearance

were proto-historic Sioux villages in Minnesota, western Wisconsin, and the eastern Dakotas? Did the size, layout, and composition of Dakota villages change during the French period? What kinds of Euro-American goods were traded to the Sioux? When were pottery vessels and stone tools (arrowheads and knives) replaced by metal kettles and tools? In which order were indigenous items replaced in space and time? How were early trade items used and altered? Is there material evidence for the presence of eastern tribal people in Dakota villages? Again, the range of questions is limited only by the scope of the imagination.

37. For what was traded to the Indians, see Anderson 1994; White 1982, 1994. Anderson (1994:10) found that clothing (either finished clothing or the materials used to make clothing) was the "cornerstone commodity of the trade," accounting for more than 50 percent of Euro-American trade items in his study. White (1994) believes the Dakota were more interested in iron products.

38. For the meaning of objects, see Thomas 1991; Moore 1993; Kopytoff 1986. For interpreting the meaning of early fur trade objects, see Hamell 1982; Miller and Hamell 1986; White 1982, 1984, 1994. For an economist's view of the fur trade (in contrast to that of an anthropologist's), see Trosper 1988:206. For examples of comparative studies of exchange in colonial situations, see Leach 1983; Thomas 1991.

39. For discussion of the mindset of the mercantile trade, see Gregory 1982 and Rabb 1967.

40. On the gift, see Mauss 1990; also see Nicholas 1991. For examples of accounts of intertribal trade in the western Great Lakes and northern Plains, see Blakeslee 1975; Wood 1980; Ewers 1968:14–33; Vehik and Baugh 1994; White 1977, 1982, 1984, 1994, 1999. In societies that lack other forms of centralized political control, alliances are regulated or managed by a complex of mechanisms, such as communal intergroup resource procurement (e.g., group bison hunts), feasting, ceremonies, ritual, and exchange. At the time early Euro-American fur traders were entering the western Great Lakes, exchange among native groups packing into the region was strongly enmeshed in alliance formation and management. Exchanged items in intertribal exchanges ranged along a continuum from commodity to gift. For the importance of economic forces in the trade, see White (1994:396, 400).

41. The Sioux usually adopted Euro-American trading goods for pragmatic reasons. For instance, they could see how the possession of muskets and steel knives affected the balance of power among eastern tribes (in particular the Iroquois), so they adopted muskets and knives as quickly as possible. Likewise, the adoption of some goods (e.g., metal axes, knives, kettles, and awls) was essential to maintain a technological balance with their neighbors (Treuer 1994:86–7). It is important to understand, too, that the Indians that the French were trading with were, for the most part, professional traders. According to Rich (1966:9–10), for example, "Despite their apparently different sense of values and their different notions of buying and selling, of giving gifts in gift exchange, and so on, the Indians with whom the Europeans were making contact were professional traders." Among the questions that could

be asked are: How did fur traders handle the relationships of commitment they were engaged in? What was the nature of the entanglement of the Sioux and these non-Indian strangers? Since the identity of things is not fixed in their structure and form, how did the Sioux recontextualize objects? Likewise, since objects are not immutable, which kinds of things moved in and out of a valuable gift state through time? Which kinds of items were treated like commodities? How were attempts to recontextualize goods affected by gender, by a glut in supplies, by the periodic collapse of the trade, or by an inability to control their distribution either within the band or to other tribes?

42. Hoover 1988:73.
43. Hassrick 1964:8–9.
44. Hoover 1988:72.
45. As a primer to problems of translation from Native American oral discourse to English, see Tedlock 1983; Swann 1992; Krupat and Swann 1987; Castro 1983; DeMallie 1984; Rice 1989, 1991.
46. For examples of Sioux discourse and its interpretation, see Around Him 1983; Black Bear and Theisz 1976; DeMallie 1984; Deloria 1954, 1978; Rice 1989, 1992a, 1992b, 1993. For statements that Sioux literature had to be turned into true literature via translation, see Clements 1992.
47. Walker 1983:206–381.
48. Clements 1992:40–2.
49. For a recent discussion of how native oral discourse should be translated and presented, see Rice and Murray 1999.
50. Powers 1992.
51. Rice 1992b:289.
52. For the image of the "squaw" who toils while her husband loafs, see Albers 1983:3 and Weist 1983. Marla Powers (1986:8–14) traces the history of this imagery in descriptions of the Oglala. For male dominance in Dakota society, see Pond 1986 [1908]:140–1. As Klein and Ackerman (1995a:3) summarize the situation, "Silence surrounds the lives of native North American women" and "the traditional literature is superficial in the discussion of women." These observations are as true in general for traditional male-oriented anthropological studies as they are for the reports of early explorers and other observers.
53. As stressed in chapter 4, gender categories and roles most likely changed over time and among tribal divisions in the Sioux cultural tradition. Not all Sioux women have shared identical or even similar lives. This variability should be of interest to all individuals interested in the Sioux. In the following discussion, the terms "women" and "men" refer to behavioral roles rather than to biological categories, even though the great majority of "women" and "men" were women and men by sex as well.
54. Work, ritual, and other such concepts in this paragraph are Western categories that would not have made much sense to nineteenth-century traditional Sioux, for work, ritual life, and all other activities were blended together in inseparable ways. These categories were developed as heuristics in the study of late capitalist societies. As Sioux society has become incorporated more fully into American life in the twentieth century, the concepts have more

relevance to its examination from an ethnohistoric perspective. For female roles in traditional Sioux culture, see DeMallie 1983; Pond 1986 [1908]; Powers 1986:53–103.

55. The case for male power over women is strong in traditional Sioux society. Among the ways women could place limits on male power or gain access to it were: (1) the strong value in Sioux society on individual autonomy; (2) the possibility of adopting alternate roles, such as that of a "manly-hearted woman"; and (3) the mythological charter for women's status in Sioux religion (a charter that stresses a greater innate spirituality within women; as a consequence, men had to go on vision quests to increase their spirituality).

56. For the loss of power by Lakota women following the adoption of a nomadic Plains lifeway, see Klein 1983a, 1983b. For studies relevant to the impact of the fur trade upon pre-horse Sioux women, see Leacock 1978; Etienne and Leacock 1980; Kirk 1983; White 1999.

57. For trends in the lifeways of Sioux women on reservations, see Maynard 1979; Medicine 1982; Albers 1982, 1983, 1985; Powers 1986:107–214; Winter 1997.

58. These tensions were expressed in some households by substance abuse. See, for example, Whittaker 1962 and May 1996.

59. In general, anthropological studies have focused on recording the memories of elders for clues to earlier cultural practices ("memory culture") rather than on the lives of contemporary Sioux. In recent years, there has been a shift from the search for the attributes of the "traditional Lakota woman" to an understanding of how the lives of Sioux women have changed over time. For the growing interest in the lives of Sioux and other North American Indian women, see Nordquist 1999; Albers 1989; Bataille and Sands 1991; Bataille 1993; Penman 2000. The forced change in residence pattern of the reservation period resulted in new opportunities for mutual support between Sioux women (e.g., the White Shawl Society at Rosebud). Increasingly, power came from economic, sexual, and marital relationships with outsiders. For an example of the voice of an unusual Sioux woman, see Crow Dog and Erdoes 1991 and Brave Bird 1993 (for an interesting contrast, see Crow Dog and Erdoes 1995). Among the many questions we might ask about the changing roles and voice of Sioux women are: What does the early silence surrounding Sioux women mean? What sources are available for making an informed assessment of male–female equality at different times and places in the Sioux cultural tradition? Has the affect of colonial pressure on the position of women been similar in all divisions of the Sioux or has it varied widely? How are contemporary Sioux women, with others, re-creating Sioux culture in the twenty-first century?

4 . The Early American Period, 1803–1850

1. See, for example, McGinnis 1990:18–21.

2. For accounts of Lewis and Clark's explorations, see Allen 1987, 1991; Jackson 1978; Moulton 1983, 1997; Hurt 1974:139–58. For accounts of the fur

trade on the northern Plains during this period, see Ewers 1972; Hanson 1975; Michael 1965; Sunder 1965; Swagerty 1988, 1994; Wishart 1979. The newly purchased Louisiana Territory was an 828,000-square-mile wilderness that stretched from the Gulf of Mexico to Canada and from the Mississippi River in the east to the foothills of the Rocky Mountains in the west.

3. On Zebulon Pike's northern travels, which passed through Sioux territory, see Anderson 1984:79–84; Coues 1895; Pike 1966.

4. According to a 1839 census, there were 1,658 Mdewakanton, 325 Wahpekute, 1,256 Sisseton, and 750 Wahpeton (Hoover 1996a:161). Tanner (1987:148) provides a figure of 5,700 Dakota for southern Minnesota for this period. During his northern expedition, Pike estimated there were over 2,000 Mdewakonton in Minnesota along with 1,000 Wahpeton, 1,100 Sisseton, and 270 Wakpekute. See Maps 20 and 28 in Tanner (1987) for locations of Dakota villages in 1810 and 1830, respectively; also see Dorsey 1897:215–16; Landes 1968:4–9; Pond 1986 [1908]:4–6; Babcock 1945. For a description of the organization of a Dakota village, see Landes 1968:28–48; for descriptions of Dakota structures and facilities, see Spector 1985; Hurt 1974:20–1; Howard 1980 [1966]:5.

5. For Dakota chiefs, see Anderson 1986; Diedrich 1987; Hughes 1969 [1927]; Landes 1968:78–94; Wilson 1905–8. There were five Dakota chiefs with the name Wabasha and four with the name Little Crow. Qualities of a Dakota leader were religious knowledge, oratorical ability, and benevolence; the word for chief in Dakota, *witshastaopi*, means "men who are fathers" (Diedrich 1987:vii). Leadership among the Dakota was semi-hereditary but one had to perform to retain credibility. According to Hurt (1974:14), "each Sioux band had at its head a chief who in his turn took his place in a council of chiefs for the tribe (here the Mdewakanton) as a whole." For a description of the status of chiefs among the Lakota in 1802, see Abel 1939:105–6. Among the many travelers through the land of the Dakota at this time who left descriptions of their culture were George Catlin (Catlin 1973), George W. Featherstonhaugh (Featherstonhaugh 1970), William H. Keating (Keating 1959 [1824]), Stephen H. Long (Kane et al. 1978), Joseph N. Nicollet (Nicollet 1970, 1993; Bray 1980; DeMallie 1975), and Henry R. Schoolcraft (1992 [1821], 1993 [1958]); also see Hurt 1974:196–201 and Howard 1980 [1966]:4–10.

6. For accounts of the Dakota–Ojibwa conflict, see Nicollet 1970:154–80; Hickerson 1988 [1970]; Pond 1986 [1908]:123–37; Robinson 1967 [1904]:112–14; Treuer 1994; Warren 1984 [1885]. According to most accounts, the Ojibwa were supplied with steel knives and muskets earlier and more steadily than the Dakota until as late as 1820 (Treuer 1994:81; Schoolcraft 1993 [1958]:xvi; Folwell 1956, I:80; Danzinger 1979:37). Landes (1968:12) suggests that the Dakota would have been pushed still further south if not for the intervention of the US military. For accounts of the fur trade among the Eastern Sioux during the late eighteenth and early nineteenth century, see Buechler 1989; Gilman 1970, 1974; Michael 1965; Nute 1930; Tohill 1928–9; Whelan 1993; White 1977; Woolworth 1986.

7. For the northern and southern boundaries of the 1825 Prairie du Chien council between the Dakota and the Ojibwa, Sauk, and Mesquakie, see Map 22 in Tanner 1987:123; also see Tanner 1987:149. For the 1825 Treaty of Prairie du Chien, see Anderson 1984:121–3; Meyer 1993:39–41; Treuer 1994:240–6. A second, more successful, treaty at Prairie du Chien was held in 1830 (Anderson 1984:133–5).

8. Tanner 1987:149. The reasons for the Dakota–Ojibwa conflict were many and varied. Two were territorial incentives (Pond 1986 [1908]:60) and revenge belief and practices. It was a social obligation among both the Dakota and Ojibwa to free the spirit of the dead of this world so that they could go on to the spirit world. This could be accomplished in several ways, one of which was to kill an enemy. This deeply held religious belief resulted in cycles of revenge killings. Another common practice, scalping, was also deeply embedded in religious beliefs. War parties were usually limited to about 6 to 50 warriors in size, for smaller groups were easier to keep undetected, to raise, and to supply. In the early 1800s, the decline of the fur trade and an increase in the availability of alcohol heightened still further the tension and violence between the two groups (Gilman 1970; Pond 1986 [1908]:75).

9. The literature on Fort Snelling is substantial. For overviews, see Hansen 1958 and Hall 1987. The building of Fort Snelling in 1819–23 marked the beginning of large-scale American involvement in Dakota affairs.

10. Wabasha II was commissioned a general in the British army and led expeditions against the Americans in the War of 1812 (Anderson 1984:87–99). Little Crow was also very active in supporting British interests. The Eastern Sioux support of the British can be traced in part to their kinship relationships with British traders, such as Robert Dickson and Joseph Renville, who promoted hostility toward the US (Buechler 1989:62–5).

11. For the Lac Qui Parle mission and Joseph Renville, see Ackermann 1931 and Willand 1964. Renville had a Sioux mother and a French father.

12. Among the artists who drew pictures of Dakota life before the Civil War were Frank B. Mayer, Robert O. Sweeny, and Seth Eastman. See "Looking Through Pictures" in chapter 5 of this text. For general accounts of the Dakota of this period, see Anderson 1984:77–176, 1986; Deloria 1967b; Dorsey 1897; Eastman 1995 [1849]; Hickerson 1974c; Howard 1960a, 1980 [1966]; Hurt 1974; Landes 1968; Meyer 1993; Pond 1986 [1908]; Riggs 1869, 1969 [1880], 1973 [1893]; Wozniak 1978; Woolworth and Woolworth 1980. The manuscript collections of Major Lawrence Taliaferro, Samuel W. Pond, John P. Williamson, H. H. Sibley, and many other nineteenth-century observers of the Dakota are archived at the Minnesota Historical Society. For Pond, Riggs, Taliaferro, Sibley, and Williamson, see Babcock 1924; Barton 1919; Blegen 1927; Pond 1893; Riggs 1969 [1880].

13. Mayer 1986 [1932]:12. For the 1837 treaty discussed in the following paragraph, see Anderson 1980b.

14. For the westward movement of the Yankton/Yanktonai, see Woolworth 1974:25–31; Champe 1974; Howard 1972:283–90; Picha 1996. For Lewis and Clark on the location of the Yankton and Yanktonai, see Hurt 1974:151–8 and Woolworth 1974:32–8. For reviews of the Yankton–Yanktonai dur-

ing this period, see Howard 1972, 1976, 1980 [1966]:11–19; Woolworth 1974:32–136; Warren 1986a, 1986b; Hoover 1988:25–31; also see Deloria 1967a. For a description of the environmental setting of the James River, the heartland of Yankton territory, see Picha 1996:13–20. For the Yankton's James River Rendezvous, see Picha 1996. Archaeologically, the two most likely Middle Sioux rendezvous locations are Drifting Goose's Village (32SP101) on Armadale Island and Dirt Lodge Village (32SP11) in the James River valley of east-central South Dakota (Haberman (1981:2, 1983). According to Truteau (Nasatir 1990 I:260), the Yankton he encountered in the Big Bend of the Missouri in 1794 told him they had moved westward because the prairies east of the Missouri "were presently stripped of wild animals." The Yankton were generally considered the best disposed of the Sioux on the Missouri River.

15. For the location of the Yanktonai, see Howard 1972:300; Tanner 1987:150; Hurt 1974:200–1, 206–7; Warren 1986a. According to Yanktonai oral tradition and the John K. Bear Winter Count, Yanktonai were wintering on the James Valley in South Dakota by the early eighteenth century (Howard 1976). According to figures collected during the Lewis and Clark expedition, the Yanktonai were the most numerous of all Sioux tribes with 500 men (warriors); estimations for numbers of men for other Sioux groups were: Yankton (200); Brulé (300); Oglala (150); Minneconjou (250); Sans Arc, Hunkpapa, Two Kettles, and Blackfeet (300); Wahepton (200); Mdewakanton (300); Wahpekute (1500; Sisseton (200) (Hurt 1974:152–5). In an 1825 War Department letter, the following total population numbers are given: Yankton (3000), Yanktonai (4,000), Brulé (1,500), Oglala (1,500), Saones (Sans Arc, Two Kettles, Blackfeet, and Minneconjou – 4,000), and Hunkpapas (1,500) (Hurt 1974:175–6).

16. As the Yankton and Yanktonai moved westward, they came into increasing contact with resident riverine tribes, such as the Arikara and Mandan, from whom they adopted many traits, including clothing styles, village plan, and seasonal economic cycle. According to Howard (1972:303), "the Yankton took over virtually intact the seasonal economic and settlement patterns characteristic of riverine groups."

17. For a review of Yankton subsistence, see Howard 1972:290–2. According to Howard (1972:295, 1980 [1966]:15), the Yankton–Yanktonai were still using stone knives and scrapers, and pottery vessels, in the early nineteenth century, although the style and historical origin of the purported vessels remain unclear. The Yankton were fairly well supplied with horses and fusees (guns), and had a few mules.

18. For Drifting Goose's Village, see Howard 1972:300, 1980 [1966]:13; Haberman 1981. Howard (1960a:258–60, 1980 [1966]:12–13) states that four earthlodge villages of the Arikara type, but built by the Yanktonai in the nineteenth century, have been found: one (Drifting Goose's Village) near Armadale Island (near Mellette), a second ("Dirt lodges") near Ashton, and a third near Fort Thompson, South Dakota; and a fourth near Fort Yates, North Dakota. Earthlodges were present, too, at least at one Yankton village (Howard 1980 [1966]:iv). According to winter counts, the Sans Arc

first attempted to build earthlodges in Peoria Bottom, north of Pierre, in 1815–16 (Hurt 1974:38).

19. Howard 1972:297. Of the various travelers along the Missouri River in the first half of the nineteenth century, Joseph N. Nicollet was the only one to travel through the interior of their territory and leave an account and a map of the region (Bray 1980; Nicollet 1993; DeMallie 1975; Howard 1972:303).

20. For early nineteenth-century reports of the Western Sioux, see Bradbury 1817; Luttig 1964 [1920]; Hurt 1974:188–191, 202–23. For general descriptions of the Lakota in the nineteenth century, see Bonvillain 1994; Hassrick 1964; Hyde 1937; Standing Bear 1928, 1931, 1933; Sandoz 1961 [1942]; Walker 1980, 1982, 1983; Howard 1980 [1966]:20–5.

21. For population estimates for the seven divisions of the Lakota in the 1830s and 1840s, see McGinnis 1990:76. Mooney (1991 [1896]:1058) thought the Lakota population was somewhat more than two-thirds the total Sioux population. Pond (1986 [1908]:5–6) estimated that there were about 7,000 Dakota at the time in Minnesota and adjacent South Dakota (also see Landes 1968:13–14).

22. For an overview of intertribal warfare between 1803 and 1850, see McGinnis 1990:17–84.

23. Epidemics had been causing imbalances in tribal power in the northern Plains for many years. The smallpox epidemic of 1780–1, which was particularly severe, is estimated to have killed half the Mandan and Hidatsa; see Trimble 1992, 1994; Sundstrom 1997. Epidemics also periodically swept through the western Great Lakes region (Ackerknecht 1945; Blegen 1975:117; Green 1993; Hickerson 1974a:106; Schoolcraft 1993 [1958]:54; Tanner 1987:170. A particularly severe smallpox epidemic struck all Indian groups west of Lake Superior in 1750. Other, mainly smallpox, epidemics in this region occurred in 1768, 1770, 1780–84, 1801–2, 1830, 1834, and 1837; cholera epidemics were reported among the Dakota in the 1840s. Indian groups often assumed that Euro-Americans intentionally caused these epidemics to reduce Indian warfare and Indian populations in general (Treuer 1994:189).

24. For the impact of the hide trade, see Klein 1983a, 1983b.

25. For Lakota plant use, see Gilmore 1991 [1919]. Hurt (1974:18) suggests that the Lakota were forced to abandon their agricultural practices when they migrated out onto the Plains because the Mandan, Arikara, and other agricultural tribes already were in control of the fertile river bottoms.

26. For explorations in the Plains, see Goetzmann 1959. A scientific expedition led by Major Stephen H. Long in 1820 was also intended to protect the fur trade. For the famous 1838–9 Nicollet–Frémont expedition, see Jackson and Spence 1970. In 1824, the federal government established the St. Louis Superintendency and the Upper Missouri Agency under the auspices of the War Department. In 1826, the first superintendent William Clark developed the policy of ending tribal war by requiring each tribe to pay for its depredations out of money due from government land purchases.

27. McGinnis 1990; Mishkin 1992 [1940]; Newcomb 1950. Divale and Harris (1976:521) define warfare as "all organized forms of intergroup homicide involving combat teams of two or more persons, including feuding and raiding."

28. Mishkin 1992 [1940]:58; Newcomb 1950.
29. For descriptions of intertribal warfare on the northern Plains, see Calloway 1982; Ewers 1975; McGinnis 1990; Mishkin 1992 [1940]; Secoy 1992 [1953]. Dakota warfare differed in many respects from that of the Lakota before the middle of the nineteenth century, when most Dakota moved westward. For example, the Minnesota Dakota used canoes rather than horses on their northern raids and did not count coup (Treuer 1994:63–83). However, when fighting the Fox and other southern groups, at least some rode to battle on horses. Also see Landes 1959, 1968a:204–14.
30. Fried et al. 1968; Reyna and Downs 1994.
31. Mishkin (1992 [1940]) has argued most forcefully for the transformative role of the horse in Plains Indian culture. He suggests the horse: (1) increased mobility on the Plains; (2) facilitated greater intertribal trade, visiting, intermarriage, and exchange of ideas; (3) provided a means of transporting large quantities of meat, bison robes, and other items of material wealth; (4) provided tangible wealth that led to increased disparities in wealth and status; (5) contributed to the formation of a more homogeneous Plains culture area; (6) increased the fluidity of bands; (7) increased material comforts (e.g., by allowing increased food surpluses and larger tipis); (8) gave rise to new patterns of warfare; (9) increased raiding because of the necessity of acquiring horses; and (10) resulted in a shift in material culture from bulky or fragile items of wood, bark, and basketry to skin, leather, and rawhide items better suited for travel by horse. For a list of Lakota raids for horses between 1700 and 1763, see Hurt 1974:85–6.
32. Disputes over the most favored hunting grounds were accelerated by the westward movement of the bison herds. By 1807, the herds had already withdrawn into the western sections of the Dakotas, Nebraska, Kansas, Oklahoma, and Texas, and by 1870 they had disappeared north and east of the Missouri River. One reason the Sioux formed large summer camps (100 to 200 tipis) at this time was to defend themselves from their many enemies as they crossed into new hunting territories.
33. Traders and agents of rival colonial powers often tried to set one group of Indians against another for one reason or another. A typical example was the successful effort by Manuel Lisa, a trader for the St. Louis–Missouri Fur Company during the War of 1812, to encourage hostilities between the Western Sioux and Indian groups along the Mississippi River to divert the Lakota from actively siding with the English (Robinson 1967 [1904]:90–1).
34. Among the Blackfoot, for example, there was a 50 percent deficit for males in the male/female ratio in 1805 and a 33 percent deficit in 1858, when horse raiding was still common; after horse raiding was banned in the reservation period, the sex ratio approached 50–50 (for discussions of death rates due to warfare, see Keeley 1996; Meggitt 1977; LeBlanc 1999). A similar impact would be expected for the warlike Lakota.
35. Sipes 1973.
36. Wied (1962 [1843]:259) reported that many Lakota were rich and had 20 or more horses, with a rich man owning 30–40 horses; in general, horses were unevenly divided among the Lakota population.

37. Fausto-Sterling 1992 [1985]; Kottak 1991:183–200. For an introduction to issues and approaches to gender in anthropology, see Brettell and Sargent 1997; Ferree et al. 1999; Mascia-Lees and Black 2000. For gender issues among North American Indians, see Albers and Medicine 1983; Albers 1989; Bataille and Sands 1991; Bataille 1993; Klein and Ackerman 1995b. Though we tend to think in terms of male and female sexes, there is in reality a continuum between these categories, which is visible in a mixture of biological markers.

38. Conkey and Spector 1984.

39. For reviews of gendered archaeology, see Balme and Beck 1995; Walde and Willows 1991; Seifert 1991; Claassen 1992; Wright 1996.

40. For examples of studies of how gender is marked materially, see Donley 1982; Hodder 1982; Welbourn 1984.

41. For the Two Spirit person (berdache), see Callender and Kochems 1983; Medicine 1983, 2001; Williams 1986, 1992; Catlin 1973:2:214–15; Pond 1986 [1908]:124; Lang 1998; Landes 1968:31–2, 50. This is a small sample of a large body of literature. Because of disapproval by Euro-Americans, the Two Spirit person was suppressed as a gender category for many years. With the resurgence of Indian culture in the 1970s and 1980s, the Two Spirit person has gained a visible presence again.

42. Whelan 1991.

43. Whelan 1991:22.

44. Pond 1986 [1908]:43–59, 140–2; DeMallie 1983. Compared to neighboring groups like the Ojibwa, gender divisions between men and women were pronounced in Sioux society, with women rarely attaining sociopolitical leadership positions. In this regard, it is interesting to note that the Dakota language (like other Plains languages and unlike most European languages) does not distinguish between masculine and feminine gender (Sherzer 1976:178).

45. Spector 1985, 1993.

46. See Hodder (1982, 1984) for archaeological examples of shifts in gender status.

47. For types of kinship systems, see Parkin 1997. See chapter 5 of this text for voluntary associations. Although their specific purpose and degree of formality might have differed, voluntary associations have been important in all known societies.

48. For examples of studies of the developmental sequences of kinship patterns and their associations, see Murdock 1949 and Dole 1972.

49. For Sioux kinship, see DeMallie's (1982a:8–13) bibliographical discussion in Walker's *Lakota Society*; also see DeMallie 1971, 1979, 1994; Lesser 1930, 1958; Stipe 1971; Albers 1982; Hassrick 1944, 1964:107–20; Walker 1914, 1982; Landes 1968:95–160; Pond 1986 [1908]:147; Wallis 1947. It is useful in studies of kinship and social organization to distinguish between the structure and cultural patterns of social relations, for they vary independently from one another. The structure of social relations (social structure) is the totality of socially recognized relations between individuals who are genetically and affinally connected. Cultural patterns of social relations

are the normative patterns of behavior associated with each structural relation. The forms of social structure are limited in number. Each is also necessarily well integrated since it provides for the orderly arrangement of society. In contrast, cultural patterns of social relations take a greater variety of forms and require much less integration. Children and outsiders who enter a society as adopted kin are trained in how to behave toward individuals in each social relationship. Many discussions of Sioux kinship focus upon proper normative behavior (e.g., mother-in-law avoidance) rather than the network of structural relations in Sioux society. See DeMallie (1994:142–3) for the advantages of both approaches in studies of Lakota kinship.

50.   Lesser 1958:295–7. Wallis (1947:31) recorded the presence of the classificatory lévirate and sororate among the Wahpeton Dakota in 1914 at the Manitoba reservation to which they had fled after the Conflict of 1862. The emphasis in Lakota kinship between cross cousins on the one hand and siblings and parallel cousins on the other is a divide as well between "aunts" and "uncles" (who are not parents' potential spouses under the lévirate and sororate) and children of "mothers" and "fathers" (parents' potential spouses under the lévirate and sororate).

51.   Polygyny is common in societies that lack commercial exchange and have a high male mortality rate (e.g., Ember 1974). For polygyny among the Sioux, see Hennepin 1938:104–23; Landes 1968:139–40; DeMallie 1983:251–2. Regarding the terms used to designate the various subdivisions of the Sioux, Hurt (1974:13) concludes that "There is no ... generally accepted set of terms to designate the various subdivisions of the Sioux." I assume that the socio-political nature of these units was not stable through time; consequently, a particular unit might historically have been a band at one time, a sub-tribe at another, a tribe at still another, and so on. When associated with the Sioux, the word "nation" does not refer to a set of political units united under a centralized government; it refers instead (in pre-reservation days) to "a large socio-political unit with a common language, which frequently acted as military allies, rarely engaged in internal warfare, and sometimes shared a hunting territory" (Hurt 1974:14). While the Eastern Sioux had divided into the Mdewakanton, the Wahpekute, the Wahpeton, and the Sisseton sometime before the end of the seventeenth century, the Lakota, with the possible exception of the Oglala, apparently had not yet differentiated into their present tribes at that time (Hurt 1974:66). This is reflected in the composition of the Seven Council Fires, where the Lakota are represented by only one fire.

52.   For bilateral residence on the Plains, see Eggan 1937, 1966:55–7. Bilateral residence was common in hunting-gathering and tribal communities with fewer than 100 people.

53.   Eggan 1955:494.

54.   See, for example, Blumberg and Winch 1972; Nimkoff and Middleton 1960.

55.   According to this reconstruction, Sioux warrior societies developed at this time as one of these associations. Sodalities of this sort, which crosscut local groups, were probably especially common if only because tribal society continued to be familistic. Clans, or gentes (corporate groups), have persistently been attributed to some bands of Sioux (Skinner 1919a; Howard 1960a:252)

However, Landes (1968:79–80) found no evidence in 1935 for the existence of clans among the Mdewakanton Dakota (also see Eggan 1966:109–10; Stipe 1971; Howard 1980 [1966]:iii). Both Pond brothers used the word "clan" to refer to a village, which was the one important fixed political unit among the Mdewakanton. For the presence of patrilineal descent groups, see Robinson 1967 [1904] and Howard 1980 [1966]:iii. The appearance of larger, more communal bison hunts in the nineteenth century may have required a degree of organization among the Lakota not present earlier, too.

56. Schusky 1971, 1986:71. Prominent leaders played a decisive role, for example, in the acquisition, control, and inheritance of land and resources. Although traditional Lakota society was basically egalitarian, it did contain elements of social stratification. These included the existence of powerful and prestigious leaders and "Big Men," hierarchically organized men's associations, and competition between groups for resources and territory. In some cases, further status and prestige were obtained through ceremonial rank, war honors, polygyny, spiritual leadership, the organization of large-scale inter-band hunts and raiding parties, and participation in extensive exchange networks.

57. For examples of kinship studies of more recent Sioux groups, see Hassrick 1944:346–7; DeMallie 1979.

58. Schusky 1994:269. While this may have been true in mid-century, the *tiospaye* is now well known through a concentrated emphasis at least since the 1970s in schools and other contexts on teaching the ways of "traditional" culture.

59. DeMallie 1979. The conclusion that significant change did not occur within the traditional Sioux kinship system during the reservation years is surprising, for, as Eggan (1966:106) notes, "kinship terminologies are sensitive indicators of change."

5.   Fighting for Survival, 1850–1889

1. The literature on the Sioux Wars is immense. For summaries and additional references see, Dunlay 1982; Goetzmann 1959; Gump 1994; Hutton 1985; McGinnis 1990; Sandoz 1966; Utley 1973, 1984; also see Price 1996. Popular writers have described the "Sioux Wars" in detail in many novels, as in *The Plainsmen* series by Terry C. Johnston.

2. Howard 1972:292. Denig (1961:38–9) notes that by 1855 the Yankton were no longer supporting other Sioux groups in their conflicts with the Americans. Among the apparent reasons were satisfaction with the Laramie Treaty, familiarity with the power of the US through visits to eastern cities, a population reduced through infectious disease, and long and friendly relationships with Euro-American traders.

3. Robinson 1967 [1904]:171, 248–9; Howard 1972:289; Hoover 1988:25–53, 1996b. The Yankton ceded 11,155 acres to the US in 1858; they retained 430,000 acres as a reservation near Fort Randall. Most Yanktonai settled on one of four reservations. After 1867, the Cut-Heads joined Sisseton–Wahpeton people at Devil's Lake in North Dakota. In 1880, 5,208 Upper

Yanktonai were place with 1,432 Assiniboin and some Dakota around Fort Peck in Montana. Other Upper Yanktonai settled with some Lower Yanktonai (also called Hunkpatinas) around the Standing Rock Agency on the border of North and South Dakota. Its 1885 census listed 631 Upper and 1,347 Lower Yanktonai. Another group of Lower Yanktonai replaced Santee Dakota at Crow Creek, near the Fort Thompson Agency in South Dakota, in 1866 when the Santee moved to a reservation in Nebraska. Crow Creek remains the only reservation set up solely for Yanktonai. When established in 1889, it contained 285,521 acres.

4.   For the 1851 treaties, see Anderson 1984:177–202; also see Kane 1951 and Hughes 1929. In all, the Dakota gave up use rights to some 21 million acres for their new reservation, agency services, and annuities.

5.   The Spirit Lake massacre of c.40 settlers in northern Iowa and southern Minnesota in 1857 by a small number of Wahpekute led by Inkpaduta terrified settlers and fueled an already heightened mistrust of Indians. See Teakle 1918; Anderson 1984:217–22, 1986:82–3; Hughes 1908.

6.   The Dakota Conflict and events leading up to it have been told from many perspectives. Examples include Anderson 1984:261–80, 1986; Anderson and Woolworth 1988; Carley 1976; Gluek 1955; Henig 1976; Lass 1963; Oehler 1997 [1959]; Roddis 1956; Russo 1976; Schultz 1992. A series of military posts, which include Fort Seward (near Jamestown), Fort Ransom, and Fort Wadsworth (modern-day Sisseton), were established in Dakota Territory in the mid-1860s and 1870s in response to the Dakota Conflict (Athearn 1967). The conflict demonstrates the nominal power of Sioux chiefs, who were unable to control rebellious members of their bands before and during the conflict. Hyde (1937, 1961) documents the difficulty Red Cloud and Spotted Tail had in controlling their bands of Lakota in the latter half of the nineteenth century.

7.   The Santee were first placed on the Crow Creek Reservation but moved to the Santee Reservation in Nebraska in 1866. Subdivisions of Sisseton and Wahpeton were place on the Lake Traverse (officially the Sisseton–Wahpeton Sioux Reservation) and Devil's Lake (now Spirit Lake Nation) reservations in the late 1860s, too. About 2,500 Dakota had fled to Canada, where several hundred eventually remained on small reservations. Still others moved to Fort Peck Reservation in Montana, where a 1909 census counted 58 Sisseton and Wahpeton. For histories of these reservations, see Meyer 1993; Allen et al. 1971; Schusky 1975; Grobsmith 1981a; Ritter 1999; Nurge 1970; Hoxie 1979; also check the Web for information about these reservations. Meyer (1993) remains the best single source for the history of the Dakota during this period.

8.   For the rise of hide trade between 1850 and 1883, see Klein 1993 and Roe 1951.

9.   For the Bozeman Trail and Red Cloud's War, see Hyde 1937, 1961. For the location and numbers of western Sioux to 1868, see Hurt 1974:224–34. For a description of an Indian agency on the Great Sioux Reservation, see Clow 1977.

10.   For references to the Battle of the Little Bighorn, see notes 27 and 28 below.

11. For Crazy Horse, see Ambrose 1996 [1975]; Grimes 2000; Sandoz 1961 [1942].

12. For Sitting Bull, see Vestal 1989 [1932]; Utley 1993; Anderson 1996. For 1877–89 raiding by the Sioux, see McGinnis 1990:149–93. The final Indian rebellion, led by Geronimo, ended in 1886. For the Sioux agreement of 1889, see Hoover 1989.

13. In October 1883, Sitting Bull and his people were involved in the last major bison hunt on the Plains, when they pursued a herd of 1,000 bison near the border of the Dakotas and Montana. This was also the last year railroads shipped large numbers of hides out of the northern Plains for sale.

14. Many Sioux men, especially Oglala, performed in Wild West shows between 1883 and 1933, during which time they toured the nation and the world; see Moses 1996 and Reddin 1999. Other famous Sioux besides Sitting Bull who appeared in Wild West shows were Black Elk, an Oglala, and Luther Standing Bear, a Brulé. As an antidote to the Wild West shows, the Indian Service promoted the growth of Indian fairs, especially agricultural fairs, in keeping with its assimilationist policy. In the 1920s and 1930s, independent Lakota rodeos also gave the Lakota opportunities to gather as a people (Fuss 1999).

15. Viola 1976.

16. For Seth Eastman, see Eastman 1995 [1849]; Densmore 1954; McDermott 1961. For Frank Blackwell, see Mayer 1986 [1932] and Page 1978. The first known sketch of a Sioux seems to be in Carver (1956:Pl. 4).

17. For photographers of the American West (e.g., William Henry Jackson, John K. Hillers, Timothy O'Sullivan, Stanley J. Morrow, J. A. Anderson, and Alexander Gardner), see DeMallie 1981; Bush and Mitchell 1994; Fleming and Luskey 1986, 1993; Glenn 1983; Bush and Mitchell 1994; Hurt and Lass 1956. Edward Curtis was the best-known photographer of nineteenth-century Native America (Brown 1972; Graybill and Boesen 1981; Lyman 1982). For the most part, their photographs avoided the harsh realities of poverty and dislocation. For early photographers in Minnesota, see Wilson 1990 and Woolworth 1994. T. W. Ingersoll took numerous photographs of the Dakota in the 1890s.

18. Albers and James 1984, 1987.

19. For issues and approaches in visual anthropology, see Banta and Hinsley 1986; Malmsheimer 1987; Scherer 1990, 1992; Blackman 1986; Weber 1985. Also see the journals *Visual Anthropology* and *Studies in the Anthropology of Visual Communication.*

20. Blackman 1986; Malmsheimer 1987.

21. On Indian stereotypes in pictures, see Malmsheimer 1985, 1987; Hales 1988:33–4; Scherer 1975; Dippie 1992; Lyman 1982; Gidley 1985.

22. Compare the photograph of Little Crow as "chief" taken by A. Z. Shindler in 1858 (e.g., Meyer 1993, following p. 108) with that as transformed Euro-American "gentleman" in a photograph in the Bettmann Archive (e.g., Bonvillain 1997:46). For the tensions involved in this imposed transformation, compare the range in dress and posture of members of a Dakota delegation to Washington in 1858 (Meyer 1993, seventh photograph following p. 108).

23. On pictographic documents, such as winter counts, and their importance in providing cultural historical information, see Praus 1962; Howard 1960b, 1976; DeMallie 1982b; Sundstrom 1997; Risch 2000. Both Wood (1990:89) and Howard (1976:16) stress that pictographic documents must be read as critically as historic written documents.

24. For examples of photographs and drawings by Sioux, see Running 1985 and Brokenleg and Hoover 1993.

25. For ethical issues in photographing (or otherwise depicting) contemporary American Indians, see Brumbaugh 1999 and Martinez 1996.

26. For overviews of references to the "last stand," see Paul Hutton's bibliographical essay in his *Custer Reader* (1992) and the 1994 reprinting of Dippie's *Custer's Last Stand* (1976).

27. For archaeological studies of the battle, see Scott and Fox 1987; Scott et al. 1989; Gray 1991; Fox 1993. For Indian accounts of the battle, see Hardorff 1991; Miller 1992 [1957]; Michno 1997; Black Elk 2000 [1932]. For the claim that there may have been no "last stand," see Fox 1993.

28. Dippie 1994 [1976]; Hutton 1976; Leckie 1993.

29. Linenthal 1993.

30. For voluntary associations, see Anderson 1971; Ember and Ember 1990:220–34. The quote is from Anderson 1971:219.

31. Driver (1961:406), for example, found that common interest groups were absent among most historic Arctic, Sub-Arctic, Plateau, Great Basin, and Northeast Mexican foraging peoples. Although Ember and Ember's (1990) and Driver's interpretations are followed here, it seems increasingly unlikely that voluntary associations were as rare in some types of societies as they suggest.

32. Driver (1961:407–13) documents the importance of common interest groups among advanced hunting and gathering peoples. Familiar US associations include the Masons, Odd Fellows, and college fraternities.

33. For Lakota men's associations, see Wissler 1912; Hassrick 1964:15–25; Walker 1982. Men's associations were more weakly developed the further east one moved among the Sioux (Landes 1968:66–78; Lowie 1913).

34. Miller 1999:265.

35. Other women's associations included the Porcupine Quill Workers, the Praiseworthy Women, the Owns-Alone, the Tanners, and the Women's Medicine Cult (Walker 1982:62–3; Wissler 1912).

36. See Ritter (1980) for a parallel argument for the development of age-set systems.

37. Lowie 1970 [1920]:334; Hassrick 1964:20.

38. As might be expected, late twentieth-century associations among the Sioux include many more associations with a non-ritual focus than in the past.

39. Beck and Walters 1977:8–32.

40. For introductions to traditional Lakota religion, see Black Elk 2000 [1932]; Black Elk and Lyon 1990; DeMallie 1987; DeMallie and Lavenda 1977; DeMallie and Parks 1987; Walker 1980, 1983; Powers 1977, 1982, 1986; Hassrick 1964:245–95. For Traditional Lakota religion as practiced in the twentieth century, see Feraca 1998; DeMallie and Parks 1987:157–216; Clow

1990. Feraca (1998:93–104) and DeMallie and Parks (1987:217–25) are good sources for additional references to Lakota traditional religion, whether in the nineteenth century or today.

41.   The story of the gift of the holy pipe has been told many times. For examples, see Black Elk 2000 [1932]; Brown 1989 [1953]; Hoover 1988:48–51; Powers 1986:42–9; Hall 1997. See DeMallie (1984) for the likelihood that Black Elk selected Seven Sacramental Rites from Lakota religious practice to substitute for the Seven Sacraments he taught as a Catholic; if this is what happened, then the notion of Seven Sacraments is Christian, not Lakota or "Sioux" in a general sense.

42.   Walker 1917, 1980; Deloria 1929; Fletcher 1883; Liberty 1980; Spier 1921. The Sun Dance was perhaps the most important ceremony of the Yankton–Yanktonai and was practiced by the Dakota, too (Howard 1980 [1966]:9, 15).

43.   For Dakota traditional religion, see Wallis 1919; Pond 1986 [1908]:85–113; Skinner 1919b, 1920, 1925; Lowie 1913.

44.   For Yankton–Yanktonai religious practices, see Gillette 1906; Howard 1953, 1955b, 1980 [1966]; Howard and Hurt 1952; Hoover 1988:48-51.

45.   Although pipes have a long history of use in North America (Odell 1998), catlinite and in particular catlinite disc pipes were not in common use in the northern Plains until after c. ad 1300. This suggests that the "coming of the pipe," if it was rooted in an actual historical event, occurred sometime after then; counting backward through the recorded number of "keeper's of the pipe" puts this event near the beginning of the nineteenth century (Hall 1997:78). For the suggestion that the White Buffalo Calf Woman's myth might refer to an actual late prehistoric or protohistoric event, see Marla Powers (1986:50–2). Tobacco, which was a gift of the White Buffalo Calf Woman, too, has been found at Mille Lacs village sites in Minnesota, where it seems to date to the late prehistoric or protohistoric period, or both.

6.   Assimilation and Allotment, 1889–1934

1.   Wissler 1916:869.

2.   At the time, the Brulé (*Sicangu*) were on the Rosebud Reservation, the *Hunkpapa* on the Standing Rock Reservation, and the *Oglala* on the Pine Ridge Reservation; the Blackfoot (*Sihasapa*), Two Kettles (*Oohenunpa*), Minneconjou (*Mnikowoju*), and Sans Arc (*Itazipco*) were in the area of the Cheyenne River Reservation, while various groups of the above tribes ended up at Crow Creek and Lower Brulé (Powers 1996a:299).

3.   The Ghost Dance was one of several new religions that spread across the Great Plains and Western North America in the 1880s and 1890s. For the origin, nature, and spread of the ghost dance, see Mooney 1991 [1896]; DeMallie 1982c; Kehoe 1989. Despite the intensity of the movement in Lakota communities, not all Western Sioux approved of the Ghost Dance.

4.   Quoted in *The Reservations*, p. 105.

5.   In the words of the Oglala holy man Black Elk, "the Nation's hoop is bro-

ken and scattered. There is no center any longer, and the sacred tree is dead"
(Black Elk 2000 [1932]:270. What devastated the Sioux was not just the
Wounded Knee deaths, but US refusal to abide by treaties now that the
bison had been exterminated and the Indians were starving. The bands had
come to Pine Ridge Agency not to dance the Ghost Dance specifically, but to
negotiate restoration of lands unilaterally taken from the Great Sioux Reservation and of rations not delivered, that is, because of US violations of treaties. By 1890, the US government could send large numbers of troops to
crisis areas quickly because of the railroads. About 5,000 soldiers were sent
to the Pine Ridge Reservation to contain the Lakota outbreak that US officials thought imminent. For the events leading up to the killing of Sitting
Bull, see Anderson 1996. For Indian policemen, see Hagan 1966; Ellis 1999.
For the Wounded Knee massacre, see Brown 1991 [1970] and McDermott
1990.

6. The murder of Spotted Tail, a Lakota, by another Lakota, Crow Dog,
   prompted Congress to pass the Major Crimes Act; the Act gave the federal
   government authority to persecute crimes committed on Indian reservations
   (Clow 1998; Williams 1986:314). The US government had experimented
   with allotment throughout the 1800s, but until the Dawes Act, allotment
   had been voluntary. The amount of land given to every individual varied
   depending upon whether they were the head of a family (160 acres), a single
   adult (80 acres), or a child (40 acres). Allotments were increased in some
   areas as an inducement to accept allotments or where the land was suitable
   only for cattle ranching. For example, special terms in the Sioux Act passed
   by Congress in 1889 doubled the amount of land given to a Lakota head of
   family from 160 to 320 acres. For the General Allotment Act of 1887 and its
   impact on the Sioux and other Indians, see Otis 1973; Kickingbird and
   Ducheneaux 1973; McDermott 1991; McDonnell 1980, 1991; Clow 1987a.
7. The Yanktonai Crow Creek Reservation shrank from 285,521 acres when
   established in 1889 to 154,872 in 1950; Fort Peck shrank from 2,094,144
   acres to 1,100,859 by 1935; Standing Rock shrank from 2,672,640 acres to
   1,064,000 by 1950; Lake Traverse shrank from 918,779 acres in 1873 to
   117,119 acres in 1952; and the Yankton Reservation dwindled from 430,000
   acres to 34,802 by 1980 (Hoover 1996a, 1996b).
8. Quoted in Bonvillain 1997:84.
9. For the Canadian Sioux, see Laviolette 1991; Meyer 1968; Wallis 1947;
   Howard 1984.
10. A key to the government's assimilationist aims was the compulsory educa-
    tion of Indian children. On Indian education during this period in general,
    see Adams 1971; Adams 1995; Coleman 1993. See chapter 7 of this text for
    a review of formal education among the Sioux.
11. For Peyotism, see La Barre 1989 [1938]; Anderson 1980; Slotkin 1956;
    Stewart 1974, 1980, 1987, 1996. The Sun Dance was seldom held at this
    time, for it had been repressed and forbidden.
12. For the Grass Dance, see Wissler 1916 and Powers 1996b:476–7.
13. Larner 1987, 1996. A goal of the Society was to preserve Indian core values
    while promoting Indian assimilation into American society. Gertrude

Simmons Bonnin, a Yankton, was one of these remarkable early-twentieth-century red progressives.

14. For Collier's pre-1934 reformist activities, see Kelly 1983.

15. For the story of the Black Hills tragedy, see Lazarus 1991. James Crow Feather, who was selected chairman of the Council, and Henry Standing Bear epitomized this new breed of boarding-school graduate red progressive. Standing Bear was also a key figure in the Society of American Indians. Between 1974 and 1989, the Sioux won over $100 million in claims. Many other tribes have followed their lead in using litigation to secure their rights.

16. For the Meriam Report, see Parman 1996 and *The Problem of Indian Administration* 1971 [1928].

17. Walker 1983; Black Elk 2000 [1932]; Deloria 1978; Brown 1989 [1953]. Also see Deloria 1954; DeMallie 1984; McLaughlin 1990 [1916]. The Yankton Sioux are particular well known for their contribution to the preservation of traditional oral literature (Hoover 1988:93). Besides Ella Deloria (Finn 1995), other Yankton who have made prominent contributions are the Episcopal father Vine Deloria, Sr., "Grandma" White Tallow, and Joseph Rockboy.

18. On the distinctive meanings of Lakota literature, see Rice 1989, 1992b. For assorted "readings" of Black Elk over the years, see McCluskey 1972; Holly 1979; Bataille 1984; Deloria 1984; DeMallie 1984; Ellen 1986; Holler 1984, 2000a; Rice 1989, 1991. For the trend to devalue Black Elk's teaching, see Holler 2000b:xiii.

19. Benjamin 1968; also see Stamps 1995:23–40. On the value of and uses of narrative discourse, see White 1980, 1987; Carr 1986; Cohen 1989; Cruikshank 1998.

20. In Rosaldo's (1989:129) reading, narrative shapes rather than reflects human conduct.

21. Rice 1989:26. The categories in this and the following paragraph are taken from Julian Rice's insightful *Lakota Storytelling* (1989). Theisz (1975:6) distinguishes three kinds of Lakota oral narratives: *ehanni woyake* (accounts of the beginning of the world, and sacred beliefs and deities), *ehanni wicooyake* (historical accounts of recent events), and *ohunkanka woyake* (stories that teach a moral or amuse).

22. Rice 1989:3, 26.

23. In Cruikshank's (1998:40) words, oral traditions have "social histories, and they acquire meaning in the situations in which they are used."

24. Innis 1972 [1950]:64–100, 215–17; Stamps 1995:48–51, 65–96; Cruikshank 1992. Again, in Cruikshank's (1998:43–4) words: "oral tradition may tell us about the past, but its meanings are not exhausted with reference to the past. Good stories from the past continue to provide legitimate insights about contemporary events. What appears to be the 'same' story, even in the repertoire of one individual, has multiple meanings depending on location, circumstance, audience, and stage of life of narrator and listener."

25. This perspective raises questions that deserve attention. Why have so many Western analysts concentrated on recovering the "authentic" voice of the Sioux rather than on their social uses of narrative in the twentieth century?

What mechanisms have been used to displace the authority of the spoken word among the Sioux with literacy? What problems occur when multilayered Sioux narratives are removed from their cultural context as though their meanings are straightforwardly obvious? What can a study of oral tradition contribute to our understanding of how images of the past and present are formulated and publicly presented by the Sioux? What do these narratives tell us about the construction of local knowledge and of worldmaking among the Sioux? Why have Sioux elders selected some rather than other narratives as important ones to pass on to younger people in the twenty-first century? How is legitimacy claimed for oral narrative (Rushforth 1992, 1994)? Will the cultural prominence of oral narrative fade in Sioux culture in the twenty-first century for the same reasons it eventually faded in importance in Western cultures in the eighteenth and nineteenth centuries? For the claim that the Dakota oral tradition is of divine origin and, therefore, must not and cannot be evaluated in Western terms, see Wilson 1997.

26. Wallace 1956:265.

27. Wallace 1956:264; also see Linton 1943. For the notion of cultural revitalization more generally among American Indians, see Miller 1996.

28. For the Ghost Dance, see ch. 6, n. 3. The Grass Dance and Peyotism, another revitalization movement, were other belief systems that spread through Plains reservations in the 1880s. For general overviews of the Peyote religion and the Native American Church, see Slotkin 1956; La Barre 1989 [1938]; Anderson 1980; Stewart 1974, 1980, 1987, 1996.

29. Most Sioux tribes to the east did not adopt the Ghost Dance for one reason or another; some, for instance, had only recently been proselytized by the Dream Dance.

30. For discussions of prophetic movements, see Hadden and Shupe 1986 and Miller 1985.

31. Since the Sioux believed that animal spirits influenced a hunter's success, the leader of a hunt was often a prophet or visionary with links to the world of spirits (Walker 1982:76; Landes 1968:33, 49).

32. For an example of the use of prophecy by contemporary Sioux elders, see Wilson 1997.

33. For concepts of time in anthropology, see Gell 1996; Hughes and Trautman 1995; Munn 1992.

34. For Sioux notions of time and work, see Hassrick 1964:8–11; Pond 1986 [1908]:84, 176; Walker 1982:111–12, 122–3. The description provided here is a composite from these sources. There were most likely differences in detail in reckoning time among divisions of the Sioux.

35. For examples of and references to Sioux winter counts, see Hassrick 1964:346–51; Howard 1955a, 1960b, 1976; Mallery 1987 [1887]; Walker 1982:124–57; Henning 1982; Hurt 1974:85–6, 112–14, 135, 182–3; Sundstrom 1997; Risch 2000; Meya 1999.

36. For day counts on sticks, see Hassrick 1964:11.

37. For discussions of the rise of the modern Western concept of time and its implication for concepts of work and history, see Gell 1996; Hughes and Trautman 1995; Thompson 1967; Whipp 1987.

38. Walker 1982:112–15.
39. For comparative readings on the colonizing of time, see Cooper 1992 and Hughes and Trautman 1995.
40. For language as a tool of colonial expansion, see Cohn 1985, 1996:16–56; Fabian 1986; Tiffin and Lawson 1994; Raheja 1996.
41. In other parts of the world such as Africa and India, where assimilation was not the objective, particular native languages, such as Swahili in central Africa, were adopted as the lingua franca. The goal in these cases was not to civilize the natives but to obtain a cheap, captive workforce.

7. Restoration and Reorganization, 1934 – 1975

1. For the Indian Reorganization Act, see Taylor 1980 and Washburn 1984. Collier was Commissioner of Indian Affairs from 1933 to 1945. To obtain support for his new policies among Indians, he convened a series of ten congresses on reservations, the first of which was on a Sioux reservation. For Collier, the IRA and assimilation were not incompatible, although many other US officials considered the IRA just an alternative route to the end goal of complete assimilation.
2. For the details of the acceptance or rejection of the IRA on Sioux reservations, see Biolsi 1992 and Meyer1993; also see Clow 1989.
3. The ERA (Emergency Relief Administration) brand on cattle earmarked for food (rather than breeding) was generally read by undernourished Indians as "eat 'em right away."
4. Quoted in *The Reservations*, p. 163. For participation by the Sioux in the Civilian Conservation Corps, see Bromert 1978.
5. Some Sioux tribes, such as the Brulé at Rosebud, the Oglala at Pine Ridge, the Sisseton–Wahpeton at Lake Traverse, and the Yanktonai at Crow Creek probably lost political power by adopting the IRA, for they had prior constitutions that did not require oversight by the Office of Indian Affairs or by the Secretary of the Interior (Clow 1987a; Hoover 1996a:162, 1996b:707). The Yankton on the Yankton Reservation adopted forms of constitutional government in 1891 and 1932 but had not yet accepted the terms of the IRA by this writing (Hoover 1996b:707). For Sioux IRA colonies, see Bromert 1984.
6. Churchill (1999:52), for example, claims that some aspects of the IRA were "a consequence of the discovery of rich resources on Indian Territory"; as a result, non-Indian Americans "looked to find a way to retain the land in trust, where they might be exploited at controlled rates by preferred corporations for designated purposes and in the most profitable fashion imaginable."
7. The "rhetoric was frequently ugly. Alice Lee Jemison, a Seneca from New York and a federation member, urged repeal of the IRA and called for the dismissal of John Collier on grounds he was a communist and an atheist. Collier said her charges were 'glimmerings on the lunatic fringe'" (*The Reservations*, p. 174). For the American Indian Federation, see Hauptman 1983, 1996 (the quote is from Hauptman 1996:33).

8. Lawson 1982a. The Crow Creek Reservation lost 15,565 acres to the Fort Randall and Big Bend Dam projects (Hoover 1996b:706).

9. For the US government's termination policy, see Fixico 1986 and Burt 1982.

10. On the Yankton Reservation, for instance, "numerous government facilities were abandoned or offered for sale, and Greenwood went into decline as a center of activity. The Indian hospital at Wagner now became a public health service facility, and Farm Station #2 at Lake Agnes, the colony facilities, and some buildings in Greenwood were turned over to the tribe" (Hoover 1988:65).

11. The relocation period in federal Indian policy was the decade of the 1950s. For the US government's 1950s relocation movement, see Burt 1986; Fixico 1986; Joe 1987. In part, the government was responding to a dramatic increase in the number of recognized Indians now on reservations, as recorded by US Census figures from 1900 to 1950. Efforts by the federal government to attract light industries to reservations in the 1950s and early 1960s had also largely failed; see, for example, Hoover (1988:67–8).

12. About 50 people lived at Prairie Island in 1935, 82 in 1937 (including some members of other tribes), 86 in 1962, and 61 in 14 families in 1968 (Landes 1968:19; also see Meyer 1961).

13. The social and economic programs of Johnson's Great Society initiative did not aid all Sioux equally. The Yankton are an example: "Besides recovering full agency status in 1969, the only benefit they received was federal aid for new housing. Both scatter and cluster housing was constructed. These looked like working-class suburban development dwellings, and were painted in bright, gaudy colors. The houses could be rented for modest fees, and the housing was the first new construction in some 50 years. However, there was still little work and almost no recreational facilities" (Hoover 1988:68–9).

14. For instance, at Prairie Island in the late 1960s: "the average income per reservation family at Prairie Island was $1600. They also received about $1700 in assistance in various forms, including pensions, tribal subsidies, tax exemption, welfare, OASI, and medical services. The average family cash income for Goodhue County for all families at the time was $4900 and $3300 for Indian Families. There was no schooling past 9th grade on average, although the average statewide schooling for non-Indian children was only 10th grade. About 25% of the Prairie Island families had telephones" (Landes 1968:20–1; also see Meyer 1961). In 1950, the lowest annual family income reported among the Western Sioux was $767 at Standing Rock (Hoover 1996b:707; also see Howard 1972:282).

15. Many of Vine Deloria, Jr.'s most popular books (e.g., *Custer Died for Your Sins*) first appeared near the end of this period. By contrast, Luther Standing Bear's books, which appeared in the late 1920s and early 1930s (and which are still being published in new editions), were an early influence in the period. Dee Brown's immensely popular *Bury My Heart at Wounded Knee*, which was published in 1970, aroused popular sympathy for the Sioux.

16. For the occupation in 1969 of Alcatraz Island and other Sioux-led protests during this period, see Smith and Warrior 1996. Demands for civil rights

had recently been supported by Congressional affirmation in the Civil Rights Act in 1964, and was part of the "counter-culture" of the late 1960s. The growing popularity of the concept of "cultural relativism" may also have played a role in this movement, for the notion made it acceptable to assert pride in one's own cultural heritage, even though (and especially if) it was different from that of a dominant society.

17. For the history of AIM and its role in Indian nationalism, see Bonney 1977 and Means 1995.

18. See Reinhardt 1999; Dewing 1985; Smith and Warrior 1996. Robert Burnette, a former tribal chairman at Rosebud, originally proposed the Indian march on Washington that became the Trail of Broken Treaties.

19. For the origins of the powwow and its styles, see Powers 1996b; also see Powers 1990b and Black Bear and Theisz 1976.

20. For general reviews, see Verano and Ubelaker 1992; Crosby 1986; Ramenosfsky 1987; Campbell 1989a.

21. Aufderheide et al. 1994. The skeletons that were examined were assumed to be late prehistoric and protohistoric Mdewakanton Dakota because they were in sites said by archaeologists to be Mdewakanton Dakota. However, a word of caution. Some individuals, in particular the major burial in the Cooper Mound (21ML16), were buried with Oneota pottery vessels. Given the complex relationships that may have existed between the Oneota and Psinomani, and the mix of individuals in historic villages, these individuals could have been allies who were ancestral Iowa or Oto rather than ancestral Dakota. An axiom of Helen Tanner's is relevant here: "no tribal village whose membership one can count and trace in detail will be found to contain only members of that tribal community" (reported in Hoxie 1997:610).

22. Green 1993; Owsley 1992:83; Ramenosfsky 1987. The argument is that disease pathogens spread along aboriginal trade routes before the arrival of Euro-American traders, with horses moving northward from the Southwest and trade goods moving westward from the Northeast.

23. Aufderheide et al. 1994:334–41; also see Myster and O'Connell 1997a, 1997b. As the authors stress, sampling problems may have influenced their conclusions. The mean stature of adult males and females was 167 cm (c.5′ 5″) and 163 cm (c.5′ 4″), respectively.

24. These numbers are based on the estimated size of the Mille Lacs site cluster population discussed in chapter 2, times the number of additional clusters that are thought to have existed. Gary Anderson (1984:18–19), an historian, has suggested that there were about 38,000 Sioux in 1650 on the basis of admittedly shaky early population reports. In broader context, population size estimates based on archaeological samples are usually lower, often much lower, than estimates found in early written records. In these cases, just what is fact and what is supposition, guesstimate, or deception has to be carefully worked out. I maintain, however, that individuals who argue for large numbers of late prehistoric Sioux must support their claims by reference to the archaeological record (i.e., numbers and sizes of habitation sites).

25. For epidemic diseases in the northern Plains, see Dobyns 1983; Ramenofsky 1987; Owsley 1992; Owsley and Jantz 1994; Decker 1991; Trimble 1979,

1989; Sundstrom 1997. For demographic studies of nomadic Plains groups during the nineteenth century, see Campbell 1989b and Taylor 1989.

26. For the devastating 1837 epidemic, see Crosby 1976; Trimble 1979, 1994. For the 1832 inoculation program on the Missouri River, which was one outcome of the Vaccination Act of 1832, see Trimble 1992. The 1837 small-pox epidemic spread rapidly among the Yankton and Santee Sioux at Sioux subagencies in central South Dakota who had refused vaccination. About 900 Lakota, 256 Yanktonai, 1,062 Yankton, and 294 other Sioux were vaccinated during the 1832 program, making the western Sioux the main beneficiaries of the program. For treaty sites as a source of disease, see Dobyns 1992:215. At the 1825 Prairie du Chien treaty session, dysentery killed some Indians at the session and many others on their way home.

27. For alcohol abuse and chemical dependency among Indians in general, see May 1989, 1996; Ebbott 1985:220–35. For body weight gains, see Johnston and Schell 1979. For a review of trends in Indian health, see Ebbott 1985:199–235 and Campbell 1989a. For depression among the early reservation Sioux, see Dewing 1991. For the relationship between identity, self-esteem, emotional well-being substance abuse, and depression among the Sioux, see Pittenger 1998; Daniels 1999; Williams 1998.

28. Ebbott 1985. Two studies among the Standing Rock Sioux in 1960 and 1980 reported a decline in drinking prevalence from 69 percent to 58 percent (May 1996:24). For the Indian Health Care Service and the Indian Health Care Improvement Act of 1976, see Campbell 1996.

29. For an overview of traditional Indian medicine and concepts of disease, see Locust 1996; Jurich 1992; Ellerby 2000. For examples of their incorporation into contemporary Sioux health-care management systems, see Lang 1985; Stone 1998; Ingram 1989; Selzler 1996; Lawrence 1999.

30. Netting et al. 1984:xx. For introductions to households, domestic groups, and families, see Bender 1967; Blanton 1994; Harris 1984; Mac Eachern et al. 1989; Miller 1999:212–33; Netting et al. 1984; Yanagisako 1979. This introduction glosses over the many conceptual and methodological problems involved in household studies. In some definitions of "household," not all members need be in residence (e.g., a husband or child working elsewhere who sends money back home). In contrast to a household, a family is made up of people who consider themselves related through kinship. An important concept not considered here is the house, whose form documents the changing sexual, social, ideological, and economic relations that produced it (Blanton 1994). Different house styles reflect different ideals and enforce different social divisions. The shape, size, adornment, and other characteristics of Sioux houses have changed through time. A related topic not considered here except in passing is the effect on Sioux lifeways of government housing.

31. Wilk and Netting 1984; Pasternak et al. 1976.

32. Hassrick 1964:11–15; DeMallie 1976:81–2. A *Tiyospaye* usually contained fewer than 30 tipis. According to DeMallie (1976:81), a single *Tiyospaye* was composed of 5 to 20 related families.

33. Hassrick 1964:119.

34. Hassrick 1964:173.
35. Hassrick 1964:171–6, 209–42. For the internal structure of a typical tipi, see Hassrick 1964:213–14. Dogs and occasionally favored horses might also occupy household space.
36. For Dakota village and household life, see Landes 1968:28–48. By contrast, the household among contemporary Ojibwa in northern Minnesota was essentially autonomous throughout the year; households coalesced only for a brief summer interval of village life, during which, however, a household retained its independence (Landes 1937).
37. Hennepin (1938:107) mentions that Aquipaguetin, a chief he encountered at Mille Lacs in 1680, "showed me five or six of his wives." The argument here is that household function and morphology changed because of a change in how and why work was done. According to the logic of this argument, the pre-reservation Ojibwa in northern Minnesota are not a good analogue for Psinomani lifeways because of their emphasis on the autonomous household unit rather than the tightly knit, cooperative village. It should be stressed that in this section I am developing a model of household change among the prehistoric Sioux; while the model fits the archaeological record as I understand it, it has not been tested in a focused study.
38. Violence between domestic partners is found in all cultures in varying forms and frequencies; males dominate as perpetrators and women as victims. For cross-cultural perspectives, see Counts et al. 1992 and Levinson 1989.
39. Even with this brief review, it should be apparent that the relationship between household function and morphology is a rich avenue of inquiry into Sioux culture and its change. Among the many questions that might be asked about Sioux households now and in the past are: How and why have households varied within and between Sioux communities at particular times in the past? What was daily life like in a typical Lakota or Dakota household in 1550, 1650, 1750, and 1850? What life phases did a nineteenth-century Sioux household go through during its existence? How and why have Sioux households changed through time? Did the shift to a tribal mode of social organization result in increased competition among the domestic units of close kin? Did a late prehistoric household form persist (with some adjustments) into the reservation period or did some groups adopt new household forms? How did the fur trade and the hide trade (and epidemics, dislocations, reservations, and casinos) affect household composition among the Sioux? How did the household of a resident fur trader married to a Sioux woman differ from a "full-blood" Sioux household (and could we tell the difference in the archaeological record)? How do ideal models of households in Sioux communities today differ from actual households?
40. For traditional Sioux education, see Pond 1986 [1908]:142–6.
41. For the role of churches in Indian education, see Morris 1996 and Bowden 1981. For mission schools among the Sioux, see Peterson 1985; Duratschek 1947; Hoover 1988; Schneider 1994:209–15; Galler 1998, 2000; Clemmons 2001; Enochs 1994; Ekquist 1999; Lamb 1998. In North Dakota, Indian Affairs allotted Sioux reservations to various denominations in 1872.

42. Adams 1995; Molin 2001.
43. For federal Indian education policy until c.1934, see Berry 1968 and Szasy 1996; for its application to Sioux children, see Erikson 1939; Ahler 1980; Beaulieu 1971; Hulston 1995; Riney 1998, 1999. For the curriculum in Sioux territory, see Olsen 1953 and Meyer 1993:185–9.
44. For trends in Indian education since 1928, see Szasy 1996; Boyer 1996; Crum 1996; Demmert 1996a, 1996b; Gipp 1996; Reyhner and Eder 1989; Trennert 1996.
45. American Indian advocacy groups that have worked toward reforms in Indian education include the Committee of One Hundred (created on a temporary basis in 1923), the Society of American Indians (founded in 1911), the national Indian Education Association (founded in 1970), and the American Indian Higher Education Consortium (founded in 1973). See Antell 1996.
46. Numerous studies and reports have focused on Indian education. For a sample involving the Sioux, see Telford 1932; Spilka 1970; Bryde 1970; Riney 1999; also see Macgregor 1946.
47. For Congressional acts, see Gipp 1996; Demmert 1996a; Szasy 1996.
48. See note 43 above for examples. Children on the Pine Ridge Reservation have been the focus of many of these studies.
49. For detailed histories of scholarship in Siouan, see Chafe (1976) and Rood (1978); for references, see Hollow and Parks 1980. Also see Sherzer 1976; Rood 1979; Boas 1937; Boas and Swanton 1911; Parks and DeMallie 1992; Grant 1971. Hollow and Parks (1980:69) state that no Siouan language has been adequately described. At the level of language, the seven major divisions of the Sioux were dialect groups, with the drift greatest between the most distant east–west groups. For criticism of the Dakota–Nakota–Lakota division as traditionally presented, see Parks and DeMallie 1992. Since the use of the word "Dakota" for both the language group and for the dialect of the Dakota (Santee) subdivision of the Sioux is confusing, the expression "Santee (Dakota)" for the latter is used here.
50. Hollow and Parks 1980:75; also see Chafe 1962.
51. For Assiniboin and Stoney, see Levin 1964; Parks and DeMallie 1992; Hollow 1970; Bellam 1975; and Lowie 1909, 1960. For the Dakota (Santee), see Riggs 1852, 1992 [1890], 1973 [1893]; Williamson 1902. For the Lakota, see Buechel 1939, 1970; Boas and Deloria 1933, 1941; Deloria 1954. Father Eugene Buechel was a Jesuit missionary and Ella Deloria a native Lakota trained in linguistics by Franz Boas. Also see Carter (1974). Because the Plains contained a rich mosaic of at least 33 distinct languages or dialects, a lingua franca was necessary for tribes to interact. Before the adoption of English for this purpose in the second half of the nineteenth century, tribes communicated through sign language (Mallery 1880a, 1880b; Tomkins 1969). The Dakota (Santee) did not practice the developed sign language of the Plains, though they did have a limited sign language (Landes 1968:86–7).
52. Gilmore 1991 [1919]; Matthews 1959. Matthews concluded that the Proto-Siouan speech community had an Omaha-like kinship system. An earlier study by Lesser (1930) based on ethnological information concluded it was

bilateral. For general introductions to sociolinguistics, see Hymes (1974) and Spolsky (1998).

53. For example, Wilson 1997:104–6.

8.   The Sioux Today: Self-Determination, 1975–2000

1.   Danzinger 1996; Trope 1996; Churchill 1999:55.
2.   Churchill 1996a; Lazarus 1991; Pommersheim 1996.
3.   For the Big Foot Memorial Riders, see *The Reservations*, p. 176. For the Mah-Kato Powwow, see Bonvillain 1997:102.
4.   For examples of studies of the Sioux economy since 1975, see Bonvillain 1997:92–5, 101; Hoover 1988:97–8; Pickering 1996; for comparison, see Mekeel 1932, 1936.
5.   For the negative effects of gaming among Sioux communities, see Cozzetto 1995; Cozzetto and Larocque 1996; Bonvillain 1997:95–100.
6.   Sioux communities and reservations west of the plush Twin Cities market have also opened casinos. Examples are the Fire Fly Casino at Upper Sioux, the Fort Totten Casino at Devil's Lake (Spirit Lake), the Fort Randall Casino on the Yankton Reservation, the Lode Star Casino on the Crow Creek Reservation, the Dakota Sioux Casino at Lake Traverse, and the Royal River Casino at the Flandreau Santee Reservation.
7.   For Sioux education since 1975, see the numerous Web pages for individual Sioux reservations and for the "bureaus of education" (which have various names) for Minnesota, Nebraska, and the Dakotas. Another informative source is the National Indian Education Association (NIEA), whose president, president-elect, and vice president at the time of writing are Lakota or Dakota.
8.   For the modern Sioux giveaway, see Hoover 1988:89–90; Grobsmith 1979, 1981b. If a group or community sponsors a giveaway to recognize or solicit cooperation beyond the community, visitors might also be honored with gifts.
9.   For examples of the revival of traditional ceremonies and arts and crafts, see Hoover 1988:81–8, 98.
10.   For modern day powwows, see Powers 1996b; Roberts 1992; Mattern 1999; Theisz 1987.
11.   For the heirship problem, the 1984 heirship bill, and the expansion of tribal land, see Bonvillain 1997:97–8 and Lawson 1982b, 1991.
12.   For an example of the blend of cultures in new housing, see Hoover 1988:69, 93.
13.   Population figures for only some Sioux reservations are listed here. Acceptable employment opportunities have been responsible in part for often soaring membership on some reservations. For instance, membership on the Yankton Reservation grew from 2,200 in 1858, to 4,500 in 1980, to about 6,000 in 1992 (with 3,400 in residence); at Lake Traverse, enrollment jumped from 1,677 in 1875, to 3,648 in 1952, to 10,073 in 1992 (Hoover 1996a:162, 1996b:708). Some reservations are shared with members of other Indian

tribes and a few have been closed. Tipiota near Wabasha in southern Manitoba closed in 1946, and the Turtle Mountain and Cypress Hills communities established by Sitting Bull lost their status as recognized reservations by 1910. For the distribution of the Sioux on reservations by division, see Howard 1980 [1966]:10, 19, 25. In the US there are now eight Sioux reservations in South Dakota, two in North Dakota, four in Minnesota, one in Nebraska, and one in Montana, which is shared with Assiniboin (see the map in Hoover 1996c:600).

14. For tension between factions, see Churchill 1999; Lazarus 1991; Daniels 1970; Anderson 1991. Contra Lazarus, Churchill (1999:43) finds no real evidence that mixed-bloods were any more responsible for the many problems that Indians had in the past than were full-bloods, though there are famous examples of this occurring. An example is Charles Picotte, a mixed-blood Yankton chief, who "allegedly profited enormously by cooperating with the Whites in alienating tribal lands" (Howard 1972:304).

15. For problems with tribal leaders, see Mihesuah 1999:27 and Reinhardt 2000. The 1973 factional dispute at Pine Ridge over Richard "Dick" Wilson's policies is the most publicized example (e.g., Churchill 1996a, 1996b).

16. Bonvillain 1997:101–2.

17. Hoover 1988:70–1, 74.

18. According to Howard (1980 [1966]:1), for example, "With respect to the subdivisions of the tribe, confusion tends to run rampant, and with increasing acculturation even the older members of the tribe have forgotten the traditional distinctions. Identifications tend to be based upon reservation or geographical area rather than division or band."

19. For the push toward sovereignty among the Sioux, see Deloria and Lytle 1998 and Fouberg 1997. For the importance of modern electronic media is promoting cultural revitalization among the Sioux, see Mizrach 1999. The Boldt decision concerned fishing rights in the state of Washington and the Voigt decision fishing, hunting, and gathering rights in the state of Wisconsin.

20. For reasons to stay on reservations, see Hoover 1988:71–3.

21. For explorations of Indian humor, see Basso 1979; Ryan 1992; Lincoln 1993; Price 1998. Since dominant societies generally consider those they dominate too dim-witted to have humor, it should be no surprise that North American Indians were once considered a rather stoic, dull-witted lot, too (Purdie 1993).

22. The word "humor" has a long and interesting history. Its modern use as denoting anything that makes us laugh is recent. For brief but informative reviews, see "Humour" in the *Encyclopedia Britannica* (1972) and Freud (1928). A more detailed review of Sioux humor would distinguish between nuances of humor, such as wit, irony, comedy, sarcasm, satire, teasing, caricature, punning, burlesque, and parody. The modern cartoon, which is alive and well in Indi'n country, is pictorial humor.

23. Lincoln 1993:6.

24. Starita 1995:247.

25. Stated tersely, "making fun is a way of making sense" (Lincoln 1993:102). In urban settings, some individuals of Indian heritage work out their iden-

tity through joking, which they occasionally do as standup comics (Price 1998). For a relevant discussion of the role of the standup comedian as anthropologist, see Koziski 1984.

26. Reported in Lincoln 1993:58.
27. Deloria 1988 [1969]:146. Deloria is a superb jokester who counts coup through comic jibes at anthropologists, clerics, Congress, and anyone else he disagrees with or he thinks needs a jibe. Although humorous, this is serious play with real things at stake, both cultural and self-definitional. See Lincoln 1993:25–6.
28. John Lame Deer, Wallace Black Elk, Guy Dull Knife Sr,. and Frank Fools Crow are examples of Sioux jokesters (Mails 1990 [1978]:8; Black Elk 1990; Starita 1995:246–7; also see Howard 1962.
29. Many activities can be interpreted as "counting coup," even scoring in basketball (Colton 2000).
30. Vine Deloria, Jr. (1988 [1969]:167) has said, "When a people can laugh at themselves and laugh at others and hold all aspects of life together without letting anybody drive them to extremes, then it seems to me that that people can survive." For introductions to Vine Deloria, Jr.'s wide-ranging thought, see Deloria et al. 1999 and Biolsi and Zimmerman 1997. Among the best known of his books are *Custer Died for Your Sins* (1969), *We Talk, You Listen* (1970), *God is Red* (1992), *Behind the Trail of Broken Treaties* (1974), and *The Nations Within: The Past and Future of American Indian Sovereignty* (with Clifford Lytle, 1998).
31. Lincoln 1993:77. Early-twentieth-century Sioux holy men, such as John Lame Deer and Nick Black Elk, were more inventive *heyoka* than tragic visionary (Brown 1979:57; Lame Deer and Erdoes 1994). For discussions of the *heyoka*, see Densmore 1992 [1918]:158–9; Howard 1954.
32. Brown 1979:56.
33. For this reason, the Western dichotomy between serious and fun is not an appropriate framework for the study of Sioux humor, for they are inextricably melded together in traditional Sioux culture. Because it was a deeply based ingredient of traditional Sioux culture, the Bureau of Indian Affairs attempted to suppress Sioux clowning into the 1920s under the "religious crimes code."
34. According to oral tradition, there always has been humor among the Sioux. One can imagine that humor served as a survival skill during the stressful tribalization process of the fourteenth century, during the movement out of the northwoods in the seventeenth and eighteenth centuries, and during their confrontations with Euro-Americans in the nineteenth century. Among the many questions that one might ask about humor in Sioux culture are: What do Sioux laugh about today? Is there a difference between what they laugh at today and what they laughed at 100 years ago, 200 years ago, and so on? How does humor among the Sioux vary by age and gender? In what ways does traditional Sioux humor differ from Euro-American humor? Are there adequate intercultural models for translating traditional Sioux humor? How have and do Sioux use humor as an intra-tribal political tool?
35. There is a large literature on Euro-American views of Indians. For a mix of

views, see Friar and Friar 1972; Green 1975, 1988; Berkhofer 1978, 1988; Bataille and Silet 1980; Lyman 1982; Stedman 1982; Ewers 1965; Albers and James 1987; Hanson and Rouse 1987; Fiedler 1988; Albers 1989; Bieder 1986; Maltz and Archambault 1995:241–5; Jojola 1996; and Mihesuah 1996. For reviews of the drunken Indian stereotype and alcohol abuse among Indians, see Whittaker 1962, 1982; May 1989, 1996, 1999. For stereotypes of Sioux women, see Albers and James 1987:35, 37, and of the Dakota, see White 1992. For the Pocahontas image, see Deloria 1988 [1969]:3–4 and Green 1975. For Indian views of the image, see "'Pocahontas': One of the best or worst films about American Indians?" (*Indian Country Today*, June 1, 1995, p. C3) and "Pocahontas Rates an F in Indian Country" (*Indian Country Today*, July 6, 1995, p. D1). For a reexamination of Pocahontas as a real woman, see Kidwell 1992:99–101. Other common stereotypes of Indian males are the Cadillac Indian and the Lonesome Polecat.

36. For the role of museums and academics in perpetuating stereotypes of Native peoples, see Ames 1992 and Nason 1996. Anthropologists have reinforced cultural stereotypes of the Sioux by emphasizing the unusual (e.g., the extremes of the Sun Dance) and by focusing disproportionately on Sioux culture in the "ethnographic present" of the nineteenth century. Because these studies dominate the bookshelves, they contribute to the perpetuation of images of the Sioux as "primitive," "warlike," "poverty-stricken," and exotic.

37. Maltz and Archambault 1995:242. Mihesuah (1996:25) suggests that the positive stereotypes of the 1960s and 1970s might account for some non-Indians and mixed-heritage peoples' decision to identity themselves as Indians, a decision that is responsible in part for the dramatic increase in numbers of Indians counted in the 1980 census; since 1960, when the US Bureau of Census began asking people to identify themselves by ethnic group or race, the American Indian population has nearly tripled.

38. For classic examples of oversimplified, negative stereotyping of white American academics (and of women in general) by a Lakota, see Deloria 1988 [1969]:83–6. For comment on his stereotypes, see Medicine 1978:4. For vested economic and social interests, see Rouse and Hanson 1991. Current examples of an escalation of negative stereotypes (of both Indians and whites) abound in those areas of the US where Indians and non-Indians are clashing over hunting and fishing rights and rights to other economic resources.

39. For efforts by the Sioux to respond to negative stereotyping, see Deloria 1988 [1969]. Activists have also challenged negative portrayals of Indians by sports teams (the Washington Redskins, the Atlanta Braves, etc.), in films and videos (e.g. Disney's 1995 *Pocahontas*), and in geographical place-names (e.g., Squaw Lake).

40. This "tough love" conclusion has been expressed by a number of students of the situation. According to Maltz and Archambault (1995:245), "What American Indian people need to have is a vision of themselves that is realistic. They need to see themselves as part of the human condition, not as images of utopia. They need to have a vision of themselves and their history that is genuinely human and not always flattering."

41. Rouse and Hanson 1991.
42. For a comprehensive list, see Churchill (1999:30–1). Other reasons are: (1) While thousands of Sioux still live on reservations, many more live in urban centers and are being acculturated to an urban lifestyle. Are second- and third-generation urban "Sioux" still Sioux? (2) Some individuals claim to be Sioux only when it is economically profitable or socially desirable to be a Sioux, or both. Are these on-again, off-again "Sioux" really Sioux? (3) Being "Sioux" in some instances determines who gets casino profits. (4) The number of individuals who identify themselves as Sioux is growing. Why? (5) Many Sioux have several ethnic and other identities depending on where they live, what they do, and who their parents are.. (6) The identity of a person as Sioux is at times a political issue (rather than a genetic or cultural issue) because of factional struggles for power, benefits, or values. (7) Since there is a growing consensus that studies of the Sioux should include Sioux voices, there is a concern that "genuine" Sioux participate in the process. What does "genuine" mean here and how is it decided? For the latter point, the notion is that Sioux or Indians in general "can best identify the forces that shape their unique self-images" (Churchill 1999:31). For discussions of the notion that a Native qua Native has a privileged perspective on the history of their cultural tradition, see Gable et al. 1992 and Hastrap 1993.
43. Churchill 1999:7. For discussions of the important issue of Sioux and Indian identity, see Clifton 1990; Daniels 1970; Green 1995; Bordewich 1996; Nagel 1996; Jaimes 1992, 1996; Mihesuah 1996, 1999; Churchill 1999; Anderson 1997. For relevant related discussions, see Friedman 1992; Bordewich 1996; Rasmussen 1997.
44. As stated by Churchill (1999:43) for Indian identity in general, "by 1830, at the latest, the notion of defining 'Indianness' in terms of race had been rendered patently absurd." Nor was degree of blood quantum a measure of loyalty to traditional Sioux interests. Crazy Horse, the Oglala Lakota leader, may have been of mixed "racial" descent, while Red Cloud, Little Big Man, Bull Head, and other "full-bloods" "did much to undercut the ability to sustain Lakota resistance" (Churchill 1999:45). Names of sizable mixed-blood families among the Lakota include Pourier, Garnier, Amiott, Robideaux, Archambault, and Mousseau (Churchill 1999:41).
45. For the notion that some groups get preferential treatment because of blood quantum, see Churchill 1999:50, 63. Also see Wilson 1992 and Jaimes 1992.
46. For instructive discussions of this issue, see Rushmore 1914; McBeth 1983; Adams 1995.
47. Although well intended and effective, the passage of the Act for the Protection of American Indian Arts and Crafts in 1990 resulted in a hunt by some for fake Lakota and other Indians. The intent of the act was to protect Indian culture by making it a criminal offense to fraudulently identify oneself as Indian in order to sell artwork (Sheffield 1997). Also, see the 1993 series of articles in *Indian Country Today* by Jerry Reynolds on "Indian" writers. This was the first major legislation to legitimize the idea that a person without tribal membership is not an Indian. For problems

associated with not looking like an Indian, see Wilson 1992 and Hilden 1995.

48. For criteria for tribal membership, see Snipp 1989:362–5. Today, the Bureau of Indian Affairs (BIA) and the US Department of Education recognize as Indian only those who are accepted as such by a federally recognized tribe. There is a deeper and more ominous issue associated with the insistence on maintaining blood quantum levels for tribal membership. If the present trend of intermarriage with non-Sioux continues, the Sioux could become extinct by legal definition in the future. Questions of identity are not only entangled with issues of sovereignty, then, but with continued existence as federally recognized tribes.

49. For examples of infighting among factions, see Hilden 1995 and Reinhardt 2000.

50. See Mihesuah 1999:26. Prominent historic examples are Gertrude Simmons Bonnin, a Yankton, and Dr. Charles Eastman, a Dakota. Both lived away from their tribes and were successful in a White world. However, neither was fully accepted as a member of their tribe. For information on Gertrude Simmons Bonnin, see Fisher 1979; Johnson and Wilson 1988; Welch 1985. Besides being a blunt-spoken red progressive, she was a teacher and prolific writer, who wrote under the pen name Zitkala Śa. For Charles Eastman, see Wilson 1983; also see Eastman 1931, 1991 [1902]. Eastman's mother, Nancy Eastman, was the daughter of Seth Eastman, the artist and Fort Snelling army officer, and Wakaninajin ("Stands Sacred"), a Santee woman. This issue is clouded, too, by the reconstructed and perhaps fabricated nature of some Lakota traditions. As expressed by William Powers (1990a:52), a good deal "of what passes for Indian culture and religion has been fabricated by the white man, or the Indian who has been trained in the white man's schools." Interestingly, anthropologists tend to side with traditionalists, for they are generally more interested in traditional culture than in the highly acculturated lifestyle of many progressive Sioux. Since they also tend to be somewhat politically liberal, they often regard Native progressives as political "conservatives." Disputes between progressives and traditionalists over the best ways to proceed are often intense, for power, values, and increasingly money are at stake. Although viewed as factionalism from the outside, these disputes are part of a process of change and preservation among contemporary Indian communities (Champagne 1999:9–10).

51. Churchill 1999:54; also see, Fixico 1986 and Burt 1982. According to the 1990 US census, somewhat over one million American Indians live in urban areas and only about 700,000 on or near a reservation. The census count is based on the number of people who check the Indian category for race. The widespread claim is that many other people of Indian descent were either overlooked, chose not to mark that category, or refused to participate in the census (Champagne 1999:7).

52. The result in some cases was the exclusion from tribal membership of thousands of children who had been adopted by non-Indian couples or orphaned, regardless of quantum of Indian blood. A group of council heads

were able through a federally funded lobbying organization called the National Tribal Chairmen's Association (NTCA) to have the definition of "Indian" changed to exclude those who were not enrolled in a federally recognized tribe.

53. I was told this beautiful story by Karri Plowman, who heard a Lakota man tell the story at the 2001 Mankato Powwow.

Bibliography

Abel, Annie H. (ed.) 1939. *Tabeau's Narrative of Loisel's Expedition to the Upper Missouri*. University of Oklahoma Press, Norman.

Ackerknecht, Erwin H. 1945. *Malaria in the Upper Mississippi Valley, 1760–1900*. Johns Hopkins University Press, Baltimore.

Ackermann, Gertrude W. 1931. Joseph Renville of Lac qui Parle. *Minnesota History* 12:231–46.

Adams, Arthur T. (ed.) 1961. *The Explorations of Pierre Esprit Radisson*. Ross & Haines, Minneapolis.

Adams, David W. 1995. *Education for Extinction: American Indians and the Boarding School Experience, 1875–1928*. University Press of Kansas, Lawrence.

Adams, Evelyn C. 1971. *American Indian Education: Government Schools and Economic Progress*. Arno Press, New York.

Ahler, Janet G. 1980. The Formal Education of Plains Indians. In *Anthropology on the Great Plains*, edited by W. Raymond Wood and Margot Liberty, pp. 245–54. University of Nebraska Press, Lincoln.

Albers, Patricia C. 1982. Sioux Kinship in a Colonial Setting. *Dialectical Anthropology* 6:253–69.

Albers, Patricia C. 1983. Sioux Women in Transition: A Study of Their Changing Status in a Domestic and Capitalist Sector of Production. In *The Hidden Half: Studies of Plains Indian Women*, edited by Patricia Albers and Beatrice Medicine, pp. 175–236. University Press of America, Lanham, Md.

Albers, Patricia C. 1985. Autonomy and Dependency in the Lives of Dakota Women: A Study in Historical Change. *Review of Radical Political Economics* 17:109–34.

Albers, Patricia C. 1989. From Illusion to Illumination: Anthropological Studies of American Indian Women. In *Gender and Anthropology*, edited by Sandra Morgen, pp. 132–70. American Anthropological Association, Washington, DC.

Albers, Patricia C., and William R. James. 1984. The Dominance of Plains Imagery on the Picture Post Card. In *Fifth Annual 1981 Plains Indians Seminar in Honor of John C. Ewers*, edited by George P. Horse Capture and Gene Balls, pp. 73–97. Buffalo Bill Historical Center, Cody, Wyo.

Albers, Patricia C., and William R. James. 1987. Illusion and Illumination: Visual Images of American Indian Women in the West. In *The Women's West*, edited by Susan Armitage and Elizabeth Jameson, pp. 35–50. University of Oklahoma Press, Norman.

Albers, Patricia C., and Beatrice Medicine (eds.). 1983. *The Hidden Half: Studies of Plains Indian Women*. University Press of America, Lanham, Md.

Allen, Clifford, Joy Knutson, Vince Pratt, Arlene Stuart, Paul Stuart, and Duwayne Weston. 1971. *History of the Flandreau Santee Sioux Tribe*. Flandreau Santee Sioux Tribe, Flandreau, S. Dak.

Allen, John L. 1987. Patterns of Promise: Mapping the Plains and Prairies, 1800–1860. In *Mapping the North American Plains: Essays in the History of Cartography*, edited by Frederick C. Luebke, Frances W. Kaye, and Gary E. Moulton, pp. 41–62. University of Oklahoma Press, Norman.

Allen, John L. 1991. *Lewis and Clark and the Image of the American Northwest*. Dover Publications, New York.

Allen, Robert S. 1976. *The British Indian Department and the Frontier in North America, 1755–1830*. Occasional Papers in Archaeology and History, no. 14. Canadian Historical Sites, Ottawa.

Ambrose, Stephen E. 1975. *Crazy Horse and Custer: The Parallel Lives of Two American Warriors*. Doubleday, New York. Reprint: New York, Anchor Books, 1996.

Ames, Michael M. 1992. *Cannibal Tours and Glass Boxes: The Anthropology of Museums*. University of British Columbia Press, Vancouver.

Anderson, Carolyn R. 1997. "Dakota Identity in Minnesota, 1820–1995." Ph.D. dissertation, Indiana University, Bloomington.

Anderson, Dean L. 1994. The Flow of European Trade Goods into the Western Great Lakes Region, 1715–1760. In *The Fur Trade Revisited: Selected Papers of the Sixth North American Fur Trade Conference, Mackinac Island, Michigan, 1991*, edited by Jennifer S. H. Brown, W. J. Eccles, and Donald P. Heldman, pp. 93–115. Michigan State University Press, East Lansing, and Mackinac State Historic Parks, Mackinac Island, Mich.

Anderson, Edward F. 1980. *Peyote: The Divine Cactus*. University of Arizona Press, Tucson.

Anderson, Gary C. 1980a. Early Dakota Migration and Intertribal Warfare: A Revision. *Western Historical Quarterly* 11:17–36.

Anderson, Gary C. 1980b. The Removal of the Mdewakanton Dakota in 1837: A Case for Jacksonian Paternalism. *South Dakota History* 10:310–33.

Anderson, Gary C. 1984. *Kinsmen of Another Kind: Dakota–White Relations in the Upper Mississippi Valley, 1650–1862*. University of Nebraska Press, Lincoln.

Anderson, Gary C. 1986. *Little Crow: Spokesman for the Sioux*. Minnesota Historical Society Press, St. Paul.

Anderson, Gary C. 1996. *Sitting Bull and the Paradox of Lakota Nationhood*. HarperCollins, New York.

Anderson, Gary C., and Alan R. Woolworth (eds.). 1988. *Through Dakota Eyes: Narrative Accounts of the Minnesota Indian War of 1862*. Minnesota Historical Society Press, St. Paul.

Anderson, Harry. 1956. An Investigation of the Early Bands of the Saone Group of Teton Sioux. *Journal of the Washington Academy of Sciences* 46:87–94.

Anderson, Harry. 1991. The Waldron–Black Tomahawk Controversy and the Status of Mixed Bloods among the Teton Sioux. *South Dakota History* 21:69–83.

Anderson, Robert T. 1971. Voluntary Associations in History. *American Anthropologist* 73:209–22.

Anfinson, John O. 1980. "The Wilford Site, 21 ML 12: The Historic Component." MA thesis, University of Minnesota, Minneapolis.

Anfinson, Scott F. 1997. *Southwestern Minnesota Archaeology: 12,000 Years in the Prairie Lake Region.* Minnesota Historical Society, St. Paul.

Antell, Will D. 1996. National Indian Education Association. In *Native America in the Twentieth Century: An Encyclopedia*, edited by Mary B. Davis, p. 373. Garland Publishing, New York.

Around Him, John. 1983. *Lakota Ceremonial Songs.* Trans. Albert White Hat, Sr. Sinte Gleska College, Rosebud, S. Dak.

Athearn, Robert G. 1967. *Forts of the Upper Missouri.* Prentice-Hall, Englewood Cliffs, NJ.

Aufderheide, Arthur C., Elden Johnson, and Odin Langsjoen. 1994. *Health, Demography, and Archaeology of Mille Lacs Native American Mortuary Populations.* Memoir 28. Plains Anthropological Society, Lincoln, Nebr.

Babcock, Willoughby M., Jr. 1924. Major Lawrence Taliaferro, Indian Agent. *Mississippi Valley Historical Review* 11:358–75.

Babcock, Willoughby M., Jr. 1945. Sioux Villages in Minnesota prior to 1837. *Minnesota Archaeologist* 12:126–46.

Bad Heart Bull, Amos, and Helen H. Blish. 1967. *A Pictographic History of the Oglala Sioux.* University of Nebraska Press, Lincoln.

Baerreis, David A., Reid A. Bryson, and John E. Kutzbach. 1976. Climate and Culture in the Western Great Lakes Region. *Midcontinental Journal of Archaeology* 1:39–57.

Bailey, Thomas W. 1997. "Evidence for Tobacco Use at the Wilford Site (21ML12), Mille Lacs County, Minnesota." M.S. thesis, University of Minnesota, Minneapolis.

Balme, Jane, and Wendy Beck. 1995. *Gendered Archaeology: The Second Australian Women in Archaeology Conference.* ANH Publications, Australian National University, Canberra.

Banta, Melissa, and Curtis M. Hinsley. 1986. *From Site to Sight: Anthropology, Photography, and the Power of Imagery.* Peabody Museum Press, Cambridge, Mass.

Barthes, Roland. 1974. *S/Z.* Translated by Richard Miller. Hill & Wang, New York.

Barthes, Roland. 1977. The Death of the Author. In *Image, Music, Text*, compiled and translated by Stephen Heath, pp. 142–8. Hill & Wang, New York.

Barton, Winifred W. 1919. *John P. Williamson: A Brother to the Sioux.* Fleming H. Revell, New York.

Basso, Keith. 1979. *Portraits of "The Whiteman": Linguistic Play and Cultural Symbols among the Western Apache.* Cambridge University Press, New York.

Bataille, Gretchen M. 1984. Black Elk – New World Prophet. In *A Sender of Words: Essays in Memory of John G. Neihardt*, edited by Vine Deloria Jr., pp.

135–42. Howe Brothers, Salt Lake City.

Bataille, Gretchen M. (ed.) 1993. *Native American Women: A Biographical Dictionary*. Garland Publishing, New York.

Bataille, Gretchen M., and Kathleen M. Sands. 1991. *American Indian Women: A Guide to Research*. Garland Publishing, New York.

Bataille, Gretchen M., and Charles L. P. Silet (eds.). 1980. *The Pretend Indians: Images of Native Americans in the Movies*. Iowa State University Press, Ames.

Beaulieu, David. 1971. *The Formal Education of Minnesota Indians: Historical Perspective until 1934*. Edited by Richard G. Woods and Arthur M. Harkins. University of Minnesota, Minneapolis.

Beck, Peggy V., and Anna L. Walters. 1977. *The Sacred: Ways of Knowledge, Sources of Life*. Navajo Community College, Tsaile, Ariz.

Bellam, Earnest. 1975. "Stoney Morphology and Phonology." MA thesis, University of Calgary, Calgary.

Belyea, Barbara. 1992a. Images of Power: Derrida/Foucault/Harley. *Cartographica* 29(2):1–9.

Belyea, Barbara. 1992b. Amerindian Maps: The Explorer as Translator. *Journal of Historical Geography* 18:267–77.

Belyea, Barbara. 1998. Inland Journeys, Native Maps. In *Cartographic Encounters: Perspectives on Native American Mapmaking and Map Use*, edited by G. Malcolm Lewis, pp. 135–55. University of Chicago Press, Chicago.

Benchley, Elizabeth D., B. Nansel, Clark A. Dobbs, Susan M. T. Myster, and Barbara H. O'Connell. 1997. *Archeology and Bioarcheology of the Northern Woodlands*. Research Series, no. 52. Arkansas Archeological Survey, Fayetteville.

Bender, Barbara. 1985. Emergent Tribal Formations in the American Midcontinent. *American Antiquity* 50:52–62.

Bender, Donald R. 1967. A Refinement of the Concept of Household: Families, Co-residence, and Domestic Functions. *American Anthropologist* 69:493–504.

Benjamin, Walter. 1968. The Storyteller. In *Illuminations*, edited by Hannah Arendt, pp. 83–109. Schocken, New York.

Benyus, Janine M. 1989. *Northwoods Wildlife: A Watcher's Guide to Habitats*. NorthWord Press, Madison, Wis.

Bergsland, Knut, and Hans Vogt. 1962. On the Validity of Glottochronology. *Current Anthropology* 3:115–53.

Berkhofer, Robert F., Jr. 1978. *The White Man's Indian: Images of the American Indian from Columbus to the Present*. Alfred A. Knopf, New York.

Berkhofer, Robert F., Jr. 1988. White Conceptions of Indians. In *History of Indian–White Relations*, edited by Wilcomb E. Washburn, pp. 522–47. Handbook of North American Indians, vol. 4. Smithsonian Institution, Washington, DC.

Berry, Brewton. 1968. *The Education of the American Indians: A Survey of the Literature*. US Department of Health, Education, and Welfare. Washington, DC.

Bieder, Robert E. 1986. *Science Encounters the Indian, 1820–1880*. University of Oklahoma Press, Norman.

Binford, Lewis R. 1980. Willow Smoke and Dog's Tails: Hunter-Gatherer Settlement Systems and Archaeological Site Formation. *American Antiquity* 45:1–

17.

Biolsi, Thomas. 1992. *Organizing the Lakota: The Political Economy of the New Deal on the Pine Ridge and Rosebud Reservations.* University of Arizona Press, Tucson.

Biolsi, Thomas, and Larry J. Zimmerman (eds.). 1997. *Indians and Anthropologists: Vine Deloria, Jr., and the Critique of Anthropology.* University of Arizona Press, Tucson.

Birk, Douglas A. 1977. The Norway Lake Site: A Multicomponent Woodland Complex in North Central Minnesota. *The Minnesota Archaeologist* 36:6–45.

Birk, Douglas A. 1982. The La Vérendryes. Reflections on the 250th Anniversary of the French Posts of La Mer de l'Ouest. In *Where Two Worlds Meet. The Great Lakes Fur Trade*, edited by Carolyn Gilman, pp. 116–19. Minnesota Historical Society, St. Paul.

Birk, Douglas A. 1991. French Presence in Minnesota: The View from Site MO20 near Little Falls. In *French Colonial Archaeology: The Illinois Country and the Western Great Lakes*, edited by John A. Walthall, pp. 237–66. University of Illinois Press, Urbana.

Birk, Douglas A. 1992. Putting Minnesota on the Map: Early French Presence in the Folle Avoine Region Southwest of Lake Superior. *The Minnesota Archaeologist* 51:7–26.

Birk, Douglas A. 1994. When Rivers Were Roads: Deciphering the Role of Canoe Portages in the Western Lake Superior Fur Trade. In *The Fur Trade Revisited: Selected Papers of the Sixth North American Fur Trade Conference, Mackinac Island, 1991*, edited by Jennifer S. H. Brown, W. J. Eccles, and Donald P. Heldman, pp. 359–76. Michigan State University Press, East Lansing, and Mackinac State Historic Parks, Mackinac Island, Mich.

Birk, Douglas A., and Elden Johnson. 1992. The Mdewakanton Dakota and Initial French Contact. In *Calumet and Fleur-de-Lys: Archaeology of Indian and French Contact in the Midcontinent*, edited by John A. Walthall and Thomas E. Emerson, pp. 203–40. Smithsonian Institution Press, Washington, DC.

Black Bear, Ben, Sr., and Ronnie D. Theisz. 1976. *Songs and Dances of the Lakota.* Sinte Gleska College, Rosebud, S. Dak.

Black Elk, Nicholas (with John G. Neihardt). 1932. *Black Elk Speaks: Being the Life Story of a Holy Man of the Oglala Sioux.* William Morrow, New York. Reprint: Lincoln, University of Nebraska Press 2000.

Black Elk, Wallace H., and William S. Lyon. 1990. *Black Elk: The Sacred Ways of a Lakota.* Harper & Row, San Francisco.

Blackman, Margaret B. 1986. Visual Ethnohistory: Photographs in the Study of Culture History. In *Ethnohistory: A Researcher's Guide*, edited by Dennis Weidman, pp. 137–66. Studies in Third World Societies Publication 35. College of William and Mary, Williamsburg, Va.

Blair, Emma H. (ed.) 1911. *The Indian Tribes of the Upper Mississippi Valley and Region of the Great Lakes.* Arthur H. Clark Co., Cleveland. Reprint: Lincoln, University of Nebraska Press, 1996.

Blakeslee, Donald J. 1975. "The Plains Interband Trade System: An Ethnohistoric and Archeological Investigation." Ph.D. dissertation, University of Wisconsin-Milwaukee.

Blanton, Richard E. 1994. *Houses and Households: A Comparative Study*. Plenum Press, New York.

Blegen, Theodore C. (ed.) 1927. The Unfinished Autobiography of Henry Hastings Sibley. *Minnesota History* 8(4):329–62.

Blegen, Theodore C. 1975. *Minnesota: A History of the State*. 2d ed. University of Minnesota Press, Minneapolis.

Blumberg, Rae L., and Robert F. Winch. 1972. Societal Complexity and Familial Complexity: Evidence for the Curvilinear Hypothesis. *American Journal of Sociology* 77:898–920.

Boas, Franz. 1937. Some Traits of the Dakota Language. *Language* 13:137–41.

Boas, Franz, and Ella Deloria. 1932. Notes on the Dakota, Teton Dialect. *International Journal of American Linguistics* 7:97–121.

Boas, Franz, and Ella Deloria. 1941. *Dakota Grammar*. Memoirs of the National Academy of Sciences, vol. 23, no. 2. Washington, DC.

Boas, Franz, and John R. Swanton. 1911. Siouan: Dakota (Teton and Santee Dialects). In *Handbook of American Indian Languages* I: 875–965. Bulletin 40, Bureau of American Ethnology, Washington, DC.

Bonney, Rachel A. 1977. The Role of AIM Leaders in Indian Nationalism. *American Indian Quarterly* 3:209–24.

Bonvillain, Nancy. 1994. *The Teton Sioux*. Chelsea House Publishers, New York.

Bonvillain, Nancy. 1997. *The Santee Sioux*. Chelsea House Publishers, New York.

Bordewich, Fergus M. 1996. *Killing the White Man's Indian: Reinventing Native Americans at the End of the Twentieth Century*. Doubleday, New York.

Bowden, Henry W. 1981. *American Indians and Christian Missions: Studies in Cultural Conflict*. University of Chicago Press, Chicago.

Boyer, Paul. 1996. Tribal Colleges. In *Native America in the Twentieth Century: An Encyclopedia*, edited by Mary B. Davis, pp. 649–51. Garland Publishing, New York.

Bradbury, John. 1817. *Travels in the Interior of America in the Years 1809, 1810, and 1811*. Sherwood, Neely, & Jones, London. Reprint: Lincoln, University of Nebraska Press 1986.

Brave Bird, Mary (with Richard Erdoes). 1993. *Ohitika Woman*. Grove Press, New York.

Bray, Martha Coleman. 1980. *Joseph Nicollet and His Map*. American Philosophical Society, Philadelphia.

Brettell, Caroline B., and Carolyn F. Sargent (eds.). 1997. *Gender in Cross-Cultural Perspective*. 2d ed. Prentice Hall, Englewood Cliffs, NJ.

Brodhead, John R. 1853–87. *Documents Relating to the Colonial History of New York*. 15 vols. Edited by Edmund B. O'Callaghan. Weed, Parsons, Albany.

Brody, Hugh. 1981. *Maps and Dreams: Indians and the British Columbia Frontier*. Jill Norman & Hobhouse, London.

Brokenleg, Martin, and Herbert T. Hoover. 1993. *Yanktonai Sioux Water Colors: Cultural Remembrances of John Saul*. Center for Western Studies, Sioux Falls, S. Dak.

Bromert, Roger. 1978. The Sioux and the Indian-CCC. *South Dakota History* 8:340–56.

Bromert, Roger. 1984. Sioux Rehabilitation Colonies: Experiments in Self-Sufficiency, 1936–1942. *South Dakota History* 14:31–47.

Brown, Dee. 1970. *Bury My Heart at Wounded Knee: An Indian History of the American West.* Holt, Rinehart, & Winston, New York. Reprint: New York, H. Holt, 1991.

Brown, Joseph E. (ed.) 1953. *The Sacred Pipe: Black Elk's Account of the Seven Rites of the Oglala Sioux.* University of Oklahoma Press, Norman. Reprint: Norman, University of Oklahoma Press, 1989.

Brown, Joseph E. 1972. *The North American Indians: A Selection of Photographs by Edward S. Curtis.* Princeton University Press, Princeton, NJ.

Brown, Joseph E. 1979. The Wisdom of the Contrary: A Conversation with Joseph Epes Brown. *Parabola* 4:54–65.

Brumbaugh, Lee P. 1999. Shadow Catchers or Shadow Snatchers? Ethical Issues for Photographers of Native Americans. In *Contemporary Native American Cultural Issues*, edited by Duane Champagne, pp. 217–24. AltaMira Press, Walnut Creek, Calif.

Bryde, John F. 1970. *The Sioux Indian Student: A Study of Scholastic Failure and Personality Conflict.* Dakota Press, Vermillion, S. Dak.

Buechel, Eugene. 1939. *A Grammar of Lakota, the Language of the Teton Sioux Indians.* St. Francis Mission, St. Francis, S. Dak.

Buechel, Eugene. 1970. *A Dictionary of the Teton Dakota Sioux Language: Lakota-English, English-Lakota, with Considerations Given to Yankton and Santee.* Edited by Paul Manhart. Red Cloud Indian School, Pine Ridge, S. Dak.

Buechler, Jeff. 1989. Eastern Dakota Social Structure and the Fur Trade. *South Dakota Archaeology* 13:55–68.

Burpee, Lawrence J. (ed.) 1968 [1927]. *Journals and Letters of Pierre Gaultier de Varennes de la Vérendrye and His Sons, with Correspondence between the Governors of Canada and the French Court, Touching the Search for the Western Sea.* Champlain Society, Toronto.

Burt, Larry W. 1982. *Tribalism in Crisis: Federal Indian Policy, 1953–1961.* University of New Mexico Press, Albuquerque.

Burt, Larry W. 1986. Roots of the Native American Urban Experience: Relocation Policy in the 1950s. *American Indian Quarterly* 10:85–99.

Bush, Alfred L., and Lee C. Mitchell. 1994. *The Photograph and the American Indian.* Princeton University Press, Princeton, NJ.

Butcher-Youngans, Sherry 1980. "The Cooper Village Site, 21 ML 9: An Historic Analysis." Plan B Master's paper, University of Minnesota, Minneapolis.

Butcher-Youngans, Sherry 1981. "The Battle of Kathio: Fact or Fiction." Plan B Master's paper, University of Minnesota, Minneapolis.

Callender, Charles, and Lee M. Kochems. 1983. The North American Berdache. *Current Anthropology* 24:443–70.

Calloway, Colin G. 1982. The Inter-tribal Balance of Power on the Great Plains, 1760–1850. *Journal of American Studies* 16:25–47.

Campbell, Gregory R. (ed.) 1989a. Contemporary Issues in Native American Health. Special Issue of *American Indian Culture and Research Journal* 13(3–4).

Campbell, Gregory R. 1989b. Plains Indian Historical Demography and Health: An Introductory Overview. *Plains Anthropologist, Memoir* 23:v–xiii.

Campbell, Gregory R. 1996. Indian Health Service. In *Native America in the Twentieth Century: An Encyclopedia*, edited by Mary B. Davis, pp. 256–61. Garland Publishing, New York.

Campbell, Lyle. 1997. *American Indian Languages: The Historical Linguistics of Native America*. Oxford University Press, New York.

Campbell, Lyle. 1998. *Historical Linguistics: An Introduction*. Edinburgh University Press, Edinburgh.

Carley, Kenneth. 1976. *The Sioux Uprising of 1862*. 2d ed. Minnesota Historical Society, St. Paul.

Carr, David. 1986. *Time, Narrative, and History*. Indiana University Press, Bloomington.

Carrithers, Michael. 1992. *Why Humans Have Cultures: Explaining Anthropology and Social Diversity*. Oxford University Press, New York.

Carter, Richard T. 1974. *Teton Dakota Phonology*. University of Manitoba Anthropological Papers, No. 10. Winnipeg.

Carver, Jonathan. 1956. *Travels through the Interior Parts of North America, in the Years 1766, 1767, and 1768*. 3d ed. Ross & Haines, Minneapolis.

Castro, Michael. 1983. *Interpreting the Indian: Twentieth-Century Poets and the Native American*. University of New Mexico Press, Albuquerque.

Catlin, George. 1973. *Letters and Notes on the Manners, Customs, and Conditions of North American Indians*. 2 vols. Dover Publications, New York.

Chafe, Wallace L. 1962. Estimates Regarding the Present Speakers of Indian Languages. *International Journal of American Linguistics* 28:162–71.

Chafe, Wallace L. 1976. *The Caddoan, Iroquoian, and Siouan Languages*. Mouton, The Hague.

Champagne, Duane (ed.) 1999. *Contemporary Native American Cultural Issues*. AltaMira Press, Walnut Creek, Calif.

Champe, John L. 1974. Yankton Chronology. In *Sioux Indians III*, pp. 247–74. Garland Publishing New York.

Churchill, Ward. 1996a. American Indian Movement. In *Native America in the Twentieth Century: An Encyclopedia*, edited by Mary B. Davis, pp. 35–8. Garland Publishing, New York.

Churchill, Ward. 1996b. Wounded Knee II. In *Native America in the Twentieth Century: An Encyclopedia*, edited by Mary B. Davis, pp. 698–700. Garland Publishing, New York.

Churchill, Ward. 1999. The Crucible of American Indian Identity: Native Tradition versus Colonial Imposition in Postconquest North America. In *Contemporary Native American Cultural Issues*, edited by Duane Champagne, pp. 39–67. AltaMira Press, Walnut Creek, Calif.

Claassen, Cheryl (ed.) 1992. *Exploring Gender Through Archaeology: Selected Papers from the 1991 Boone Conference*. Prehistory Press, Madison.

Clements, William M. 1992. "Tokens of Literary Faculty": Native American Literature and Euroamerican Translation in the Early Nineteenth Century. In *On the Translation of Native American Literatures*, edited by Brian Swann, pp. 33–50. Smithsonian Institution Press, Washington, DC.

Clemmons, Linda. 2001. "We find it a difficult work": Educating Dakota Children in Missionary Homes, 1835–1862. *American Indian Quarterly* 24:570–

600.

Clifton, James A. (ed.) 1990. *The Invented Indian: Cultural Fictions and Government Policies*. Transaction Publishers, New Brunswick, NJ.

Clow, Richmond C. 1989. Tribal Populations in Transition: Sioux Reservations and Federal Policy, 1934–1965. *South Dakota History* 19:362–91.

Clow, Richmond C. 1990. The Lakota Ghost Dance after 1890. South Dakota History 20:323–33.

Clow, Richmond C. 1998. The Anatomy of a Lakota Shooting: Crow Dog and Spotted Tail, 1879–1881. *South Dakota History* 28:209–27.

Clow, Richmond L. 1977. The Whetstone Indian Agency, 1868–1872. *South Dakota History* 7:291–308.

Clow, Richmond L. 1987a. The Indian Reorganization Act and the Loss of Tribal Sovereignty: Constitutions on the Rosebud and Pine Ridge Reservations. *Great Plains Quarterly* 7:125–34.

Clow, Richmond L. 1987b. Cattlemen and Tribal Rights: The Standing Rock Leasing Conflict of 1902. *North Dakota History* 54(2):23–30.

Cohen, David. 1989. The Undefining of Oral Tradition. *Ethnohistory* 36:9–18.

Cohn, Bernard S. 1985. The Command of Language and the Language of Command. In *Subaltern Studies* IV: *Writings on South Asian History and Society*, edited by Ranajit Guha, pp. 276–329. Oxford University Press, Delhi.

Cohn, Bernard S. 1996. *Colonialism and Its Forms of Knowledge: The British in India*. Princeton University Press, Princeton, NJ.

Coleman, Michael C. 1993. *American Indian Children at School, 1850–1930*. University Press of Mississippi, Jackson.

Colton, Larry. 2000. *Counting Coup: A True Story of Basketball and Honor on the Little Big Horn*. Warner Books, New York.

Conkey, Margaret, and Janet Spector. 1984. Archaeology and the Study of Gender. *Advances in Archaeological Method and Theory* 7:1–38.

Cooper, Frederick. 1992. Colonizing Time: Work Rhythms and Labor Conflict in Colonial Mombasa. In *Colonialism and Culture*, edited by Nicholas B. Dirks, pp. 209–45. University of Michigan Press, Ann Arbor.

Corum, Charles R. 1975. A Teton Tipi Cover Depiction of the Sacred Pipe Myth. *South Dakota History* 5:229–44.

Cosgrove, Denis, and Stephen Daniels (eds.). 1988. *The Iconography of Landscape: Essays on the Symbolic Representation, Design, and Use of Past Environments*. Cambridge University Press, New York.

Coues, Elliott. 1895. *The Expeditions of Zebulon Montgomery Pike*. 2 vols. F. P. Harper, New York. Reprint: New York, Dover Publications, 1987.

Counts, Dorothy A., Judith K. Brown, and Jacquelyn C. Campbell. 1992. *Sanctions and Sanctuary: Cultural Perspectives on the Beating of Wives*. Westview Press, Boulder.

Cozzetto, Don A. 1995. The Economic and Social Implications of Indian Gaming: The Case of Minnesota. *American Indian Culture and Research Journal* 19(1):119–31.

Cozzetto, Don A., and Brent W. Larocque. 1996. Compulsive Gambling in the Indian Community: A North Dakota Case Study. *American Indian Culture and Research Journal* 20(1):73–86.

Crosby, Alfred W. 1976. Virgin Soil Epidemics as a Factor in the Aboriginal Depopulation in America. *William and Mary Quarterly* 33:289–99.

Crosby, Alfred W. 1986. *Ecological Imperialism: The Biological Expansion of
Europe, 900–1900*. Cambridge University Press, New York.

Crow Dog, Leonard, and Richard Erdoes. 1995. *Crow Dog: Four Generations of
Sioux Medicine Men*. HarperCollins, New York.

Crow Dog, Mary, and Richard Erdoes. 1991. *Lakota Woman*. HarperPerennial,
New York.

Cruikshank, Julie. 1992. Oral Tradition and Material Culture: Multiplying Meanings of "Words" and "Things." *Anthropology Today* 8(3):5–9.

Cruikshank, Julie. 1998. *The Social Life of Stories: Narrative and Knowledge in
the Yukon Territory*. University of Nebraska Press, Lincoln.

Crum, Steven J. 1996. Higher Education. In *Native America in the Twentieth
Century: An Encyclopedia*, edited by Mary B. Davis, pp. 237–9. Garland Publishing, New York.

Daniel, Glenda, and Jerry Sullivan. 1981. *The North Woods of Michigan, Wisconsin, Minnesota, and Southern Ontario*. Sierra Club Books, San Francisco.

Daniels, Mark C. 1999. "Type 2 Diabetes Mellitus among Lakota/Dakota: Associated Mental Health Factors and Treatment Implications." Ph.D. thesis, University of Toledo, Toledo, Ohio.

Daniels, Robert E. 1970. Cultural Identities among the Oglala Sioux. In *The
Modern Sioux: Social Systems and Reservation Culture*, edited by Ethel Nurge,
pp. 198–245. University of Nebraska Press, Lincoln.

Danzinger, Edmund J., Jr. 1979. *The Chippewas of Lake Superior*. University of
Oklahoma Press, Norman.

Danzinger, Edmund J., Jr. 1996. Government Policy: Self-Determination. In *Native America in the Twentieth Century: An Encyclopedia*, edited by Mary B.
Davis, pp. 223–5. Garland Publishing, New York.

Decker, Jody F. 1991. Depopulation of the Northern Plains Natives. *Social Science and Medicine* 33:381–93.

Delanglez, Jean. 1943. Franquelin, Mapmaker. *Mid-America: An Historical Review* 14:29–74.

Delanglez, Jean. 1946. The Joliett Lost Map of the Mississippi. *Mid-America: An
Historical Review* 17:67–144.

Deloria, Barbara, Kristen Foehner, and Sam Scinta. 1999. *Spirit & Reason: The
Vine Deloria, Jr., Reader*. Fulcrum Publishing, Golden, Colo.

Deloria, Ella C. 1929. The Sun Dance of the Oglala Sioux. *Journal of American
Folk-Lore* 42:354–413.

Deloria, Ella C. 1944. *Speaking of Indians*. Friendship Press, New York. Reprint:
Lincoln, University of Nebraska Press, 1998.

Deloria, Ella C. 1954. Short Dakota Texts, Including Conversations. *International
Journal of American Linguistics* 20:17–22.

Deloria, Ella C. 1967a. Some Notes on the Yankton. *Museum News* 28(3–4):1–
30. W. H. Over Dakota Museum, University of South Dakota, Vermillion.

Deloria, Ella C. 1967b. Some Notes on the Santee. *Museum News* 28(5–6):1–21.
W. H. Over Dakota Museum, University of South Dakota, Vermillion.

Deloria, Ella C. 1978. *Dakota Texts*, edited by Agnes Picotte and Paul N. Pavich.

Dakota Press, Vermillion, S. Dak.

Deloria, Vine, Jr. 1969. *Custer Died for Your Sins: An Indian Manifesto*. Macmillan, New York. Reprint: Norman, University of Oklahoma Press, 1988.

Deloria, Vine, Jr. 1970. *We Talk, You Listen: New Tribes, New Turf*. Macmillan, New York.

Deloria, Vine, Jr. 1974. *Behind the Trail of Broken Treaties: An Indian Declaration of Independence*. Delacorte Press, New York. Reprint: Austin, University of Texas Press, 1985.

Deloria, Vine, Jr. (ed.) 1984. *A Sender of Words: Essays in Memory of John G. Neihardt*. Howe Brothers, Salt Lake City.

Deloria, Vine, Jr. 1992. *God is Red: A Native View of Religion*. 2d ed. North American Press, Golden, Colo.

Deloria, Vine, Jr., and Clifford M. Lytle. 1998. *The Nations Within: The Past and Future of American Indian Sovereignty*. 2d ed. University of Texas Press, Austin.

DeMallie, Raymond J. 1971. "Teton Dakota Kinship and Social Organization." Ph.D. dissertation, University of Chicago, Chicago.

DeMallie, Raymond J. 1975. Joseph N. Nicollet's Account of the Sioux and Assiniboin in 1839. *South Dakota History* 5:343–59.

DeMallie, Raymond J. 1976. Sioux Ethnohistory: A Methodological Critique. *Journal of Ethnic Studies* 4(3):77–83.

DeMallie, Raymond J. 1979. Change in American Indian Kinship Systems: The Dakota. In *Currents in Anthropology, Essays in Honor of Sol Tax*, edited by Robert Hinshaw, pp. 221–41. Mouton, New York.

DeMallie, Raymond J. 1981. Scenes in the Indian Country: A Portfolio of Alexander Gardner's Stereographic Views of the 1868 Fort Laramie Treaty Council. *Montana, The Magazine of Western History* 31(3):42–59.

DeMallie, Raymond J. 1982a. Introduction. In *Lakota Society*, by James R. Walker, edited by Raymond J. DeMallie, pp. 3–13. University of Nebraska Press, Lincoln.

DeMallie, Raymond J. 1982b. Time and History. In *Lakota Society*, by James R. Walker, edited by Raymond J. DeMallie, pp. 111–22. University of Nebraska Press, Lincoln.

DeMallie, Raymond J. 1982c. The Lakota Ghost Dance: An Ethnohistorical Account. *Pacific Historical Review* 51:385–405.

DeMallie, Raymond J. 1983. Male and Female in Traditional Lakota Culture. In *The Hidden Half: Studies of Plains Indian Women*, edited by Patricia Albers and Beatrice Medicine, pp. 237–65. University Press of America, Lanham, Md.

DeMallie, Raymond J. (ed.) 1984. *The Sixth Grandfather: Black Elk's Teachings Given to John Neihardt*. University of Nebraska Press, Lincoln.

DeMallie, Raymond J. 1987. Lakota Belief and Ritual in the Nineteenth Century. In *Sioux Indian Religion: Tradition and Innovation*, edited by Raymond J. DeMallie and Douglas R. Parks, pp. 25–43. University of Oklahoma Press, Norman.

DeMallie, Raymond J. 1994. Kinship and Biology in Sioux Culture. In *North American Indian Anthropology: Essays on Society and Culture*, edited by Raymond J. DeMallie and Alfonso Ortiz, pp. 125–46. University of Oklahoma

Press, Norman.

DeMallie, Raymond J., and Robert H. Lavenda. 1977. Wakan: Plains Siouan Concepts of Power. In *The Anthropology of Power: Ethnographic Studies from Asia, Oceania, and the New World,* edited by Raymond D. Fogelson and Richard N. Adams, pp. 153–65. Academic Press, New York.

DeMallie, Raymond J., and Douglas R. Parks (eds.). 1987. *Sioux Indian Religion: Tradition and Innovation.* University of Oklahoma Press, Norman.

Demmert, William G., Jr. 1996a. Indian Education Act, 1972. In *Native America in the Twentieth Century: An Encyclopedia,* edited by Mary B. Davis, pp. 255–6. Garland Publishing, New York.

Demmert, William G., Jr. 1996b. Public Schools. In *Native America in the Twentieth Century: An Encyclopedia,* edited by Mary B. Davis, pp. 486–9. Garland Publishing, New York.

Denig, Edwin T. 1961. *Five Indian Tribes of the Upper Missouri, Sioux, Arickaras, Assiniboines, Crees, Crows.* Edited by John C. Ewers. University of Oklahoma Press, Norman.

Densmore, Frances. 1954. *The Collection of Water-Color Drawings of the North American Indian by Seth Eastman.* James Jerome Hill Reference Library, St. Paul.

Densmore, Frances. 1918. *Teton Sioux Music.* Bureau of American Ethnology Bulletin 61. Washington, DC. Reprint: Lincoln, University of Nebraska Press, 1992.

Dewing, Rolland. 1985. *Wounded Knee: The Meaning and Significance of the Second Incident.* Irvington Publishers, New York.

Dewing, Rolland. 1991. Depression on South Dakota's Indian Reservations: The SDERA Survey of 1935. *South Dakota History* 21:84–96.

Dickson, Dennis W. 1968. "The Vineland Bay Site: An Analysis." MA thesis, University of Minnesota, Minneapolis.

Diedrich, Mark. 1987. *Famous Chiefs of the Eastern Sioux.* Coyote Books, Minneapolis.

Dincauze, Dena F., and Robert J. Hasenstab. 1989. Explaining the Iroquois: Tribalization on a Prehistoric Periphery. In *Centre and Periphery: Comparative Studies in Archaeology,* edited by Timothy C. Champion, pp. 67–87. Unwin Hyman, Boston.

Dippie, Brian W. 1994. *Custer's Last Stand: The Anatomy of an American Myth.* University of Nebraska Press, Lincoln (reprint of the original 1976 edition with a new preface by the author).

Dippie, Brian W. 1992. Representing the Other: The North American Indian. In *Anthropology and Photography, 1860–1920,* edited by Elizabeth Edwards, pp. 132–6. Yale University Press, New Haven.

Divale, William T., and Marvin Harris. 1976. Population, Warfare, and the Male Supremacist Complex. *American Anthropologist* 78:521–38.

Dobyns, Henry F. 1983. *Their Number Become Thinned: Native American Population Dynamics in Eastern North America.* University of Tennessee Press, Knoxville.

Dobyns, Henry F. 1992. Native American Trade Centers as Contagious Disease Foci. In *Disease and Demography in the Americas,* edited by John W. Verano and Douglas H. Ubelaker, pp. 215–22. Smithsonian Institution Press, Washington, DC.

Dole, Gertrude E. 1972. Developmental Sequences of Kinship Patterns. In *Kinship Studies in the Morgan Centennial Year*, edited by Priscilla Reining, pp. 134–66. The Anthropological Society of Washington, Washington, DC.

Donley, Linda W. 1982. House Power: Swahili Space and Symbolic Markers. In *Symbolic and Structural Archaeology*, edited by Ian Hodder, pp. 63–73. Cambridge University Press, New York.

Dorsey, James O. 1897. Siouan Sociology. *Bureau of American Ethnology Annual Report* 15:205–44. U.S. Government Printing Office, Washington, DC.

Driver, H. E. 1961. *Indians of North America*. University of Chicago Press, Chicago.

Dunlay, Thomas. 1982. *Wolves for the Blue Soldiers: Indian Scouts and Auxiliaries with the United States Army, 1860–90*. University of Nebraska Press, Lincoln.

Duratschek, Sister Claudia. 1947. *Crusading along Sioux Trails: A History of the Catholic Indian Missions of South Dakota*. Abbey Press, St. Meinrad, Ind.

Eastman, Charles. 1902. *Indian Boyhood*. Little, Brown, Boston. Reprint: Lincoln, University of Nebraska Press, 1991.

Eastman, Charles. 1931. *From the Deep Woods to Civilization*. Little, Brown, Boston.

Eastman, Mary. 1849. *Dahcotah: or, Life and Legends of the Sioux around Fort Snelling*. John Wiley, New York. Reprint: Afton, Minn., Afton Historical Society Press, 1995.

Ebbott, Elizabeth. 1985. *Indians in Minnesota*, edited by Judith Rosenblatt. 4th ed. University of Minnesota Press, Minneapolis.

Eder, James F. 1987. *On the Road to Tribal Extinction: Depopulation, Deculturation, and Adaptive Well-being among the Batak of the Philippines*. University of California Press, Berkeley.

Eggan, Fred. 1937. The Cheyenne and Arapaho Kinship System. In *Social Anthropology of North American Tribes*, edited by Fred Eggan, pp. 31–95. University of Chicago Press, Chicago.

Eggan, Fred. 1955. Social Anthropology: Methods and Results. In *Social Anthropology of North American Tribes*, edited by Fred Eggan, pp. 483–551. Enlarged ed. University of Chicago Press, Chicago.

Eggan, Fred. 1966. *The American Indian: Perspectives for the Study of Social Change*. Aldine Publishing, Chicago.

Ehrenberg, Ralph E. 1987a. Exploratory Mapping of the Great Plains before 1800. In *Mapping the North American Plains: Essays in the History of Cartography*, edited by Frederick B. Luebke, Frances W. Kaye, and Gary E. Moulton, pp. 3–26. University of Oklahoma Press, Norman.

Ehrenberg, Ralph E. 1987b. Mapping the North American Plains: A Catalog of the Exhibition. In *Mapping the North American Plains: Essays in the History of Cartography*, edited by Frederick B. Luebke, Frances W. Kaye, and Gary E. Moulton, pp. 173–230. University of Oklahoma Press, Norman.

Ekberg, Carl J., and William E. Foley (eds.). 1989. *An Account of Upper Louisiana* (by Nicholas de Finiels). Translated by Carl J. Ekberg. University of Missouri Press, Columbia.

Ekquist, Karla L. 1999. "Federal Indian Policy and the St. Francis Mission School on Rosebud Reservation, South Dakota: 1886–1908." Ph.D. dissertation, Iowa State University, Ames.

Ellen, Roy F. 1986. What Black Elk Left Unsaid: On the Illusory Images of Green Primitivism. *Anthropology Today* 2(6):8–12.

Ellerby, Jonathan H. 2000. "Spirituality, Holism, and Healing among the Lakota Sioux." MA thesis, University of Manitoba, Winnipeg.

Ellis, Mark R. 1999. Reservation *Akicitas*: The Pine Ridge Indian Police, 1879–1885. *South Dakota History* 29:185–210.

Ember, Carol R., and Melvin Ember. 1990. *Cultural Anthropology*. 6th ed. Prentice Hall, Englewood Cliffs, NJ.

Ember, Melvin. 1974. Warfare, Sex Ratio, and Polygyny. *Ethnology* 13:197–206.

Emerson, Thomas E. 1999. The Langford Tradition and the Process of Tribalization on the Middle Mississippian Borders. *Midcontinental Journal of Archaeology* 24(1):3–56.

Emerson, Thomas E., and James A. Brown. 1992. The Late Prehistory and Protohistory of Illinois. In *Calumet Fleur-De-Lys: Archaeology of Indian and French Contact in the Midcontinent*, edited by John A. Walthall and Thomas E. Emerson, pp. 77–128. Smithsonian Institution Press, Washington, DC.

Encyclopedia Britannica. 1972. "Humour." 11:839–41. William Benton, Chicago.

Enochs, Ross A. 1994. "Lakota Mission: Jesuit Mission Method and the Lakota Sioux, 1886–1945." Ph.D. dissertation, University of Virginia, Charlottesville.

Erikson, Erik H. 1939. Observations on Sioux Education. *Journal of Psychology* 7:101–56.

Etienne, Mona, and Eleanor Leacock (eds.). 1980. *Women and Colonization: Anthropological Perspectives*. Praeger, New York.

Ewers, John C. 1965. The Emergence of the Plains Indian as the Symbol of the North American Indian. *Smithsonian Institution Annual Report for 1964*:531–44. Gov. Pub., Washington, DC. Reprinted in *The American Indian: Past and Present*, edited by Roger L. Nichols 1986, pp. 1–13. 2d ed. John Wiley & Sons, New York.

Ewers, John C. 1968. *Indian Life on the Upper Missouri*. University of Oklahoma Press, Norman.

Ewers, John C. 1972. The Influence of the Fur Trade upon the Indians of the Northern Plains. In *People and Pelts: Selected Papers of the Second North American Fur Trade Conference*, edited by Malvina Bolus, pp. 1–26. Peguis Publishers, Winnipeg.

Ewers, John C. 1975. Intertribal Warfare as the Precursor of Indian–White Warfare on the Northern Great Plains. *Western Historical Quarterly* 6:397–410.

Fabian, Johannes. 1986. *Language and Colonial Power: The Appropriation of Swahili in the Former Belgian Congo, 1880–1938*. Cambridge University Press, New York.

Fausto-Sterling, Anne. 1985. *Myths of Gender: Biological Theories about Women and Men*. Basic Books, New York. Reprint: New York, Basic Books, 1992.

Featherstonhaugh, G. W. 1970. *A Canoe Voyage up the Minnay Sotor; with an*

Account of the Lead and Copper Deposits in Wisconsin; of the Gold Region in the Cherokee Country; and Sketches of Popular Manners. Minnesota Historical Society, St. Paul.

Fenton, William N. 1952. The Training of Historical Ethnologists in America. *American Anthropologist* 54:328–39.

Feraca, Stephen E. 1998. *Wakinyan: Lakota Religion in the Twentieth Century.* University of Nebraska Press, Lincoln.

Ferguson, R. Brian, and Neil Whitehead. 1992. The Violent Edge of Empire. In *War in the Tribal Zone: Expanding States and Indigenous Warfare*, edited by R. Brian Ferguson and Neil L. Whitehead, pp. 1–30. School of American Research Press, Santa Fe, N. Mex.

Ferree, Myra M, Judith Lorber, and Beth B. Hess (eds.). 1999. *Revisioning Gender.* Sage, Thousand Oaks, Calif.

Fiedler, Leslie A. 1988. The Indian in Literature in English. In *History of Indian-White Relations*, edited by Wilcomb E. Washburn, pp. 573–81. Handbook of North American Indians, vol. 4. Smithsonian Institution, Washington, DC.

Finn, Janet. 1995. Ella Cara Deloria and Mourning Dove: Writing For Cultures, Writing Against the Grain. In *Women Writing Culture*, edited by Ruth Behar and Deborah A. Gordon, pp. 131–47. University of California Press, Berkeley.

Fisher, Dexter. 1979. Zitkala Ša: The Evolution of a Writer. *American Indian Quarterly* 5:229–38.

Fixico, Donald L. 1986. *Termination and Relocation: Federal Indian Policy, 1945–1960.* University of New Mexico Press, Albuquerque.

Flax, Jane. 1990. *Thinking Fragments: Psychoanalysis, Feminism, and Postmodernism in the Contemporary West.* University of California Press, Berkeley.

Fleming, Paula R., and Judith L. Luskey. 1986. *The North American Indians in Early Photographs.* Harper & Row, New York.

Fleming, Paula R., and Judith L. Luskey. 1993. *Grand Endeavors of American Indian Photography.* Smithsonian Institution Press, Washington, DC.

Fletcher, Alice. 1883. The Sun Dance of the Oglala Sioux. *Proceedings of the American Association for the Advancement of Science, 1882*, pp. 580–4. Salem, Mass.

Folwell, William W. 1956–69. *History of Minnesota.* 4 vols. Minnesota Historical Society, St. Paul.

Fouberg, Erin K. H. 1997. "Tribal Territory and Tribal Sovereignty: A Study of the Cheyenne River and Lake Traverse Indian Reservations." Ph.D. dissertation, University of Nebraska, Lincoln.

Foucault, Michel. 1979. What is an Author? In *Textual Strategies: Perspectives in Post-Structuralist Criticism*, edited by Josué V. Harari, pp. 141–60. Cornell University Press, Ithaca, NY.

Fox, Richard Allan, Jr. 1993. *Archaeology, History, and Custer's Last Battle: The Little Bighorn Reexamined.* University of Oklahoma Press, Norman.

Freud, Sigmund. 1928. Humour. *International Journal of Psycho-Analysis* 9:1–6.

Friar, Ralph E., and Natasha A. Friar. 1972. *The Only Good Indian: The Hollywood Gospel.* Drama Book Specialists, New York.

Fried, Morton H. 1967. *The Evolution of Political Society: An Essay in Political*

Anthropology. Random House, New York.

Fried, Morton H. 1968. On the Concept of "Tribe" and "Tribal Society." In *Essays on the Problem of Tribe*, edited by June Helm, pp. 3–20. Proceedings of the 1967 Annual Spring Meeting of the American Ethnological Society. University of Washington Press, Seattle.

Fried, Morton H. 1975. *The Notion of Tribe*. Cummings Press, Menlo Park, Calif.

Fried, Morton, Marvin Harris, and Robert Murphy (eds.). 1968. *War: The Anthropology of Armed Conflict and Aggression*. Natural History Press, Garden City, NY.

Friedman, Jonathan. 1992. The Past in the Future: History and the Politics of Identity. *American Anthropology* 94:837–59.

Fuss, Allison. 1999. Cowboys on the Reservation: The Growth of Rodeo as a Lakota National Pastime. *South Dakota History* 29:211–28.

Gable, Eric, Richard Handler, and Anna Lawson. 1992. On the Uses of Relativism: Fact, Conjecture and Black and White Histories at Colonial Williamsburg. *American Ethnologist* 19:791–805.

Galler, Robert W., Jr. 1998. A Triad of Alliances: The Roots of Holy Rosary Indian Mission. *South Dakota History* 28:144–60.

Galler, Robert W., Jr. 2000. "Environment, Culture, and Social Change on the Great Plains: A History of Crow Creek Tribal School (South Dakota)." Ph.D. dissertation, Western Michigan University, Kalamazoo.

Gates, Charles M. (ed.) 1965. *Five Fur Traders of the Northwest*. Minnesota Historical Society Press, St. Paul.

Gelb, Norman (ed.) 1993. *Jonathan Carver's Travels Through America 1766-1768: An Eighteenth Century Explorer's Account of Uncharted America*. John Wiley and Sons, New York.

Gell, Alfred. 1985. How to Read a Map. *Man* 20:271–86.

Gell, Alfred. 1996. *The Anthropology of Time: Cultural Constructions of Temporal Maps and Images*. Berg, Washington, DC.

Gibbon, Guy. 1987. Battle Island (21AK9): A Multi-Component Site on Big Sandy Lake, Aitkin County, Minnesota. *The Minnesota Archaeologist* 46(1):3–30.

Gibbon, Guy. 1989. *Explanation in Archaeology*. Blackwell, New York.

Gibbon, Guy. 1994. Cultures of the Upper Mississippi River Valley and Adjacent Prairies in Iowa and Minnesota. In *Plains Indians, A.D. 500–1500: The Archaeological Past of Historic Groups*, edited by Karl H. Schlesier, pp. 128–48. University of Oklahoma Press, Norman.

Gibbon, Guy. 2001. Oneota. In *Encyclopedia of Prehistory*, Vol. 6: *North America*, edited by Peter N. Peregrine, pp. 389–407. Kluwer Academic/Plenum, New York.

Giddens, Anthony. 1984. *The Constitution of Society: Outline of the Theory of Structuration*. University of California Press, Berkeley.

Gidley, Mick. 1985. North American Indian Photographs/Images (review essay). *American Indian Culture and Research Journal* 9(3):37–47.

Gillette, John M. 1906. The Medicine Society of the Dakota Indians. *Collections of the State Historical Society of North Dakota* 1:459–74.

Gilman, Carolyn. 1992. *The Grand Portage Story*. Minnesota Historical Society Press, St. Paul.

Gilman, Rhoda R. 1970. Last Days of the Upper Mississippi Fur Trade. *Minnesota History* 42:122–40.

Gilman, Rhoda R. 1974. The Fur Trade in the Upper Mississippi Valley, 1630–1850. *Wisconsin Magazine of History* 58:3–18.

Gilmore, Melvin R. 1919. *Uses of Plants by the Indians of the Missouri River Region. Bureau of American Ethnology Annual Report* 33:43–154. Reprint: Lincoln, University of Nebraska Press, 1991.

Gipp, Gerald E. 1996. Johnson O'Malley Act. In *Native America in the Twentieth Century: An Encyclopedia*, edited by Mary B. Davis, pp. 281–2. Garland Publishing, New York.

Glenn, Elizabeth J. 1974. *Physical Affiliations of the Oneota Peoples.* Report no. 7, Office of the State Archaeologist, University of Iowa, Iowa City.

Glenn, J. R. 1983. De Lancey W. Gill: Photographer for the Bureau of American Ethnology. *History of Photography* 7:7–22.

Gluek, Alvin C., Jr. 1955. The Sioux Uprising: A Problem in International Relations. *Minnesota History* 34:317–24.

Goetzmann, William H. 1959. *Army Exploration in the American West 1803-1863.* Yale University Press, New Haven.

Goodman, Ronald. 1992. *Lakota Star Knowledge: Studies in Lakota Stellar Theology.* 3d ed. Sinte Gleska College, Rosebud, S. Dak.

Grant, Paul WarCloud. 1971. *Sioux Dictionary: Over 4,000 Words, Pronunciation-at-a-Glance.* State Publishing Co., Pierre, S. Dak.

Graves-Brown, Paul, Siân Jones, and Clive Gamble (eds.). 1996. *Cultural Identity and Archaeology: The Construction of European Communities.* Routledge, New York.

Gray, John S. 1991. *Custer's Last Campaign: Mitch Boyer and the Little Bighorn Reconstructed.* University of Nebraska Press, Lincoln.

Graybill, Florence Curtis, and Victor Boesen. 1981. *Edward Sheriff Curtis: Visions of a Vanishing Race.* American Legacy Press, New York.

Green, Michael K. 1995. *Issues in Native American Cultural Identity.* Peter Lang, New York.

Green, Rayna. 1975. The Pocahontas Perplex: The Image of Indian Women in American Culture. *Massachusetts Review* 16:698–714.

Green, Rayna. 1988. The Indian in Popular American Culture. In *History of Indian–White Relations*, edited by Wilcomb E. Washburn, pp. 587–606. Handbook of North American Indians, vol. 4. Smithsonian Institution, Washington, DC.

Green, William. 1993. Examining Protohistoric Depopulation in the Upper Midwest. *The Wisconsin Archeologist* 74(1-4):290–323.

Gregg, Michael L. 1994. Archaeological Complexes of the Northwestern Plains and Prairie-Woodland Border, A.D. 500–1500. In *Plains Indians, A.D. 500–1500: The Archaeological Past of Historic Groups*, edited by Karl H. Schlesier, pp. 71–95. University of Oklahoma Press, Norman.

Gregg, Susan A. 1991. Introduction. In *Between Bands and States*, edited by Susan Gregg, pp. xxvii–xxix. Occasional Paper No. 9. Center for Archeological Investigations, Southern Illinois University at Carbondale.

Gregory, C.A. 1982. *Gifts and Commodities.* Academic Press, New York.

Grimes, Richard S. 2000. The Making of a Sioux Legend: The Historiography of Crazy Horse. *South Dakota History* 30:277–302.

Grimm, Eric C. 1985. Vegetation History Along the Prairie–Forest Border in Minnesota.. In *Archaeology, Ecology and Ethnohistory of the Prairie–Forest Border Zone of Minnesota and Manitoba*, edited by Janet Spector and Elden Johnson, pp. 9–30.

J & L Reprint Co., Lincoln, Nebr.

Grimm, Thaddeus C. 1985. Time-Depth Analysis of Fifteen Siouan Languages. *Siouan and Caddoan Linguistics*, June. Department of Linguistics, University of Colorado.

Grobsmith, Elizabeth S. 1979. The Lakhota Giveaway: A System of Social Reciprocity. *Plains Anthropologist* 24(1984):123–31.

Grobsmith, Elizabeth S. 1981a. *The Lakota of the Rosebud: A Contemporary Ethnography*. Holt, Rinehart, & Winston, New York.

Grobsmith, Elizabeth S. 1981b. The Changing Role of the Giveaway Ceremony in Contemporary Lakota Life. *Plains Anthropologist* 26(1981):75–9.

Grove, Jean M. 1988. *The Little Ice Age*. Methuen, New York.

Gudschinsky, Sarah C. 1956. The ABC's of Lexicostatistics (Glottochronology). *Word* 12:17-5-210.

Gump, James O. 1994. *The Dust Rose Like Smoke: The Subjugation of the Zulu and the Sioux*. University of Nebraska Press, Lincoln.

Haarland, R. 1977. Archaeological Classification and Ethnic Groups: A Case Study from Sudanese Nubia. *Norwegian Archaeological Review* 10:1–31.

Haas, Jonathan (ed.) 1990. *The Anthropology of War*. Cambridge University Press, New York.

Haberman, Thomas W. 1981. *Evaluation of 39SP101: Drifting Goose's Village at Armadale Island*. Contract Investigation Series 111. South Dakota Archaeological Research Center, Rapid City.

Haberman, Thomas W. 1983. Historic Aspects of the Dirt Lodge Village Site in Spink County, South Dakota. *South Dakota Archaeology* 7:35–62.

Hadden, Jeffrey K., and Anson Shupe. 1986. *Prophetic Religions and Politics*. Paragon House, New York.

Hagan, William T. 1966. *Indian Police and Judges: Experiments in Acculturation and Control*. Yale University Press, New Haven.

Hales, Peter B. 1988. *William Henry Jackson and the Transformation of the American Landscape*. Temple University Press, Philadelphia.

Hall, Robert L. 1997. The Gifts of White Buffalo Calf Maiden. In Hall's *An Archaeology of the Soul: North American Indian Belief and Ritual*, pp. 77–85. University of Illinois Press, Urbana.

Hall, Stephen P. 1987. *Fort Snelling, Colossus of the Wilderness*. Minnesota Historical Society Press, St. Paul.

Hamell, George R. 1982. Trading in Metaphors: The Magic of Beads. In *Proceedings of the 1982 Glass Trade Bead Conference*, edited by Charles F. Hayes III, pp. 5–28. Research Records, No. 16. Rochester Museum and Science Center, Rochester, NY.

Hansen, Marcus L. 1958. *Old Fort Snelling, 1819–1858*. Ross & Haines, Minneapolis. Originally published in 1918 by the State Historical of Iowa, Iowa

City.

Hanson, James A. 1975. *Metal Weapons, Tools, and Ornaments of the Teton Dakota Indians*. University of Nebraska Press, Lincoln.

Hanson, Jeffrey R., and Linda P. Rouse. 1987. Dimensions of Native American Stereotypes. *American Indian Culture and Research Journal* 11(4):33–58.

Hardorff, Richard G. 1991. *Lakota Recollections of the Custer Fight: New Sources of Indian-Military History*. Arthur H. Clark, Spokane.

Harley, John B., and David Woodward (eds.). 1987. *Cartography in Prehistoric, Ancient, and Medieval Europe and the Mediterranean*, vol. 1 of *The History of Cartography*. University of Chicago Press, Chicago.

Harris, Olivia. 1984. Households as Natural Units. In *Of Marriage and the Market: Women's Subordination Internationally and Its Lessons*, edited by Kate Young, Carol Wolkowitz, and Roslyn McCullagh, pp. 136–55. Routledge & Kegan Paul, Boston.

Hassrick, Royal B. 1944. Teton Dakota Kinship System. *American Anthropologist* 46:338–47.

Hassrick, Royal B. 1964. *The Sioux: Life and Customs of a Warrior Society*. University of Oklahoma Press, Norman.

Hastrap, Kirsten. 1993. Native Anthropology: A Contradiction in Terms? *Folk* 35:147–61.

Hauptman, Laurence M. 1983. The American Indian Federation and the Indian New Deal: A Reinterpretation. *Pacific Historical Review* 52:378–402.

Hauptman, Laurence M. 1996. American Indian Federation. In *Native America in the Twentieth Century: An Encyclopedia*, edited by Mary B. Davis, pp. 33. Garland Publishing, New York.

Helm, June (ed.) 1968. *Essays on the Problem of Tribe*. Proceedings of the 1967 Annual Spring Meeting of the American Ethnological Society. University of Washington Press, Seattle.

Henig, Gerald S. 1976. A Neglected Cause of the Sioux Uprising. *Minnesota History* 45:107–10.

Hennepin, Louis. 1903. *A New Discovery of a Vast Country in America*. Edited by Reuben G. Thwaites. A. C. McClurg & Co., Chicago. Reprint: Toronto, Coles Publishing, 1974.

Hennepin, Louis. 1938. *Father Louis Hennepin's Description of Louisiana*. Edited and translated by Marion E. Cross. University of Minnesota Press, Minneapolis.

Henning, Elizabeth R. P. 1982. Western Dakota Winter Counts: An Analysis of the Effects of Westward Migration and Culture Change. *Plains Anthropologist* 27(95):57–65.

Hickerson, Harold. 1965. The Virginia Deer and Intertribal Buffer Zones in the Upper Mississippi Valley. *Publication No. 78 of the American Association for the Advancement of Science*. Washington, DC.

Hickerson, Harold. 1974a. Ethnohistory of Chippewa in Central Minnesota. *Chippewa Indian* IV. Indian Claims Commission. Garland Publishing, New York.

Hickerson, Harold. 1974b. Ethnohistory of the Chippewa of Lake Superior. *Chippewa Indians* III. Indian Claims Commission. Garland Publishing, New

York.

Hickerson, Harold. 1974c. Mdewakanton Band of Sioux Indians. *Sioux Indians* I:1–301. Garland Publishing, New York.

Hickerson, Harold. 1988 [1970]. *The Chippewa and Their Neighbors: A Study in Ethnohistory*. Waveland, Prospect Heights, Ill.

Hilden, Patricia P. 1995. *When Nickels Were Indians: An Urban Mixed-Blood Story*. Smithsonian Institution Press, Washington, DC.

Hodder, Ian. 1982. *Symbols in Action*. Cambridge University Press, New York.

Hodder, Ian. 1984. Burials, Houses, Women and Men in the European Neolithic. In *Ideology, Power and Prehistory*, edited by Daniel Miller and Christopher Tilley, pp. 51–68. Cambridge University Press, New York.

Holler, Clyde. 1984. Lakota Religion and Tragedy: The Theology of *Black Elk Speaks*. *Journal of the American Academy of Religion* 52:19–45.

Holler, Clyde (ed.) 2000a. *The Black Elk Reader*. Syracuse University Press, Syracuse, NY.

Holler, Clyde. 2000b. Introduction. In *The Black Elk Reader*, edited by Clyde Holler, pp. xiii–xxvi. Syracuse University Press, Syracuse.

Hollow, Robert C. 1970. A Note on Assiniboine Phonology. *International Journal of American Linguistics* 36:296–8.

Hollow, Robert C., and Douglas R. Parks. 1980. Studies in Plains Linguistics: A Review. In *Anthropology on the Great Plains*, edited by W. Raymond Wood and Margot Liberty, pp. 68–97. University of Nebraska Press, Lincoln.

Holly, Carol T. 1979. *Black Elk Speaks* and the Making of Indian Autobiography. *Genre* 12:117–36.

Holzkamm, Tim E. 1983. Eastern Dakota Population Movements and the European Fur Trade: One More Time. *Plains Anthropologist* 28(101):225–33.

Hoover, Herbert T. 1988. *The Yankton Sioux*. Chelsea House Publishers, New York.

Hoover, Herbert T. 1989. The Sioux Agreement of 1889 and Its Aftermath. *South Dakota History* 19:56–94.

Hoover, Herbert T. 1996a. Dakota. In *Native America in the Twentieth Century: An Encyclopedia*, edited by Mary B. Davis, pp. 161–4. Garland Publishing, New York.

Hoover, Herbert T. 1996b. Yankton and Yanktonai. In *Native America in the Twentieth Century: An Encyclopedia*, edited by Mary B. Davis, pp. 706–8. Garland Publishing, New York.

Hoover, Herbert T. 1996c. Sioux Federation. . In *Native America in the Twentieth Century: An Encyclopedia*, edited by Mary B. Davis, p. 600. Garland Publishing, New York.

Howard, James H. 1953. Notes on Two Dakota "Holy Dance" Medicines and Their Uses. *American Anthropologist* 55:608–9.

Howard, James H. 1954. The Dakota Heyoka Cult. *Scientific Monthly* 78:254–8.

Howard, James H. 1955a. Two Dakota Winter Count Texts. *Plains Anthropologist* 5:13–30.

Howard, James H. 1955b. The Tree Dweller Cults of the Dakota. *Journal of American Folklore* 68(268):169–74.

Howard, James H. 1960a. The Cultural Position of the Dakota: A Reassessment.

In *Essays in the Science of Culture, in Honor of Leslie A. White*, edited by Gertrude E. Dole and Robert L. Carneiro, pp. 249–68. Thomas Y. Crowell, New York.

Howard, James H. 1960b. Dakota Winter Counts as a Source of Plains History. *Anthropological Papers No. 61, Bureau of American Ethnology, Bulletin* 173:335–416. Smithsonian Institution, Washington, DC.

Howard, James H. 1962. Peyote Jokes. *Journal of American Folklore* 75:10–14.

Howard, James H. 1966. *The Dakota or Sioux Indians: A Study in Human Ecology.* Anthropological Papers, no. 2, Dakota Museum, University of South Dakota, Vermillion. Reprint: Lincoln, J & L Reprint Co. 1980.

Howard, James H. 1972. Notes on the Ethnogeography of the Yankton Dakota. *Plains Anthropologist* 17(58–1):281–307.

Howard, James H. 1976. *Yanktonai Ethnohistory and the John K. Bear Winter Count.* Memoir 11. Plains Anthropological Society, Lincoln, Nebr.

Howard, James H. 1984. *The Canadian Sioux.* University of Nebraska Press, Lincoln.

Howard, James H., and Wesley R. Hurt, Jr. 1952. A Dakota Conjuring Ceremony. *Southwestern Journal of Anthropology* 8(3):286–96.

Hoxie, Frederick E. 1979. From Prison to Homeland: The Cheyenne River Indian Reservation before WWI. *South Dakota History* 10:1–24.

Hoxie, Frederick E. 1997. Ethnohistory for a Tribal World. *Ethnohistory* 44(4):595–615.

Hughes, Diane O., and Thomas R. Trautmann (eds.). 1995. *Time: Histories and Ethnologies.* University of Michigan Press, Ann Arbor.

Hughes, Thomas. 1908. Causes and Results of the Inkpaduta Massacre. *Collections of the Minnesota Historical Society* 12:263–82.

Hughes, Thomas. 1929. *Old Traverse des Sioux.* Herald Publishing Co., St. Peter, Minn.

Hughes, Thomas. 1927. *Indian Chiefs of Southern Minnesota.* Free Press, Mankato, Minn. Reprint: Minneapolis, Ross & Haines 1969.

Hulston, Nancy J. 1995. Federal Children: Indian Education and the Red Cloud–McGillycuddy Conflict. *South Dakota History* 25:81–94.

Hurt, Wesley R. 1974. Dakota Sioux Indians. *Sioux Indians* II. Garland Publishing, New York.

Hurt, Wesley R., and William E. Lass. 1956. *Frontier Photographer: Stanley J. Morrow's Dakota Years.* University of South Dakota, Vermillion.

Hutton, Paul A. 1976. From Little Bighorn to Little Big Man: The Changing Image of a Western Hero in Popular Culture. *The Western Historical Quarterly* 7:19–45.

Hutton, Paul A. 1985. *Phil Sheridan and His Army.* University of Nebraska Press, Lincoln.

Hutton, Paul A. 1992. *The Custer Reader.* University of Nebraska Press, Lincoln.

Hyde, George E. 1937. *Red Cloud's Folk: A History of the Oglala Sioux Indians.* University of Oklahoma Press, Norman.

Hyde, George E. 1961. *Spotted Tail's Folk: A History of the Brulé Sioux.* University of Oklahoma Press, Norman.

Hymes, Dell. 1974. *Foundations in Sociolinguistics: An Ethnographic Approach.*

University of Pennsylvania Press, Philadelphia.

Ingram, Mary R. 1989. "Ethnohealth and Ethnocaring Practices among the Lakota." Ph.D. dissertation, University of Utah, Salt Lake City.

Innis, Harold Adams. 1950. *Empire and Communications.* Clarendon Press, Oxford. Reprint: Toronto, University of Toronto Press 1972.

Jackson, Donald D. (ed.) 1978. *Letters of the Lewis and Clark Expedition, with Related Documents, 1783–1854.* 2d ed. University of Illinois Press, Urbana.

Jackson, Donald D., and Mary L. Spence (eds.) 1970. *The Expeditions of John Charles Frémont, vol. 1, Travels from 1838 to 1844.* University of Illinois Press, Urbana.

Jacobson, Clair. 1980. A History of the Yanktonai and Hunkpatina Sioux. *North Dakota History* 47(1):4–24.

Jahner, Elaine A. 1987. Lakota Genesis: The Oral Tradition. In *Sioux Indian Religion: Tradition and Innovation,* edited by Raymond J. DeMallie and Douglas R. Parks, pp. 45–65. University of Oklahoma Press, Norman.

Jaimes, M. Annette. 1992. Federal Indian Identification Policy: A Usurpation of Indigenous Sovereignty in North America. In *The State of Native America: Genocide, Colonization, and Resistance,* edited by M. Annette Jaimes, pp. 123–38. South End Press, Boston.

Jaimes, M. Annette. 1996. Indian Identity. In *Native America in the Twentieth Century: An Encyclopedia,* edited by Mary B. Davis, pp. 261–2. Garland Publishing, New York.

Joe, Jennie R. 1987. Forced Relocation and Assimilation: Dillon Myer and the Native American. *Amerasia Journal* 13(2):161–5.

Johnson, David L., and Raymond Wilson. 1988. Gertrude Simmons Bonnin, 1876–1938: "Americanize the First American." *American Indian Quarterly* 12:27–40.

Johnson, Elden. 1962. Notes on the Mdewakanton Bark House. *Minnesota Archaeologist* 24:49–52.

Johnson, Elden. 1971. The Northern Margin of the Prairie Peninsula. *Journal of the Iowa Archaeological Society* 18:13–21.

Johnson, Elden. 1984. *Cultural Resource Survey of the Mille Lacs Area.* University of Minnesota, Minneapolis. Report prepared for the Minnesota Historical Society, St. Paul.

Johnson, Elden. 1985. The 17th Century Mdewakanton Dakota Subsistence Mode. In *Archaeology, Ecology and Ethnohistory of the Prairie–Forest Border Zone of Minnesota and Manitoba,* edited by Janet Spector and Elden Johnson, pp. 154–65. J & L Reprint Co., Lincoln, Nebr.

Johnson, Elden. 1991. Ceramic Stratigraphy at the Creech Site (21CA14). *The Minnesota Archaeologist* 50(1):3–6.

Johnston, Francis E., and L. M. Schell. 1979. Anthropometric Variation of Native American Children and Adults. In *The First Americans: Origins, Affinities, and Adaptations,* edited by William S. Laughlin and A. B. Harper, pp. 275–91. Gustav Fischer, New York.

Jojola, Theodore S. 1996. Public Image. In *Native America in the Twentieth Century: An Encyclopedia,* edited by Mary B. Davis, pp. 483–6. Garland Publishing, New York.

Jones, Siân. 1997. *The Archaeology of Ethnicity: Constructing Identities in the Past and Present*. Routledge, New York and London.

Jurich, Katarin. 1992. "Health and Being in the World: An Interpretive Work on Lakota Health." Ph.D. dissertation, University of California, San Francisco.

Justin, Michael A., and Lynn Schuster. 1994. The Basswood Shores Site, 21DL90, a Late Woodland Habitation. *Minnesota Archaeologist* 53:77–85.

Kane, Lucile M. 1951. The Sioux Treaties and the Traders. *Minnesota History* 32:65–80.

Kane, Lucile M., June D. Holmquist, and Carolyn Gilman (eds.). 1978. *The Northern Expeditions of Stephen H. Long: The Journals of 1817 and 1823 and Related Documents*. Minnesota Historical Society, St. Paul.

Kaufman, Kevin. 1989. *The Mapping of the Great Lakes in the Seventeenth Century*. The John Carter Brown Library, Providence, RI.

Keating, William H. 1824. *Narrative of an Expedition to the Source of St. Peter's River*. H. C. Carey & I. Lea, Philadelphia. Reprint: Minneapolis, Ross & Haines, 1959.

Keeley, Lawrence. 1996. *War before Civilization: The Myth of the Peaceful Savage*. Oxford University Press, Oxford.

Kehoe, Alice Beck. 1989. *The Ghost Dance: Ethnohistory and Revitalization*. Holt, Rinehart, & Winston, New York.

Keller, Steve, and Renee Keller. 1982. *James River Valley Survey, Spink County, South Dakota, 1982*, vol. 3. Contract Investigations Series 68-III. South Dakota Archaeological Research Center, Rapid City.

Kellogg, Louise P. 1917. *Early Narratives of the Northwest, 1634–1699*. C. Scribners's Sons, New York. Reprint: New York, Barnes & Noble 1967.

Kellogg, Louise P. 1925. *The French Regime in Wisconsin and the Northwest*. State Historical Society of Wisconsin, Madison.

Kellogg, Louise P. 1927. Fort Beauharnois. *Minnesota History* 8:232–46.

Kellogg, Louise P. 1935. *The British Regime in Wisconsin and the Northwest*. State Historical Society of Wisconsin, Madison.

Kelly, Lawrence C. 1983. *The Assault on Assimilation: John Collier and the Origins of Indian Policy Reform*. University of New Mexico Press, Albuquerque.

Key, Patrick J. 1983. *Craniometric Relationships Among Plains Indians: Culture-Historical and Evolutionary Implications*. Report of Investigations No. 34, Department of Anthropology, University of Tennessee, Knoxville.

Key, Patrick J. 1994. Relationships of the Woodland Period on the Northern and Central Plains: The Craniometric Evidence. In *Skeletal Biology in the Great Plains: Migration, Warfare, Health, and Subsistence*, edited by Douglas W. Owsley and Richard L. Jantz, pp. 179–87. Smithsonian Institution Press, Washington, DC.

Kickingbird, Kirke, and Karen Ducheneaux. 1973. *One Hundred Million Acres*. Macmillan, New York.

Kidwell, Clara S. 1992. Indian Women as Cultural Mediators. *Ethnohistory* 39:97–107.

Kimes, T., C. Haselgrove, and I. Hodder. 1982. A Method for the Identification of the Location of Regional Cultural Boundaries. *Journal of Anthropological Archaeology* 1:113–31.

Kirk, Sylvia Van. 1983. *Many Tender Ties: Women in Fur-Trade Society, 1670–1870.* University of Oklahoma Press, Norman.

Klein, Alan M. 1983a. The Plains Truth: The Impact of Colonialism on Indian Women. *Dialectical Anthropology* 7:299–313.

Klein, Alan M. 1983b. The Political-Economy of Gender: A 19thcentury Plains Indian Case. In *The Hidden Half: Studies of Plains Indian Women,* edited by Patricia Albers and Beatrice Medicine, pp. 143–73. University Press of America, Lanham, Md.

Klein, Alan M. 1993. Political Economy of the Buffalo Hide Trade: Race and Class on the Plains. In *The Political Economy of North American Indians,* edited by John H. Moore, pp. 133–60. University of Oklahoma Press, Norman.

Klein, Laura F., and Lillian A. Ackerman. 1995a. Introduction. In *Women and Power in Native North America,* edited by Laura F. Klein and Lillian A. Ackerman, pp. 3–16. University of Oklahoma Press, Norman.

Klein, Laura F., and Lillian A. Ackerman (eds.). 1995b. *Women and Power in Native North America.* University of Oklahoma Press, Norman.

Kohl, Johann G. 1857. *Reisen im Nordwestern der Vereinigten Staaten.* D. Appleton & Co., New York.

Kopytoff, Igor. 1986. The Cultural Biography of Things: Commoditization as Process. In *The Social Life of Things: Commodities in Cultural Perspective,* edited by Arjun Appadurai, pp. 64-91. Cambridge University Press, New York.

Kottak, Conrad P. 1991. *Cultural Anthropology.* 5th ed. McGraw-Hill, New York.

Koziski, Stephanie. 1984. The Standup Comedian as Anthropologist: Intentional Culture Critique. *Journal of Popular Culture* 18(2):57–76.

Krupat, Arnold, and Brian Swann (eds.). 1987. *Recovering the Word: Essays on Native American Literature.* University of California Press, Berkeley.

La Barre, Weston. 1938. *The Peyote Cult.* Yale University Press, New Haven. Reprint: Norman, University of Oklahoma Press, 1989.

La Hontan, Louis Armand de Lom D'Arce, baron de. 1703. *New Voyages to North America.* H. Bonwicke, London. Reprint: Chicago, A. C. McClurg & Co., 1905.

Lamb, Mary B. 1998. "First Contact: Swiss Benedictine Sisters at Standing Rock Missions in a Cross-Cultural Frame, 1881-1890 (South Dakota, North Dakota)." Ph.D. dissertation, Graduate Theological Union, Berkeley, Calif.

Lame Deer, John (Fire), and Richard Erdoes. 1994. *Lame Deer, Seeker of Visions.* Rev. ed. Washington Square Press, New York.

Landes, Ruth. 1937. *Ojibwa Sociology.* Columbia University Contributions to Anthropology, vol. 29. Columbia University Press, New York.

Landes, Ruth. 1959. Dakota Warfare. *Southwestern Journal of Anthropology* 15:43–52.

Landes, Ruth. 1968. *The Mystic Lake Sioux, Sociology of the Mdewakantonwan Santee.* University of Wisconsin Press, Madison.

Lang, Gretchen C. 1985. Diabetics and Health Care in a Sioux Community. *Human Organization* 44:251–60.

Lang, Sabine. 1998. *Men as Women, Women as Men: Changing Gender in Native American Cultures.* University of Texas Press, Austin.

Larner, John W. (ed.) 1987. *The Papers of the Society of American Indians.* Scholarly Resources, Wilmington, Del.

Larner, John W. 1996. Society of American Indians. In *Native America in the Twentieth Century: An Encyclopedia*, edited by Mary B. Davis, pp. 603–5. Garland Publishing, New York.

Lass, William E. 1963. The Removal from Minnesota of the Sioux and Winnebago Indians. *Minnesota History* 38:353–64.

Laviolette, Gontran. 1991. *The Dakota Sioux in Canada*. Rev. ed. DLM Publications, Winnipeg.

Lawrence, Elden E. 1999. "Returning to Traditional Beliefs and Practices: A Solution for Indian Alcoholism." Ph.D. dissertation, South Dakota State University, Brookings.

Lawson, Michael L. 1982a. *Dammed Indians: The Pick-Sloan Plan and the Missouri River Sioux, 1944–1980*. University of Oklahoma Press, Norman.

Lawson, Michael L. 1982b. Indian Heirship Lands: The Lake Traverse Experience. *South Dakota History* 12:213–31.

Lawson, Michael L. 1991. The Fractional Estate: The Problem of American Indian Heirship. *South Dakota History* 21:1–42.

Lazarus, Edward. 1991. *Black Hills, White Justice: The Sioux Nation versus the United States, 1775 to the Present*. HarperCollins, New York.

Leach, Jerry W. (ed.) 1983. *The Kula: New Perspectives on Massim Exchange*. Cambridge University Press, New York.

Leacock, Eleanor. 1978. Women's Status in Egalitarian Society: Implications for Social Evolution. *Current Anthropology* 19:247–75.

LeBlanc, Steven A. 1999. *Prehistoric Warfare in the American Southwest*. University of Utah Press, Salt Lake City.

Leckie, Shirley A. 1993. *Elizabeth Bacon Custer and the Making of a Myth*. University of Oklahoma Press, Norman.

Lees, Robert B. 1953. The Basis of Glottochronology. *Language* 29:113–27.

Lees, William B. 1985. Dakota Acculturation during the Early Reservation Period: Evidence from the Deerbly Site (39LM39), South Dakota. *Plains Anthropologist* 30(108):103–21.

Lesser, Alexander. 1930. Some Aspects of Siouan Kinship. In *Proceedings of the Twenty-third International Congress of Americanists*, 1928, 563–71. New York.

Lesser, Alexander. 1958. "Siouan Kinship." Ph.D. dissertation, Columbia University, New York.

Lévi-Strauss, Claude. 1966. *The Savage Mind*. University of Chicago Press, Chicago.

Levin, Norman. 1964. *The Assiniboine Language*. Indiana University Research Center in Anthropology, Folklore, and Linguistics, Publication 32. Bloomington.

Levinson, David. 1989. *Family Violence in Cross-Cultural Perspective*. Sage Publications, Newbury Park, Calif.

Lewis, G. Malcom. 1987. Indian Maps: Their Place in the History of Plains Cartography. In *Mapping the North American Plains: Essays in the History of Cartography*, edited by Frederick C. Luebke, Francis W. Kaye, and Gary E. Moulton, pp. 63–80. University of Oklahoma Press, Norman.

Lewis, G. Malcom (ed.) 1998. *Cartographic Encounters: Perspective on Native American Mapmaking and Map Use*. University of Chicago Press, Chicago.

Liberty, Margot. 1980. The Sun Dance. In *Anthropology on the Great Plains*, edited by W. Raymond Wood and Margot Liberty, pp. 164–78. University of Nebraska Press, Lincoln.

Lincoln, Kenneth. 1993. *Indi'n Humor: Bicultural Play in Native America*. Oxford University Press, New York.

Linenthal, Edward T. 1993. *Sacred Ground: Americans and Their Battlefields*. Rev. ed. University of Illinois Press, Urbana.

Linton, Ralph. 1943. Nativistic Movements. *American Anthropologist* 45:230–40.

Little, Bryce. 1985. Early Mdewakanton Dakota Culture and Interpretations for Archaeology: A Re-evaluation, 1640–1780. In *Archaeology, Ecology and Ethnohistory of the Prairie-Forest Border Zone of Minnesota and Manitoba*, edited by Janet Spector and Elden Johnson, pp. 146–53. J & L Reprint Co., Lincoln, Nebr.

Locust, Carol S. 1996. Traditional Medicine. In *Native America in the Twentieth Century: An Encyclopedia*, edited by Mary B. Davis, pp. 642–4. Garland Publishing, New York.

Lothson, Gordon A. 1972. "Burial Mounds of the Mille Lacs Lake Area." 3 vols. MA thesis, University of Minnesota, Minneapolis.

Lourandos, Harry. 1997. *Continent of Hunter-Gatherers: New Perspectives in Australian Prehistory*. Cambridge University Press, New York.

Lowie, Robert H. 1909. *The Assiniboine*. Anthropological Papers, vol. 4, pt. 1. American Museum of Natural History, New York.

Lowie, Robert H. 1913. Dance Associations of the Eastern Dakota. *Anthropological Papers of the American Museum of Natural History*, vol. 11, pt. 2, pp. 101–42.

Lowie, Robert H. 1920. *Primitive Society*. Boni & Liveright, New York. Reprint: New York, Liveright, 1970.

Lowie, Robert H. 1960. A Few Assiniboine Texts. *Anthropological Linguistics* 2(8):1–30.

Lund, Duane R. 1980. *Our Historic Boundary Waters: From Lake Superior to Lake of the Woods*. Nordell Graphic Communications, Staples, Minn.

Luttig, John C. 1920. *Journal of a Fur-Trading Expedition on the Upper Missouri, 1812–1813*. Edited by Stella M. Drumm. Missouri Historical Society, St. Louis. Reprint: New York, Argosy-Antiquarian, 1964.

Lyman, Christopher M. 1982. *The Vanishing Race and Other Illusions: Photographs of Indians by Edward S. Curtis*. Smithsonian Institution Press, Washington, DC.

MacEachern, Scott, David J. W. Archer, and Richard D. Garvin (eds.). 1989. *Households and Communities*. Archaeological Association, University of Calgary, Calgary.

Macgregor, Gordon. 1946. *Warriors without Weapons: A Study of the Society and Personality Development of the Pine Ridge Sioux*. University of Chicago Press, Chicago.

Mails, Thomas E. 1978. *Fools Crow*. Doubleday, Garden City, NJ. Reprint: Lincoln, University of Nebraska Press, 1990.

Mallery, Garrick. 1880a. *Introduction to the Study of Sign Language among the*

North American Indians. Govt. Print. Off., Washington, DC.

Mallery, Garrick. 1880b. The Sign Language of the Indians of the Upper Missouri. *American Antiquarian and Oriental Journal* 2:218–28.

Mallery, Garrick. 1887. The Dakota and Corbusier Winter Counts. *Fourth Annual Report of the Bureau of American Ethnology*, pp. 89–146 and plates V1–L1. Smithsonian Institution, Washington, DC. Reprint: Lincoln, J & L Reprint Co., 1987.

Malmsheimer, Lonna M. 1985. "Imitation White Man": Images of Transformation at the Carlisle Indian School. *Studies in Visual Communication* 11(4):54–75.

Malmsheimer, Lonna M. 1987. Photographic Analysis as Ethnohistory: Interpretive Strategies. *Visual Anthropology* 1:21–36.

Maltz, Daniel, and JoAllyn Archambault. 1995. Gender and Power in Native North America. In *Women and Power in Native North America*, edited by Laura F. Klein and Lillian A. Ackerman, pp. 230–49. University of Oklahoma Press, Norman.

Martinez, Natasha B. 1996. Photography. In *Native America in the Twentieth Century: An Encyclopedia*, edited by Mary B. Davis, pp. 449–52. Garland Publishing, New York.

Mascia-Lees, Frances E., and Nancy J. Black. 2000. *Gender and Anthropology.* Waveland Press, Prospect Heights, Ill.

Mather, David. 2000. *Archaeological Overview of the Mille Lacs Locality.* Loucks Project Report 96506-2 (prepared for the Minnesota Department of Transportation, St. Paul). Loucks Associates, Minneapolis.

Mather, David, and Elizabeth J. Abel. 2000. *The Lake Onamia-Trunk Highway 169 Recovery Project, Mille Lacs County, Minnesota.* 2 vols. Loucks Project Report 96506-1 (prepared for the Minnesota Department of Transportation, St. Paul). Loucks Associates, Minneapolis.

Mather, David, Mary Whelan, and Sarah Nicholas. 2000. Mille Lacs Regional Zooarchaeology. In *The Lake Onamia-Trunk Highway 169 Data Recovery Project, Mille Lacs County, Minnesota*, vol. 1, pp. 17.1–17.10. Loucks Project Report 96506-1 (prepared for the Minnesota Department of Transportation, St. Paul). Loucks Associates, Minneapolis.

Mattern, Mark. 1999. The Powwow as a Public Arena for Negotiating Unity and Diversity in American Indian Life. In *Contemporary Native American Cultural Issues*, edited by Duane Champagne, pp. 129–43. AltaMira Press, Walnut Creek, Calif.

Matthews, G. Hubert. 1959. Proto-Siouan Kinship Terminology. *American Anthropologist* 61:252–78.

Mauss, Marcel. 1990. *The Gift: The Form and Reason for Exchange in Archaic Societies.* Routledge, New York.

May, Philip A. 1989. Alcohol Abuse and Alcoholism among American Indians: An Overview. In *Alcoholism in Minority Populations*, edited by Thomas D. Watts and Roosevelt Wright, pp. 95–119. Charles C. Thomas, Springfield, Ill.

May, Philip A. 1996. Alcohol Abuse. In *Native America in the Twentieth Century: An Encyclopedia*, edited by Mary B. Davis, pp. 23–7. Garland Publishing, New York.

May, Philip A. 1999. The Epidemiology of Alcohol Abuse among Native Americans: The Mythical and Real Properties. In *Contemporary Native American Cultural Issues*, edited by Duane Champagne, pp. 227–44. AltaMira Press, Walnut Creek, Calif.

Mayer, Frank B. 1932. *With Pen and Pencil on the Frontier in 1851: the Diary and Sketches of Frank Blackwell Mayer*. Minnesota Historical Society, St. Paul. Reprint: St. Paul, Minnesota Historical Society Press 1986, edited by Bertha L. Heilbron.

Maynard, Eileen. 1979. Changing Sex-roles and Family Structure among the Oglala Sioux. In *Sex-roles in Changing Cultures*, edited by Ann McElroy and Carolyn Matthiasson, pp. 11–19. Occasional Papers in Anthropology, vol. 1. State University of New York at Buffalo, Buffalo.

McBeth, Sally J. 1983. *Ethnic Identity and the Boarding School Experience of West–Central Oklahoma American Indians*. University Press of America, Washington, DC.

McCluskey, Sally. 1972. *Black Elk Speaks*: and So Does John Neihardt. *Western American Literature* 6:231–42.

McDermott, John D. 1990. Wounded Knee: Centennial Voices. *South Dakota History* 20:245–98.

McDermott, John D., Jr. 1991. Allotment and the Sissetons: Experiments in Cultural Change, 1866–1905. *South Dakota History* 21:43–68.

McDermott, John F. 1961. *Seth Eastman, Pictorial Historian of the Indian*. University of Oklahoma Press, Norman.

McDonnell, Janet A. 1980. Competency Commissions and Indian Land Policy, 1913–1920. *South Dakota History* 11:21–34.

McDonnell, Janet A. 1991. *The Dispossession of the American Indian, 1887–1934*. Indiana University Press, Bloomington.

McGinnis, Anthony. 1990. *Counting Coup and Cutting Horses: Intertribal Warfare on the Northern Plains, 1738–1889*. Cordillera Press, Evergreen, Colo.

McKern, Will C. 1963. *The Clam River Focus*. Publications in Anthropology 9, Milwaukee Public Museum, Milwaukee.

McLaughlin, Marie L. 1916. *Myths and Legends of the Sioux*. Bismarck Tribune Co., Bismarck. Reprint: Lincoln, University of Nebraska Press, 1990.

Means, Russell. 1995. *Where White Men Fear to Tread: The Autobiography of Russell Means*. St. Martin's Press, New York.

Medicine, Beatrice. 1978. *The Native American Woman: A Perspective*. National Educational Laboratory Publishers, Austin.

Medicine, Beatrice. 1982. The American Indian Family: Culture Change and Adaptive Strategies. *Journal of Ethnic Studies* 8:13–23.

Medicine, Beatrice. 1983. "Warrior Women" – Sex Role Alternatives for Plains Indian Women. In *The Hidden Half: Studies of Plains Indian Women*, edited by Patricia Albers and Beatrice Medicine, pp. 267–80. University Press of America, Lanham, Md.

Medicine, Beatrice. 2001. *Learning to Be an Anthropologist while Remaining Native*. University of Illinois Press, Urbana.

Meer, R., P. Trocki, and J. A. Schwegman. 1994. *Clam River Narrows Revisited: Data Recovery of a Portion of the Clam Rivers Narrows Site (47Bt-200), Burnett*

County, Wisconsin. Museum Archaeology Program, Report in Archaeology No. 26. State Historical Society of Wisconsin, Madison.

Meggitt, M. 1977. *Blood is Their Argument.* Mayfield, Palo Alto, Calif.

Mekeel, Scudder. 1932. A Discussion of Culture Change as Illustrated by Material from a Dakota Community. *American Anthropologist* 34:274–85.

Mekeel, Scudder. 1936. The Economy of a Modern Teton Dakota Community. *Yale University Publications in Anthropology* 6:1–14. New Haven.

Mekeel, Scudder. 1943. A Short History of the Teton-Dakota. *North Dakota Historical Quarterly* 10(3):137–205.

Meya, Wilhelm K. 1999. "The Calico Winter Count, 1825–1877: An Ethnohistorical Analysis (Lakota)." MA thesis, University of Arizona, Tucson.

Meyer, Roy W. 1961. The Prairie Island Community: A Remnant of Minnesota Sioux. *Minnesota History* 37:271–82.

Meyer, Roy W. 1968. The Canadian Sioux: Refugees from Minnesota. *Minnesota History* 41:13–28.

Meyer, Roy W. 1993. *History of the Santee Sioux: United States Indian Policy on Trial.* Rev ed. University of Nebraska Press, Lincoln.

Michael, Ronald L. 1965. "Fur Trade of the Red River Valley of the North: 1763–1812." MA thesis, University of North Dakota, Grand Forks.

Michlovic, Michael G. 1985. The Problem of Teton Migration. In *Archaeology, Ecology and Ethnohistory of the Prairie–Forest Border Zone of Minnesota and Manitoba,* edited by Janet Spector and Elden Johnson, pp. 131–45. J & L Reprint Co., Lincoln, Nebr.

Michlovic, Michael G. 1987. The Archaeology of the Mooney Site (21NR29). *The Minnesota Archaeologist* 46(2):39–66.

Michlovic, Michael G., and Fred E. Schneider 1993. The Shea Site: A Prehistoric Fortified Village on the Northeastern Plains. *Plains Anthropologist* 38:117–37.

Michno, Gregory F. 1997. *Lakota Noon: The Indian Narrative of Custer's Defeat.* Mountain Press Publishing Co., Missoula.

Mihesuah, Devon A. 1996. *American Indians: Stereotypes and Realities.* Clarity, Atlanta, Ga.

Mihesuah, Devon A. 1999. American Indian Identities: Issues of Individual Choice and Development. In *Contemporary Native American Cultural Issues,* edited by Duane Champagne, pp. 13–38. AltaMira Press, Walnut Creek, Calif.

Miller, Barbara D. 1999. *Cultural Anthropology.* Allyn & Bacon, Boston.

Miller, Christopher L. 1985. *Prophetic Worlds: Indians and Whites on the Columbia Plateau.* Rutgers University Press, New Brunswick, NJ.

Miller, Christopher L., and George R. Hamell. 1986. A New Perspective on Indian–White Contact: Cultural Symbols and Colonial Trade. *The Journal of American History* 73:311–28.

Miller, David H. 1957. *Custer's Fall: The Native American Side of the Story.* Duell, Sloan, & Pearce, New York. Reprint: New York, Meridian, 1992.

Miller, Jay. 1996. Cultural Revitalization. In *Native America in the Twentieth Century: An Encyclopedia,* edited by Mary B. Davis, pp. 156–8. Garland Publishing, New York.

Milner, George R. 1999. Warfare in Prehistoric and Early Historic Eastern North America. *Journal of Archaeological Research* 7:105–51.

Milner, George R., Eve Anderson, and Virginia G. Smith. 1991. Warfare in Late Prehistoric West-Central Illinois. *American Antiquity* 56:581–603.

Mishkin, Bernard. 1940. *Rank and Warfare among the Plains* Indians. Monograph 3, American Ethnological Society, University of Washington Press, Seattle. Reprint: Lincoln, University of Nebraska Press, 1992.

Mizrach, Steven E. 1999. "Natives on the Electronic Frontier: Technology and Cultural Change on the Cheyenne River Sioux Reservation (South Dakota)." Ph.D. dissertation, University of Florida, Gainesville.

Molin, Paulette F. 2001. "To Be Examples to … Their People": Standing Rock Sioux Students at Hampton Institute, 1878–1923 (Part One). *North Dakota History* 68:2–23.

Mooney, James. 1896. *The Ghost-Dance Religion and the Sioux Outbreak of 1890.* Bureau of American Ethnology, Annual Report 14, pt. 2. Smithsonian Institution, Washington, DC. Reprint: Lincoln: University of Nebraska Press, 1991.

Moore, Henrietta. 1993. Things Ain't What They Seem. *Social Analysis* 34:126–31.

Morris, Joann S. 1996. Churches and Education. In *Native America in the Twentieth Century: An Encyclopedia*, edited by Mary B. Davis, pp. 113–16. Garland Publishing, New York.

Moses, Lester G. 1996. *Wild West Shows and the Images of American Indians, 1883–1933.* University of New Mexico Press, Albuquerque.

Moulton, Gary E. (ed.) 1983. *Atlas of the Lewis and Clark Expedition.* University of Nebraska Press, Lincoln.

Moulton, Gary E. (ed.) 1997. *The Journals of the Lewis and Clark Expedition*, 12 vols. University of Nebraska Press, Lincoln.

Munck, Thomas. 2000. *The Enlightenment: A Comparative Social History 1721–1794.* Oxford University Press, New York.

Munn, Nancy D. 1992. The Cultural Anthropology of Time: A Critical Essay. *Annual Review of Anthropology* 21:93–123.

Murdock, George P. 1949. *Social Structure.* Macmillan, New York.

Myster, Susan M. T. 2001. "Ten Thousand Years of Population Relationships at the Prairie–Woodland Interface: Cranial Morphology in the Upper Midwest and Contiguous Areas of Manitoba and Ontario." Ph.D. dissertation, University of Tennessee, Knoxville.

Myster, Susan M. T., and Barbara H. O'Connell. 1997a. Bioarchaeology of Iowa, Wisconsin, and Minnesota. In *Bioarchaeology of the North Central United States*, edited by Douglas W. Owsley and J. C. Rose, pp. 147–239. Research Series, No. 49. Arkansas Archeological Survey, Fayetteville.

Myster, Susan M. T., and Barbara H. O'Connell. 1997b. Bioarcheology. In *Archeology and Bioarcheology of the Northern Woodlands*, edited by Elizabeth D. Benchley, B. Nansel, Clark A. Dobbs, Susan M. T. Myster, and Barbara H. O'Connell, pp. 215–302. Research Series, No. 52. Arkansas Archeological Survey, Fayetteville.

Nagel, Joane. 1996. *American Indian Ethnic Renewal: Red Power and the Resurgence of Identity and Culture.* Oxford University Press, New York.

Nasatir, Abraham P. 1931. The Anglo-Spanish Frontier on the Upper Missouri

1786–1796. *Iowa Journal of History and Politics* 29:155–232.

Nasatir, Abraham P. (ed.) 1990. *Before Lewis and Clark: Documents Illustrating the History of the Missouri, 1785–1804*, 2 vols. University of Nebraska Press, Lincoln.

Nason, James D. 1996. Museums. In *Native America in the Twentieth Century: An Encyclopedia*, edited by Mary B. Davis, pp. 359–63. Garland Publishing, New York.

Neill, Edward D. 1902. Dakota Land and Dakota Life. *Collections of the Minnesota Historical Society* 1:254–94.

Netting, Robert McC., Richard R. Wilk, and Eric J. Arnould (eds.). 1984. *Households: Comparative and Historical Studies of the Domestic Group*. University of California Press, Berkeley.

Newcomb, W. W., Jr. 1950. A Re-examination of the Causes of Plains Warfare. *American Anthropologist* 52:317–30.

Nicholas, Thomas. 1991. *Entangled Objects: Exchange, Material Culture, and Colonialism in the Pacific*. Harvard University Press, Cambridge, Mass.

Nicollet, Joseph N. 1970. *The Journals of Joseph N. Nicollet: A Scientist on the Mississippi Headwaters, with Notes on Indian Life, 1836–37*. Edited by Martha C. Bray, translated by André Fertey. Minnesota Historical Society, St. Paul.

Nicollet, Joseph N. 1993. *Joseph N. Nicollet on the Plains and Prairies: The Expeditions of 1838–39, with Journals, Letters, and Notes on the Dakota Indians*. Translated and edited by Edmund C. Bray and Martha C. Bray. Minnesota Historical Society Press, St. Paul.

Nimkoff, M. F., and Russell Middleton. 1960. Types of Family and Types of Economy. *American Journal of Sociology* 66:215–25.

Nordquist, Joan. 1999. *The Native American Woman: Social, Economic, and Political Aspects: A Bibliography*. Reference and Research Services, Santa Cruz, Calif.

Nurge, Ethel (ed.) 1970. *The Modern Sioux: Social Systems and Reservation Culture*. University of Nebraska Press, Lincoln.

Nute, Grace L. 1930. Posts in the Minnesota-Fur Trading Area, 1660–1855. *Minnesota History* 11:353–85.

Nute, Grace L. 1938. Introduction. In *Father Hennepin's Description of Louisiana*, Louis Hennepin, pp. vii–xv. University of Minnesota Press, Minneapolis.

Nute, Grace L. 1943. *Caesars of the Wilderness: Médard Chouart, Sieur des Groseilliers and Pierre Esprit Radisson, 1618–1710*. D. Appleton-Century Co., New York. Reprint: St. Paul, Minnesota Historical Society Press, 1978.

Odell, George H. 1998. Pipe. In *Archaeology of Native North America: An Encyclopedia*, edited by Guy Gibbon, pp. 647–8. Garland Publishing, New York.

Oehler, Chester M. 1959. *The Great Sioux Uprising*. Oxford University Press, New York. Reprint: New York, Da Capo Press, 1997.

Olsen, Louise P. 1953. The Problem of Language in the Indian Schools of Dakota Territory, 1885–1888. *North Dakota History* 20(1):47–57.

Ossenberg, Nancy S. 1974. Origins and Relationships of Woodland Peoples: The Evidence of Cranial Morphology. In *Aspects of Upper Great Lakes Anthropology: Papers in Honor of Lloyd A. Wilford*, edited by Elden Johnson, pp. 15–39. Minnesota Prehistoric Archaeology Series No. 11. Minnesota Historical Society, St. Paul.

Otis, Delos S. 1973. *The Dawes Act and the Allotment of Indian Lands*. Edited by Francis P. Prucha. University of Oklahoma Press, Norman.

Overstreet, David F. 1995. The Eastern Wisconsin Oneota Regional Continuity. In *Oneota Archaeology: Past, Present, and Future*, edited by William Green, pp. 33–64. Report 20, Office of the State Archaeologist, University of Iowa, Iowa City.

Owsley, Douglas W. 1992. Demography of Prehistoric and early Historic Northern Plains Populations. In *Disease and Demography in the Americas*, edited by John W. Verano and Douglas H. Ubelaker, pp. 75–86. Smithsonian Institution Press, Washington, DC.

Owsley, Douglas W., and Richard L. Jantz (eds.). 1994. *Skeletal Biology in the Great Plains: Migration, Warfare, Health, and Subsistence*. Smithsonian Institution Press, Washington, DC.

Owsley, Douglas W., and J. C. Rose (eds.) 1997. *Bioarchaeology of the North Central United States*. Research Series, No. 49. Arkansas Archeological Survey, Fayetteville.

Page, Jean J. 1978. Frank Blackwell Mayer: Painter of the Minnesota Indian. *Minnesota History* 46:66–74.

Parker, John. 1976. *The Journals of Jonathan Carver and Related Documents, 1766–1770*. Minnesota Historical Society Press, St. Paul.

Parkin, Robert. 1997. *Kinship: An Introduction to the Basic Concepts*. Blackwell Publishers, Malden, Maine.

Parks, Douglas R. 1988. The Importance of Language Study for the Writing of Plains Indian History. In *New Directions in American Indian History*, edited by Colin G. Calloway, pp. 153–97. University of Oklahoma Press, Norman.

Parks, Douglas R., and Raymond J. DeMallie. 1992. Sioux, Assiniboine, and Stoney Dialects: A Classification. *Anthropological Linguistics* 34:233–55.

Parman, Donald L. 1996. Meriam Commission. In *Native America in the Twentieth Century: An Encyclopedia*, edited by Mary B. Davis, pp. 335–6. Garland Publishing, New York.

Pasternak, Burton, Carol R. Ember, and Melvin Ember. 1976. On the Conditions Favoring Extended Family Households. *Journal of Anthropological Research* 32:109–23.

Penman, Sarah (ed.) 2000. *Honor the Grandmothers: Lakota and Dakota Women Tell Their Stories*. Minnesota Historical Society Press, St. Paul.

Peterson, Jacqueline, and John Anfinson. 1984. The Indian and the Fur Trade: A Review of Recent Literature. In *Scholars and the Indian Experience*, edited by W. R. Swagerty, pp. 223–57. Indiana University Press, Bloomington.

Peterson, Susan C. 1985. Doing "Women's Work": The Grey Nuns at Fort Totten Indian Reservation, 1874–1900. *North Dakota History* 52(2):18–25.

Picha, Paul R. 1996. "Rivière à Jacque and the James River Dakota Rendezvous: An Exploratory Study of Dakota Sioux Ethnohistory." Master's thesis, University of Missouri-Columbia, Columbia.

Pickering, Kathleen A. 1994. Articulation of the Lakota Mode of Production and the Euro-American Fur Trade. In *The Fur Trade Revisited: Selected Papers of the Sixth North American Fur Trade Conference, Mackinac Island, 1991*, edited by Jennifer S. Brown, W. J. Eccles, and Donald P. Heldman, pp. 57–69. Michigan State University Press, East Lansing, and Mackinac State Historic Parks, Mackinac Island, Mich.

Pickering, Kathleen A. 1996. "Lakota Culture, World Economy: An Experience of American Indian Economic Incorporation." Ph.D. dissertation, University of Wisconsin-Madison, Madison.

Pike, Zebulon M. 1966. *Journals, with Letters and Related Documents*, 2 vols. Edited by Donald D. Jackson. University of Oklahoma Press, Norman.

Pittenger, Susan M. 1998. "The Relationship between Ethnic Identity, Self-Esteem, Emotional Well-Being and Depression among Lakota/Dakota Sioux Adolescents." Psy.D. dissertation, Old Dominion University, Norfolk, Va.

Pommersheim, Frank. 1996. Black Hills. In *Native America in the Twentieth Century: An Encyclopedia*, edited by Mary B. Davis, pp. 72–5. Garland Publishing, New York.

Pond, Samuel W. 1908. The Dakota or Sioux in Minnesota as They Were in 1834. *Minnesota Historical Society Collections* 12:319–501. Reprint: St. Paul, Minnesota Historical Society Press, 1986.

Pond, Samuel W., Jr. 1893. *Two Volunteer Missionaries among the Dakota; or, The Story of the Labors of Samuel W. and Gideon H. Pond*. Congregational Sunday-school and Publishing Society, Boston.

Powers, Marla N. 1986. *Oglala Women: Myth, Ritual, and Reality*. University of Chicago Press, Chicago.

Powers, William K. 1977. *Oglala Religion*. University of Nebraska Press, Lincoln.

Powers, William K. 1982. *Yuwipi: Vision and Experience in Oglala Ritual*. University of Nebraska Press, Lincoln.

Powers, William K. 1986. *Sacred Language: The Nature of Supernatural Discourse in Lakota*. University of Oklahoma Press, Norman.

Powers, William K. 1990a. When Black Elk Speaks, Everybody Listens. *Social Text* 24:43–56.

Powers, William K. 1990b. *War Dance: Plains Indian Musical Performance*. University of Arizona Press, Tucson.

Powers, William K. 1992. Translating the Untranslatable: The Place of the Vocable in Lakota Song. In *On the Translation of Native American Literatures*, edited by Brian Swann, pp. 293–310. Smithsonian Institution Press, Washington, DC.

Powers, William K. 1996a. Lakota. In *Native America in the Twentieth Century: An Encyclopedia*, edited by Mary B. Davis, pp. 299–303. Garland Publishing, New York.

Powers, William K. 1996b. Powwow. In *Native America in the Twentieth Century: An Encyclopedia*, edited by Mary B. Davis, pp. 476–80. Garland Publishing, New York.

Praus, Alexis A. 1962. *The Sioux, 1798–1922: A Dakota Winter Count*. Bulletin No. 44, Cranbrook Institute of Science, Bloomfield Hills, Mich.

Price, Catherine. 1996. *The Oglala People 1841–1879: A Political History*. University of Nebraska Press, Lincoln.

Price, Darby L. P. 1998. Laughing Without Reservation: Indian Standup Comedians. *American Indian Culture and Research Journal* 22:255–71.

The Problem of Indian Administration. 1928. Johns Hopkins University Press, Baltimore. Reprint: New York, Johnson Reprint Co., 1971.

Purdie, Susan. 1993. *Comedy: The Mastery of Discourse.* Toronto University Press, Toronto.

Rabb, Theodore K. 1967. *Enterprise and Empire: Merchant and Gentry Investment in the Expansion of England, 1575–1630.* Harvard University Press, Cambridge, Mass.

Raheja, Gloria G. 1996. Caste, Colonialism, and the Speech of the Colonized: Entextualization and Disciplinary Control in India. *American Ethnologist* 23(3):494–513.

Ramenofsky, Ann F. 1987. *Vectors of Death: The Archaeology of European Contact.* University of New Mexico Press, Albuquerque.

Rasmussen, Marilyn F. 1997. "Lakota Women's Traditional Dress of the Last Half of the Twentieth Century." Ph.D. dissertation, University of Nebraska, Lincoln.

Reddin, Paul. 1999. *Wild West Shows.* University of Illinois Press, Urbana.

Reinhardt, Akim D. 1999. Spontaneous Combustion: Prelude to Wounded Knee 1972. *South Dakota History* 29:229–44.

Reinhardt, Akim D. 2000. "A Government Not of Their Choosing: Pine Ridge Politics from the Indian Reorganization Act to the Siege of Wounded Knee." Ph.D. dissertation, University of Nebraska, Lincoln.

The Reservations. 1995. Time-Life Books, Alexandria, Va.

Reyhner, Jon A., and Jeanne Eder. 1989. *A History of Indian Education.* Eastern Montana College, Billings.

Reyna, Stephen P., and R. E. Downs (eds.). 1994. *Studying War: Anthropological Perspectives.* Gordon & Breach, Langhorne, Pa.

Rice, Julian. 1989. *Lakota Storytelling: Black Elk, Ella Deloria, and Frank Fools Crow.* Peter Lang, New York.

Rice, Julian. 1991. *Black Elk's Story: Distinguishing Its Lakota Purpose.* University of New Mexico Press, Albuquerque.

Rice, Julian. 1992a. *Deer Women and Elk Men: The Lakota Narratives of Ella Deloria.* University of New Mexico Press, Albuquerque.

Rice, Julian. 1992b. Narrative Styles in *Dakota Texts.* In *On the Translation of Native American Literatures,* edited by Brian Swann, pp. 276–92. Smithsonian Institution Press, Washington, DC.

Rice, Julian (ed.) 1993. *Ella Deloria's Iron Hawk.* University of New Mexico Press, Albuquerque.

Rice, Keren, and Laura Murray. 1999. *Talking on the Page: Editing Aboriginal Oral Texts.* University of Toronto Press, Toronto.

Rich, Edwin E. 1966. The French Background. In *Montreal and the Fur Trade,* pp. 1–34. McGill University Press, Montreal.

Richter, Daniel K., and James H. Merrell (eds.) 1987. *Beyond the Covenant Chain: The Iroquois and Their Neighbors in Indian North America, 1600–1800.* Syracuse University Press, Syracuse.

Riggs, Stephen R. (ed.) 1852. *Grammar and Dictionary of the Dakota Language.* Smithsonian Contribution to Knowledge, vol. 4. Smithsonian Institution, Washington, DC.

Riggs, Stephen R. 1869. *Tah-koo Wah-kan; or, The Gospel among the Dakotas.* Congregational Sabbath-School and Publishing Society, Boston.

Riggs, Stephen R. 1880. *Mary and I: Forty Years with the Sioux.* W. G. Holmes, Chicago. Reprint: Minneapolis, Ross & Haines, 1969.

Riggs, Stephen R. (ed.) 1890. *A Dakota-English Dictionary.* Edited by James Owen Dorsey. Contributions to North American Ethnology, vol. 7. Washington, DC. Reprint: St. Paul, Minnesota Historical Society Press, 1992.

Riggs, Stephen R. 1893. *Dakota Grammar, Texts, and Ethnography.* Edited by James O. Dorsey. Contributions to North American Ethnology, vol. 2. Washington, DC. Reprint: Minneapolis, Ross & Haines, 1973.

Riney, Scott. 1998. "I Like the School So I Want to Come Back": The Enrollment of American Indian Students at the Rapid City Indian School. *American Indian Culture and Research Journal* 22(2):171–92.

Riney, Scott. 1999. *The Rapid City Indian School 1898–1933.* University of Oklahoma Press, Norman.

Risch, Barbara. 2000. A Grammar of Time: Lakota Winter Counts, 1700–1900. *American Indian Culture and Research Journal* 24(2):23–48.

Ritter, Beth R. 1999. "Dispossession to Diminishment: The Yankton Sioux Reservation, 1858–1998." Ph.D. dissertation, University of Nebraska, Lincoln.

Ritter, Madeline L. 1980. The Conditions Favoring Age-Set Organization. *Journal of Anthropological Research* 36:87–104.

Ritzenthaler, Robert E. 1966. Radiocarbon Dates for Clam River Focus. *The Wisconsin Archeologist* 47:219–20.

Roberts, Chris. 1992. *Powwow Country.* American and World Geographic Publishing, Helena, Mont.

Roberts, John M. Jr., Carmella C. Moore, and A. Kimball Romney. 1995. Predicting Similarity in Material Culture among New Guinea Villages from Propinquity and Language. *Current Anthropology* 36:769–88.

Robinson, Doane. 1904. *A History of the Dakota or Sioux Indians.* South Dakota Historical Collections, vol. 2, Part II. Aberdeen, S. Dak. Reprint: Minneapolis, Ross & Haines, 1967.

Roddis, Louis H. 1956. *The Indian Wars of Minnesota.* Torch Press, Cedar Rapids.

Roe, Frank G. 1951. *The North American Buffalo.* University of Toronto Press, Toronto.

Ronda, James P. 1994. Peter Pond and the Exploration of the Greater Northwest. In *Encounters With a Distant Land: Exploration and the Great Northwest,* edited by Carlos A. Schwantes, pp. 71–85. University of Idaho Press, Moscow.

Rood, David S. 1978. Siouan Linguistics: An Assessment. *Newsletter of Siouan and Caddoan Linguistics,* August, pp. 1–16. Department of Linguistics, University of Colorado.

Rood, David S. 1979. Siouan. In *The Languages of Native America: Historical and Comparative Assessments,* edited by Lyle Campbell and Marianne Mithun, pp. 236–98. University of Texas Press, Austin.

Rosaldo, Renato. 1989. *Culture and Truth.* Beacon, Boston.

Rosenau, Pauline M. 1992. *Post-Modernism and the Social Sciences.* Princeton

University Press, Princeton, NJ.

Rouse, Linda P., and Jeffrey R. Hanson. 1991. American Indian Stereotyping, Resource Competition, and Status-based Prejudice. *American Indian Culture and Research Journal* 15(3):1–17.

Ruggles, Richard I. 1991. *A Country So Interesting: The Hudson's Bay Company and Two Centuries of Mapping, 1670–1870*. McGill-Queen's University Press, Montreal.

Running, John. 1985. *Honor Dance: Native American Photographs*. University of Nevada Press, Reno.

Rushforth, Scott. 1992. The Legitimation of Beliefs in a Hunter-Gatherer Society: Bearlake Athapaskan Knowledge and Authority. *American Ethnologist* 19:483–500.

Rushforth, Scott. 1994. Political Resistance in a Contemporary Hunter-Gatherer Society: More about Bearlake Athapaskan Knowledge and Authority. *American Ethnologist* 21:335–52.

Rushmore, Elsie M. 1914. *The Indian Policy during Grant's Administrations*. Marion Press, New York.

Russo, Priscilla A. 1976. The Time to Speak is Over: The Onset of the Sioux Uprising. *Minnesota History* 45:97–106.

Ryan, Allan J. 1992. Postmodern Parody: A Political Strategy in Contemporary Canadian Native Art. *Art Journal* 51(3):59–65.

Ryan, Simon. 1994. Inscribing the Emptiness: Cartography, Exploration, and the Construction of Australia. In *De-Scribing Empire: Post-Colonialism and Textuality*, edited by Chris Tiffin and Alan Lawson, pp. 115–30. Routledge, New York.

Sahlins, Marshall D. 1968. *Tribesmen*. Prentice-Hall, Englewood Cliffs, NJ.

Sandoz, Mari. 1942. *Crazy Horse, the Strange Man of the Oglalas*. Alfred Knopf, New York. Reprint: Lincoln, University of Nebraska Press, 1961.

Sandoz, Mari. 1966. *The Battle of the Little Bighorn*. Lippincott, Philadelphia.

Sandoz, Mari. 1961. *These Were the Sioux*. Hastings House, New York. Reprint: New York, Dell, 1967.

Saylor, Barbara J. 1980. Prehistoric Skeletal Analysis in Manitoba: An Overview. In *Directions in Manitoba Prehistory: Papers in Honour of Chris Vickers*, edited by Leo Pettipas, pp. 303–16. Association of Manitoba Archaeologists and Manitoba Archaeological Society, Winnipeg.

Scherer, Andrew K. 1998. "Late Precontact Dental Morphology and Biological Relationships in the Upper Midwest." Undergraduate thesis, Hamline University, St. Paul.

Scherer, Joanna C. 1975. You Can't Believe Your Eyes: Inaccuracies in Photographs of North American Indians. *Studies in the Anthropology of Visual Communication* 2(2):67–79.

Scherer, Joanna C. (ed.) 1990. *Picturing Cultures: Historical Photographs in Anthropological Inquiry*. Special issue, *Visual Anthropology* 3(2–3).

Scherer, Joanna C. 1992. The Photographic Document: Photographs as Primary Data in Anthropological Enquiry. In *Anthropology and Photography, 1860–1920*, edited by Elizabeth Edwards, pp. 32–41. Yale University Press, New Haven.

Schneider, Mary Jane. 1994. *North Dakota Indians: An Introduction*. 2d ed. Kendall/Hunt Publishing Co., Dubuque.

Schoolcraft, Henry R. 1821. *Narrative Journal of Travels, through the Northwestern Region of the United States*. E. & E. Hosford, Albany. Reprint: East Lansing, Michigan State University Press, 1992.

Schoolcraft, Henry R. 1853–7. *Information Respecting the History, Condition, and Prospects of the Indian Tribes of the United States*. 6 vols. Lippincott, Grambo, & Co., Philadelphia.

Schoolcraft, Henry R. 1958. *Schoolcraft's Expedition to Lake Itasca: The Discovery of the Source of the Mississippi*. Edited by Philip P. Mason. Michigan State University Press, East Lansing. Reprint: East Lansing, Michigan State University Press 1993.

Schultz, Duane. 1992. *Over the Earth I Come: The Great Sioux Uprising of 1862*. St. Martin's Press, New York.

Schusky, Ernest L. 1971. The Upper Missouri Indian Agency. *Missouri Historical Review* 65:249–69.

Schusky, Ernest L. 1975. *The Forgotten Sioux: An Ethnohistory of the Lower Brulé Reservation*. Nelson-Hall, Chicago.

Schusky, Ernest L. 1986. The Evolution of Indian Leadership on the Great Plains, 1750–1950. *American Indian Quarterly* 10:65–82.

Schusky, Ernest L. 1994. The Roots of Factionalism among the Lower Brulé. In *North American Indian Anthropology: Essays on Society and Culture*, edited by Raymond J. DeMallie and Alfonso Ortiz, pp. 258–77. University of Oklahoma Press, Norman.

Scott, Douglas D., and Richard A. Fox, Jr. 1987. *Archaeological Insights into the Custer Battle*. University of Oklahoma Press, Norman.

Scott, Douglas D., Richard A. Fox, Jr., Mellissa A. Connor, and Dick Harmon. 1989. *Archaeological Perspectives on the Battle of the Little Bighorn*. University of Oklahoma Press, Norman.

Searle, John R. 1995. *The Construction of Social Reality*. Free Press, New York.

Secoy, Frank R. 1953. *Changing Military Patterns on the Great Plains (17th Century through Early 19th Century)*. J. J. Augustin, Locust Valley, N.Y. Reprint: Lincoln, University of Nebraska Press, 1992.

Seifert, D. (ed.) 1991. Gender in Historical Archaeology. *Historical Archaeology* 25(4):82–108.

Selzler, Bonnie K. 1996. "The Health Experience of Dakota Sioux and Their Perception of Culturally Congruent Nursing Care." Ph.D. dissertation, University of Colorado Health Sciences Center, Boulder.

Service, Elman R. 1971. *Primitive Social Organization: An Evolutionary Perspective*. 2d ed. Random House, New York.

Service, Elman R. 1979. *The Hunters*. 2d ed. Prentice-Hall, Englewood Cliffs, NJ.

Sheffield, Gail K. 1997. *The Arbitrary Indian: The Indian Arts and Crafts Act of 1990*. University of Oklahoma Press, Norman.

Shennan, Stephen J. (ed.) 1989. *Archaeological Approaches to Cultural Identity*. Unwin & Hyman, London.

Shennan, Stephen J. 1991. Some Current Issues in the Archaeological Identification of Past Peoples. *Archaeologia Polona* 29:29–37.

Sherzer, Joel. 1976. An Areal-Typological Study of North American Indian Languages North of Mexico. *North-Holland Linguistic Series* 20. North-Holland Publishing Co., Amsterdam.

Sipes, Richard G. 1973. War, Sports, and Aggression: An Empirical Test of Two Rival Theories. *American Anthropologist* 75:64–86.

Skinner, Alanson. 1919a. A Sketch of Eastern Dakota Ethnology. *American Anthropologist* 21:164–74.

Skinner, Alanson 1919b. Notes on the Sun Dance of the Sisseton Dakota. *Anthropological Papers of the American Museum of Natural History*, vol. 16, pt. 4, pp. 381–5.

Skinner, Alanson. 1920. Medicine Ceremony of the Menomini, Iowa, and Wahpeton Dakota. *Indian Notes* 4:262–302.

Skinner, Alanson 1925. Tree-Dweller Bundles of the Wahpeton Dakota. *Indian Notes* 2:66–73.

Slotkin, James S. 1956. *The Peyote Religion: A Study in Indian–White Relations.* Free Press, Glencoe, IL.

Smith, David G., R. S. Malhi, J. Eshleman, J. G. Lorenz, and F. A. Kaestle. 1999. Distribution of mtDNA Haplogroup X Among Native North Americans. *American Journal of Physical Anthropology* 110:271–84.

Smith, G. Hubert. 1947. Trade among the Dakota. *Minnesota Archaeologist* 13:65–9.

Smith, Paul C., and Robert A. Warrior. 1996. *Like a Hurricane: The Indian Movement from Alcatraz to Wounded Knee.* New Press, New York.

Snipp, C. Matthew. 1989. *American Indians: The First of This Land.* Russell Sage Foundation, New York.

Snortland, J. Signe. 1994. Northern Plains Woodland Mortuary Practices. In *Skeletal Biology in the Great Plains: Migration, Warfare, Health, and Subsistence*, edited by Douglas W. Owsley and Richard L. Jantz, pp. 51–70. Smithsonian Institution, Washington, DC.

Spector, Janet D. 1985. Ethnoarchaeology and Little Rapids: A New Approach to 19thCentury Eastern Dakota Sites. In *Archaeology, Ecology, and Ethnohistory of the Prairie-Forest Border Zone of Minnesota and Manitoba*, edited by Janet Spector and Elden Johnson, pp. 167–203. J & L Reprint Co., Lincoln, Nebr.

Spector, Janet D. 1993. *What This Awl Means: Feminist Archaeology at a Wahpeton Dakota Village.* Minnesota Historical Society Press, St. Paul.

Spier, Leslie. 1921. The Sun Dance of the Plains Indians: Its Development and Diffusion. *Anthropological Papers of the American Museum of Natural History*, vol. 16, pt. 7, pp. 451–527.

Spilka, Bernard. 1970. *Alienation and Achievement among Oglala Sioux Secondary School Students, Final Report.* National Institute of Mental Health, Bethesda, Md.

Spolsky, Bernard. 1998. *Sociolinguistics.* Oxford University Press, New York.

Springer, James W., and Stanley R. Witkowski. 1982. Siouan Historical Linguistics and Oneota Archaeology. In *Oneota Studies*, edited by Guy Gibbon, pp. 69–83. University of Minnesota Publications in Anthropology, No. 1. Minneapolis.

Stamps, Judith. 1995. *Unthinking Modernity: Innis, McLuhan, and the Frankfurt*

School. McGill-Queen's University Press, Montreal.

Standing Bear, Luther. 1928. *My People the Sioux.* Houghton Mifflin, Boston. Reprint: Lincoln, University of Nebraska Press, 1975.

Standing Bear, Luther. 1931. *My Indian Boyhood.* Houghton Mifflin, Boston. Reprint: Lincoln, University of Nebraska Press, 1988.

Standing Bear, Luther. 1933. *Land of the Spotted Eagle.* Houghton Mifflin, Boston. Reprint: Lincoln, University of Nebraska Press, 1978.

Starita, Joe. 1995. *The Dull Knives of Pine Ridge: A Lakota Odyssey.* Putnam, New York.

Stedman, Raymond W. 1982. *Shadows of the Indians: Stereotypes in American Culture.* University of Oklahoma Press, Norman.

Stewart, Omer C. 1974. Origin of the Peyote Religion in the United States. *Plains Anthropologist* 19:211–23.

Stewart, Omer C. 1980. The Native American Church. In *Anthropology on the Great Plains,* edited by W. Raymond Wood and Margot Liberty, pp. 188–96. University of Nebraska Press, Lincoln.

Stewart, Omer C. 1987. *Peyote Religion: A History.* University of Oklahoma Press, Norman.

Stewart, Omer C. 1996. Peyote Religion. In *Native America in the Twentieth Century: An Encyclopedia,* edited by Mary B. Davis, pp. 446–9. Garland Publishing, New York.

Stipe, Claude E. 1971. Eastern Dakota Clans: The Solution of a Problem. *American Anthropologist* 73(5):1031–5.

Stone, Joseph B. 1998. "Traditional and Contemporary Lakota Death, Dying, Grief, and Bereavement Beliefs and Practices: A Qualitative Study." Ph.D. dissertation. Utah State University, Logan.

Sullivan, Louis R. 1919. Anthropometry of the Siouan Tribes. *Anthropological Papers of the American Museum of Natural History,* vol. 23, pt. 3.

Sunder, John E. 1965. *The Fur Trade on the Upper Missouri, 1840–1865.* University of Oklahoma Press, Norman.

Sundstrom, Linea. 1997. Smallpox Used Them Up: References to Epidemic Disease in Northern Plains Winter Counts. *Ethnohistory* 44:305–43.

Swadesh, Morris. 1952. Lexico-Statistic Dating of Prehistoric Ethnic Connections. *Proceedings of the American Philosophical Society* 96:453–63.

Swagerty, William R. 1988. Indian Trade in the Trans-Mississippi West to 1870. In *History of Indian–White Relations,* edited by Wilcomb E. Washburn, pp. 351–74. Handbook of North American Indians, vol. 4. Smithsonian Institution, Washington, DC.

Swagerty, William R. 1994. The Upper Missouri Outfit: The Men and the Fur Trade in the 1830s. In *Fort Union Fur Trade Symposium Proceedings, September 13–15, 1990,* pp. 25–42. Fort Union Monograph Series, Publication No. 2. Friends of Fort Union Trading Post, Williston, N. Dak.

Swann, Brian (ed.) 1992. *On the Translation of Native American Literatures.* Smithsonian Institution Press, Washington, DC.

Swanton, John R. 1943. Siouan Tribes and the Ohio Valley. *American Anthropologist* 45:49–66.

Syms, E. Leigh. 1985. Fitting People into the Late Prehistory of the Northeastern

Plains: A Need to Return to a Holistic Anthropological Approach. In *Archaeology, Ecology and Ethnohistory of the Prairie–Forest Border Zone of Minnesota and Manitoba*, edited by Janet Spector and Elden Johnson, pp. 73–107. J & L Reprint Co., Lincoln, Nebr.

Szasy, Margaret C. 1996. Education Policy. In *Native America in the Twentieth Century: An Encyclopedia*, edited by Mary B. Davis, pp. 182–4. Garland Publishing, New York.

Tanner, Helen H. (ed.) 1987. *Atlas of Great Lakes Indian History*. University of Oklahoma Press, Norman.

Taylor, Graham D. 1980. *The New Deal and American Indian Tribalism: The Administration of the Indian Reorganization Act, 1934–45*. University of Nebraska Press, Lincoln.

Taylor, John F. 1989. Counting: The Utility of Historic Population Estimates in the Northwestern Plains, 1800–1880. *Plains Anthropologist, Memoir* 23:17–30.

Teakle, Thomas. 1918. *The Spirit Lake Massacre*. State Historical Society of Iowa, Iowa City.

Tedlock, Dennis. 1983. *The Spoken Word and the Work of Interpretation*. University of Pennsylvania Press, Philadelphia.

Telford, C. W. 1932. Test Performance of Full and Mixed Blood North Dakota Indians. *Journal of Comparative Psychology* 14:123–45.

Temple, Wayne C. 1975. *Indian Villages of the Illinois Country, Part 1, Atlas Supplement*. Scientific Papers, vol. II. Illinois State Museum, Springfield.

Tester, John R. 1995. *Minnesota's Natural Heritage: An Ecological Perspective*. University of Minnesota Press, Minneapolis.

Theisz, Ronnie D. (ed.) 1975. *Buckskin Tokens: Contemporary Oral Narratives of the Lakota*. Sinte Gleska College, Rosebud, S. Dak.

Theisz, Ronnie D. 1987. Song Texts and Their Performers: The Centerpiece of Contemporary Lakota Identity Formulation. *Great Plains Quarterly* 7:116–24.

Thomas, Nicholas. 1991. *Entangled Objects: Exchange, Material Culture, and Colonialism in the Pacific*. Harvard University Press, Cambridge, Mass.

Thompson, E. P. 1967. Time, Work-discipline, and Industrial Capitalism. *Past and Present* 38:56–97.

Thompson, Robert G. 2000. Phytolith Analysis of Selected Ceramic Sherds from the Mille Lacs Region. In *The Lake Onamia-Trunk Highway 169 Data Recovery Project, Mille Lacs County, Minnesota*, by David Mather and Elizabeth J. Abel, vol. 1, pp. 19.1–19.21. Loucks Project Report 96506-1 (prepared for the Minnesota Department of Transportation, St. Paul). Loucks Associates, Minneapolis.

Thwaites, Rueben G. 1902–8. *The French Regime in Wisconsin, 1634–1760*. 3 vols. State Historical Society of Wisconsin, Madison.

Thwaites, Rueben G. (ed.) 1896–1901. *The Jesuit Relations and Allied Documents. Travels and Explorations of the Jesuit Missionaries in New France 1610–1791*. 73 vols. Burrows Brothers Co., Cleveland. Reprint: New York, Pageant Book Co., 1959.

Tiffin, Chris, and Alan Lawson (eds.). 1994. *De-scribing Empire: Post-colonialism and Textuality*. Routledge, New York.

Tohill, Louis A. 1928–9. Robert Dickson, British Fur Trader on the Upper Mississippi. *North Dakota Historical Quarterly* 3(1–3):5–49, 83–128, 182–203.

Tomkins, William. 1969. *Indian Sign Language*. Dover Publications, New York.

Trennert, Robert A. 1996. Bureau of Indian Affairs Schools. In *Native America in the Twentieth Century: An Encyclopedia*, edited by Mary B. Davis, pp. 84–7. Garland Publishing, New York.

Treuer, Anton Steven. 1994. "Ojibwe–Dakota Relations: Diplomacy, War and Social Union, 1679–1862." 2 vols. Master's thesis, University of Minnesota, Minneapolis.

Trimble, Michael K. 1979. *An Ethnohistorical Interpretation of the Spread of Smallpox in the Northern Plains Utilizing Concepts of Disease Ecology*. Midwest Archeological Center, National Park Service, Lincoln, Nebr.

Trimble, Michael K. 1989. Infectious Disease and the Northern Plains Horticulturalists: A Human Behavioral Model. *Plains Anthropologist Memoir* 23:41–59.

Trimble, Michael K. 1992. The 1832 Inoculation Program on the Missouri River. In *Disease and Demography in the Americas*, edited by John W. Verano and Douglas H. Ubelaker, pp. 257–64. Smithsonian Institution, Washington, DC.

Trimble, Michael K. 1994. The 1837–1838 Smallpox Epidemic on the Upper Missouri. In *Skeletal Biology in the Great Plains: Migration, Warfare, Health, and Subsistence*, edited by Douglas W. Owsley and Richard L. Jantz, pp. 81–9. Smithsonian Institution Press, Washington, DC.

Trope, Jack F. 1996. American Indian Religious Freedom Act. In *Native America in the Twentieth Century: An Encyclopedia*, edited by Mary B. Davis, pp. 39–40. Garland Publishing, New York.

Trosper, Ronald L. 1988. That Other Discipline: Economics and American Indian History. In *New Directions in American Indian History* edited by Colin G. Calloway, pp. 199–222. University of Oklahoma Press, Norman.

Tucker, Sarah J. 1942. *Atlas: Indian Villages of the Illinois Country*. Scientific Papers 2(1). Illinois State Museum, Springfield.

Upham, Steadman (ed.) 1990. *The Evolution of Political Systems: Sociopolitics in Small-scale Sedentary Societies*. Cambridge University Press, New York.

Upham, Warren. 1905. Groseilliers and Radisson, the First White Men in Minnesota, 1655–56, and 1659–60, and Their Discovery of the Upper Mississippi River. *Collections of the Minnesota Historical Society* 10(2):449–594.

Upham, Warren (ed.) 1908. *Minnesota in Three Centuries, 1655–1908*. 4 vols. Publishing Society of Minnesota, New York.

Utley, Robert M. 1973. *Frontier Regulars: The United States Army and the Indian, 1866–1891*. Macmillan, New York.

Utley, Robert M. 1984. *The Indian Frontier of the American West 1846–1890*. University of New Mexico Press, Albuquerque.

Utley, Robert M. 1993. *The Lance and the Shield: The Life and Times of Sitting Bull*. Henry Holt, New York.

Valppu, Seppo H. 2000. Archaeobotanical Analysis. In *The Lake Onamia-Trunk Highway 169 Data Recovery Project, Mille Lacs County, Minnesota*, by David Mather and Elizabeth J. Abel, vol. 1, pp. 18.1–18.18 Loucks Project Report 96506-1 (prepared for the Minnesota Department of Transportation, St. Paul).

Loucks Associates, Minneapolis.

Van Dyke, Allen P., and Edgar S. Oerichbauer. 1988. The Clam River Focus Revisited: Excavations at 47 BT-36, Burnett County, Wisconsin. *Wisconsin Archeologist* 69:139–62.

Vehik, Susan C., and Timothy G. Baugh. 1994. Prehistoric Plains Trade. In *Prehistoric Exchange Systems in North America*, edited by Timothy G. Baugh and Jonathan E. Ericson, pp. 249–74. Plenum Press, New York.

Verano, John W., and Douglas H. Ubelaker (eds.). 1992. *Disease and Demography in the Americas*. Smithsonian Institution Press, Washington, DC.

Vestal, Stanley. 1932. *Sitting Bull, Champion of the Sioux*. Houghton Mifflin, Boston. Reprint: Norman, University of Oklahoma Press, 1989.

Viola, Herman J. 1976. *The Indian Legacy of Charles Bird King*. Doubleday, New York.

Walde, Dale, and Noreen D. Willows (eds.). 1991. *The Archaeology of Gender*. Archaeological Association, University of Calgary, Calgary.

Walker, James R. 1914. Oglala Kinship Terms. *American Anthropologist* 16:96–109.

Walker, James R. 1917. The Sun Dance and Other Ceremonies of the Oglala Division of the Teton Dakota. *Anthropological Papers of the American Museum of Natural History*, vol. 16, pt. 1, pp. 51–221.

Walker, James R. 1980. *Lakota Belief and Ritual*. Edited by Raymond J. DeMallie and Elaine A. Jahner. University of Nebraska Press, Lincoln.

Walker, James R. 1982. *Lakota Society*. Edited by Raymond J. DeMallie. University of Nebraska Press, Lincoln.

Walker, James R. 1983. *Lakota Myth*. Edited by Elaine A. Jahner. University of Nebraska Press, Lincoln.

Wallace, Anthony F. C. 1956. Revitalization Movements. *American Anthropologist* 58:264–81.

Wallis, Wilson D. 1919. The Sun Dance of the Canadian Dakota. *Anthropological Papers of the American Museum of Natural History*, vol. 16, pt. 4, pp. 317–80.

Wallis, Wilson D. 1947. *The Canadian Dakota*. Anthropological Papers of the American Museum of Natural History, vol. 41, pt. 1.

Warkentin, John, and Richard I. Ruggles (eds.). 1970. *Manitoba Historical Atlas*. Historical and Scientific Society of Manitoba, Winnipeg.

Warren, Robert E. 1986a. Comparative Analysis. In *Papers in Northern Plains Prehistory and Ethnohistory, Ice Glider 32OL110*, edited by W. Raymond Wood, pp. 109–10. Special Publication No. 10. South Dakota Archaeological Society, Sioux Falls.

Warren, Robert E. 1986b. Ice Glider Faunal Remains and Yanktonai Ethnohistory. In *Papers in Northern Plains Prehistory and Ethnohistory, Ice Glider 32OL110*, edited by W. Raymond Wood, pp. 146–83. Special Publication No. 10. South Dakota Archaeological Society, Sioux Falls.

Warren, William W. 1984 [1885]. *History of the Ojibway People*. Minnesota Historical Society, St. Paul.

Washburn, Wilcomb E. 1984. A Fifty-year Perspective on the Indian Reorganization Act. *American Anthropologist* 86:279–89.

Watrall, Charles R. 1968. Virginia Deer and the Buffer Zone in the Late Prehistoric–Early Protohistoric Periods in Minnesota. *Plains Anthropologist* 13(40):81–6.

Weber, Ronald L. 1985. Photographs as Ethnographic Documents. *Arctic Anthropology* 22(1):67–78.

Wedel, Mildred M. 1974. Le Sueur and the Dakota Sioux. In *Aspects of Upper Great Lakes Anthropology, Papers in Honor of Lloyd A. Wilford*, edited by Elden Johnson, pp. 157–71. Minnesota Prehistoric Archaeology Series No. 11. Minnesota Historical Society, St. Paul.

Weist, Katherine. 1983. Beasts of Burden and Menial Slaves: NineteenthCentury Observations of Northern Plains Indian Women. In *The Hidden Half: Studies of Plains Indian Women*, edited by Patricia Albers and Beatrice Medicine, pp. 29–52. University Press of America, Lanham, Md.

Welbourn, Alice. 1984. Endo Ceramics and Power Strategies. In *Ideology, Power and Prehistory*, edited by Daniel Miller and C. Tilley, pp. 17–24. Cambridge University Press, Cambridge.

Welch, Deborah. 1985. "Zitkala Ša: An American Indian Leader, 1876–1938." Ph.D. dissertation, University of Wyoming, Laramie.

Wheat, Carl I. 1957. *Mapping the Transmississippi West: 1540–1861*, vol. 1, *the Spanish Entrada to the Louisiana Purchase*. Institute of Historical Cartography, San Francisco.

Whelan, Mary K. 1990. Late Woodland Subsistence Systems and Settlement Size in the Mille Lacs Area. In *The Woodland Tradition in the Western Great Lakes: Papers Presented to Elden Johnson*, edited by Guy Gibbon, pp. 55–75. University of Minnesota Publications in Anthropology no. 4. Minneapolis.

Whelan, Mary K. 1991. Gender and Historical Archaeology: Eastern Dakota Patterns in the 19th Century. *Historical Archaeology* 25(4):17–32.

Whelan, Mary K. 1993. Dakota Indian Economics and the Nineteenth-Century Fur Trade. *Ethnohistory* 40:246–76.

Whipp, Richard. 1987. "A Time to Every Purpose": An Essay on Time and Work. In *The Historical Meanings of Work*, edited by Patrick Joyce, pp. 210–36. Cambridge University Press, Cambridge.

White, Bruce M. 1977. *The Fur Trade in Minnesota: An Introductory Guide to Manuscript Sources*. Minnesota Historical Society, St. Paul.

White, Bruce M. 1982. Parisian Women's Dogs: A Bibliographical Essay on Cross-Cultural Communication and Trade. In *Where Two Worlds Meet: The Great Lakes Fur Trade*, edited by Carolyn Gilman, pp. 120–6. Museum Exhibit Series No. 2. Minnesota Historical Society, St. Paul.

White, Bruce M. 1984. "Give Us a Little Milk": The Social and Cultural Significance of Gift Giving in the Lake Superior Fur Trade. In *Rendezvous: Selected Papers of the Fourth North American Fur Trade Conference, 1981*, edited by Thomas C. Buckley, pp. 185–98. North American Fur Trade Conference, St. Paul, Minn.

White, Bruce M. 1988. "The Dakota at Mille Lacs in the 17th Century: A Historical Ethnography." Unpublished manuscript on file at the Wilford Archaeology Laboratory, University of Minnesota, Minneapolis.

White, Bruce M. 1992. Stereotypes of Minnesota's Native People. *Minnesota His-

tory 53:99–111.

White, Bruce M. 1994. Encounters with Spirits: Ojibwa and Dakota Theories about the French and Their Merchandise. *Ethnohistory* 41(3):369–405.

White, Bruce M. 1999. The Woman Who Married a Beaver: Trade Patterns and Gender Roles in the Ojibwa Fur Trade. *Ethnohistory* 46(1):109–47.

White, Hayden. 1980. The Value of Narrativity in the Representation of Reality. *Critical Inquiry* 7(1):169–90.

White, Hayden. 1987. *The Content of the Form: Narrative Discourse and Historical Representation.* John Hopkins University Press, Baltimore.

White, Richard. 1978. The Winning of the West: The Expansion of the Western Sioux in the Eighteenth and Nineteenth Centuries. *Journal of American History* 65(2):319–43.

White, Richard. 1991. *The Middle Ground: Indians, Empires, and Republics in the Great Lakes Region, 1650–1815.* Cambridge University Press, New York.

Whittaker, James O. 1962. Alcohol and the Standing Rock Sioux Tribe. *Quarterly Journal of Studies on Alcohol* 23:468–79.

Whittaker, James O. 1982. Alcohol and the Standing Rock Sioux Tribe: A Twenty-year Follow-up Study. *Journal of Studies on Alcohol* 43:191–200.

Wied, Maximilian, Prinz von. 1843. *Travels in the Interior of North America*, translated from the German by H. Evans Lloyd. Ackermann, London. Reprint: Norman, University of Oklahoma Press, 1962, translated and edited by Seymour Feiler.

Wilford, Lloyd A. 1937. "Minnesota Archaeology with Special Reference to the Mound Area." Ph.D. dissertation, Harvard University, Cambridge.

Wilford, Lloyd A. 1944. The Prehistoric Indians of Minnesota: The Mille Lacs Aspect. *Minnesota History* 25(4):329–41.

Wilford, Lloyd A. 1949. "Excavations at Mille Lacs in 1949." Manuscript on file, Minnesota Historical Society, Fort Snelling.

Wilk, Richard R., and Robert McC. Netting. 1984. Households: Changing Forms and Functions. In *Households: Comparative and Historical Studies of the Domestic Group*, edited by Robert McC. Netting, Richard R. Wilk, and Eric J. Arnould, pp. 1–28. University of California Press, Berkeley.

Willand, Jon. 1964. *Lac qui Parle and the Dakota Mission.* Lac qui Parle County Historical Society, Madison, Minn.

Willey, Patrick S. 1990. *Prehistoric Warfare on the Great Plains: Skeletal Analysis of the Crow Creek Massacre Victims.* Garland Publishing, New York.

Williams, David (ed.) 1999. *The Enlightenment.* Cambridge University Press, New York.

Williams, Michael S. 1998. "An Investigation of Internalizing Social-Emotional Characteristics in a Sample of Lakota Sioux Children." Ph.D. dissertation, Utah State University, Logan.

Williams, Robert A. 1986. Law. In *Native America in the Twentieth Century: An Encyclopedia*, edited by Mary B. Davis, pp. 312–16. Garland Publishing, New York.

Williams, Walter L. 1986. Persistence and Changes in the Berdache Tradition among Contemporary Lakota Indians. *Journal of Homosexuality* 11(3/4):191–200.

Williams, Walter L. 1992. *The Spirit and the Flesh: Sexual Diversity in American Indian Culture.* 2d ed. Beacon Press, Boston.

Williamson, John P. 1902. *An English-Dakota Dictionary.* American Tract Society, New York. Reprint: St, Paul, Minnesota Historical Society Press, 1992.

Wilson, Angela C. 1997. Power of the Spoken Word: Native Oral Traditions in American Indian History. In *Rethinking American Indian History*, edited by Donald L. Fixico, pp. 101–16. University of New Mexico Press, Albuquerque.

Wilson, Bonnie G. 1990. Working the Light: Nineteenth-Century Professional Photographers in Minnesota. *Minnesota History* 52:42–60.

Wilson, Charles C. 1905–8. The Successive Chiefs Named Wabasha. *Minnesota Historical Society Collections* 12:504–12.

Wilson, Raymond. 1983. *Ohiyesa: Charles Eastman, Santee Sioux.* University of Illinois Press, Urbana.

Wilson, Terry P. 1992. Blood Quantum: Native American Mixed Bloods. In *Racially Mixed People in America*, edited by Maria P. P. Root, pp. 108–25. Sage Publications, Newbury Park, Calif.

Winchell, Newton H. 1911. *The Aborigines of Minnesota: A Report Based on the Collections of Jacob V. Brower, and on the Field Surveys and Notes of Alfred J. Hill and Theodore H. Lewis.* Minnesota Historical Society, St. Paul.

Winter, Elaine M. 1997. "Women in Transition: An Analysis of Lakota Leadership Models." Ed.D. dissertation, Northern Illinois University, Dekalb.

Wishart, David J. 1979. *The Fur Trade of the American West, 1807–1840: A Geographical Synthesis.* University of Nebraska Press, Lincoln.

Wissler, Clark. 1907. Some Protective Designs of the Dakota. *Anthropological Papers of the American Museum of Natural History*, vol. 1, pt. 2, pp. 19–53.

Wissler, Clark, 1912. Societies and Ceremonial Associations in the Oglala Division of the Teton-Dakota. *Anthropological Papers of the American Museum of Natural History*, vol. 11, pt. 1, pp. 3–99.

Wissler, Clark. 1916. General Discussion of Shamanistic and Dancing Societies. *Anthropological Papers of the American Museum of Natural History*, vol. 11, pt. 12, pp. 853–76.

Wolf, Eric R. 1982. *Europe and the People without History.* University of California Press, Berkeley.

Wood, W. Raymond. 1980. Plains Trade in Prehistoric and Protohistoric Intertribal Relations. In *Anthropology on the Great Plains*, edited by W. Raymond Wood and Margot Liberty, pp. 98–109. University of Nebraska Press, Lincoln.

Wood, W. Raymond. 1981. The John Evans 1796–97 Map of the Missouri River. *Great Plains Quarterly* 1:39–53.

Wood, W. Raymond (comp.). 1983. *An Atlas of Early Maps of the American Midwest.* Scientific Papers, vol. 18. Illinois State Museum, Springfield.

Wood, W. Raymond. 1987. Mapping the Missouri River Through the Great Plains, 1673–1895. In *Mapping the North American Plains: Essays in the History of Cartography*, edited by Frederick B. Luebke, Francis W. Kaye, and Gary E. Moulton, pp. 27–40. University of Oklahoma Press, Norman.

Wood, W. Raymond. 1990. Ethnohistory and Historical Method. In *Archaeological Method and Theory*, vol. 2, edited by Michael B. Schiffer, pp. 81–109. University of Arizona Press, Tucson.

Wood, W. Raymond (comp.) 1993. *Joseph N. Nicollet's 1839 Manuscript Maps of the Missouri River and Upper Mississippi Basin.* Scientific Papers, vol. 24. Illinois State Museum, Springfield.

Woolworth, Alan R. 1974. Ethnohistorical Report on the Yankton Sioux. In *Sioux Indians III*, pp. 1–245. Garland Publishing, New York.

Woolworth, Alan R. 1994. Adrian J. Ebell, Photographer and Journalist of the Dakota War of 1862. *Minnesota History* 54:87–92.

Woolworth, Alan R., and Nancy L. Woolworth. 1980. Eastern Dakota Settlement and Subsistence Patterns Prior to 1851. *Minnesota Archaeologist* 39:70–89.

Woolworth, Nancy L. 1986. The Sisseton–Wahpeton Dakota Indian Fur Trades, 1820–1838. In *The Prairie: Past, Present, and Future*, edited by Gary K. Clambey and Richard H. Pemble, pp. 15–20. Tri-College University Center for Environmental Studies, Fargo, N. Dak.

Wozniak, John S. 1978. *Contact, Negotiation, and Conflict: An Ethnohistory of the Eastern Dakota, 1819–1839.* University Press of America, Washington, DC.

Wright, Rita P. (ed.) 1996. *Gender and Archaeology.* University of Pennsylvania Press, Philadelphia.

Yanagisako, Sylvia. 1979. Family and Household: The Analysis of Domestic Groups. *Annual Review of Anthropology* 8:161–205.

Index